"Jon Isaak's *New Testament Theology* is a fine introduction to the thought of the writings of the New Testament and to the larger themes that run through these writings. The book helpfully points out the diversity and unity of theology within the New Testament. Isaak offers a rich menu at the table. Some readers will be enriched by it, others may suffer indigestion."
 —**John E. Toews**
 Professor Emeritus of New Testament
 Mennonite Brethren Biblical Seminary

"With scintillating style, Jon Isaak sets forth a rigorously descriptive and constructive *New Testament Theology* from an Anabaptist-evangelical Christian perspective. Using Caird's metaphor of a conference table, Isaak 'listens' sensitively to the various historical-theological witnesses represented in the writings of the NT. Insightful diagrams, tables, and exercises focus the issues engaging the participants in conference table talk. I heartily recommend this fresh approach for classroom, group study, and personal enrichment."
 —**V. George Shillington**
 Professor Emeritus of Biblical and Theological Studies
 Canadian Mennonite University

"Imagine a round-table discussion involving the writers of the New Testament. Each writer shares deeply held theological convictions. After each has spoken comes the convener's constructive task of discerning common viewpoints among the diverse voices around the table. Isaak creatively utilizes this conference table image to craft this stimulating book. His readers will find themselves drawn into this conversation, as it continues among participants in God's creative and redemptive work today."
 —**Jacob W. Elias**
 Professor Emeritus of New Testament
 Associated Mennonite Biblical Seminary

"Missionary-teacher Jon Isaak writes confidently from the perspective of his life of service to the church and academic research to introduce New Testament readers to God's mission to save humans from sin through the power of the Lord Jesus and to issues raised by scholars."
 —**Lynn Jost**
 Dean of the Seminary
 Fresno Pacific University

"In his *New Testament Theology: Extending the Table* Jon Isaak has invented a new kind of text book. Too often the rather boring, sometimes prideful, but necessary old kind of academic introduction (who wrote this, when, where, why . . . ?) has been ruthlessly separated from any thought about how the early Christian texts might today inform living faith and vital theological debate in our day. Isaak builds especially on the work of George Caird and of Luke T. Johnson, yet he also draws on his own Anabaptist sense of faithful conversation and charitable conflict. The result is an accessible yet gently challenging book which systematically introduces the writings of the New Testament as diverse voices in a theological conversation in which readers are also active yet mutually and biblically accountable participants. Historically and theologically, Isaak is generally respectful of traditional positions, occasionally he over-simplifies, but unlike some 'conservative' authors, he does not pretend that the conversation of theologies in and around the New Testament is always an easy harmony of voices. Readers, teachers, and groups will particularly appreciate the creative exercises and discussion topics at the end of each chapter. Isaak consistently articulates problems and proposes possible solutions with a candor that invites readers to discern, to argue, and even to disagree among themselves in a spirit of generous friendship. Isaak approaches the challenges of biblical scholarship in a way that is pastoral and evangelical in spirit without being defensive or evasive."

—**Ian H. Henderson**
   Associate Professor of New Testament Studies
   McGill University

New Testament Theology

New Testament Theology

New Testament Theology

Extending the Table

JON M. ISAAK

CASCADE *Books* • Eugene, Oregon

NEW TESTAMENT THEOLOGY:
Extending the Table

Copyright © 2011 Jon M. Isaak. All rights reserved. Except for brief quotations in critical publications or reviews, no part of this book may be reproduced in any manner without prior written permission from the publisher. Write: Permissions, Wipf and Stock Publishers, 199 W. 8th Ave., Suite 3, Eugene, OR 97401.

Cascade Books
An Imprint of Wipf and Stock Publishers
199 W. 8th Ave., Suite 3
Eugene, OR 97401

www.wipfandstock.com

Unless otherwise indicated, biblical quotations are from the New Revised Standard Version Bible, copyright 1989, Division of Christian Education of the National Council of the Churches of Christ in the United States of America. Used by permission. All rights reserved.

ISBN 13: 978-1-55635-293-5

Cataloging-in-Publication data:

Isaak, Jon M., 1960–

New testament theology : extending the table / Jon M. Isaak.

xx + 382 p. ; 23 cm. — Includes bibliographical references and indexes.

ISBN 13: 978-1-55635-293-5

1. Bible—N.T.—Theology. 2. Bible—N.T.—Criticism, interpretation, etc. I. Title.

BS2397 .I73 2011

Manufactured in the USA.

For Mary Anne, Peter, *and* Rianna

Contents

List of Tables | viii
Preface | xi
Acknowledgments | xv

1. Introduction to New Testament Theology | 1
2. New Testament Theology as a Historical and Theological Discipline | 23
3. The Theological Contribution of Paul | 55
4. The Theological Contribution of the Synoptic Gospel Writers | 103
5. The Theological Contribution of the Johannine Traditions | 146
6. The Theological Contribution of the Remaining Canonical Witnesses | 186
7. Conference Intermission | 224
8. Christology: The Person and Work of Messiah Jesus | 238
9. Revelation: God's Self-Disclosure to Humanity and all Creation | 255
10. Theology: God-Talk and Imagination | 271
11. Anthropology: What It Means to Be Human | 288
12. Pneumatology: God's Living Presence through the Resurrected Lord | 301
13. Ecclesiology: The Identity and Mission of the Gathered Messianic Community of God | 311
14. Eschatology: Picturing the Goal and Completion of Creation | 330

Epilogue | 351
Bibliography | 355
Index of Authors | 361
Index of Scriptural Passages and Other Ancient Writings | 364

Tables

2.1 Mrs. Khokhlakov's Conversation with Father Zossima in *The Brothers Karamazov* | 53–54
3.1 Beginnings of Christian Literary Development | 56
3.2 Ancient Jewish Covenant Theology | 82
3.3 Jewish Apocalyptic Theology | 82
3.4 Paul's Modification of Jewish Apocalyptic Theology | 83
3.5 The Concentration-Expansion Dynamic of the Cross-Resurrection | 87
3.6 English Language Development and the Translation of "Faith" and "Righteousness" | 96
3.7 Comparison of Three Translations of Romans 3:21–26 | 99
3.8 E-mail Sent to Mennonite Brethren Pastors, Dated September 14, 2001 | 101–2
4.1 Jesus Foretells His Betrayal in Synoptic Parallels | 105
4.2 Lament over Jerusalem in Synoptic Parallels | 106
4.3 Two- or Four-Source Hypothesis for Solving the Synoptic Problem | 107
4.4 Conclusion to Parable of the Evil Tenants in Synoptic Parallels | 127
4.5 Parable of the Royal Wedding Feast or Great Feast in Synoptic Parallels | 128
4.6 Pronouncement of True Greatness in Synoptic Parallels | 132
4.7 Letter to Friend in Response to Christmas Article in *Newsweek* | 142–45
5.1 Conceptualizing the Framing of the Jesus Tradition | 157
5.2 The Structure of the Fourth Gospel's "Father" Christology/Theology | 159
6.1 General Schema of the Letter to the Hebrews according to Vanhoye | 196
6.2 Comparing the Rhetoric of Paul and James regarding Faith | 203

6.3   Comparing the Pagan Worldview with the NT Writers' Judeo-Christian Worldview | 210
6.4   Traditional View: Orthodoxy Precedes Heresy | 222
6.5   Critical Response to Traditional View: Heresy Precedes Orthodoxy | 223
6.6   Alternative View: Heterodoxy Precedes Orthodoxy | 223
8.1   Two-Player Salvation Model | 248
8.2   Three-Player Salvation Model | 248
8.3   Short Essay on Who Jesus Is and Why It Matters | 251–53
9.1   The NT Writers' Model of God's Self-Disclosure over Time | 257
9.2   Three Views on Conceptualizing the Christian Bible | 258
9.3   Biblical Revelation as a Static Deposit | 260
9.4   Biblical Revelation as a Compelling Vision | 262
10.1 Comparing the Western Worldview with the NT Writers' Judeo-Christian Worldview | 287
11.1 The Sixteenth Century Marks a Divergence of Anthropological Views in the Western Church | 298–99
11.2 Jesus as the Anthropological Norm and "First Fruits" of the "New" Creation | 300
12.1 Traditional "Isolated" View the Trinity | 303
12.2 Relational understanding of the Trinity | 304
13.1 The Church as Sign to Culture and Outpost of God's Coming Reign | 323
14.1 A Reflection on the Resurrection of the Dead occasioned by Lisa's Funeral | 345–46
14.2 Three Views on the Church's Relation to Israel | 346–48

Preface

IN THE PAGES THAT follow, I will argue that New Testament (NT) theology is both a descriptive and a constructive enterprise. It is *descriptive* in that it deals with the accounts that the NT writers narrate of their experience with Yahweh, the God of Israel, in light of Easter—an experience that transformed their understanding of Jesus and their reading of Torah. It is *constructive* in that it joins the diverse testimonies of these writers into a textured and thick space (i.e., fertile, generative, nutritious) within which contemporary followers of Jesus continue together to resonate with and to be shaped by the ancient yet living Spirit of God.

This book is historical, thematic, and theological. It explores the conversation taking place around a "conference table," to borrow George B. Caird's image. In this way, "to write a NT Theology is to preside at a conference of faith and order," where the conference chair engages the writers of the NT "in a colloquium about theological matters which they themselves have placed on the agenda" (Caird 1994:18). As the NT writers share their vision of God's saving work among them and their passion for the Christian church engaged in God's mission, we hear differing perspectives developed on the agenda items that hold the conference together. On most any topic, a spectrum of conviction emerges. The result is a creative tension. Differing perspectives are held together without reduction within a vision for God's mission. The product is a deep and richly textured space within which ongoing community reflection and praxis can take place. In this sense, the conference remains "in session," as these conversations are explored, organized, and extended by faith communities around the world through the centuries under topical headings like Christology, anthropology, ecclesiology, eschatology, and so on. In this way, the NT impulse toward theological reflection and praxis continues to nurture communities of Jesus through time until the new-creation age is fully realized.

It is my conviction that the back-and-forth dialogue of these conference proceedings creates the space within which the church in any context continues to be shaped by the living voice of the risen Lord. In this way, NT Theology plays the role of "extending the conference table" through time, giving contemporary faith communities a way of connecting with God's people who have engaged in theological reflection from the dawn of time and who will continue to do so until the end of time.

Like all interpreters or conference chairpersons, I am also bound to influence the direction of the conference discussion by the questions that get on the agenda, the order in which speakers are called to speak, the assessment of the sense of the meeting, and so on. While I may try to remain neutral and allow the panel of speakers the freedom to speak for themselves, I come to the task of chairing the conference of theological reflection and construction from a perspective, one that I would describe as anabaptist-evangelical.

Sometimes people ask me, what is an anabaptist-evangelical perspective? How might one recognize this strand within Christianity? For me, there are at least two emphases: (1) a large optimism about human transformation as a journey of growth and development, including commitments to community building, nonviolent peacemaking, and lifelong discipleship—a few of the key *anabaptist* ideals; and (2) a deep conviction that such transformation is best rooted in a personal connection to Jesus, including a commitment to participation in the ongoing life of Jesus, the one who was uniquely grounded in the active pursuit of the mission of God to reconstitute the people of God for the transformation of all creation—a key *evangelical* ideal. These two emphases shape my reading, reception, and assessment of the conference proceedings and of the vision narrated by the Christian Bible in two testaments.

Of course, there are other valid receptions and interpretive frameworks besides mine, each with varying degrees of merit—and I certainly do not claim to speak for Evangelicals, Anabaptists, Mennonites, or the Mennonite Brethren Biblical Seminary. The multiplicity of our perspectives makes conversation, correction, and improvement possible for those who gather at the table around the subject matter that continues to draw God's people together for the realization of God's purpose.

Paul offers genuine encouragement at just this point, giving credibility to the task of theological construction and community building. He says, "Each builder must choose with care how to build . . . For no one can lay any foundation other than the one that has been laid; that foundation is Jesus Christ . . . The work of each builder will become visible, for the Day will disclose it . . . If the work is burned up, the builder will suffer loss; the builder will be saved, but only as through fire" (1 Cor 3:10–15). Apparently, the evaluative issue is not so much about constructing the right theological wording to ensure access to God's salvation (like getting the right password), but about how *representative* each of our community theological constructions is of what God is doing and where God is taking creation. The only exam that really counts is this one.

So, welcome to the table! If you choose to participate in this grand building project, my hope is that this book will prove a constructive invitation to engage in the ways that God is partnering with humanity to bring about the completion of the creation enterprise begun so long ago.

Acknowledgments

NONE OF US COMES to theological reflection without guides and mentors. I am no exception. In particular, I want to acknowledge professors Elmer A. Martens and John E. Toews, two of my professors at Mennonite Brethren Biblical Seminary in Fresno, California. Both men were instrumental to my introduction to and eventual embrace of biblical theology in the early 1990s. I was fascinated by its *potential* to explain some of the confusing features of the Bible and its *power* to draw contemporary faith communities into its story in a transformative way. Martens's own textbook on biblical theology, *God's Design* (1998, 1981), focused on Old Testament (OT) theology and became a key text in my own formation.

It was only much later that I learned how hard-fought the battle for biblical theology was at the seminary. Speaking about the early years, Martens writes, "In the beginning [i.e., in 1955] the curriculum had a theologically dispensational cast. That changed with the coming of J. B. Toews in 1964. He sought a mandate from the U.S. Conference to color the seminary program Anabaptist and hired A. J. Klassen as academic dean to see to the implementation" (2005:14).

Evidently one of the key ways to wrestle the curriculum from dispensationalism and fundamentalism was to focus on biblical theology, which insisted instead on using only scriptural categories for theological discussions. Martens continues: "Intent on highlighting biblical theology, President Toews phoned, wrote and personally visited me, then a doctoral student at Claremont University Graduate school and eventually persuaded me (for I had other aspirations) that it was God's will that I join the faculty" (2005:14).

In very simple but incredibly profound terms, and without directly addressing the underlying cultural, religious, and social issues related to dispensationalism and fundamentalism, Martens explained the difference between biblical theology and systematic theology: "Quite clearly there are other ways of talking about God, even for the Christian, than in the ways that the Bible talks about [God]. For instance, in Systematic Theology one speaks of God in philosophical terms and resorts to terms such as being, attribute, and existence. In Biblical Theology one attempts to discuss God according to the categories such as deliverance, promise, covenant" (1975:35).

Who could argue with such a passionate plea for reshaping the seminary curriculum so that it would be more biblical? And yet, unhooking the seminary "wagon" from systematic theology and hooking it instead to biblical theology was part of a much larger objective, namely, to move the seminary into the anabaptist-evangelical orbit, with concern for the reign and mission of God, as well as with concern for the church's cultural and social engagement.

So, in 1967 a two-part biblical theology course—one semester of OT theology and one of NT theology—was launched that would eventually become one of the centerpieces of the seminary curriculum, ultimately replacing the series of systematic theology courses as the standard degree requirement (Martens 1975:35–40). Martens began teaching OT Theology in 1969, continuing to do so until 2004. NT Theology was taught by professors David Ewert (1975–1981), John E. Toews (1982–1995), and Timothy J. Geddert (1996–). All four men were my teachers at different times, and each of them strengthened my appreciation for biblical theology.

However, it was John E. Toews's imprint that significantly shaped the NT Theology course at Mennonite Brethren Biblical Seminary. For Toews, NT theology was a historical, thematic, and theological enterprise—all at once! The first seven weeks of his semester-long course were devoted to the theologies of the NT: Paul's, Mark's, Matthew's, James's, and so on—and the next seven to the contributions that these theologies made to themes like Christology, ecclesiology, eschatology, and so on. Toews's NT theology was *descriptive*; it attended to the NT writers' interpretations of their experience with the God of Israel, in light of Easter—an experience that profoundly transformed their understanding of Jesus, their reading of Torah, and their life together. But it was also *constructive*; it joined the diverse testimonies of the NT writers into a textured space within which contemporary followers of Jesus could continue to be shaped by the testimony to the living Spirit of God.

When I was first asked to teach NT theology at the seminary in 2002, Toews was gracious enough to allow me to use his lecture notes as a foundation. So along with my own notes from my student days in the early 1990s, I had a place from which to begin. Many traces of his outline and formulations remain in the manuscript that follows. While I take full responsibility for the ways that I have developed these ideas over the years, I acknowledge my indebtedness to Toews's foundational work for framing the task of NT theology.

One of the ways that I supplemented Toews's notes was by asking students to engage three authors, each from different but related NT fields, in a seminar format of discussion and interaction. First, I felt it was necessary to strengthen my students' grasp of the introductory and historical matters associated with the NT writings. So, I asked them to interact with Luke T. Johnson's widely used textbook, *The Writings of the New Testament* (1999). Johnson's attention to the historical *method* (as opposed to the historical *model*) and his promotion of the experience-interpretation model gave students a solid way of locating the NT writings and their ongoing significance for the believing community. Johnson's NT introduction helped to clarify the voices of the NT writers and their particular concerns, as they gave witness to God's surprising activity among them and engaged one another in the conference proceedings that came to be known as the NT.

Second, I felt that in the move away from systematic theology to biblical theology at the seminary, sometimes questions of systematic theology were not well developed or even appreciated. Students needed help to see that not all systematic theologies are suspect; some are more sensitive to the narrative character of the biblical witness. Here I had students interact with C. Norman Kraus's anabaptist systematic-theology textbook, *God Our Savior* (1991). Kraus's systematic theology begins with the conviction that Jesus is the normative self-revelation of God. The largeness of this claim provided students with the language to explore the task of theology: namely, to contextualize the message of the Bible so that its true meaning can be appropriated in any culture. Kraus helped students think theologically and systematically about the multiple dimensions of our life together in this world, by providing an alternative to some popular systematic theologies. Too often these seem aimed at reducing the biblical narrative to a set of propositions, believed to transfer easily to other cultures. Unlike this kind of "suitcase theology," Kraus argued for a dynamic theological system intent on relating the gospel message to cultures across time and space—a contextual systematic theology.

Third, at the same time that students worked through Kraus, they also read George B. Caird's textbook, *New Testament Theology* (1994). This text was completed and edited by Lincoln Hurst following Caird's untimely death in 1984. It is to Caird that I owe the controlling image of NT theology as an "apostolic conference" of faith and order. I found Caird's work extremely helpful in that he pushed students to consider new ways of understanding the NT. Not only did he pay attention to the diversity of theological voices represented by the NT writers; he was able to hear the underlying unity without forcing them to sing the same line. For Caird, "the music of the New Testament choir is not written to be sung in unison" (1994:24). Such sensibilities enabled Caird to see *both/and* scenarios in the biblical narratives and arguments, where many see only *either/or* possibilities. No doubt, his classical training as a biblical scholar, which included Hebrew Bible as well as NT, helped him place the NT squarely within the world of the ancient Near East with its appreciation for both/and solutions. Finally, Caird's assertion that "we shall not find Jesus even indirectly relevant to our age unless we first find him directly relevant to his own" (1994:351) grounded his theology in Jesus's Jewishness. The hopes and dreams that Jesus had first for Israel and then for all the peoples of the earth testify to Israel's conviction that God had deliberately left creation incomplete, so that it could be completed with human cooperation—something that finally became a genuine possibility in Jesus.

This book is my attempt to write a NT theology in a popular format that is *historically* rigorous in its reconstruction of the NT voices (in the tradition of Johnson), *theologically* grounded in Jesus's story as witnessed by the NT writers (in the tradition of Caird), and *thematically* constructive for the church in its ongoing witness to the watching world (in the tradition of Kraus). I acknowledge my indebtedness to all three authors and trust that my ambitious attempt to do all three things in one book will prove useful to students of biblical literature, theology, culture, and mission.

In addition, I acknowledge the contribution of my students during these twelve years of seminary teaching; their good questions and solid critique helped me to reformulate and reimagine the ideas that now find their place in this book. The careful editing eye of Jim Neudorf saved me from many blunders. My two mentors, professors Tim Geddert and John E. Toews, read the entire manuscript and gave many helpful suggestions for improvement. To all of you, including to my wife, Mary Anne, and to our children, Peter and Rianna, I say thank you for your encouragement and company along the way.

My hope is that communities of Christian faith may find the rich enabling presence of God to be theirs as together they fill out, in contemporary and relevant ways, the newly reconfigured people of God that is taking shape around Messiah Jesus. It is through such communities of the Spirit of the risen Lord that God's mission to disarm the powers of evil and move all creation forward toward completion is being accomplished.

Jon M. Isaak
Fresno, California
Christmas 2009

1

Introduction to New Testament Theology

IN THIS CHAPTER MY aim is to set out some of the framework from within which I propose to do the work of NT theology. The chapter has five objectives: (1) to review the history of biblical theology, (2) to make a case for biblical theology, (3) to assess the three main models of doing NT theology today, (4) to set out criteria for assembling a NT theology, and (5) to develop the controlling metaphor of a conference table for conceptualizing the task of NT theology.

THE HISTORY OF BIBLICAL THEOLOGY

The term *biblical theology* was first used in print by Wolfgang J. Christmann in 1629, but it was Henricus A. Diest's 1643 book that functioned to establish the emerging discipline (Hasel 1978:17). These early biblical theologies amounted to collections of Bible verses collated and organized to demonstrate the biblical basis for certain points of traditional Christian doctrine. On the doctrine of God, for example, authors listed all the texts they could find in the Bible that expressed some attribute of God. Typically, they devoted one chapter to citing OT texts and one to listing NT texts. Then they proceeded on to contributions from early-church theologians and significant figures in Christian history, concluding with formulations of contemporary importance for churchly life. These scholars did not see themselves as writing biblical theology, as opposed to some other kind of theology. At this early stage, they were simply writing theology. The interests of biblical studies and doctrinal studies were completely integrated: they were one and the same thing.

The discourse was shaped primarily by the traditional doctrines of the Christian creed.

The integrated situation, where doctrine governed the direction of biblical and theological discussion, was followed by two reactionary movements. They were different, but related. First, there was the pietistic reaction of the seventeenth century. In Germany, scholars like Philip J. Spener (1635–1705) voiced concerns about doctrinally dominated biblical theology. Spener felt that the situation had become altogether too scholastic and dry, serving the purposes of doctrine alone. In his 1675 book, Spener advocated a biblical theology aimed at nurturing the individual spiritual lives of Christian believers. His basic criterion for sound theology was personal significance. Others in this period of German Romanticism were instrumental in launching the home Bible-study movement that spread through Reformation churches and denominations of the time period.

Second, and a little later, there was the rationalistic reaction of the eighteenth century. Still in Germany, scholars like Johann P. Gabler (1753–1826) also began to voice criticism of biblical theology's servitude to dogmatic theology. However, instead of calling for the criterion of personal significance as Spener had done, these scholars argued that science should be the determining criterion for sound theology. Gabler argued that human reason could be used to determine the *universal* truths from the biblical narrative and that these could be and should be separated from the time-bound *particularities* of the ancient Near Eastern culture out of which the Bible emerged. The resultant truth, distilled from the raw material, was real biblical theology. Gabler's famous speech, delivered in 1787 at the University of Altdorf, argued for a complete separation between biblical theology (that which was descriptive, historical, and scientific) and dogmatic theology (that which was prescriptive, religious, and churchly). A few key lines from that speech read as follows:

> But let those things that have been said up to now be worth this much: that we distinguish carefully the divine from the human, that we establish some distinction between biblical and dogmatic theology, and after we have separated those things which in the sacred books refer most immediately to their own times and to the [people] of those times from those pure notions which divine providence wished to be characteristic of all times and places, let us then construct the foundation of our philosophy upon religion

and let us designate with some care the objectives of divine and
human wisdom. Exactly thus will our theology be made more
certain and more firm . . . We must diligently investigate what in
the books of the New Testament was said as an accommodation
to the ideas or the needs of the first Christians and what was said
in reference to the unchanging idea of the doctrine of salvation;
we must investigate what in the sayings of the Apostles is truly
divine, and what perchance merely human. (Sandys-Wunsch and
Eldredge 1980:138, 142–43)

One result of this turn of events was that an "iron curtain" was eventually erected between biblical theology and doctrinal theology. Increasingly, biblical theology was done independently of the church and almost exclusively in large universities. This was the situation as it developed in the various sectors of the Protestant Reformation tradition. Catholic theology faced its struggle with biblical theology later in the twentieth century.

By the nineteenth century few biblical-theology textbooks on the whole Bible were being written. Instead, given the shift toward history, biblical theology was replaced by the writing of OT and NT theologies. Both these kinds of books were essentially historical in nature. OT theologies reconstructed the historical development of Israel's religion. Typical questions included the following: How did Israel's concept of God compare to its pagan neighbors? How did Israel's monotheism come to be? How was Canaan settled? What are the sources behind the OT books that we have today? In this period, for the first time in Christian history, the OT prophets were allowed to speak for themselves, without the NT adding anything to them. With the same independence, NT theologies reconstructed the historical development of early Christianity. Here, typical questions included the following: How did Jesus come to understand his mission? When did he come to think of himself as the Messiah? What was the nature of Paul's struggle with Palestinian and Hellenistic Judaism? What was the relationship between the early Jesus movements? How did the formation of the Christian Bible and orthodoxy come about? What are the sources behind the NT books?

While such historical questions are certainly significant, they typically did not lead to much theological discussion. In many cases, the conversations shifted to a discussion of religion as a developing social phenomenon within a historical model of cause and effect. In the academy, this kind of biblical theology came to be known as *Religionsgeschichte* or the history-of-religion, which addressed the history of the traditions or confessions behind and embedded in the biblical text. The highpoint of this period came in the 1950s with the work of Gerhard von Rad on the OT and Rudolf Bultmann on the NT.

Of course, more conservative biblical theologies were produced during this time, but these only seemed to emphasize the growing wedge between biblical and dogmatic theology. Biblical theology, as practiced in the academy, came to be associated with those who thought of it as a descriptive discipline primarily interested in how humanity developed and articulated its thinking about God. Dogmatic theology, on the other hand, came to be associated with those in churchly institutions, who had much less interest in historical questions. For these scholars, theology was a confessional or normative discipline, setting out how God is to be known and worshiped by human beings.

In 1970, Brevard S. Childs named the wedge between the historical and the theological concerns as the "crisis of Biblical Theology." The crisis erupted largely because of the stubborn insistence that a choice must be made: either biblical theology is about what *humanity* thinks about God, or it is about what *God* thinks about humanity. Either biblical theology is a dispassionate study of the *development* of the Judeo-Christian tradition as it emerged out of its Mediterranean cradle, or it is a study that reads the biblical texts as a *witness* to what God intends or desires for humanity. The polarization of purpose that marked the "crisis in Biblical Theology" for Childs in the 1970s continues today in the twenty-first century. As with most polarized debates, there seldom are only two choices. In fact, as indicated, I will argue that a strong case can be made for a biblical theology that is *both* descriptive (i.e., tracing the historical development of the Judeo-Christian tradition) *and* constructive (i.e., confessing that the voice of God's intentions can be discerned in the collection of texts that now form the Christian Bible).

A CASE FOR BIBLICAL THEOLOGY

For some, it is difficult to speak confidently of doing biblical theology in the twenty-first century (see Via 2002; Penner and Vander Stichele 2005; Olson 2006; Mead 2007). In the decades since Childs named the crisis in biblical theology, two further challenges have made the prospects of doing biblical theology even more daunting. If a compelling case is to be made for a biblical theology that is both descriptive (i.e., historical) and constructive (i.e., theological), it must be able to respond to these two contemporary challenges.

First, the Western world's diminishing confidence in the possibility of objective truth outside human subjectivity presents a challenge to the assumptions of biblical theology. This plays itself out in a growing mistrust in the historical approach. What can be said with certainty about the ancient world? Whose perspective on past events is going to be named as the "historical" account? There is a growing loss of confidence in the Enlightenment synthesis that claims there are universal, self-evident, objective truths foundational to our world, which keep it all working in order. In the same way, there is a growing loss of confidence that a biblical theology exists "out there" to discover, if we just keep looking. The shift away from the modern synthesis to an increasingly postmodern worldview presents new challenges for doing biblical theology.

The issue is that in the Western world the very nature of truth is questionable. In our increasingly postmodern world, many would say that there is only one truth: namely, my truth or perhaps the truth held by my community. Put another way, the only absolute is that there is no absolute outside ourselves and our community. The Enlightenment idea that the machine-like nature of the material world can be unlocked by human reason has fallen out of fashion. Appreciation for randomness, chaos, and chance is replacing the older fascination with the classical laws of gravitation and motion that explained the movements of planets and satellites, but that are not sufficient to explain motion at the subatomic level or at the speed of light.

Postmodernity is a reaction to the idea that there is a universal, overarching story; a unifying theory of everything; and a master plan holding everything together—all of which modernity thought could be discerned through the proper application of specific procedures. For the postmodern person such a worldview is seen as "the tyranny of the one," as the domination of the powerful over the powerless, and as the privileged speaking for the marginalized. Attempts to find common ground on which to resolve differences are mostly futile, because there is no common ground and no master story. Therefore, attempts to construct a biblical theology that holds the message of the Bible together become questionable. Some suggest it is better to abandon the effort. Clearly the shift away from the assumption that God exists outside us, making claims on humanity through the witness of the biblical writers, presents new challenges for doing biblical theology.

Second, the emergence of multiple reading strategies has also proved to be a challenge to the task of doing biblical theology. Related to postmodernity's challenge to the existence or nature of truth is the emergence of many different reading approaches to the Bible, which have become fashionable in the last decades.

Until recently, the only acceptable exegetical method for interpreting the Bible was the grammatical-historical method (sometimes called the historical-critical method), a product of the Enlightenment. Here, the biblical text was explored in its grammatical context (with attention to the meanings of words, to the flow of the argument or narrative, and to similar concerns) and in its historical context (with attention to the social setting of the author, the occasion of the writing, and the audience). By thoroughly considering the grammatical and the historical contexts, interpreters felt confident in determining the author's intentions, which were assumed to be directly applicable to reading communities regardless of time or location.

Such confidence in the grammatical-historical method popularized by modernity is no longer shared by all. During the twentieth century numerous other reading strategies emerged: literary, social-scientific, rhetorical, structuralist, reader-response, feminist, liberationist, postcolonial, to name some. The obvious issue raised is one of adjudicating. Is one method better or more productive? Or perhaps each method is just as legitimate as another, since each person or community is involved in their own meaning-making enterprise. Some wonder if anyone other than the reader can determine the meaning of a biblical text, since access to the author's intentions or to the text's meaning is questionable. Rather than speaking of the *text's* meaning, it is fashionable to speak of the *community's* meaning of the text. The text funds the meaning-making enterprise and is governed by the reader's preferred reading strategy, not by something located in the text. Clearly the shift away from the notion that a text *has* meaning to a more postmodern appreciation for multiple textual meanings presents new challenges for doing biblical theology.

To sum up, the earlier crisis in biblical theology is exacerbated by two of postmodernity's assertions. First, the modern project has erred by searching for absolute, objective knowledge that is accessible through a precisely definable method. Thus, the very idea of a biblical theology is ruled out from the start. Second, all understanding is tentative, personal, subjective, and ad hoc. Thus, the plurality of meanings undercuts the enterprise of discerning an overarching biblical theology.

Now, before abandoning the enterprise of biblical theology altogether, let's look at the postmodern challenge a little more closely. While twenty-first-century people in the West have no choice as to the worldview in which they find themselves located, they do have a choice as to how to live in an increasingly postmodern world. Some choose an isolationist approach and pretend that postmodernity is an aberration that will go away if left alone. They might say, "Retreat to the hills. Let's set up a commune and wait it out." This is the *ostrich* approach. Others choose the polar opposite, a more ambivalent approach. They concede that their theological construct is just one among many, equally good constructions, since there is really no overarching truth out there anyway. Since this understanding appears more sophisticated and tolerant, all attempts to engage others in conversation and dialogue are abandoned. They might say, "There is no point. Let's agree not to talk about truth claims." This is the *chameleon* approach.

Neither the isolationist (ostrich) nor the ambivalent (chameleon) response seems to offer much of a path forward. Instead, I suggest that the Christian community continue to embrace the posture that has characterized at least some groups of God's people from the beginning of time. In every age, God's people have recognized their place within the culture where they find themselves (to varying degrees, of course) and at the same time have tried self-critically to transform and reform the status-quo cultural worldview, based on their primary allegiance to God's kingdom (again, to varying degrees). This is a policy of engagement—not isolation or ambivalence. By engaging interactively and critically with culture, ways of extending the biblical witness to God and to God's creation enterprise emerge laced with potential and promise. This is the *raccoon* approach. How so? Perhaps it is an urban legend, but apparently raccoons wash and examine the food they scavenge before eating it, setting some things aside and embracing others: this is a marvelous image of critical engagement, invitation, and discernment.

So, with the disposition of a raccoon, let me suggest three ways that the challenges of postmodernity can contribute to a responsive and functional biblical theology and thus make the case for a twenty-first-century kind of biblical theology—one that is both descriptive (i.e., historical) and constructive (i.e., theological). This is the way of the raccoon, not the ostrich or the chameleon; it is about taking some lines and leaving others.

First, postmodernity offers a corrective to an overly mechanical view of doing biblical theology. Often there is a mechanical feel to the way the Bible is read theologically. Much like a cookbook, encyclopedia, or repair manual, biblical theologies sometimes claim to offer the biblical answers to all sorts of questions (even those not addressed in the Bible) by following "three easy steps." Here, exploration is reduced to a matter of correctly applying certain external rules and principles (often quite arbitrary) to the biblical text. But is this really how biblical literature functions? It sounds so reductionistic, so modern. Instead, is not the Bible the prophetic and apostolic witness to the living and dynamic Word of God? It is not the thing itself, but the *witness* to God's self-disclosure to and in the world. In this way, the Bible functions not as an object of veneration, but as a *window* through which God and humanity are seen more clearly. In every generation, biblical theology then works to "keep the window glass clean."

Second, postmodernity urges us to acknowledge that biblical interpretation and biblical theology are human constructions. Often, zealous claims are made that a proposed interpretation speaks for God. Dissenting voices are suppressed; such suppression suggests that personal fears or self-interest really lie behind these affirmations. But would God really want to own every one of the ideas (ideas that are sometimes mutually exclusive) purported to represent God's character and purpose? Would it not be better to speak with more humility, acknowledging that any claim to possess the knowledge of God is irresponsible? However, claiming to be attentive to and shaped by God's character and God's way (always subject to correction) is at least plausible. With postmodernity's help, we can now more boldly say, "This is how I hear God speaking through these biblical texts to our time." Then, confident that God's heartbeat will eventually become known, we invite people to come and listen with us and to live among us to see if there is any truth behind these words of ours. In this way, community discernment and assessment is built into the truth-telling enterprise of doing biblical theology.

Third, postmodernity urges us to admit that some biblical interpretations and biblical theologies have led to domination and oppression. Where modernity is confident in the power of knowledge, postmodernity questions that confidence and all concentrations of power wherever they are located—in government, in the academy, in the church, in families, in industry, in business, and so on. This is called a "hermeneutic of suspicion." And there is good reason to be suspicious: the history of Christianity is full of stories where convictions or constructions held by well-meaning people have led to domination or oppression of the powerless. The tendency of totalizing visions often results in systematic violence against the marginalized and voiceless (e.g., in foreign policy, in economics, in immigration, in gender equity). The problem that postmodernity identifies is that most authoritative interpretations end up doing some sort of violence either to other people or to other interpretations. This is a helpful critique.

Christians should be ready to acknowledge that at points they have overestimated the kind of knowledge they possess and have used it for evil and not only for good. Nevertheless, it does not automatically follow that a vision of the transcendent/immanent God to which the Bible testifies must be abandoned. The fault of oppressive biblical theologies need not be pinned on God. Instead, biblical theology—and all theology, given its character as a human construct—must take full responsibility for its abusive constructions, knowing that it must answer to God for how representative of God's way its constructions really are.

To sum up, postmodernity needs to be affirmed for helping the Christian community realize its inclination to make overly mechanical theologies, constructions often driven by fear or self-interest, and interpretations tending toward domination or oppression. These criticisms function as a much-needed wake-up call. However, there are some aspects of postmodernity's critique of biblical theology that are overstated and need to be "washed off," in the way that a raccoon cleans its food before eating. Is postmodernity correct in making the leap, based on some oppressive interpretations (e.g., justifications for the Crusades, for slavery, for apartheid, for war, or for exclusion) that God is abusive, absent, impotent, nonexistent, or remote? Should not responsibility for these interpretations that have led to injustice rest with human beings? We should not blame God for oppressive theologies. So with chastened humility, the Christian community continues to renew its faith and conviction that the Bible does give witness to the Word of God, and that together in the Spirit of the risen Lord, the church can discern its meaning and be shaped by its vision.

If biblical theology is to have any currency in the twenty-first century, it must find a way between the *overconfident* modern application of method and the *despairing* exercise of unbounded postmodern interpretation. It must correct modernity's overconfidence with a greater measure of chastened humility, appreciation for mystery, and openness to change. But then, too, biblical theology must correct postmodernity's despair with a greater measure of assurance and trust that God exists, that God loves creation, that God's creation project is still in process, and that God invites all to participate in the completion of the creation enterprise. A biblical theology that is both descriptive (i.e., historical) and constructive (i.e., theological) holds the most promise for delivering correctives on both of these fronts—overconfidence and despair—in the emerging postmodern Western world.

THREE MAIN MODELS OF DOING NT THEOLOGY

If the above case for doing biblical theology descriptively and constructively is at all compelling, it is still not clear just how such a biblical theology would proceed. What are the possibilities? Three models—each with strengths and weaknesses—are current today. What can be learned from each approach? Let's look at each one in turn.

First, there is the *thematic* model, sometimes also called the topical approach to NT theology. A quick survey of the table of contents in the NT theologies written by Alan Richardson (1958), Donald Guthrie (1981), and Thomas R. Schreiner (2008) reveals a model that moves through a list of doctrinal themes. For these authors, biblical theology serves as the "raw material" for systematic theologians and their constructions. Biblical texts are organized as proofs or as *prolegomena* supporting a prior systematic formulation of Christian doctrine. In the thematic model, doctrinal affirmations tend to take the lead, and the Bible is used to anchor these themes.

The strength of the thematic model is that it addresses the common criticism that church folk sometimes have of biblical scholars: namely, that they seldom come up with anything of value for the ongoing life of the church. The thematic model is exempt from this complaint. It is completely in the service of the church. Here, biblical theology is normative for contemporary Christian faith and practice.

While the pragmatic advantages are real, several cautions are necessary. (1) There is the problem of confusing categories. Doctrines are human constructions made to represent the character of God and God's world, but they should not be confused with God. This model tends to confuse doctrines *about* God *with* God. These are two different categories. (2) Then there is the problem of unchecked self-interest. The criteria for selecting the themes or doctrines are arbitrarily chosen by the scholar. Plus, the arbitrariness is exacerbated by the imposition of external categories (doctrinal and/or philosophical) onto the NT writings almost as in some systematic theologies. Such structural impositions run the risk of constructing a NT Theology that skews or mutes some NT voices.

A second model is the *historical* model, sometimes called history-of-religions or chronological approach to NT theology. Following this approach are the scholars mentioned earlier who led the attack on dogmatic theology, beginning with Gabler in the eighteenth century. For these scholars, the aim is to transform NT theology into a study of the history of NT thought. Instead of NT theology (singular), the argument is that there are only NT theologies (plural). Furthermore, the result is not necessarily normative for Christian faith and practice. Questions of belief, confession, and religion are of a different order. Why? Because in this model, theology is primarily a historical discipline. Typically, this approach traces the chronological movement from the Israelite people's ancient Near Eastern world through Greco-Roman influences and finally to an early catholic church of the second century—a trajectory viewed as either progression or regression, depending on the scholar's persuasion.

The historical approach to NT theology has two distinct forms, because history is read differently depending on one's philosophical assumptions. Hegelian dialectical philosophy describes one kind of historical approach. Here, the key word is *development*. For scholars like William Wrede (1973, orig. 1897), Paul is the second founder of Christianity in that he corrupted the attractively simple religion of Jesus, the teacher of true morality, making Christianity into a religion of redemption dominated by the proclamation of the cross and resurrection. Here, the development is viewed as regressive. For Ferdinand Christian Baur (1973, orig. 1863) and his Tübingen School, the development is less about progression or regression and more about a traceable *tendency* that can be used to locate each NT writing. By employing the three-step pattern of thesis, antithesis, and synthesis, the trajectory of NT writings can be traced.

For Baur, the apostolic age was dominated by the opposition between the narrowminded Jewish Christianity of the original apostles (i.e., Peter) and the law-free, universalistic gospel of Paul. Only in the postapostolic period did the opposition ease in the period known as emerging early catholicism (e.g., Luke's unified account of Paul and Peter in Acts). Through compromises and concessions the two parties came together in a middle way, united in their opposition to the threats of gnosticism, Montanism, and Marcionism of the second century. The contention here is that theology is only seen within historical developments as people interact and movements evolve over time. More recent NT theologies by Walter Schmithals (1997) and Georg Strecker (2000) carry forward similar commitments to a developmental-historical model, confident of being able to chart, say, the various theological strata within the Jesus tradition or Paul's letters.

The other form of the historical approach to NT theology follows existentialist philosophy. Here, the key word is *self-actualization*. Sometimes called the kerygmatic approach (from *kerygma* or proclamation), this way of doing theology actually doubts history's usefulness for faith. According to Bultmann (1951, 1955), the only truly valuable theological experiences are those that transcend history, where people self-actualize in spite of their miserable historical situation. What *is* historical is each person's responsibility to rise above her or his situation, not whether this or that story of Jesus really happened as narrated in the NT.

Bultmann's program of demythologization is based on the conviction that modern people need to peel away the ancient mythological layers in which the gospel is wrapped so that they too can make courageous decisions of faith, just as the first followers of Jesus did. By separating out the timeless invitation to decide for faith from those time-conditioned features of the ancient world, the biblical narratives can again be read as examples of hope and courage. This explains why Bultmann has little interest in the historical Jesus or in what Jesus thought of himself. Such historical pursuits undermine true faith for Bultmann, since faith would now be based on some facts of history, and not on the courage to self-actualize in the face of evidence to the contrary. According to Bultmann, "the acknowledgment of Jesus as the one in whom God's word decisively encounters [a person], whatever title be given him—'Messiah (Christ),' 'Son of Man,' 'Lord'—is a pure act of faith independent of the answer to the historical question whether or not Jesus considered himself the

Messiah. Only the historian can answer this question—as far as it can be answered at all—and faith, being personal decision, cannot be dependent upon a historian's labor" (1951:26).

One advantage of both historical approaches—dialectic and existential—is that their practitioners have uncovered vast amounts of background material that shed light on the context of earliest Christianity. Their aim has not usually been apologetic (i.e., to prove the veracity of Christian claims) but descriptive (i.e., to document how early Christian groups thought and lived their faith). The last 150 years have seen a remarkable quantity of material discovered or published relating to NT times (e.g., Nag Hammadi gnostic library [1945] and Dead Sea Scrolls [1947]) and relating to the manuscript transmission history of biblical texts, e.g., parchment copies of the complete Christian Bible dated to the fourth century (Sinaiticus [1859] and Vaticanus [1889]) and papyrus copies of NT texts dated to the second and third centuries (A. C. Beatty 1931; J. Rylands 1934; and M. Bodmer 1952). Much more is known about the time period in which the NT was written and about the history of manuscript transmission simply because historically-oriented research has uncovered a great deal. (See Stegemann and Stegemann 1999; Crossan and Reed 2001; Ferguson 2003; Lampe 2003.)

But the problems with the historical-chronological approach are vast too. For all the background material that has been found, there has been little payoff for establishing the chronology of specific NT writings. NT chronology remains notoriously problematic. Leaving aside the challenges of sorting out the chronology of Jesus's life from the gospel accounts, even for Paul, where the *documentary* evidence is the strongest, it is difficult to situate his life and writings within the three neat missionary journeys that Luke narrates in Acts. While we may now know much about the Greco-Roman world within which the NT writers lived, this does not necessarily help to situate the NT writings within ideological trajectories. The problem is that apart from Paul's documentary letters, the rest of the NT writings are largely *literary* in nature. As authors, the NT writers write persuasively and rhetorically artful texts aimed at shaping their communities of Jesus. This means they do not obviously reflect their sources or the beliefs of their home communities. Without external evidence, only this much can be said: literary texts of the NT represent the views of their authors, and apparent parallels to certain ideological views do not necessarily prove genetic linkages. (For example, try sorting out the background of the Letter to the Hebrews; is the background from Philo? from Qumran? Is the background Pauline? Petrine? gnostic?)

Evidently, the Christian movement is not merely the mathematical product of existing forces (as in the dialectic historical model); an element of novelty also breaks into the Mediterranean world with the power to transform Judaism and give it new meaning. Furthermore, the assumption that it is possible to distinguish the timeless themes from the time-conditioned NT material (as in the existentialist historical model) also begins to break down. Why? Because everything in the NT is historically and culturally conditioned! The real question is, what do these time-conditioned texts say about the subject matter to which they give witness? For all the critique leveled at dogmatic theology by Gabler and his heirs practicing the historical model, the way these two historical models are controlled by philosophical commitments threatens to distort NT Theology in a way surprisingly similar to dogmatic theology.

The third model is the *Heilsgeschichte* or history-of-salvation approach to NT theology. Conservative scholars responded to the historical-chronological approaches with a counterproposal: an overarching single-theme approach. Scholars like Adolf Schlatter (1973, orig. 1909), Oscar Cullmann (1967), Werner G. Kümmel (1973), and George E. Ladd (1993) represent the contrary voice to the history-of-religions approach to NT theology. This contrary voice stresses the theological unity of God's saving work that spans the diverse theologies of the NT writings. Recent writers of NT theologies in this tradition include I. Howard Marshall (2004), Frank Thielman (2005), and Frank J. Matera (2007). For these scholars, the Bible records the acts of God's saving history that give witness to God's aim of redeeming humanity—a process begun long ago, but one that remains incomplete until the eschatological consummation at the end of time. The diverse theological witnesses of the NT voices (and of the entire Bible, for that matter) are held together by a particular theological grid governed by one theme: namely, salvation history. *Heilsgeschichte* is promoted as the best way to understand the inner unity that binds together the diverse testimonies of the NT writings.

The obvious attraction of the salvation-history approach is that it is explicitly theological, when many biblical theologies have worked so hard to remove any overtly theological dimension from their NT theologies, in favor of a uniquely historical or descriptive enterprise. Now, it is true that Bultmann's kind of historical approach (existentialist) is very theological; however, he refuses to put much stock in the historicity of the narrated events of the biblical story. By way of contrast, the more recent NT theologies by James D. G. Dunn (1990) and N. T. Wright (1992; 1996; 2003, the first three of his major five-book project) are explicit in their attempt to do something that Bultmann refused to do: namely, to read NT texts through lenses that are *both* rigorously historical *and* unashamedly theological. In any case, it is precisely salvation history's insistence on tracing a theological arc through the NT that makes it an alternative model for NT theology. Claiming a convergence between God's activity and the events narrated in the Bible, the thrust of God's salvation project is revealed in the unfolding history of the biblical witness.

The salvation-history approach is not without problems, however. (1) Because the approach claims there is "one thread" that traverses the NT witnesses and holds them together, the model risks imposing a systematic structure on the NT texts—much like the earlier dogmatic approach. This can be especially troubling when NT texts that do not fit the structure are hindered from speaking for themselves or are silenced completely. Forcing texts to line up somewhere in the salvation-history grid leads to some inevitable distortions. (2) The salvation-history model is often unaware that it tends to ignore the hermeneutical challenge of contemporary significance. Readers are left with only the ancient stories of Paul and others, without offering a NT faith that is a live option for today. For example, Paul's modified eschatology of "already/not yet" is thoroughly explained in salvation-historical terms, but what that would look like today, two thousand years later, is rarely discussed.

Each of these three models—thematic, historical, and theological—has large benefits and some significant pitfalls, as indicated above. The issues and questions that each wrestles with will not be far from our attention. Thematic interpreters ask: Is there a center that unifies the NT writings, or does their diversity make such an enterprise impossible? Historical interpreters ask: Is NT theology primarily an investigation into human theological writing, or does it also somehow connect with God's activity? Theological interpreters ask: Is there an underlying vision of God to which the NT writers give witness, or is it best to characterize the NT as a collection of divergent theologies? While the binary (either/or) form of these questions may not be the most helpful, it does set out the poles of the spectrum within which all NT theologies must work. For a NT Theology to be both serviceable and responsive, it must be able to engage these questions, plus to take advantage of the best of the thematic, historical, and theological models, working at all three agendas at once.

CRITERIA FOR ASSEMBLING A NT THEOLOGY

In order to assemble a serviceable and responsive NT theology, as noted above (one that is both descriptive and constructive, and one that is thematic, historical, and theological), the project must be guided by several criteria. What follows, recast in my own words, are the six criteria for assembling a NT theology set out by my mentor, Prof. John E. Toews; these are the six that I propose guide the presentation of what follows in this book.

First, NT Theology must be firmly rooted in the language of the NT writings themselves. This may seem too obvious to mention. But this criterion is necessary to protect against reading the NT through philosophies like Hegelianism, existentialism, or dispensationalism. By our using the language and the categories of the NT itself, the organizing themes and topics emerge from the biblical texts.

Second, NT theology must incorporate in some way all the theologies represented in the NT writings or groups of writings. It begins with a straightforward inquiry into the theological center or vision guiding each NT writing. It is not that the Bible is "raw material" waiting for theology to be "done to it" later. The NT is already a theological construction. NT theology enables the various themes and concepts to emerge, and discusses their relatedness. Similarities and differences are noted between NT voices, but individual voices are not forced to sing in unison. Tensions are allowed to remain so that space, spectrum, and dimension emerge. Thus, NT theology searches for the unified theology underlying the whole (i.e., the theology behind the advice or driving the story), based on the conviction that, while fragmentary and diverse, each writing is a witness to God's activity.

Third, NT theology must be able to organize and to set out the themes that the NT writers are discussing so that a coherent and consequential conversation can happen across time and culture. Whether students follow the canonical order (from Matthew to Revelation) or a chronological order from earliest to latest (e.g., 1 Thessalonians to 2 Peter), the voices speaking to topics like revelation, God, Jesus, humanity, the Holy Spirit, and so on, can be collated, compared, and contrasted.

Both the diversity and the unity ought to be noted, and the relationship explored between unity and difference, because this gives texture and depth to the theological construction.

Fourth, NT theology must be both historical and theological, just as the writings themselves come from a particular historical era and express theological interests. NT theology will acknowledge the NT writers' conviction that God is doing something special in these last days, and this connects to the ancient promise and purpose of God. Contemporary NT theology, however, will also recognize the creative pastoral theology in which the writers are engaged as they embrace the invitation to join in God's mission. Thus, worthwhile NT theology will reject as false the dichotomy established by the question: Is NT theology a *historical* discipline or a *theological* discipline? It is both. The task of NT theology is to *describe* the guiding convictions characteristic of each writing and then to *construct* ways of extending these views for contemporary appropriation. It is both descriptive and constructive.

Fifth, NT theology must be a theology of the whole Christian Bible as well. It must be able to integrate the Hebrew Bible (OT) and the early Christian writings (NT) without falling into the trap of reading the OT only for its clues to Jesus's identity. The gains made by the biblical theology movement, which freed the OT to speak for itself, must not be lost. Recognizing that the OT prophets spoke the Word of God to their own generation, a NT theology must be able to overcome the wall between OT and NT. It will not be *supersessionist* with regard to Israel (claiming that the church has superseded, replaced, or displaced Israel), but instead it will trace the links that the NT writers themselves sketch between the Torah and Jesus. Key to this understanding will be the realization that the OT sees itself as incomplete—not in the sense of lacking something, but in the sense of anticipating the day when evil is undone and God's creation purpose is finally realized. In this way, NT theology must be able to connect with OT's vision for creation.

Sixth, NT theology ought to emerge from and also shape local ecclesial communities of biblical interpretation. NT theology must be translatable into contemporary forms as it leads to and comes from theological reflection. However, such an enterprise is necessarily partial and contingent. The project always gets a grade of IP (i.e., "in process"), since it takes place within a particular ecclesial and theological location that is still itself in process. In other words, the best NT theology emerges from within those communities actively engaged in biblical interpretation and theological reflection and appropriation. These communities offer self-critical engagement of culture and its values. Thus, NT theology takes place in the context of the church in mission (the mission of God), continually *reaching back* (rooted in the biblical witness) and *extending forward* (powered by the biblical witness) to live the missional imperative. Therefore, NT theology finds ways to re-express the theology of the NT in order to shape the norms of the contemporary church's life within the culture in which it finds itself.

To do NT theology according to these six criteria is not about collecting raw material excavated from the gold mine of the Bible so that it can then be presented to the church for its theological work of constructing doctrines (i.e., the so-called conservative option, for lack of a better term). In this view, the Bible is seen as a deposit to be mined for the propositions useful in contemporary settings. Neither is NT theology largely a sociological study of what the ancients thought about God (i.e., the so-called liberal option). In this view, the Bible is seen as an antiquated museum piece and as something to be either updated or set aside so that life can proceed in a politically correct manner. On the contrary, the NT theology that I am proposing is better compared to a community support group or recovery group, where newcomers learn and old-timers review the vision of God's reconstituted, resistance people. While they live in the shadow of the empire, they refuse its death-dealing ways, choosing to embrace their life-affirming vocation of promoting God's creation purposes.

NT theology, then, amounts to an invitation to come and live in the community where God's ongoing and gracious purposes are being explored and lived, with the NT writers setting the agenda. In a real way the NT is already a theological construction, a theological witness to God's deliverance, promise, and covenant faithfulness. There is no need to revise or update the biblical narratives to conform to any particular cultural reality. Instead, NT theology invites people within their particular cultural reality to participate in the NT witness to God's creative enterprise. The project is not about "cutting new ground"—the temptation is always to say *more* or *less* than the biblical witness—but instead to find ways to re-express and extend the biblical witness in contemporary patterns. In this way, people in each generation can recover their true identity as narrated by the biblical story, so that this story becomes theirs, actualized within faith communities everywhere. Without embarrassment, these communities embrace the Christian Bible as scripture, not as simply one narrative among others, but as one privileged above all others and expected to shape their community's life by its story.

A "CONFERENCE TABLE" MODEL OF NT THEOLOGY

To optimize the benefits of the three models that have been attempted over the years (thematic, historical, and salvation-history) and to avoid some of their pitfalls, I propose to build on Caird's "conference table" model. In this model, the writers of the NT are invited to speak to the issues that they themselves raise. Just exactly how many authors there are, or who they are, is less important than hearing their voices. In this way, a context is created within which there is room to explore ongoing implications and to keep the conference in session—thus, a model that is both descriptive and constructive.

Good precedent exists for such a conference. The first apostolic conference was held in Jerusalem (Acts 15; Galatians 2), less than twenty years after Pentecost. This meeting serves as a guide for our own conference proceedings. The point of discussion at the first conference was the unity of the young church. Paul's Gentile mission was under review: What was it? Was it legitimate? What were the implications? At the meeting, Paul set before the conference his gospel, because it had implications for the church. Paul was convinced that Jesus, "who had died under the curse of the Law had been vindicated by God, and was now able to offer to those whose penalty he had shared a share in his own victorious life" (Caird 1994:23). But if "being righteoused" was about identifying with Jesus's victory and not counting on one's ethnicity, this had as a corollary the equality of Jew and Gentile in the church, something not yet fully accepted in Jerusalem.

The Jerusalem-council debate was critical. If the church in Jerusalem failed to see the gospel as Paul did, then his missionary venture would receive a serious setback. The issue was church unity. In the end, the apostles did come to consensus, even if there remained differences of opinion about which they agreed to differ. They reached unity, having heard enough to be satisfied with Paul's construal of God's mission. However, they did not write up a "statement of faith" to be signed, or even attempt to reach unanimity! Peter and Paul were to go on their own separate missionary ventures: Peter to the Jews and Paul to the Gentiles.

They separated not out of disunity, but agreeing on essentials (namely, that both their missions were really part of God's mission) and recognizing different practices with regard to the Jewish ethnic identity markers (i.e., circumcision, dietary laws, and laws of ritual purity).

The deliberations at the Jerusalem conference are of signal importance for understanding the unity of the NT, the unity of the church, and the task of NT theology. Caird notes:

> The New Testament itself provides a criterion for judging its own unity. The question we must ask is not whether these books all say the same thing, but whether they all bear witness to the same Jesus and through him to the many splendored wisdom of the one God. If we are persuaded that the second Moses, the Son of Man, the friend of sinners, the incarnate *logos*, the firstborn of all creation, the Apostle and High Priest of our calling, the Chief Shepherd, and the Lamb opening the scroll are the same person in whom the one God has achieved and is achieving his mighty work, we shall neither attempt to press all our witnesses into a single mould nor captiously complain that one seems at points deficient in comparison with another. (1994:24)

Thus, the conference recounted in Acts 15 and Galatians 2 helps to conceptualize how the collection of NT writings function to map out the parameters within which Christian churches can discern their share in the unity that is theirs in spite of their diversity, and helps to visualize the task of NT theology.

The implementation of the conference-table model for NT theology involves two steps with two corresponding assumptions. (1) The NT writers are invited to speak of their driving vision or passion. While they are not expected to say exactly the same thing, the operative assumption is that they "bear witness to the same Jesus and through him to the many splendored wisdom of the one God" (Caird 1994:24). Our task, as conference chairpersons, will be to interrogate the NT witnesses and to articulate the sense of the meeting, even if it can only ever be an "interim report" from the conference. (2) The contributions of the NT writers are then sorted out and organized around the topics that appear to get significant attention, topics like Christology, theology, ecclesiology, anthropology, eschatology, and so on. Here, the operative assumption is that God, the Master of the Universe, chooses to be revealed over time through the testimony of many independent and diverse witnesses.

Thus, the NT writers testify to the remarkable program of God's self-revelation, one where "the music of the NT choir is not written to be sung in unison" (ibid.:24). The multivoiced choir also enables all to be able to find voices in the choir with which to resonate. Our task, as conference chairpersons, will be to supervise and facilitate the extension of the NT witnesses, enabling the inclusion of all who choose to add their voice to the choir.

Probably the biggest advantage of the conference-table model is that it combines the strengths of the three current models (it is thematic, historical, and theological), and it works in such a way as to reduce the pitfalls that so easily trip up these three when they are practiced in isolation from one another. In the back-and-forth dialogue between the members of the conference, space is created within which successive faith communities are empowered by the Spirit of the risen Christ to do their theological reflection, constructing ways to appropriate the witness of God's Word.

As the microphone is passed around the conference table from one NT writer to the next, we hear the unity that reverberates through their different theologies, as well as the "symphonic effect" produced by the diversity of their theological expressions. The full-bodied, multivoiced chorus summons successive faith communities in the Spirit of the risen Lord to do their own theological thinking and appropriation, embodying the subject matter to which the NT gives witness. Thus, the watching world is invited to participate in God's shalom project (Ott 2004), as local faith communities hear the living Word of the Lord again in fresh ways and are shaped by its testimony. In this way, participants find themselves drawn to and added to the "cloud of witnesses" (Heb 12:1), those who have also responded to God's call from the beginning of time.

In the next chapter, the focus turns to clarifying the subject matter under discussion around the NT conference table.

EXERCISES

1. Read Reginald Fuller's essay, "New Testament Theology," in *The New Testament and Its Modern Interpreters*, 565–84.

    Trace the development of NT theology through the twentieth century. How compelling is Fuller's assessment of the future of NT theology? What has the twenty-first century revealed so far?

2. Read Robert Morgan's essay, "Theology (NT)," in *The Anchor Bible Dictionary*, 6:473–83.

    Morgan reviews the nature and purpose of NT theology and makes some analysis of critical junctures in its history. He concludes with a list of nine challenges faced by practitioners of NT theology. Which do you find most pressing? Why?

3. Read Krister Stendahl's essay called "Biblical Theology, Contemporary," in *The Interpreter's Dictionary of the Bible*, 1:418–32; and Dennis T. Olson's essay titled "Biblical Theology," in *The New Interpreter's Dictionary of the Bible*, 1:461–65.

    Stendahl's classic treatment of biblical theology is known for making a sharp distinction between what a biblical text *meant* in its original setting and what it *means* in the present. Why was such a distinction viewed as a welcome corrective in 1962? What new challenges did his sharp distinction between the descriptive task and the hermeneutical task introduce?

    Compare and contrast Stendahl's 1962 article with Olson's 2006 article.

4. Visit a theological library and browse the NT theology section (BS2397). Pull from the shelves several texts and review their introductions and tables of contents.

    What do the introductory comments and the topics under discussion reveal about the assumptions made by these theologians?

5. Read Dan O. Via's small book, in the Guides to Biblical Scholarship series, called *What Is New Testament Theology?* He provides a helpful summary of the different ways NT theologies are organized. Via's special interest is the interface of NT theology with history, hermeneutics, and postmodernity.

    Make a concept map linking the forms of NT theology with their key proponents. Share your map with someone else, explaining the differences and various emphases of each type of NT theology. Assess the merits of Via's prognosis for the future of NT theology.

2

New Testament Theology as a Historical and Theological Discipline

IN THIS CHAPTER, WE turn our attention to the subject matter under discussion at the NT conference, exploring both its historical and theological dimensions. The chapter has five objectives: (1) to explore the subject matter being discussed at the NT meeting, (2) to clarify what happened to launch the Jesus movement, (3) to examine the dissonance between the early Christian experience and their inherited symbolic world (i.e., the way first-century Jews traditionally made sense of the world), (4) to show how interpretation mediated the tension between experience and symbolic world, and (5) to list the convictions emerging from the interplay of experience and interpretation that will become central to NT theology.

THE SUBJECT MATTER OF THE CONFERENCE TABLE MEETING

So, who called this meeting anyway? What is to be discussed? What is the reason for the meeting? Before we pass the microphone to each NT panelist to hear them respond to such questions, one issue needs to be addressed. We must inquire about the nature of the early Christian experience we are about to hear described. Most everyone would agree that the panelists are going to talk about an experience in which they share in some way. But what is the nature of this experience? Where did it start? Some clarification is needed.

Clearly the NT writers are writing about a story that they found to be significant. Evidently others resonated with the same story as well—so much so that the NT writings were circulated, copied, and expanded in communities of faith around the Mediterranean. But was this founding story an event that happened to a particular person upon which the first Christians then elaborate? Or was it an experience that emerged from within the first Christians themselves? Or perhaps was it some combination? Just exactly what kind of story or experience is being discussed anyway?

At the outset, it is important to recognize that NT scholars do not assess the generating experience in the same way. During the first half of the twentieth century, the nature of the experience was read largely as a historical experience that happened to Jesus, which was then witnessed by the early followers of Jesus and then later framed by the NT writers in various forms: in letters, speeches, biographies, histories, and apocalypses. However, even with scholarly agreement at this level, the implication of that historical event witnessed by Jesus's followers was read quite differently. Two options emerged: one nonnormative and one normative. These are the two that would later contribute to the "iron curtain" dividing biblical theology from theological concerns described in chapter 1 as the "crisis" in biblical theology.

For one set of scholars, including Wrede (1973), the historical experience of the early disciples was unique to "primitive" Christianity. Following the chronological, history-of-religion model, mixed with strong elements of Hegelian dialectical philosophy, these scholars understood NT theology as a historical or descriptive discipline with no normative value for contemporary faith. For these scholars, the Easter faith experienced by the primitive church disappeared long ago and is no longer available. Since there was virtually no connection between the early Jesus movement (lost forever) and the institutional form of contemporary Christianity, NT theology could have no normative value for Christianity today.

For another set of scholars, including Schlatter (1973), the encounter of the early disciples with Jesus was indeed normative in that it formed the basis for normative theology addressing the contemporary church. These scholars followed the theological model, claiming that NT theology was a historical discipline that also had normative value. While contemporary Christianity certainly differed in some aspects from early

Christianity, a strong link still held between them, such that those early experiences could indeed be used as proclamation/exhortation for the believing community today. Schlatter agreed with Wrede that NT theology was a historical discipline; but on theological grounds he found Wrede's nonnormative reading lacking. For Schlatter, history was the arena of God's actions, and therefore, NT theology remained normative and instructive to successive generations of Jesus followers.

The situation changed in the Western world during the second half of the twentieth century, largely due to Bultmann's *New Testament Theology*. Bultmann (1951, 1955) proposed a solution to the dilemma represented by the growing divide between NT theologians who lined up behind either Schlatter (NT as normative) or Wrede (NT as nonnormative). Bultmann's solution was quite novel. Why not divide the NT into two groups? Treat some of the NT material as Wrede did (as nonnormative and purely descriptive of a time no longer available) while treating other NT parts as normative and constructive for contemporary appropriation, as Schlatter did?

The question, however, remained: By what method could the NT be separated into these two groups? The answer was found in some of the new critical tools used by scholars. Form criticism and source criticism were becoming quite fashionable instruments in the toolbox of scholars in the history-of-religion school. These scholars assumed multiple sources and settings went into the composition of the gospel narratives (and biblical material in general), and that the footprints of these sources and settings were often still visible in the literary seams left over from the not-so-careful stitching together of various literary forms (e.g., Jesus sayings, parables, teaching material, miracle stories, healing accounts, passion narratives). Bultmann suggested that one could magnify these editorial moves by assuming that the framers of gospel narratives—the ones who sorted through the oral traditions in the decades after Easter, organizing and editing them into the final gospel forms which we have today—were working with *two* Jesus figures: Jesus of Nazareth (the pre-Easter historical figure) and the Christ of faith (the post-Easter religious figure).

In the post-Easter period, so the argument goes, the search for self-understanding in the wake of great disappointment (i.e., their teacher's execution) caused the early disciples to merge the two Jesus figures in the interests of Christian devotion and proclamation. The "Christ of faith" represented the struggle of each Christian to find for himself or herself the redemptive significance of the cross, transcending reason, emotion, and the materialism of the world. As an existentialist, Bultmann was convinced that to lead an authentic life a person must *choose* a life, not live one shaped by the material world. Similar convictions guided the early disciples, Bultmann believed, which caused them to conflate the pre-Easter Jesus with the post-Easter Christ through fictionalized/mythological stories of Jesus developed after the crucifixion, during a period of oral transmission. Eventually these sources and settings were combined by the NT writers into the written form that we now have.

Bultmann developed criteria by which, he argued, the NT historian could assess the historicity of a Jesus narrative. These tools helped him decide which stories could be traced to Jesus of Nazareth, and which stories should be attributed to the early community's witness to the Christ of faith. Only that which could be traced back to Jesus of Nazareth (using his critical tools) was historical. Actually Bultmann did not think there would be very much left after the layers of mythology added by the later Christians were peeled away. About the only thing that passed through his criteria was Jesus's message that the Son of Man is coming, and that the kingdom of God is near. These could be certain, in Bultmann's view, to go all the way back to Jesus of Nazareth; the rest (e.g., miraculous healing stories and resurrection accounts) was retrojection, or editorial reworking at the hands of the young church, which wanted to connect its idea of the Christ of faith with Jesus of Nazareth using fictional/mythical stories of Jesus.

The key criterion that Bultmann used was called "dissimilarity." The tool worked like this: Anything that appeared in Jesus's mouth that would also likely be affirmed by the early church was assumed to be retrojection by the early church (i.e., words placed in Jesus's mouth). Employing this tool, he worked to peel away the layers that he suspected were added by later Christians to make Jesus fit the affirmations that these Christians were making about the Christ of faith. As one can imagine, the remaining profile of Jesus was quite meager. Since the early church confessed Jesus as Messiah, so the argument goes, this title as a self-designation could not have been something that goes back to Jesus. According to the criterion of dissimilarity, Jesus could not have claimed to be the Messiah, since that is what the post-Easter community believed. Only those sayings of Jesus dissimilar to what one would expect a post-Easter Christian community to say could be assured of being truly the words of Jesus. Not much passes this criterion. About all that remains is a shadowy figure calling or longing for God's liberation of Israel.

Of course many have argued with good reason that Bultmann's criterion of dissimilarity is far too restrictive, eliminating all of the Jesus tradition that was also valued by the church. It is skewed against Jesus's teaching, suspicious of anything also affirmed by the church. The tool has some value in *confirming* aspects of Jesus's teaching (e.g., those sayings that later Christians might have found troubling or embarrassing and could easily have eliminated from the record; but because they did not, their authenticity increases). However, the criterion of dissimilarity is not useful for *refuting* the authenticity of Jesus's teaching, since in order to work, it presumes that Jesus's followers affirmed and passed on *nothing* of Jesus's life and teaching. Only those things completely lost on the disciples could pass through this criterion. However, surely Jesus's disciples must have received, remembered, and transmitted much of Jesus's teaching—even if they did not understand all of its significance. Jesus was after all known as a good teacher.

For Bultmann, however, the meager historical sketch of Jesus of Nazareth was not really a problem, since it could not be used for authentic faith anyway according to his existentialist theology. Why? Because faith based on evidence is not real faith. So for Bultmann, Jesus was merely "a presupposition for the theology of the New Testament rather than part of that theology itself" (1951:3). The "proclaimer became the proclaimed" (ibid.:33) in the preaching of the early church. Jesus announced God's coming kingdom, but it was his followers who filled out this assertion in remarkable ways (i.e., with the kerygma). What is necessary for Christian faith to flourish is that each person mimics such faith by courageously deciding to live authentically and faithfully, rising above disappointments and failure, just as Paul and John did. This was real NT theology, according to Bultmann. The Christ of faith must be embodied existentially by each authentic disciple of Jesus.

According to Bultmann, Paul and John wrote profound existential theology, since their embrace of the Christ of faith involved genuine obedience to the proclamation of the Easter faith (i.e., the kerygma), resulting in a new understanding of the self and of God. For Bultmann, "every assertion about God is simultaneously an assertion about [humanity] and vice versa" (ibid.:191). In this way, Bultmann's theology had an essentially anthropological core: to engage in theology was to engage in anthropology—not anthropology in the sense of social-scientific research, but in the broader sense of understanding what it means to be human. At the very center was the affirmation that when Jesus died, it was not Jesus who arose, but it was the *church* that arose in its proclamation of the Easter faith (i.e., the kerygma).

Thus, existentialism's invitation to live authentically extends to all people; come one and all; live courageously in the hope that animated the first disciples in the face of incredible odds, and thereby share in their Easter faith. This explains Bultmann's demythologization program. By stripping away the ancient mythological and legendary features (e.g., the empty tomb), contemporary disciples have an opportunity to embrace the theological vision that leads to authentic living. Choose life in the face of death! Share in the Easter faith that rises above horrible situations and evidence to the contrary in order to live an authentic, self-actualized life.

Unlike Wrede and Schlatter, for Bultmann the experience that the conference delegates are talking about is not something that happened to Jesus, which was then witnessed by the early followers, circulated orally within the Jesus communities for several decades, and finally fixed in the form we now have by the NT writers. No, the experience being shared at the conference table is the writers' own, and one that must be replicated by every person of faith if they are to be persons of Easter faith, like Paul and John.

To sum up, according to Bultmann, the confession of the church is a function of the Easter experience in the hearts of the disciples as they make sense of the loss of their teacher and rabbi, finding new ways to carry on in spite of their disappointment. Jesus really is not messianic. He is the proclaimer of the Jewish apocalyptic kingdom of God, who is looking for the coming of the future messiah. The early church confessed Jesus as that Messiah on the basis of their own Easter experience and conflated the two. Thus, the church made a nonmessianic Jesus into a messianic Jesus. But instead of this being a horrible hoax, it is exemplary! Just as the disciples created the empty tomb and resurrection stories to deal with their profound disappointment, so contemporary followers of Jesus must also existentially make the "leap of faith" in their personal struggle to overcome the messiness and disappointment of life.

Where are things now in the period following Bultmann? The influence of Bultmann extends far and wide so that whether scholars agree or disagree with his assessments, they must deal with Bultmann. Contemporary scholars have mostly abandoned his skepticism about finding any value in the historical Jesus. In fact, historical-Jesus research has become fashionable once again. Many scholars continue to use his critical tools (like the criterion of dissimilarity) for separating the sayings or events they think reach back to Jesus of Nazareth from those thought to be added later by the early Christian community. However, where Bultmann saw such reconstructions as having no bearing on contemporary faith (since true faith is about overcoming disappointments), a new generation of critical scholars argues that the meager and nontraditional picture of Jesus extracted from the gospel narratives is indeed constructive for faith. How so? For these scholars, the nontraditional picture of Jesus undermines and challenges the convictions of the established church or of civil religion, which are often held with much suspicion and disdain by these same scholars.

Still, Bultmann's assessment is not the only way to appreciate the Easter faith that sent the first disciples into the world to preach the good news of God's salvation and victory over death. There are many (including me!) whose presuppositions and conclusions are quite different from Bultmann's. Three points of challenge are noteworthy. First, the disconnect that Bultmann proposed between Jesus of Nazareth and the Christ of faith undermines the very faith that Bultmann wants to promote. Why? Because it makes Christianity basically docetic, gnostic, and ahistorical. By disconnecting the spiritual from the earthly, Bultmann fails to appreciate the implications of Christianity's location within Judaism, where disembodied souls have no legitimate place (1 Cor 15:38). Even Paul identifies the risen Lord as having a "spiritual body," although not of "flesh and blood" (1 Cor 15:44, 50); and Luke stresses the risen Lord is not a ghost but truly a body, albeit of another dimension, of the new-age dimension (Luke 24:39). Bultmann's affirmations miss this vital continuity by separating body from soul, separating history from faith, and separating Jesus from the Christ. By promoting faith as an out-of-body, existential decision, faith borders on the neurotic, illusory, and psychosomatic. If faith becomes an experience that is self-generated, Christian faith is not rooted in a human response to historical acts of God's liberation but in psychological wishful thinking.

It may be praiseworthy for its bravery, but in the end it is unable to deliver much more than just that, bravery.

Second, Bultmann's assumption of what is possible and what is not, of what is historical and what is mythical, undermines the testimony of the first witnesses of the Easter event in a way that approaches arrogance. For the moment, leaving aside the exact nature of the resurrection, which we will discuss below, the gospel narratives remain univocal in their affirmation that those who spoke about the resurrection of Jesus believed themselves to be speaking about an event that happened to Jesus several days after his crucifixion. In the words of Caird, "It was not a private, interior illumination which sent them out into the world as preachers of the gospel, but a conviction that they had been witnesses to an event exterior to their own minds, an event which happened to someone else" (1997:217). Of course, one could argue that they were mistaken, or that they misinterpreted their experience (something Bultmann does not claim). But that they declare to be speaking about a matter of fact is hard to get around, given the memory of eyewitnesses that remained in control at that stage.

Third, Bultmann's dismissal of the continuity between the Easter proclamation (kerygma) and Jesus's own proclamation misconstrues the character of the disciples' Easter experience of Jesus's resurrection. The NT writers do not characterize the resurrection of Jesus as a resuscitation of a dead corpse. On the contrary, the NT writers speak of the resurrection appearances as Jesus with his disciples in a *new* way—as the ongoing, personal, and transcendent presence of Jesus among his followers through the power of the Holy Spirit. See, for example, Luke Johnson's helpful study titled *The Religious Experience in Earliest Christianity* (1998), examining baptism, speaking in tongues, and meals in common. And the same resurrection presence of the risen Lord Jesus continues to be experienced in the regular activities of the church—worship, signs and wonders, healing, instruction, discernment, forgiveness, deliverance, mission, and so on—as it actively anticipates *now* the completion of the resurrection transformation of all things, something that still remains a *future* hope (variously called: the "coming" of the Lord, the "end of time," the "resurrection," the "new heaven and earth," the "new Jerusalem").

In fact, it was only after the disciples' Easter encounter with the risen Lord that they came to know who Jesus *really was* as "the Christ."

And it was that same experience which also forced them to recognize who Jesus *had been* before his exaltation to God's right hand. This explains why the gospel stories explicitly indicate that they are written after and in light of the disciples' Easter experience (e.g., John 12:33). The gospel stories themselves represent the continuity between Jesus's own proclamation and the Easter proclamation (kerygma), a continuity that always was there, but only discerned in hindsight.

Recall Luke's portrayal of an incident where Jesus joins the two travelers to Emmaus, chiding them for not realizing that the Christ would have to suffer "these things" before his victory and glorification. "Beginning with Moses and all the prophets, he interpreted to them the things about himself in all the scriptures" (Luke 24:27). It had not been obvious before Easter. But after Easter, it was the risen Lord who "opened their minds to understand the scriptures" (24:45). They had to learn how to find Jesus in Scripture and thus to hear for the *first time* what Jesus had been saying *all along*: "these are my words that I spoke to you while I was still with you" (24:44).

Instead of courageous stories of the disciples' bravery and innovation in the face of disappointment (Bultmann), the gospel accounts represent eyewitness testimonies of an enormous world-transforming power that radically changed the disciples' assessment of what was, what is, and what will be. But this means that, as Johnson points out, "the Christian experience of the resurrection . . . did not follow as a natural result of the ministry of Jesus as recounted in the Gospels. It is rather the reverse: the Gospels follow as a natural process of reflection on Jesus' human ministry as a result of the Christian experience of him as resurrected Lord" (2003:108). Even so, while it is not now possible to detail exactly the extent to which the Easter experience shaped the NT writers' narration of the circulating memories of Jesus's life, teaching, and ministry, it is enough to affirm that Easter made an impact, and at the same time to claim a basic continuity between Jesus's own proclamation and the way that the NT writers presented and elaborated the Easter proclamation (kerygma) later in their gospel narratives and exhortations.

So, in the rest of this book, I assume that our conference participants are going to be relating, in a seamless whole, both the transmitted memories of Jesus's proclamation *and* their interpretation of the shocking event that happened to Jesus, the significance of which they struggled to comprehend using the symbols available to them.

CLARIFYING WHAT HAPPENED TO LAUNCH THE MOVEMENT

So, what was that event that the NT writers claim to have happened to, in, and among the first disciples? Whatever it was, the obscurity of the early Christian movement certainly does complicate investigation into its origin. Consider these facts: Its founder was executed, but his followers were not—although they scattered in fear (Mark 16:8). Plus, the first missionaries were common folk who proclaimed a radical message that seemed foolish to the sophisticated (Acts 17). And yet, it was precisely this radical message that made the early Christian movement appealing to those who were typically disenfranchised by society: transients, slaves, freed folk, and women (1 Cor 1:26–31). Many of these had achieved a status in society that was inconsistent with their attributed status for one reason or another (Meeks 1983). While they may have achieved a high status in the eyes of those whose opinion counted by their hard work, outstanding talent, or remarkable ingenuity, if they were not of a certain race, social class, or gender, a corresponding attributed status could not be granted to them in the highly stratified society of the ancient world: attributed status depended largely on birth (Malina 2001:32–33). Doubtless, these marginalized folk saw in the Easter proclamation of new creation something to correct their lack of attributed status.

Baptismal confessions like the following must have been very attractive: "There is no longer Jew or Greek, there is no longer slave or free, there is no longer male and female; for all of you are one in Christ" (Gal 3:28). Perhaps this explains the disproportionate number of wealthy women (Lydia, Phoebe, Chloe, and others) providing leadership along with men in the early house churches. These wealthy women had nothing to lose and much to gain. They, and other disenfranchised folk, found the apostolic testimony to Jesus's story so compelling that they threw in their lot with this radical messianic group, forming small house churches around the Mediterranean world and giving witness to the contrast-society of God's reign.

The early church was initially ridiculed, persecuted, and dismissed by those with attributed status. During the first one hundred years (until about 130 CE) only rarely are Christians mentioned in the sources still available to us outside the NT. Josephus, the Jewish historian, refers briefly to Jesus and the movement that sprang up following his execution, noting also the stoning in 62 CE of James, the brother of Jesus and the leader of the Jerusalem church (*Antiquities* 18.3.3; 20.9.1).

From the Greco-Roman world only three citations can be found before 130 CE: Pliny, the Roman governor, writing to Emperor Trajan in 112 CE, asks for advice on how to deal with this secret society (i.e., Christians), which threatens worship at pagan temples by drawing people out of paganism and into what he calls "superstition." Pliny gives the only direct evidence by an outsider of early Christian worship practice. By means of torture, he obtained the following information:

> They maintained, moreover, that the amount of their fault or error had been this, that it was their habit on a fixed day to assemble before daylight and recite by turns a form of words to Christ as to a god; and that they bound themselves with an oath, not for any crime, but not to commit theft or robbery or adultery, not to break their word, and not to deny a deposit when demanded. After this was done, it was their custom to depart, and to meet again to take food, but ordinary food and harmless food . . . I discovered nothing else than a perverse and extravagant superstition. (Pliny *Letters* 10.96)

Roman historian Suetonius reports the expulsion of Jews from Rome during the reign of Claudius (41–54 CE), probably because of conflict and rioting within the Jewish community over the Christian claim that Jesus was the Messiah (*Claudius* 5.25.4). The report corresponds with Acts 18:2, where we learn that Paul meets Aquila and Priscilla in Corinth, after they had been expelled from Rome due to Claudius's edict.

Tacitus, another Roman historian, reports in 115 CE the persecution of Christians under Nero. They were accused of setting fire to Rome in 64 CE. "Nero fastened the guilt and afflicted the most exquisite tortures on a class hated for their abominations, called Christians by the populace. Christus, from whom the name had its origin, suffered the extreme penalty during the reign of Tiberius at the hands of one of our procurators, Pontius Pilate, and a deadly superstition, thus checked for the moment, again broke out, not only in Judaea, the first source of the evil, but also in the city, where all things hideous and shameful from every part of the world meet and become popular" (Tacitus *Annals* 15.44.2–8). These three pagan sources confirm that Christianity was first considered a sect within Judaism, that it spread from Jerusalem through

Asia Minor and to Rome, and that it was occasionally persecuted by Jewish and Roman authorities.

By the fourth century, however, Christianity had surprisingly become the dominant religious force in the Greco-Roman world. What happened? It was not esoteric teaching on the part of the early Christians that brought about this transformation. Instead it was ushered in by power. What kind of power? The experience of God's power lay in the claim to actualize the very presence of God in their meetings together and in making this claim plausible and persuasive to anyone interested.

The early Christians like Paul and his associates, sewing and mending at their workbenches in the open markets, did not offer philosophical or rational proofs, but conversed with passersby and invited interested folk to come and to see for themselves. They might have said something like, "We are having a potluck this Sunday evening at Chloe's house after we finish up here at the market. Why not stop by, and we can talk further? You do not have to bring any food this time; it is your first visit. I can tell you already that we are seeing some amazing things in the life and teaching of Jesus, in the Torah, and in our own lives: things that we never saw before." For those who wanted to see, there was plenty of evidence to confirm the veracity of the Easter proclamation: healings, signs, and release from oppressive powers of fear, guilt, and shame; there was reconciliation, mutual caring, and sharing.

These early Christians were filled with the Spirit's power, representing God's inbreaking rule within the world. They were convinced that they were part of a new creation, that the new age was dawning, and that the revelation of God's end-time rule was now taking shape among them. This experience of power was not self-generated but something initiated by God and to which they were invited to respond with vital participation: this inaugurated a real transformation within them and within their world. Paul captures this sentiment by asserting that God "was pleased to reveal his Son to (in) me" (Gal 1:16).

Something happened in the lives of real people. Something caused them to perceive their lives in radically new ways, which in turn compelled them to interpret their experience by means of the available symbols. The point is that the NT writers were not involved in self-generated creative writing; they were involved in the very work of processing the memories of Jesus's remarkable life *and* sorting out their powerful experience of his ongoing life among them with the symbols at hand. Of course they were creative, but not creative for creativity's sake. They were creative in finding ways to talk about Jesus and their experience of resurrection power: they used argumentation, narrative, metaphor, exhortation, eschatology, myth, and so on.

Still the NT is incomprehensible if seen as a collection of creative writings, even theological writings in an abstract or individual way. Why? Because, as Johnson says, "The NT is the furthest thing from such a scholastic enterprise. There is theology to be found in it, to be sure, but it is a theology that consists not in working out corollaries to propositions but in pursuing reflection on a present and continuing experience of the most fundamental sort—religious experience" (1999:104).

What was that religious experience that launched the movement? Put quite simply, it was the first disciples' experience of the resurrected Lord and how this event connected with Jesus's own teaching. Even so, this *experience* was mediated through the available symbols. So in the act of perception—in the experience itself—there is already a form of interpretation. After all, "there is no naked experience of the holy. The totally other is mediated by that which is not totally other: human symbols" (ibid.:109). In the end, religious experience lives in constantly moving "circular patterns: from experience to interpretation, from interpretation to experience" (ibid.:94). While circular, the pattern of religious experience is not like spontaneous combustion; that is, it is not generated from a number of internal factors; something from outside must initiate the circular pattern. That something was the resurrection of Jesus. This was the event that transformed their interpretation of Jesus's ministry.

The NT writers we will hear from at the conference give us a variety of interpretations of Easter and its significance for Jesus, as they attempt to articulate their religious experience of God's profound intervention at this point in human history. They also use a variety of genres to give expression to their interpretations: gospels, persuasive speeches, sermons, apocalypses, narratives, exhortations, and so on. But behind them all is the conviction that Jesus must have been telling the truth, that he was raised from the dead, that he is alive, and that the new-creation age has dawned. So while there are multiple religious experiences, there is but one shared experience. This is the one originating or generating experience without which there would be no Christian movement, without which there would be nothing to explain or interpret, and without which there would be no NT.

To sum up, the experience that launched the first Jesus movement has been described variously. Bultmann says, "If the event of Easter Day is in any sense an historical event additional to the event of the cross, it is nothing else than the rise of faith in the risen Lord, since it was this faith which led to the apostolic preaching. The resurrection itself is not an event of past history. All that historical criticism can establish is the fact that the first disciples came to believe in the resurrection" (1953:41). Caird counters, offering a more helpful explanation, "historical criticism can and must establish something rather different. The first disciples did not come to believe in the resurrection as an event which happened to themselves, comparable with Gautama's illumination, but as an event which happened to Jesus" (1997:217). The resurrection faith of the first disciples had the objective content of their experience of Jesus, now alive in a new way following his execution; this is the event that launched the movement.

From the starting point of Jesus's resurrection, the movement renewed its commitment to the story of Jesus, to the unfolding plan of God from the beginning of time, and to the nature of community life. The point is that these stories are not stories of "great psychological struggle" that resulted finally in conviction, but more of a "surprising and totally unexpected encounter" that resulted in the mission to proclaim the good news of freedom and newness of life with boldness, joy, and perseverance in suffering (Johnson 1999:113, 115).

Resurrection faith was not limited to a conviction that Jesus had resumed his life for a time, appearing to a handful of disciples. It was much more. It seems most appropriate to assume that the NT writers were moved to write out of their conviction—demonstrated in their present lives together—(1) that Jesus was alive in a new and powerful way among them because he really did rise from the dead, and (2) that this reality worked to confirm the circulating memories of all that Jesus taught and did during his ministry. Moreover, resurrection faith served to deepen appreciation of the significance of Jesus's ministry within the kingdom of God. It established that Jesus shared God's life in a unique way, making this new life accessible to all through the faith community animated by his life-giving Spirit.

THE DISSONANCE BETWEEN THE EXPERIENCE OF EARLY CHRISTIANS AND THEIR SYMBOLIC WORLD

Still, the Easter experience of the disciples was scandalous because it clashed with their inherited *symbolic world*, "the social structures in which people live, and the symbols attached to and supporting those structures" (Johnson 1999:21). With reference to the pagan symbolic world, the Easter story was confusing. Jesus faced death with fear and trembling, not with the heroic calm characteristic of the tragic hero in Greek mythology. He could be misunderstood to have left his followers not with words of consolation but desolation: "God, why have you forsaken me" (Mark 15:34)? It was not a dignified suicide like those of other heroes, but an excruciatingly painful crucifixion. Neither did Jesus try to bypass death by magic; he was executed like a common criminal. Jesus's death was foolishness, according to the Hellenistic worldview (1 Cor 1:23).

With regard to the Jewish symbolic world, the Easter story was equally confusing and even offensive. It was particularly offensive to Jews who expected a general resurrection of all the righteous to accompany the coming of the Messiah (Dan 12:2). Jesus followers were saying that the resurrection had happened to one man, who was now able to include others in the same resurrection power that would culminate in a general resurrection at the end of time. Equally problematic for many Jews was the observation that this man, Jesus, was executed by crucifixion on a wooden cross like a common criminal. Every Jew knew that "anyone hung on a tree is under God's curse" (Deut 21:23). This was scandalous: an embarrassment to Judaism and, worse, blasphemous (Acts 9:1–2). The notion that such a crucified sinner was actually the resurrected Messiah made no sense according to the Jewish worldview.

Not only was Jesus's death a contradiction to Jews, so was his life. Jews who looked for signs of Jesus's messiahship were disappointed. Why? Because he was not a revolutionary freedom fighter working for Israel's liberation like a Zealot. He did not fulfill the popularly recognized messianic texts; he was not an unambiguous king (2 Sam 7:11–16), and he was not a sword-wielding liberator (Ps 45:4–5). He was a contradiction, an enigma, a disappointment for many.

INTERPRETATION MEDIATES THE TENSION BETWEEN EXPERIENCE AND SYMBOLIC WORLD

How could the conflict be resolved for the first Jewish disciples? Their experience of Jesus' life, ministry, and now resurrection triumph *and* their deeply engrained Torah conviction that God did not dwell among the cursed were at odds. Evidently, the disciples' cognitive dissonance (between their experience and their old symbolic world or *symbolic map*) was the impetus for the interpretation that fills the pages of the NT. The symbolic map inherited from their Jewish traditions "fell to the ground and broke." Why? Because what happened to Jesus was so shocking and so unanticipated. However, as they picked up the pieces of the shattered map, these same old pieces came together in a new way, forming a *new* (but not really new) map to explain what had happened to their now risen Lord. There were no new pieces added to the map; these were the same old Torah pieces. However, from the resurrection perspective, these the old pieces radiated new meaning.

The cognitive dissonance between their experience of the risen Lord and their popular messianic expectations drove these early Christians, careful Jewish interpreters, back to the Torah. There, they found texts that they had never before read as messianic. Reading intertextually (that is, reading old texts from the perspective of their new experience), they found these old texts began to *speak* in new ways, in ways never before appreciated. Actually, this intertexual reading (sometimes called *midrash*) was a classic example of common Jewish interpretive reading strategy.

Johnson lists four texts that were not likely used messianically until the postresurrection reflection of early Christianity (1999:147). A text like "Sit at my right hand until I make your enemies your footstool" (Ps 110:1) became a favorite of Christians and was used extensively by NT writers (Mark 12:36; Matt 22:44; Luke 20:42; Acts 2:34; Heb 1:13). Why? Probably because it reminded them of the remarkable Torah interpretations that Jesus himself was remembered to have made about himself and his ministry. Furthermore, Psalm 110 also suggested that God's agent of salvation could be exalted and glorified, even though the full realization of his rule on earth was set for some time later when the dismantling of evil's rule was complete. The introduction of a *temporal space* helped the early Christians explain the beginning of the resurrection age now, even though it would not be complete until the end of time. Only then would a general resurrection of the righteous be realized. Psalm 110:1 was used regularly to show how Jesus's resurrection fit within the parameters of the ancient biblical witness and made sense of the early Christians' lived experience "between the times."

Another example is an obscure text: "Lo, your king comes to you; triumphant and victorious is he, humble and riding on a donkey" (Zech 9:9), which speaks not of a dominating king, but of a lowly one who is nevertheless triumphant. Again, this is not an image anyone anticipated for the Messiah from a basic reading of Torah before Jesus's ministry. Additional texts like "The stone that the builders rejected has become the chief cornerstone" (Ps 118:22) and Isaiah's servant songs ("He was wounded for our transgressions, crushed for our iniquities; upon him was the punishment that made us whole, and by his bruises we are healed" [Isa 53:5]) came to prominence in light of post-Easter reflection. These obscure texts came into focus because they illuminated the life of Jesus and called to mind things that he likely said about himself: words about one who suffered not because of his rebellion, but because of his faithfulness to the way of Israel's God. His loyalty to God was misunderstood (or perhaps understood all too well!) and he was found to be threatening to those whose loyalty resided elsewhere. And so, he was eliminated, as are all other threats to the empire.

As Israel had during the Babylonian exile, the early Christians experienced the dissonance of trying to match their experience with their symbolic world. They too wondered, "How could we sing the LORD's song in a foreign land" (Ps 137:4)? Gradually these early Christians found within the old symbols ways to talk of their new experience. They began to sing. Or to change the metaphor to one of sight, Luke describes how Paul abandoned his campaign of terrorizing Christians when he too encountered the risen Lord and could no longer dismiss their claims as an embarrassment to Judaism. Finally, he saw what they saw: "Something like scales fell from his eyes, and his sight was restored" (Acts 9:18).

Paul's religious experience was multiplied countless times and continues to characterize the response people of faith have to Jesus's ongoing transforming presence today. The personal and transcendent presence of Jesus among his followers through the power of the Holy Spirit continues to characterize assemblies of Jesus followers in communities around the world. Through worship, signs, instruction, and discernment, the resurrected Lord continues to animate the lives of God's people worldwide.

While the symbolic world of the early disciples gave them some terms of reference with which to interpret their experience, this was not all that happened. The dynamic went in the other direction as well: The powerful, world-shattering experience of the risen Lord compelled his followers to reshape their symbolic world. No longer could they look at the world with old-order eyes—according to the flesh—given their experience of the risen Lord. Instead, their new identification with the resurrected Jesus gave them a new way of seeing things, a new way of looking at the world. They no longer saw things only in one dimension or in one perspective. As participants in the new-creation age, they saw Jesus as not merely human, but as the *truly* human one—the way God had intended humanity to live all along (2 Cor 5:16). They recognized Jesus now as "the image of the invisible God, the firstborn of all creation" (Col 1:15), taking humanity and all of creation one huge step closer toward the goal God intended from the beginning.

Stretched beyond its elastic capacity, the symbolic world that before had worked so well for the earliest disciples suddenly snapped on that first Easter. Yet the meaning-making imperative of being human forced the earliest Christians to reshape their symbolic world to account for their new reality. This dynamic is brilliantly illustrated by Johnson's analogy of the handshake.

> [Suppose] I extend my hand to greet a stranger, and smile. The stranger approaches me the same way. Because of our shared symbolic world, we both perceive the interchange as friendly. In the ordinary course of things, it is—and the experience confirms the perception. When it does, the symbolic world is strengthened, and the symbolic structure that legitimates handshakes is renewed. But the process can go the other way. What if the stranger should grasp my hand violently and slap me in handcuffs? What if he seizes my hand and cuts it off at the wrist? Then my experience radically disconfirms my symbolic world, which says that handshakes are signs of friendship. This experience shakes my view of the world, and the symbolic structure is threatened. In light of this experience, I must now struggle to find meaning where it appears to be absent. The quest for meaning is relentless; life cannot continue without it. We try first to stretch our symbols to cover the experience. Perhaps the stranger was an enemy in disguise, and his handshake was a camouflage. That makes his act of violence anomalous, the exception that proves the rule. Thus our myth is saved, our world secure . . . The elastic

capacity of myths and symbols is, however, finite. Some experiences are so powerful and radical that they threaten to collapse the very structure of the world, the very structure of meaning. (1999:15)

Johnson's back-and-forth, experience-interpretation model illustrated by the handshake is useful for describing both the origin and shape of the NT writings as well. It helps us see why these texts were written. The model pays attention to the early Christian experience (those things that happened in the presence of the disciples), which generated and drove the process of interpretation (the meaning that the disciples attributed to those experiences). Plus the model helps us understand why these writings look as they do; it pays attention to the symbolic world of first-century Judaism and Hellenism that was reshaped in light of Jesus's life and ministry, the crucified and raised Messiah. Some chose to write life stories of Jesus, elaborating on their significance; others chose to compose histories of the movement in good Greco-Roman form; and for others, letters, speeches, and metaphorical apocalyptic poems were the literary genres of choice.

To illustrate the process of meaning making within Judaism's symbolic world, consider Paul's testimony. While Paul's traditional symbolic world helped make some sense of his encounter with Messiah Jesus, it broke under the stress of that surprising meeting with the crucified and risen Lord (1 Cor 15:1–8). Paul's ancient language of "powers and principalities" was profoundly re-formed because of Easter; he was forced to reshape his inherited map. For Paul the powers are those spiritual beings ("sons of God," "host of heaven," or angels) that are created by God and present within our world to help in God's work (e.g., in battle [Josh 5:13–15], in court [1 Kgs 22:19], in giving Torah [Gal 3:19]). While initially loyal, some powers act in defiance of God's purpose, drawing energy from human loyalty and siphoning away human allegiance to God. In return, the rebellious powers turn around and enslave all humankind and all creation in their death-dealing grip (Wink 1998:31–32).

The rebellious powers find representation in political, social, economic, familial, and religious structures of the old-world order that are now tottering toward their demise. So when Paul uses language such as "He disarmed the rulers and authorities and made a public example of them, triumphing over them in it [i.e., the cross]" (Col 2:15), he is using the ancient mythical language of his symbolic world to talk about what happened through Jesus's death and resurrection. The impact of the cross exposed the death-dealing ways of these disloyal powers that infiltrate all aspects of our corporate life as human beings and as peoples of the earth.

Paul is using ancient *mythical symbols* (like powers and principalities involved in the battle between the forces of good and forces of evil) to interpret the *historical event* of the cross: the powers are disarmed by the cross. The death-dealing ways of Satan were shown for what they truly are, draining the lie of its power. Jesus confronts the evil powers, who respond in anger and fear. Overreaching their legitimate jurisdiction, they kill Jesus. In the execution of Jesus, the "scapegoat mechanism" (the notion that someone must pay in order to keep the order of things intact for the rest of us) and the operative myth of "redemptive violence" (the notion that violence can be used redemptively if it is used in defense of justice) are exposed for the lies that they are. No longer can these ideas and the systems founded on them masquerade with promises of security and order; the real character of these dominating and oppressive ideas and systems is exposed for all who care to see. The charade is over; evil unwittingly undoes itself. It neither knew what God was doing through Jesus nor grasped the consequences of killing Jesus. As Paul says, "None of the rulers of this age understood this; for if they had, they would not have crucified the Lord of glory" (1 Cor 2:8).

But then Paul also uses the *historical event* of the cross to reinterpret those same *mythical symbols*. The cross is taken up into the myth of redemptive violence and transforms it. How? From now on, the self-blinding ways of the scapegoat mechanism will never again be free to rule unchallenged. Plus, Jesus's life and ministry, culminating in the cross, reveal God's way of engagement: a way more in line with God's character. Taking the side of the victim, God undoes the ancient death-dealing domination system in a new way, breaking the myth of redemptive violence. From now on, argues Caird, "the victories of God over all the forces in the universe which are resistant to [God's] will are to be won, not by thunderbolts of coercive might, but by the persuasive constraints of self-sacrificing love" (1997:242).

This reconfigured map caused Paul to revise his inherited symbolic world accordingly. Convinced as he was of playing a key role in the final unfolding of God's mission to gather the people of God from all nations, Paul's encounter with the resurrected Jesus and further reflection convinced him of three ways that his understanding of Judaism needed to change.

First, Paul is compelled to redraw the traditional map of the Jewish Day of the Lord. If Jesus is the Messiah (and Paul is now convinced that Jesus is the Messiah), and if the "capital-E" end of the world has not come, then a revision of the old religious map is obviously needed. The coming of the Messiah (and the Day of the Lord that it represents) must be expanded from an abrupt transition to a period of time. The coming of the Messiah needs to be stretched to include both the beginning of the end (i.e., the cross and resurrection of Jesus) and the end of the end (i.e., the public confirmation of Jesus's reign). The old image of the Messiah's coming needed to be reconceptualized; no longer could the line dividing the old age and the new age be seen so narrowly. Just as in medicine an angioplasty procedure expands arterial passageways around the heart, so in early Christian thinking proclamation (the kerygma filled out the transition between the end's beginning and its end. This means God's people now live with both realities at the same time, with a double vision; God's people live *now* out of the reality that is *not yet* complete. Already the transforming presence of the resurrected Jesus is present in the ongoing experience of Christians (both personally and communally), but their own resurrection remains a future reality. This gives the followers of Jesus in the meantime a peculiar eschatological imagination—already, but not yet.

Second, Paul must also remap God's mission and salvation timetable. If Jesus is the Messiah, then now is the time of the Gentile mission. The tradition is clear: "In the days to come.... Peoples shall stream to it [i.e., Mount Zion or Jerusalem] and many nations shall come and say: 'Come, let us go up to the mountain of the LORD, to the house of the God of Jacob; that he may teach us his way and that we may walk in his paths'" (Mic 4:1-2). But here is the problem: Paul's Jewish brothers and sisters are not recognizing Jesus as the Messiah in any large numbers, while other people are leaving their pagan commitments and identifying themselves as Christians, sharing in the communities of Jesus all around the Mediterranean. These Pauline communities have some Jewish members but are predominantly Gentile in background. Perhaps this explains why Paul challenges these mixed churches to take seriously their identity as participants in the reconfigured people of God, sharing in the new Israel by raising money to help the struggling Jews in

Jerusalem (Gal 2:10; 1 Cor 16:1–4; 2 Cor 8–9). Since his Jewish brothers and sisters have not yet recognized Messiah Jesus, maybe these mixed house churches, with their transformed lives, with their generous offering of aid to suffering Jewish Christians in Zion, will make his kin jealous enough to change their minds about Jesus. The eschatological imagery is profound: Gentiles helping Jews counter suffering and death! Perhaps this is the way God intends the nations to stream toward Zion. The traditional formula of "to the Jew first and also to the Greek" (Rom 1:16) has temporarily been reversed, but God's purpose remains the same: "and so all Israel will be saved" (Rom 11:26). In this way creation's longing for rest and wholeness will ultimately be brought to completion (1 Cor 15:20–26).

Third, Paul remaps the final form of God's people and its relation to Torah. If Jesus is the Messiah who has conquered the power of sin, evil, and death (as witnessed by Jesus's ongoing resurrection life), then the Torah, God's gift to Israel for keeping the power of sin in check, must not have been strong enough to deliver the promise. But then why did God give such an ineffectual gift to Israel? This is a problem that Paul must overcome. Is God playing fair? What good are gifts that do not work? Can God be trusted? After some reflection (Gal 1:15–20), Paul concludes that the problem cannot lie with Torah but with the power of sin (Rom 7:7–11). The Torah is the passive instrument of sin. Intended by God for good (to point to life), Torah is weakened by sin, the personification of the rebellious powers (i.e., Satan). However, God used the Torah to focus and concentrate sin in Israel (no one else had the Torah) in order to expose sin's enormously destructive ways. This, Paul argues, must have been God's plan. It cannot be a mistake. Sin was gathered into one place (Israel) so that it could be dealt with and defeated by Israel's representative, Messiah Jesus (Toews 2004:215, 293). So, the goal of Torah is realized by Jesus (Rom 10:4), who embodies God's intention for Israel and fills out the final form of God's people in these last days. Therefore, the old ethnic identity markers of circumcision, holy days, and food laws are no longer necessary to identify members of God's family. It is the "obedience of faith" (Rom 1:5) that testifies to the Gentile inclusion into God's people; this is God's end-time people (both Jewish and Gentile), who are now defined by the Spirit of the risen Christ, symbolized by their baptism into the Jesus community. Paul was not the only early Christian interpreter, neither was his the only path to interpretation.

But the way he processed his new experience with new interpretation is easiest to see because he chose to write letters with direct argumentation and exhortation. Other early Christians also interpreted and wrote, finding ways to mediate the dissonance between their experience and their symbolic world in genres other than the letter. They wrote gospels, histories, and apocalypses. Later, in the second century, Christians realized that all these early interpretations they had collected were an extremely useful guide for assessing and discerning the appropriateness of other interpretations and expressions of Christianity that continued to emerge. When new expressions were measured against the collection of early Christian writings, it quickly became evident which interpretations were helpful contemporary expressions and which were distracting or even dangerous. The collection of writings eventually called the Christian Bible, made up of both OT and NT (with their diverse genres and interpretations) began to be identified as the church's "rule of faith," useful for guiding the ongoing theological reflection of successive communities of the risen Lord.

To sum up, the first disciples' need to interpret and reread the Torah argues for the basic historicity of their experience of what happened to Jesus at the Easter, cross/resurrection event. The early Christian community could not have invented a crucified-and-raised messiah since all their intertextual work was designed to escape the problematic implications of Easter: that Jesus was *not* a failure, weak, or sinful, but in fact triumphant and victorious; that the cross was *not* some random, accidental event of mistaken identity, or a case of Jesus being caught in the wrong place at the wrong time, but something consistent with both Jesus's prior ministry and his vision for the future of creation; that God had *not* abandoned Jesus; that in spite of appearances to the contrary, God was still fair, one, faithful, righteous, sovereign; that evil had *not* won—while the whole thing looked like "business as usual," with the powerful scapegoating the powerless, nothing could be further from the truth. Therefore, we have behind these NT writings a memory (not something invented or created). Something happened to Jesus that powerfully shaped the early Christian experience and interpretation, that provided a framework—a new symbolic world—to guide the ongoing religious experience and interpretation of Christians everywhere.

THE CONVICTIONS EMERGING FROM THE INTERPLAY OF EXPERIENCE AND INTERPRETATION

The early Christians were convinced that the Easter event, Jesus's prior ministry, and his ongoing resurrection presence in their midst, were "God's deeds of power" (Acts 2:11). They described all this in hindsight, as something "in accordance with the scriptures" (1 Cor 15:4). Yet what did these early Christians understand by it all? How were they able to hold Torah in one hand *and* their disturbing, exhilarating experience of Jesus's life, death, and resurrection presence in the other? To save Torah at the expense of their experience with Jesus did not seem right; the signs, wonders, and transformed presence of Jesus undeniably signaled the dawn of "the new creation" (2 Cor 5:17). To save their experience with Jesus at the expense of Torah did not seem right either; this would call into question God's faithfulness to the ancient promises to Israel. And so, it must be that "all this is from God" (2 Cor 5:18). But how?

We have already explored some of the ways that Paul felt compelled to change his understanding of Judaism in order to hold together both Torah and his new convictions about Jesus. Are there other examples? Choosing a different genre than Paul's letters, Caird (1994:27) suggests that Luke's narrative is directly aimed at answering the question of how Easter (i.e., Jesus) fits with God's purpose for Israel (i.e., Torah). In Acts, Luke casts the speeches of both Peter (Acts 2:14–39; 3:12–26; 10:34–43) and Paul (Acts 13:26–41; 17:16–34; 22:1–21; 24:2–21; 26:2–23) in theological terms that he presumably believes to be representative of the common theology of the early church. From these speeches a list of seven basic convictions emerges for how early Christians held together Torah and Jesus (Caird 1994:30). These convictions will form the opening remarks for the NT conference, setting the parameters and the scope of the theological deliberations that are to follow.

First, there is the conviction that God was personally present and active in the events of Jesus's life, ministry, death, and resurrection and in their sequel with the young churches. The whole of it is a story "of power, wonders, and signs that God did through [Jesus]" (Acts 2:22). And so the NT is entirely a book about Israel's God, and about how this God, who is also Master of the universe, is indeed faithfully keeping promises and moving all creation toward completion. While often it seems that God is absent, remote, or impotent (consider Jesus's cry of dereliction: "God, why have you forsaken me?" [Mark 15:34]), it is precisely in these times when God is most fully and effectively present. God's victory is never in doubt.

Second, the human characters in the gospel story are actors in a drama with a preordained plot of such power and flexibility that not only their obedience but their disobedience contributes to its fulfillment. Luke casts this conviction in Peter's Pentecost sermon: "This man, handed over to you according to the definite plan and foreknowledge of God, you crucified and killed by the hands of those outside the law. But God raised him up, having freed him from death, because it was impossible for him to be held in its power" (Acts 2:23–24). This should not be construed as fatalism or determinism; God does not need disobedience in order to accomplish creation's goal. However, the confession is that God is large enough to use even disobedience to complete the goal of creation. The classical distinction remains helpful: God's *antecedent will* emerges from God's character, nature, and purpose, while God's *consequent will* is that which is permitted by God and arises from the acts of human beings and the created order (John of Damascus *De fide orthodoxa* 2.29).

God's predestined purpose is for creation to be completed and fully glorified, living in unalienated relationships. This has not yet been realized on earth. And so, Jesus's prayer makes sense: let "your will be done on earth, as it is in heaven" (Matt 6:10). While the beginning and the end are clear, the middle is yet unknown and subject to the choices and actions of humanity (God's consequent will). The way God works this purpose is a mystery, in the sense that it is previously undisclosed and must be revealed, together with an invitation for humanity to interact with God's purpose. Paul's post-Easter reflection illustrates this. "We speak God's wisdom, secret and hidden, which God decreed before the ages for our glory. None of the rulers of this age understood this; for if they had, they would not have crucified the Lord of glory" (1 Cor 2:7–8). Evil sought to secure its worldwide domination and to scuttle God's purpose by eliminating Jesus; however, unbeknownst to the powers of evil, God was able to transform this act of rebellion and violence into an instrument serving God's eternal purpose.

The gospel story narrates how Jesus reveals, embodies, and implements God's eternal purpose. Furthermore, Jesus is that eternal purpose. The union of the human and the divine, which Jesus demonstrates in his words and works, now makes God's founding purpose for creation accessible to all. As a result of Easter, evil's grip on humanity is undone. Jesus, the embodiment of God's purpose, is both Torah (Rom 10:4) and temple (Mark 11:15-19; 13:1-36; 14:58; Eph 2:19-22; Rev 21:22), opening the way for humanity at last to participate truly in God's purpose (1 Cor 3:16-17). Because of Easter, humanity can now have a share in the purpose for which God set the universe in motion.

Third, the plot of this divine drama is God's plan of salvation for Israel and through Israel for the world. Luke is convinced of the universal implications of the gospel story and of Israel's instrumental role: "By being the first to rise from the dead, [the risen Lord] would proclaim light both to our people and to the Gentiles" (Acts 26:23). Even though this was later misunderstood (Judaism and Christianity unfortunately separated from each other by the end of the first century), for Luke it is clear that the offer of salvation extends to the entire human race and to all creation for that matter. However, this confession with large global implications does not cancel the hope of salvation for Israel. Christianity was never intended to be a new religion, separate from Judaism.

The NT writers are convinced that the church does not supersede Israel or leave Israel unmodified. The church with mixed membership of Jews and Gentiles represents a re-configured Israel, a renewed Israel, one that at last lives out God's promise that "in [Abraham] all the families of the earth shall be blessed" (Gen 12:3): Israel as "a light to the nations" (Isa 49:6). This explains Jesus's association with John the Baptist and Jesus's primary concern to reform Israel so that it might at last be and do what God had always intended for Israel. A renewed Israel could be entrusted with the Gentile mission since the mission would flow directly from Israel's own mandate to be God's *saved* people and God's *saving* people. Only by being a Jewish messiah could Jesus also be the savior of the world.

Fourth, the plan of salvation is present in outline or in explicit promise throughout the OT. While the novelty of a crucified-and-risen messiah is undeniable, at its core the gospel story connected deeply with Israel's ancient story, according to Luke: "All the prophets, as many as have spoken, from Samuel and those after him, also predicted these days" (Acts 3:24). This conviction also needs to be read carefully. It is not that Jesus's life or his crucifixion is self-evident from the OT. As we have seen earlier, Jesus did not appear to fulfill the certified messianic texts. However, with the lens of Easter and the instruction of the risen Lord,

OT texts never before read messianically triggered memories of Jesus's own teaching and came to be understood as speaking of Jesus (e.g., Ps 110:1; 118:22; Isa 53:4–5; Zech 9:9).

At the same time, it must be said that built into the OT literature is a sense of being incomplete—not in any lacking sort of way, but in the lively sense of actively anticipating the fulfillment of its ancient promise. This sense of anticipation present throughout the OT helped to boost Christian interpretation. Psalm 8 speaks of the vision for humanity's participation in God's creation enterprise—something that remained unfulfilled until Jesus entered into the glory of the new-creation age (i.e., resurrection) as leader and representative of all those who would associate with him and thereby have a share in his victory even before its completion. Psalm 95 speaks of entering God's rest—something that the old order could not deliver, having been outfoxed by the power of evil and rebellion; but something that now has become a possibility at the dawn of the messianic age. Speaking of the OT heroes of faith, the author of Hebrews states, "All of these died in faith without having received the promises, but from a distance they saw and greeted them" (11:13).

Fifth, this way of reading the OT originated with Jesus, who understood God's plan from the beginning and conducted his ministry in conformity to it. While in one sense Jesus is not present at the conference table of NT writers, in another sense he is present, because the NT writings bear witness to Jesus's concern for Israel's role in God's plan for the world. According to Luke, "God anointed Jesus of Nazareth with the Holy Spirit and with power; . . . he went about doing good and healing all who were oppressed by the devil, for God was with him" (Acts 10:38). The conviction here is that the oral traditions about Jesus, which circulated, developed, and eventually became the heart of the gospel story, did not originate with the NT writers themselves. The genuine piece of creative thinking and novelty rests in the person of Jesus, who directed the minds of his followers to certain passages in the OT—such as the "Son of Man" texts (Dan 7:13), the "servant" texts (Isa 42, 49, 52, 53, and 61), and others—that would illuminate the meaning of his mission and destiny (Jeremias 1958:55).

According to Luke, Jesus knew himself to be the agent of the divine purpose, but it was the Scriptures that provided the framework of God's characteristic way of being-for-others. Jesus allowed that purpose to determine his mission; he was the God-filled man. Jesus's novel interpretations of Scripture led even his closest friends to misunderstand him, and led his enemies to vigorously oppose him; Jesus found in the Son of Man and servant texts of Scripture that which no one else had found before. So while the OT appears to bear witness to Jesus, it only confirms truths derived from something more basic than the coming of Jesus as Messiah. In other words, simply reading the OT could not by itself have produced an obvious profile of Jesus of Nazareth as the Messiah. According to Paul, in Jesus "the righteousness of God has been manifested apart from law, although the law and the prophets bear witness to it" (Rom 3:21 [RSV]). This is not a contradiction. Jesus's life and ministry were based on being more than Torah observant; what guided Jesus's words, ministry, mission, and suffering was his obedience to the redemptive purpose of God revealed in the Torah—a purpose in which he was destined to play a leading role.

Sixth, in the light of the events in which God's plan had been put into operation, the risen Jesus explained to his disciples the scriptural necessity, which they had previously failed to understand. Luke renders the tradition of Peter's sermon like this: "God raised [Jesus] on the third day and allowed him to appear, not to all the people but to us who were chosen by God as witnesses . . . He commanded us to preach to the people and to testify that he is the one ordained by God as judge of the living and the dead" (Acts 10:40-42). But how did the early followers of Jesus come to understand the OT as Jesus himself understood it? As we have seen above, Luke's answer to this question is that the Lord instructed them.

In Luke's rendition of the commissioning of the disciples, the risen Lord states, "'These are my words that I spoke to you while I was still with you—that everything written about me in the law of Moses, the prophets, and the psalms must be fulfilled.' Then he opened their minds to understand the scriptures" (Luke 24:44-45). Put another way, the Spirit of truth or the Spirit of the risen Lord functions to take the words and works of Jesus and to interpret them to the minds and hearts of believers (John 16:13-15). As the church continues in these last days of the old age, it is animated at the dawn of the new age by the ongoing presence of the risen Lord. Thus, the Spirit of the risen Lord guides, illumines, and instructs within the collective experience of the community gathered, empowering it for worship, correction, discernment, and encouragement.

Seventh, Jesus's interpretation of the OT had much in it that was offensive to his opponents and much that was puzzling to his friends; but his interpretation rested on theological convictions already held by pious Jews before his coming. Luke witnesses to the basic continuity between Jesus and Israel's archetypal self-understanding in the following observation: "When the meeting of the synagogue broke up, many Jews and devout converts to Judaism followed Paul and Barnabas, who spoke to them and urged them to continue in the grace of God" (Acts 13:43). Already in the period of the Deuteronomistic historians, when Israel's story was cast in a cyclical pattern of election-disobedience-humiliation-deliverance, the conviction that God is working out a purpose in history was well understood.

From the prophetic literature it is clear that God has set a creation enterprise in motion such that all history is under the control of God. All the nations participate in this project and are subject to God's judgment regarding their involvement (by their obedience or disobedience). Referring to the role of Cyrus, king of Persia, during Israel's exile in Babylon, Isaiah frames the ancient conviction this way: "I am God, and there is no other; I am God, and there is no one like me, declaring the end from the beginning and from ancient times things not yet done, . . . My purpose shall stand, . . . calling a bird of prey from the east, the man for my purpose from a far country. I have spoken, and I will bring it to pass" (Isa 46:9–11). Here we see affirmation of the conviction that the purpose that Yahweh is pursuing in the history of humanity, with Israel's leading the way, is the purpose for which the world was created in the first place.

These core convictions framed by Luke function well as the opening remarks of the NT meeting gathered at the large conference table. From Luke's remarks we hear reference to one launching experience witnessed by the first disciples: the Easter, cross-and-resurrection experience of Jesus—the event instrumental to both confirming Jesus's prior ministry *and* reshaping the symbolic world of God's people Israel. Without Easter there would be no conference, no NT. Even though the presenters who will now be taking the podium and speaking at the microphone are doing their own theologizing, they are all rooted in one founding experience or event. What emerges as central to NT theology is that Jesus is God's Messiah, who gives shape to the final form of God's people during the last act of the redemption drama, and that the church is the manifestation of the end-time people of God in the world, which needs its witness and its invitation to transformation.

In other words, NT theology is fundamentally *theological*: it is about God's character, mission, and creation project. NT theology is also *christological*: it is about Jesus, who is at once both the normative self-expression of God and the truly human one living out God's purpose from the dawn of time. And finally, NT theology is *ecclesiological*: it is about the church as the tangible expression of the Spirit of the risen Lord, representing at last the end-time form of God's people and inviting all creation to abandon its rebellion and find its true identity in God's purpose.

Compressed into a sound byte, the central conviction that calls all the NT writers to the conference is this: *God's people-gathering activity has now taken final shape around Messiah Jesus in communities of the Spirit of the risen Lord, through whom God's mission to disarm the powers and to move all creation forward toward completion is being accomplished.*

In the next chapter, the conference proceedings get underway, with Paul's taking the microphone first.

EXERCISES

1. Read Bart Ehrman's essays "What Is the New Testament? The Early Christians and their Literature" and "The World of the Early Christian Traditions" in *The New Testament: A Historical Introduction to the Early Christian Writings* (4th ed.), 1–16 and 17–35.

    Become familiar with the following terms:

    Jewish-Christian Adoptionists, Marcionite Christians, gnostic Christians, proto-Orthodox Christians, Christian canon, Greco-Roman religiosity, polytheism, monotheism, and *early Judaism.*

    Using these terms, describe the distinctive character of the various expressions of second-century Christianity and the world in which they existed.

2. Read Luke Timothy Johnson's essays "The Greco-Roman World," "Judaism in Palestine," and "Diaspora Judaism" in *The Writings of the New Testament: An Interpretation*, 21–41, 43–70, and 73–91.

    Become familiar with the following terms: *symbolic world, Hellenistic ideals, religious self-definition, apocalyptic literature, rabbinic tradition, midrash, Qumran,* and *Diaspora Judaism*. Using these terms, describe the social, religious, and political context within which Christianity emerged, especially with relation to Judaism.

3. In Fyodor Dostoyevsky's novel *The Brothers Karamazov*, Mrs. Khokhlakov visits Father Zossima with a question. See the excerpt below.

   Discuss answers to the following questions: What does Mrs. Khokhlakov want from Father Zossima? What does Father Zossima offer her? Elaborate on the significance of Zossima's counsel. What relations do you see between the concept of symbolic maps and Christian faith? What is the significance of this relation for talking about and doing NT theology?

'I'm suffering from—from lack of faith.'

'Lack of faith in God?'

'Oh, no, no! I dare not even think of that! But life after death—it's such a mystery! And there's no one, absolutely no one, who can solve it. Listen, you are a healer, you're an expert on the human soul. I have no right, of course, to expect you to believe me entirely, but I give you my solemn word that I'm saying this not because I haven't thought it over carefully, but because this idea of a future life upsets me so much that it positively hurts me. It frightens and horrifies me. . . . And I don't know whom to turn to—I haven't dared to all my life. . . . And now I dare to turn to you. . . . Oh dear, what will you think of me now?' She clasped her hands.

'Don't worry about what I think,' replied the elder. 'I quite believe in the sincerity of your anguish.'

'Oh, I *am* so grateful to you! You see, I close my eyes and think: if everyone has faith, then where does it come from? And then I hear people say that it all arose at first from fear of the terrible manifestation of nature, and that there's nothing in it at all. Well, I say to myself, I've been believing all my life, but what if I die and there's nothing at all and all that will happen is that, as one writer put it, "burdock will be growing on my grave"? It's awful! How, how am I to get back my faith? Mind you, I believed only when I was a little girl, mechanically, without thinking of anything. . . . But how, how am I to prove it? That's why I've come now to throw myself at your feet and ask you about it. If I miss this opportunity too now, I won't be able to get an answer for the rest of my life. How is one to prove it? How is one to be convinced? Oh, poor me! Everyone around me, almost everyone, doesn't seem to care one bit, no one worries about it now, but I'm the only one who can't stand it. It's dreadful—dreadful!'

'I daresay it is. But it's something one cannot prove. One can be convinced of it, though.'

'How? In what way?'

'By the experience of active love. Strive to love your neighbors actively and indefatigably. And the nearer you come to achieving this love, the more convinced you will become of the existence of God and the immortality of your soul. If you reach the point of complete selflessness in your love of your neighbors, you will most certainly regain your faith and no doubt can possibly enter your soul. This has been proven. This is certain.'

TABLE 2.1 Mrs. Khokhlakov's conversation with Father Zossima, from *The Brothers Karamazov*, translated by David Magarshack, 60–61.

3

The Theological Contribution of Paul

IN THIS CHAPTER WE turn our attention to Paul's testimony at the NT conference. The chapter has seven objectives: (1) to explain why I begin with Paul's testimony, (2) to outline the controversy over authentic and inauthentic Pauline letters, (3) to trace the debate over the center of Paul's theology, (4) to sketch the content of Paul's gospel message, (5) to explore the possible sources of Paul's gospel message, (6) to observe the ways Paul modifies traditional Jewish apocalyptic theology, and (7) to list Paul's convictions about the significance of Jesus.

WHY BEGIN WITH PAUL'S TESTIMONY?

The first person to the microphone at the NT conference is Paul. Now, some might ask why go to Paul first? It is not that Paul is the only or even first voice of early Christianity. He is, however, its first writer, turning out to be very instrumental in giving shape to the interpretation of Jesus's life (2 Pet 3:15–16). He writes in the first person and provides the first written witness of Easter and its significance. As an itinerant church planter, energetic missionary pastor, team leader and organizer, and creative Jewish interpreter and theologian, Paul takes a very significant role at the NT conference. Almost half the NT books are attributed to him (thirteen out of twenty-seven).

Paul chose to write letters (*documentary* texts) occasioned by problems in the young churches he had planted or with which he kept up relationships. His writings combine theological argumentation, scriptural interpretation, exhortation, encouragement, correction, logistical planning, and promotional material. Scholars date his letters as the earliest that remain (40s to 60s CE) for reasons I will set out in a moment. They represent some of the most direct testimony of early Christian interpretation and appropriation of the legacy of Jesus. The remaining NT writings are dated later (from the 60s to the close of the first century CE), written by anonymous authors or at least by authors no longer known to us (see diagram below). Such anonymity makes sense since these writers chose more poetic genres (and so left *literary* texts) to interpret the significance of Jesus: their gospel narratives, histories, speeches, exhortations, and apocalypses carry their message; these writers do not use the first-person viewpoint of an occasional letter, as Paul did.

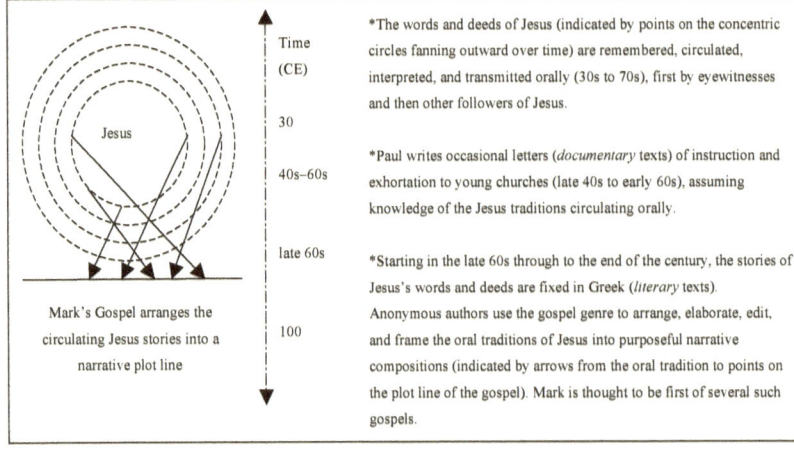

TABLE 3.1 Beginnings of Christian Literary Development

Paul's testimony is especially important because his genre of choice, documentary text, gives direct access to his convictions about the risen Lord and the historical Jesus—especially to the theological reflection that transformed his received symbolic world. Literary texts, like the Gospels, give voice to testimony that is equally vivid and significant; however, framed in a narrative rather than in direct discourse, the views of the authors are less obvious. Using a mathematical analogy, Paul does the calculation "showing all his work," while the gospel writers only give the result. So, we begin with the documentary evidence—Paul's letters—and turn to the literary evidence in subsequent chapters.

Paul's connection to Christianity, however, begins not through interpretation for the church but through persecution of the church (Phil 3:6). The persecutor was then called by God through a revelation of the risen Lord in order to be an apostle "among the Gentiles" (Gal 1:15). But why did Paul persecute the church? Most likely it was because he was already a missionary long before he was a Christian. As a Pharisee, he was a zealous promoter and defender of Israel's faith (Phil 3.6). At the time, he genuinely felt that the claims of Christianity were an embarrassment to Israel's faith and an offense against God. If God truly was at work in Jesus, as these Jewish Christians claimed, the whole symbolic framework of popular Judaism was threatened. Jesus had not restored Israel to prosperity or safety; neither had Jesus established the rule of Torah. How could he be the Messiah? Yet, it was Paul's encounter with the resurrected Jesus that forced him to reconcile that experience with the testimony of Scripture.

Paul's received symbolic map stretched to the breaking point and finally snapped, hitting the floor with a crash. However, with the pieces picked up from the floor, Paul was able to reconfigure the symbolic map of Judaism around the revelation of Jesus without adding any new pieces. In the end, he could say with conviction something that he never could have said prior to his encounter with the risen Lord. What was that? It is this: "that Christ died for our sins in accordance with the scriptures, and that he was buried, and that he was raised on the third day in accordance with the scriptures" (1 Cor 15:3–4). The subtext here is that only by looking through his new lens of a crucified-raised messiah could Paul say that all this was in "accordance with the scriptures."

Given Paul's new Easter perspective, Scriptures like Ps 110:1; 118:22; Zech 9:9; and Isa 53:4–5 could indeed be seen to confirm God's leading in Jesus's life. Even Jesus's own interpretation of God's intentions for Israel and God's cosmic design for all creation became clear in the light that shone from the empty tomb. So Paul the Pharisee and zealous advocate of Israel's faith gladly accepted the revision of his missionary mandate to be God's agent and Christ's apostle to the Gentiles (Gal 1:16). Apparently, this was the way that God was working to move creation forward toward its completion. Who was he to argue?

Even though Paul wrote the lines that later became known as the *kerygma* or the proclamation ("Christ died . . . he was buried . . . he was raised . . . he appeared," 1 Cor 15:3–4) some twenty years after his initial experience with the risen Jesus, it is not as if nothing was going on during this twenty-year window. We may not have textual evidence from this early period, but Christianity was a literary movement from the beginning. Harry Gamble argues, "Arising within the matrix of a broadly literate Judaism, early Christianity was never without a literary dimension, even though it did not immediately generate a large literature of its own" (1995:29).

At the time, all writing and reading was a form of oral presentation. Thus, oral presentations were actually literary, in that they were designed to persuade an audience to embrace a certain perspective or to adopt a certain behavior. The point is that while we have no Christian written texts that remain from the time prior to Paul's letters, it would be wrong to assume that nothing was circulating. The oral tradition of Jesus's words and deeds circulated as remembered and interpreted tradition; and thus, Christianity had a literary dimension from the start.

On two occasions, Paul refers to the circulating Jesus tradition. Regarding Jesus's eucharistic meal tradition, Paul writes: "For I received from the Lord, what I also handed on to you" (1 Cor 11:23). Concerning the tradition of Jesus's prohibition of divorce, Paul writes: "To the married I give this command—not I but the Lord—that the wife should not separate from her husband . . . and that the husband should not divorce his wife" (1 Cor 7:10). So, while Paul writes occasional letters of instruction and exhortation to young churches, he assumes knowledge of the Jesus traditions circulating orally and widely during the years of Paul's missionary work. The Jesus traditions would later be framed within the literary plotlines of the gospel writers.

Paul's letters are usually dated from the late 40s to early 60s, representing the earliest Christian writings that remain. How do we get this dating assessment? What about the gospel accounts? Are they not earlier? Since Paul makes no reference to fully composed gospels as we know them, yet assumes the Jesus traditions either explicitly (in the two examples above) or implicitly (with allusions to the Sermon on the Mount in Rom 12:9–21), his writings are usually assumed to predate the Gospels. Furthermore, Mark's gospel is usually thought to be the earliest gospel, presupposing a setting just before the Jerusalem temple is destroyed during the Jewish War between 66 and 70 CE (Mark 13:4). Paul's writings, however, do not give evidence of such heightened political tension with Rome in Jerusalem; Paul is reported to have even appealed to Caesar in

Rome to try his case (Acts 25:11). Thus, it is very likely that Paul is already dead by the time of the destruction of the temple (70 CE)—most probably killed during Nero's persecution of Christians in 64 CE.

So if the upper limit for dating Paul's writings is the early 60s, how is the lower limit of the late 40s determined—the time marking the beginning of his correspondence? In Acts 18:12, Luke notes that Gallio began his rule as proconsul when Paul left Corinth. Archeologists have unearthed an inscription that dates Gallio's appointment with some precision to summer 51 CE (Kümmel 1975:253). Since Paul left Corinth when the proconsul Gallio took office, we can date several key points in Paul's life with the additional evidence from Paul's own description of his early years as a Christ follower (Gal 1:18—2:1).

Paul relates the timeline of his own ministry as follows: conversion—three years—first Jerusalem trip—fourteen years—second Jerusalem trip. So if the second Jerusalem trip for the Jerusalem council (Acts 15) took place shortly before Paul's year-and-a-half-long Corinthian sojourn (Acts 18:11), which must have begun in the winter of 49, then we can date two key events: (1) His earliest writings to the young churches can be dated to the late 40s, following the affirmation of his Gentile mission by the Jerusalem council (Acts 15:1–29). (2) Working backward seventeen years (3 + 14) from the Jerusalem council meeting, we arrive at 49 − 17 = 32, the date of Paul's religious experience with the risen Lord. This date is within a year or two of Jesus's crucifixion and resurrection, which is dated usually around 30 CE (Sanders 1993:282–90).

Acts mentions a total of five visits that Paul makes to Jerusalem (9:23–31; 11:27–30; 15:6–29; 18:22; 21:17–26), while Paul only speaks explicitly of three in his letters (Gal 1:18; 2:1; Rom 15:31). Trying to sort out the exact chronology of such key events is not without challenges (see Alexander 1993:115–23). It is possible that the discrepancy in the number of trips could be explained as misplacement or duplication or simply omission based on differing priorities; the genres of Greco-Roman history (Acts) and occasional letter (Paul) are sufficiently different to account for the discrepancy. In any case, Paul gained affirmation for the Gentile mission from the Jerusalem church (compare Acts 15:28–29 and Gal 2:9–10) and spent the rest of his days giving leadership to a team of missionaries, gathering a collection for Jerusalem's poor, planting churches around the Mediterranean, and writing letters of encouragement and exhortation to these young, mixed (Jew-and-Gentile) house churches.

The end of Paul's ministry involved a final trip to Jerusalem, both to deliver the collection and to report on the progress of the Gentile mission. At the time, he was also preparing for westward expansion of the mission to Spain, hopefully from a base in Rome (Rom 15:28; 16:1–2). When he arrived in Jerusalem, trouble erupted and he was arrested because his Gentile mission was misunderstood by some as encouraging Jews to forsake Moses, the Torah, and the temple (Acts 21:17–26). Paul appealed to Caesar rather than be tried in Jerusalem (Acts 25:9–12) and began the long journey to Rome by ship in Roman custody. This is the last we hear of him, languishing under house arrest in Rome, awaiting trial. While it remains difficult to fit each of his letters into Luke's framework in Acts, the broad strokes of Paul's missionary career are clear.

What can we say about Paul? Clearly he was a remarkably gifted team leader, exegete, and writer, who demonstrated unflagging zeal for the ways of Israel's God, both before and after he encountered the risen Lord. It is technically incorrect to call his religious experience a conversion, since he did not convert from one religion to another. Throughout Paul's life he remained a Jew, convinced of Israel's role in God's global salvation plan, committed to the goal of Torah and to the place of the temple in God's economy. While his post-Easter experience with Messiah Jesus clarified for him the role of Israel, Torah, and temple—all three now gathered up in Jesus—Paul the apostle to the Gentiles, *and* Paul the Jewish Pharisee remain the same in two important ways: (1) Both are committed to God—firmly convinced that God is behind this move to reconstitute Israel in order to be and do what God had always intended for Israel. (2) Both are confident of their leadership role in serving God's global mission—firmly convinced of their role in helping to re-constitute Israel as the end-time form of God's people.

Furthermore, Paul claims that his encounter with the risen Lord was life changing. He talks about his encounter as something "received through a revelation of Jesus Christ" (Gal 1:12). He also talks about having and promoting "the knowledge of God's mystery, that is, Christ himself" (Col 2:2). Here Paul is using special definitions of *mystery* and *revelation* popularized by Jews during the Jewish apocalyptic period (from 250 BCE to the second century CE). In this religious usage, *mystery* is not to be confused with "riddle" or "puzzle," with something that can be solved by logical deduction and persistence. For Paul, a mystery is something that though previously hidden is divinely revealed in a surprising, unanticipated way.

So, what was Paul's personal vision statement? After traveling throughout the then-known world with his missionary team proclaiming the kerygma, what would he say is central to his gospel? Around what concept can all the things that he wrote about over the years be organized? Since most people have only a couple lines reflecting the core values of the symbolic map they use to make sense of their world, we should be able to ask the same question of Paul. We are asking about Paul's underlying convictions: the core out of which he gives pastoral advice to the young house churches around the Mediterranean world. What would he say if given the microphone?

The question of Paul's center has been answered in various ways. Each involves trying to ascertain his central conviction. How can this be done? The most obvious way is to survey Paul's letters and see what issues Paul continues to circle around. Which does he repeat? Which does he emphasize? These will give a clue as to his center. While our strategy for homing in on Paul's center appears logical, it is not as simple as it first seems. Why? Because it is not obvious when we talk about Paul's letters, which letters we are talking about. Since the eighteenth century, the authenticity of some of the NT letters attributed to Paul has been debated.

THE CONTROVERSY OVER AUTHENTIC AND INAUTHENTIC PAULINE LETTERS

Which letters can be included in the assessment of Paul's center? If some are inauthentic, their contribution to the assessment of Paul's guiding conviction is questionable. Evidently, the debate over authenticity is important.

Paul wrote many letters, but in the NT thirteen are attributed to Paul. Seven are *undisputed* by contemporary scholars (Romans, 1 and 2 Corinthians, Galatians, Philippians, 1 Thessalonians, and Philemon). Six are *disputed* (Colossians, Ephesians, 2 Thessalonians, and the Pastoral Epistles: 1–2 Timothy and Titus). The reasons for uncertainty stem from problems of style, theological content, and fit within the chronology of Paul's ministry and life (Ehrman 2008:380–402). The first two considerations (style and content) are slippery, because these are pieces of internal evidence that often can be read in several ways. A change in style or theme would not automatically suggest that someone else is writing the letter. There may be another explanation. The only consideration that has some merit is the question of fit within Paul's ministry life. But this too is hard to establish, since we do not have a complete picture of Paul's life and ministry to use for locating his correspondence. Recall the difficulty sorting out the number and nature of Paul's visits to Jerusalem according to Luke and according to Paul himself.

At this point, it must be stressed that the historical question of authenticity aims neither at removing the inauthentic letters (if any) from the NT nor at diminishing the canonical authority of any such letters. The issue is more narrowly construed. How many of the thirteen letters attributed to Paul can be used for understanding Paul's thought? For some historians, there is a great difference between the *historical* Paul and the *canonical* Paul. For these scholars almost half the Pauline corpus is pseudonymous, written by others attempting to reshape or redirect the post-Pauline-era churches with letters of instruction attributed to the well-respected Paul. The argument is that these six disputed letters cannot be used to determine Paul's ministry pattern or to represent his thinking. They can only be used to document the permutations of the Pauline tradition that followed his death and carried on through the next generation.

This, however, is not the only way to understand the literary evidence. For example, it may not be so helpful to make such a hard-line distinction between the historical Paul and the canonical Paul. Why not? Because the evidence points to a Paul who worked collaboratively in all aspects of his missionary enterprise. He used a secretary to write his letters (Rom 16:22). He dictated letters, signing some with his own hand (Gal 6:11). He coauthored letters with Timothy (2 Cor 1:1; Phil 1:1; Col 1:1; Phlm 1), with Silas and Timothy (1 Thess 1:1; 2 Thess 1:1), with Sosthenes (1 Cor 1:1), and with "all the members of God's family who are with me" (Gal 1:1). Thus, it seems that some of the stylistic and formal differences among the thirteen letters attributed to Paul could be explained by his cosponsorship and collaboration with others in his team: collaborators with whom Paul would have had essential agreement. Some letters were probably written "at arm's length" from Paul, but still congruent with the "spirit and tradition" of the Pauline missionary team. This simpler, pragmatic explanation for the differences in content, style, and vocabulary should be given priority, barring evidence to the contrary (i.e., the principle of Ockham's razor). This assessment offers a strong alternative to some of the critical reconstructions, which tend to be overly skewed toward conspiracy theories. Johnson offers this succinct summary: "The whole Pauline corpus is one that Paul 'authored' but did not necessarily write" (1999:273).

Even if the six disputed letters can be traced to the Pauline missionary team, some attention to the causes of the disputes is merited. How would a Paul-at-arm's-length conception account for the difficulties scholars have raised regarding the disputed letters since the eighteenth century? Consider 2 Thessalonians. It is often doubted as Pauline. Why? Whereas 1 Thessalonians stresses the immanence of the return or consummation of Jesus's end-time rule, 2 Thessalonians brings an emphasis on events that must transpire before the *parousia* or coming of Messiah Jesus to establish God's victory everywhere (compare 1 Thess 4:13–18 and 2 Thess 2:1–12). However, this change in emphasis need not rule out Pauline authorship. Both of these emphases represent the modified apocalyptic eschatology characteristic of early Christians.

The eschatological language of 1 and 2 Thessalonians is not something new: it is foundational for early Christianity. That the end happens suddenly, without warning, *and* that there are historical antecedents are assertions typical of the dialectical tension in Jewish apocalyptic thought (Dan 12:1–12; Mark 13:3–37; 1 Cor 7:25–35). Both assertions are held as true, even though some might see them as contradictory at one level. Thus, Kümmel (1975:268) holds that 2 Thessalonians is a second letter of Paul to the Thessalonians, likely written several weeks after the first letter. Paul includes left-out material, reminders, and complementary emphases not made in his first letter. The fact that not everything is transparent or spelled out actually raises the probability that this letter is from Paul and not pseudepigraphic.

Colossians is also doubted to be an authentic letter of Paul. Why? Because new language appears (new vocabulary, a poetic style, a shift in Pauline eschatology). Again, these need not disqualify Paul as author. Letter cosponsorship with its particular aims could explain the new language and style. Even the striking co-resurrection language ("raised with Christ" [3:1]) is not so unlike Paul, since Paul uses participationist salvation language in the undisputed letters ("joint heirs with Christ" [Rom 8:17]).

The polemical tone of Colossians (its accusation of false teaching and false wisdom, 2:8; 2:20–23) is often presumed to be aimed at opponents who were full-blown gnostics. If this were the case, it would indeed rule out Paul's authorship, since these groups were not yet present during Paul's ministry; they emerged later, in the second century (Ehrman 2008:3–7). However, it is more likely that the polemical tone is part of the Pauline team's use of stock rhetorical patterns of persuasive speech (counterexamples, generic warnings) aimed at discouraging the Colossians from some behaviors and encouraging them toward behaviors more congruent with their new identity in Christ (1:18).

Finally, there is a clear literary dependence between Colossians and Ephesians. This too does not rule out Pauline authorship. The collaboration and cosponsorship of Paul's letters likely also meant that team members referred to and even used parts of letter drafts and copies of letters to other communities as they recycled some of the arguments, exhortations, and teachings for other pastoral situations and purposes (compare "household codes" in Col 3:18—4:1 and Eph 5:21—6:9). However, such literary dependence does push one of the two, either Colossians or Ephesians, further from Paul. So, which is more at arm's length? Arguments for the dependence of Colossians on Ephesians are weak. The flow of development is likely in the other direction: Ephesians is stylistically smoother and more general. Thus, it is still reasonable to imagine Paul as the author of Colossians (Kümmel 1975:346).

What then about Ephesians? The surprising lack of concrete details and personal greetings is strange if Paul was active in Ephesus for three years as Luke reports (Acts 20:31). The superscription (i.e., letter title), "to the Ephesians," can only be dated with some certainty to the end of the second century, and the prescript, "in Ephesus" (1:1), is lacking in the earliest manuscripts (P46, Vaticanus, and Sinaiticus) and is unlikely present before the end of the fourth century. Probably there was no addressee originally, because the letter was not addressed to a particular community. Unlike Paul's usual occasional letters, this letter should be thought of as a literary product aimed at persuading a general Christian audience.

For some scholars, Ephesians is one of those letters not directly from Paul (Kümmel 1975:361). The language and style differ from Paul's usage elsewhere (in vocabulary, in complex sentences, and the piling up of phrases). The relationship to Colossians shows close dependence and yet significant differences. In Colossians, "mystery" is reserved for the eschatological act of God in Christ (1:27), whereas in Ephesians "mystery" means several things: the joining of the universe in Christ (1:10), the participation of Gentiles in salvation (3:6), and the relationship of Christ to the church, depicted using the image of marriage (5:32). Finally, there are differing theological emphases. In Colossians, believers are rooted in Christ (2:7), while in Ephesians, they are built on the foundation of the apostles (2:20). While it is doubtful that Ephesians came directly from Paul, calling it a pseudonymous letter is not the best way to characterize Ephesians. Is there another explanation for the linguistic, literary, and theological differences?

One important observation to be made is that Paul is never the object of the witness (there is no effort to plant details of Paul's life in order to persuade readers that it truly is Paul writing), but he retains the role of acting subject in the letter (Childs 1984:324). Therefore, it is not really accurate to call Ephesians pseudonymous, as the term can suggest falsifying an attribution for some often dubious gain. A more helpful conceptualization is to think of Ephesians as a first-person witness of the apostle and the founding traditions, written by a member of the Pauline missionary team and later *particularized* by the addition of an addressee (1:1). In an ironic way, this served to *generalize* the letter's address and to extend it to all believers, since this is the way Paul's occasional or particular letters had come to be regarded—for general usage everywhere. The potential for generalization and for addressing a future generation, however, was *already* embedded within the letter, given the nonparticular nature of the letter in the first place. The key question is not who wrote Ephesians, but how the witness of Paul is *extended* (not updated) for the ongoing life of the church. Ephesians is a good example of a Pauline letter that he "authored" but probably did not write.

Then there are the so-called Pastoral Letters (1–2 Timothy and Titus). These three were first called Pastorals in the eighteenth century. Not like Paul's occasional letters to young churches, these letters address individuals, offering instruction for the pastoral leadership. They are letters to Paul's delegates Timothy and Titus. All three letters are similar in style, language, and content. However, the historical and theological problems raised in the Pastorals are linked to how they are viewed in relation to the undisputed Pauline letters. The three are not in Marcion's second-century collection of Paul's letters, and it is doubtful that they were in the earliest manuscript collection of Paul's letters (P46, usually dated at 200 CE), since they could not have fit in only the missing pages of the manuscript (Kümmel 1975:370; Gamble 1995:272 n. 74). Still, from the end of the second century, their place in the Pauline corpus was established.

From the nineteenth century to the present, however, objection to direct Pauline authorship has increased. What are some of the reasons for questioning the authenticity of the Pastorals? Kümmel (1975:370–85) notes several problems: The historical situation presupposed by the Pastorals, if historical, requires a second imprisonment in Rome (2 Tim 1:8) after a release from the first imprisonment. However, we do not know what happened to Paul after his two years in Rome (Acts 28:30). It is doubtful that he returned to the east only to get in trouble again; he wanted to go west to Spain (Rom 15:28). The differences in community setting are also large. During his ministry in Corinth, Paul recommends that widows remain single (1 Cor 7:8). They and the other leading women are to learn to participate actively along with the men in the leadership of the church and the Pauline missionary team (1 Cor 11:2–16; 14:33–36; Rom 16:1–16). In the Pastorals, however, widows are expected to remarry (1 Tim 5:14). Furthermore, the participation of the leading women is muted; rather than receiving encouragement to participate in church life, women are instead encouraged to marry (1 Tim 4:3), to have children (1 Tim 2:15), and to be silent (1 Tim 2:11).

The differences in instructions about church structures between Paul's undisputed letters and the Pastorals are striking as well. Paul does not impose strict conformity in his mission churches but argues for tolerance and freedom (Romans 14), except in cases of sexual immorality (1 Corinthians 5) and idolatry (1 Cor 8:6–7), the two traditional Gentile sins (Sanders 1977:455). The ecclesiastical structure that Paul sets out for the Corinthians is remarkably spare. There is no need for a bishop to lead the meetings, because the Holy Spirit presides! "When you come together, each one has a hymn, a lesson, a revelation, a tongue, or an interpretation. Let all things be done for building up . . . one by one, so that all may learn and be encouraged . . . all things should be done decently and in order" (1 Cor 14:26–40). The lack of formal leadership structures and the stress on spiritual gifts probably contributed to the heterodox situation. By way of contrast, the Pastorals set out an ecclesiastical structure with bishops and deacons (1 Tim 3:1–13; 5:17–22), who are charged with managing the ongoing life of the church and carrying forward the Pauline witness (2 Tim 1:13–14). These and other points of difference are often used to characterize the Pastorals as a "drift" away from Paul's ideal (Banks 1994:193–200) or, worse, as a conspiracy plot to redirect the Pauline church practice (Ehrman 2008:396–401).

Is there is another way to conceptualize these apparently post-Pauline developments? While the pseudepigrapha option has grown in popularity, it has led to serious exegetical problems. Why? Because the term *pseudepigrapha* is unhelpful and misleading; it makes historical referentiality centrally important. When categorized as pseudepigrapha, the letters are characterized as "pseudo" or false until the real historical author can be reconstructed, resulting in an almost complete dismissal of their witness. All attention is directed toward reconstructing the real author. Too often the Pastorals are treated like second-century, postapostolic works by either a pious domesticator or a manipulative conspirator. However, the issue is not whether there is a temporal and material distance between Paul and the Pastorals; this has already been shown. The issue is how to interpret this distance. Is it necessary to establish the real, historical author in order to understand the distance, or is the distance an essential part of the canonical shape, useful for understanding the new dimensions of the Pauline witness? I believe the second way of formulating the operative question provides more exegetical traction.

According to Johnson, "No real progress will be made in the understanding of the Pastorals until they are restored to separate but equal status within the Pauline tradition" (1999:430). Childs offers several helpful ways to do just this (1984:380–95). First, recognize that the Pastorals are post-Pauline but not inferior in quality. While sound doctrine is emphasized, the backdrop of heresy is not concretized. This shows that the Pastorals are not about updating Paul to head off a particular false teaching. On the contrary, they are about directing the future church to the teaching of Paul, which had already been given as the normative theological context to resolve controversy. In short, the Pastoral Paul does not break new theological ground.

Second, appreciate the genuine theological continuity that the Pastorals share within the Pauline tradition. There is no need to first reconstruct the historical Paul in order to determine the legitimate scope of the Pastorals. The question is, how has the tradition been *extended*? The broad exegetical function of a Pauline collection provides a check against a narrow equation of authorship and authority either from historical-critical scholars (not by Paul, therefore automatically not useful for determining Paul's center) or from traditionalists (by Paul, therefore automatically useful for determining Paul's center). Instead, the Pauline corpus, as canonically shaped by postapostolic editors to serve the needs of successive generations of Christians, stands as a unit, bookended by Romans and the Pastorals. While Romans was assigned the introductory role, the Pastorals functioned to valorize Paul as the church's doctrinal model and to guide the church's reading of Pauline teaching (Childs 2008).

Third, acknowledge the reality of the lively ministry experience and team practice of the Apostle Paul and his missionary colleagues. The Pastorals are not a conspiracy plot promoting a new ideology, or a clever forgery aimed at securing "market share," or a patronization of Paul by a group of "personality-cult" worshipers. Rather, the Pastorals are most likely the result of a practical necessity within a *leader-oriented heterodoxy* of the first one hundred years of Christianity's charismatic and sometimes turbulent beginnings; appeal could not yet be made to a standard "rule of faith" or established doctrine (such did not exist), but only to the teaching of respected leaders like Paul (Wisse 1986:185; Gamble 1995:107). Later, in the second and third centuries, the initial leader-oriented heterodoxy generated even more diverse expressions of Christianity before some of the more institutionally minded bishops in Alexandria and Rome found the situation intolerable. Armed with greater power and new state resources (thanks to the Roman emperor's initiatives), the fourth-century church gradually replaced the leader-oriented heterodoxy with a *hierarchical orthodoxy*, complete with institutional structures of "office" and "doctrinal standards."

To sum up, Paul gave leadership to a team of missionary pastors, mobilizers, and community organizers. Part of his work involved collaborating and cosponsoring letters of encouragement and challenge to the young mission churches with whom he associated. It is not impossible to imagine that during the rocky first decades (and perhaps even shortly after Paul's death), the Pauline missionary team might have thought that the current situation was so important that a letter from the team leader on "company letterhead" needed to be distributed and circulated. So using some of the drafts in the collection of previous letters, Paul's missionary colleagues extended Paul's vision to particular situations unknown to Paul. Such pragmatic necessities are not best described as a sales gimmick or a conspiracy, but as a practical way of extending the Pauline tradition into new settings using the means available at the time. No other means were available at this early date. There was no authoritative canon, no head office, and no established church structure. In fact, this reality probably hastened the gathering of the Pauline letters into a collection, with letters to churches (e.g., Romans) at the head and with letters to delegates (e.g., the Pastorals) at the end. Thus the canonical shaping of the Pauline corpus was designed to promote the ongoing appropriation of the Pauline tradition and the gospel of Messiah Jesus to which it gave witness (2 Pet 3:15–16).

So even if the assessment of an "arm's-length" Paul makes a sharp profile of Paul harder to discern, I assume that the "disputed" letters extend the Pauline tradition in such a way that a coherent center is still discernible through the varying styles, vocabulary, and emphases within the Pauline collection of thirteen letters.

THE DEBATE OVER THE CENTER OF PAUL'S THEOLOGY

Regardless of how one assesses the Pauline authorship question, most scholars are agreed that a central vision guides Paul's theological writing; but widespread disagreement surrounds what constitutes the center. What are the classical options for Paul's center? First, ever since the Protestant Reformation, *justification by faith* has been held up as Paul's center. For Martin Luther (1960:357–62), justification by faith constitutes the center of Paul's thought—indeed the center of the entire NT. The NT books that did not sufficiently support this center were relegated to an appendix in Luther's translation of the Bible. This explains why Hebrews, James, Jude, and Revelation were set off at the back of Luther's 1522 German Bible. Part of the problem with this assessment is that Luther understood the Greek term *dikiosynē* as a judicial term (*justification*), as God's declared gift of right standing to the individual. Most likely this was a projection from his constant debate with the Roman Catholic Church and his own introspective personality (Stendahl 1976). The problem is that Luther's forensic translation (where justice is about scales, weights, and measures; and correction is retributive) took in a different direction Paul's Hebrew relational understanding (where justice is relational, and correction is restorative).

Certainly justification by faith plays a key role in Paul's missionary practice, but probably not for the reasons that Luther thought. Why not? Because first-century Judaism was not a "works-righteousness" religion, and Judaism cannot be equated with medieval Catholicism. Luther's views *overplayed* justification by faith; Paul's sense of *justification* is not anti-law (just more effective); neither is it an alternative to salvation by works (Sanders 1977:57). Judaism typically understood salvation to be by grace or election, which was then maintained by works (i.e., salvation by grace and judgment by works). Instead, Paul used justification by faith in a more limited way (to defend the inclusion of Gentiles into God's end-time people).

Luther's views also *underplayed* justification by faith; Paul's sense of *justification* describes more than just a new "imputed status" or "alien righteousness," which tends to be almost fictional since the converted individual really is still a sinner with one foot remaining in the worldly kingdom. Instead, Paul used "justification by faith" to describe something real and dynamic: namely, the *participation* in the Spirit, the new life that has begun now at the turn of the ages (Sanders 1977:514). Such participation entails the transfer from one sphere of power or existence to another that brings a transformation of behavior along with it.

If Martin Luther proposed "justification by faith" as Paul's center, Ferdinand C. Baur (1875) proposed pneumatology (spirit) as the core of Paul's vision. Baur embraced Hegelian philosophy, especially the dynamic of thesis, antithesis, and synthesis. For Baur, the center of Pauline theology was pneumatology (Romans 8), the spirit in conflict with the flesh. In the spirit, humanity shares the Spirit of God, experienced liberty from the finite, and attained absolute freedom. The center of Paul's gospel is the supremacy of the universal spirit, the eternal and infinite over the temporal and finite. In his view, this center was developed in opposition to primitive Christianity with its Jewish, legalistic orientation. So Paul helped to transform primitive Christianity into a major religious force with its new emphasis on life in the Spirit.

According to Baur, there was an antithetical relationship between Paul (law-free gospel of spirit = thesis) and Peter (law-bound Jewish-Christianity = antithesis). Out of this interaction (spirit vs. law) emerged the synthesis known as *early catholicism*. Luke's Acts, in this view, represents the accord between Peter and Paul; any prior tensions are smoothed over. The problem with this view is twofold: (1) Baur misrepresents first-century Judaism. For the most part, Judaism never thought of salvation as an achievement earned by completing works of law. That would make God a debtor, something unthinkable in Judaism. What distinguished the Israelite conception of God from concepts of its pagan neighbors was that salvation was always a gift of grace or election. (2) Baur's Hegelianism, with its machine-like algorithm, has fallen into disfavor today because it does not adequately account for the actual growth of the early Christian movement (or of any other movements for that matter). More satisfying is the explanation that history develops by paradigm shifts characterized by revolutionary spurts of one kind or another (Kuhn 1970).

Third, William Wrede (1907) argued that Paul's center is basically christological. For Wrede, Paul constructed a theological masterpiece, shaping the person and work of Jesus by using a popular gnostic redeemer myth. What he meant was that the center of Paul's thought was occupied with transforming the life of Jesus into redemptive assertions. Following the history-of-religion approach, Wrede saw Paul as the second founder of Christianity, who transformed the "historical" Jesus into the "redeemer" Christ via the pagan mythology available to him at the time. Wrede believed he could find in the mystery religions of Hellenistic mysticism and gnosticism a mythology that Paul used to transform Jesus of Nazareth, the teacher of true morality into the universal, cosmic Christ of faith.

It is true that religious texts speaking of a descending and ascending redeemer are known to have been popular in several ancient religious groups. Wrede claimed, however, that these gnostic myths were "parallel" to Paul's christological construction, and that this, therefore, was sufficient to establish a common tradition presumably available to Paul also. According to Wrede's reconstruction, the scenario is as follows: at Jesus's baptism the Christ descended upon him, and then just before he died on the cross, the Christ returned to heaven. Later, after the crucifixion, the Christ reanimated Jesus, causing him to appear to the disciples. Thus, the cosmic Christ of faith conveyed special knowledge to the disciples so that they too could survive death and return to the heavenly realm.

The problem with this view is that recent discoveries of gnostic texts point against this chronology. How so? The 1945 discovery of gnostic spiritual writings at the Egyptian village of Nag Hammadi, near the Pachomian monasteries at Tabennesi, Phbow, and Sheneset suggests that these texts may have been collected by Christian monks. They were likely used as supplementary spiritual reading during the heterodox period of early Christianity, before they were banned as heretical by the church hierarchy in Athanasius's thirty-ninth Easter festival letter in the year 367 CE (Wisse 1978:436–37). The discovery of these contraband texts is significant.

Prior to 1945, gnostics were known only indirectly from what Christian theologians (such as Irenaeus) said about them in the many tracts written against them. No doubt some of the accusations were exaggerated and their claims distorted in order to discredit them and dissuade any Christians from adopting their heterodox views. Whether intentional or not, the misrepresentation likely came from the Christian theologians' practice of systematizing the gnostic sects in terms of dogma and teaching.

The evidence from the Nag Hammadi library does *not* confirm these systematizations of gnostic thought (Wisse 1986:188). The collection itself shows an amazing variety of beliefs and practices, including the mixing of some Christian themes with other spiritualities. There is no "smoking gun." Yes, the gnostic writings do feature cosmic dualism (i.e., the belief that souls of people are imprisoned in an evil world of the flesh and long to shed this earthly existence in order to realize their essential, divine nature), and they do tell of a divine redeemer who opens up pathways to light and knowledge for those "in the know" (i.e., for those who were "gnostic"), but the writings are not uniform about what characterizes a gnostic. If there is any common theme, it is the call to an ascetic life, which may explain why some monks near Nag Hammadi found aspects of these gnostic texts interesting and worth reading, collecting, and hiding (Wisse 1978:440). In any case, it would be too much to say that the gnostic redeemer mythology was readily available and used by Paul.

If anything, the evidence points in the other direction: namely, that gnosticism in the second century, and those with gnostic tendencies, found Christian writings attractive and useful for their purposes. For example, the first commentary on the Gospel of John was written by a gnostic named Heracleon, living around 170 CE. This should not be surprising, since gnostics could use almost any spiritual text to promote their particular aims during the heterodox period of early Christianity before 200 CE.

What then are the contemporary options for a Pauline center? Justification by faith continues to be promoted as Paul's center, but with different nuances. George Eldon Ladd, for example, insists that justification by faith must have more than an individual orientation; he says, "The unifying center is rather the redemptive work of Christ as the redemptive center of history" (1993:412). Bultmann, by contrast, gives Paul's preaching of justification by faith central importance, but with an existentialist twist: it is not so much about God, but about how individuals can now finally take full responsibility for their own salvation (1951:191).

Other contenders for Paul's center are reconciliation (Martin 1981), participation and union with Christ (Sanders 1977), and an apocalyptic eschatology—one where God's promised triumph over evil is revealed to be what Jesus's life and ministry were all about, ushering in a new way of living in these last days of the old age (Beker 1980).

Is there a way to adjudicate between these contenders for Paul's center? What can be ruled out when determining the center? At minimum, it cannot be something derivative. Whatever depends on another, more comprehensive conviction cannot be the center. This calls into question contenders like reconciliation, mystical union, theology of the cross, or justification by faith. Why? Because each of these is derived from Paul's missionary argumentation aimed at solving a variety of pastoral challenges. They are contingent applications of a more basic conviction. The center must be comprehensive enough to embrace the diversity of ideas and applications that characterize the Pauline tradition.

Two clues point to apocalyptic eschatology as the Pauline center. First, Paul's starting point for his pastoral and missionary discourse is *not* the memory of Jesus's life and ministry. If Paul did spend time in Jerusalem, he does not tell us much about Jesus's life. Neither is the starting point of his gospel Jesus's life as a Torah-observant Jew. Instead, it is the resurrection of Jesus and Paul's encounter with the risen Lord that launch his reflection, interpretation, mission, collaboration, and writing. In other words, his transforming encounter with the risen Lord is the decisive moment for all of Paul's thought.

While Paul's encounter with the risen Lord can be described as revelation (the core meaning of the word *apocalyptic*), it would be wrong to call Paul an apocalypticist in the tradition of those who wrote *1 Enoch*, *2 Baruch*, *2 Esdras*, the Revelation of John, and so on. These apocalyptic writings fit a particular genre called apocalyptic, characterized by numerous vision reports and surveys of history in the form of prophecy. Still, the basic content of apocalyptic thought drives Paul's theological reflection. We see the reality of two ages (1 Cor 10:11); the coming of the Messiah, which grants believers access to the heavenly world and resurrection (1 Cor 15:23); and the nearness of the coming age (Phil 4:5), where the coming Lord brings both judgment and salvation (Phil 2:11).

A second clue that points to apocalyptic eschatology as a description of Paul's center is that virtually every issue that Paul addresses in his letters is predicated on the new reality that Easter represents. The evidence for this is the overwhelming predominance of eschatological and apocalyptic terms of reference. Some eschatological terms include "last days" (2 Tim 3:1-8), "end time" (1 Cor 15:24-26), "now" (Rom 13:11), "new creation" (2 Cor 5:17), "first fruits" (1 Cor 15:23), firstborn (Col 1:15-20), "ages overlap" (1 Cor 10:11), "hope" (Tit 1:1-3), and "peace" (Eph 2:14). Some apocalyptic categories include "revelation" (Gal 1:12), "mystery" (Rom 16:25), "gospel" (Rom 1:1-6), "righteousness" (Rom 3:21-26), "promise" (Eph 2:12-21), "kingdom" (Col 1:13), "victory" (1 Cor 15:57), "triumph" (2 Cor 2:14), "resurrection" (Phil 3:10-11), "life" (1 Tim 6:11-19), "power" (Rom 1:16), "coming" (1 Cor 15:23)," appearing" (2 Tim 1:8-10), "salvation" (Phil 1:28), "judgment" (2 Cor 5:10), "light" and "darkness" (1 Thess 5:5), "principalities" and "powers" (Eph 6:12), "sin" (Rom 5:12-21), and "wrath" (1 Thess 5:9).

Even Paul's imagery depicting the saving significance of the cross makes use of apocalyptic eschatology: "[God] disarmed the rulers and authorities and made a public example of them, triumphing over them in [the cross]" (Col 2:15). The Christ event inaugurates the *end-time age* (i.e., eschatology) in which God is triumphing over hostile cosmic powers locked in battle for ultimate lordship over God's creation. The Christ event *reveals* (a word whose meaning underlies *apocalypse* and *apocalyptic*) that God is saving and creating a people in the world through which to express God's lordship and to bring the creation enterprise to completion.

Given these two clues (that the starting point is not the memory of Jesus's life and that all argumentation is influenced by the new Easter reality), only apocalyptic eschatology emerges as the Pauline center that best explains the data. Paul is convinced that he is witnessing the final act in God's redemption drama. If he would speak into the microphone to give his vision statement, it would probably be something like this: *God is triumphing over evil through Jesus in order to redeem and reconfigure Israel into a people, which is both Jewish and Gentile. The initial victory over personal, structural, and cosmic evil occurred at Easter, and now the Spirit of the risen Lord empowers God's people to live as outposts of God's coming reign and invites all creation to abandon its rebellion and to rediscover its true identity in God. All this is happening now because God is doing this in Jesus, who is the messianic Son of God.*

There are two implications flowing from such a center: (1) The many diverse themes and emphases that characterize the Pauline tradition can all be rooted in an apocalyptic, eschatological view of Jesus. Pauline themes like the righteousness of God, justification by faith, the victory of the cross, baptism into Christ, reconciliation, and life in the Spirit can all be grounded in apocalyptic eschatology. Thus, an apocalyptic eschatology explains the rise of other emphases, strengthening its claim to be central. (2) An apocalyptic eschatology helps frame the Pauline corpus of missionary and pastoral letters. While the pastoral situations that Paul and his missionary team addressed are various, each one can be derived from an articulation of an apocalyptic eschatological center, strengthening its claim to be central.

Furthermore, development of the apocalyptic eschatological center can be traced in the Pauline letters from the early ones through to the later ones of the Pauline tradition. In the *early* writings (1–2 Thessalonians), the Pauline missionary team promotes apocalyptic eschatology as vindication in the face of suffering and oppression. That is, Jesus's ongoing resurrected life assures the faithful that the new age is dawning, and that it will one day be complete, in spite of evil's efforts to carry on causing hardship, pain, and death. In the *middle* writings (Galatians, Romans, 1–2 Corinthians, Philippians, Philemon, Colossians, and Ephesians), apocalyptic eschatology is developed to explain several ideas: God's salvation plan, the work of Christ in defeating the rebellious powers, the gift of God's Spirit to empower the church in its witness, the church's invitation to the watching world, and the church's mandate to join in God's mission to reconcile all things and complete creation. In the *later* writings (1–2 Timothy and Titus), the Pauline missionary team works to give structure to the apocalyptic eschatological vision during a time of engaged waiting and significant turbulence when the new age overlaps with the old age. There is encouragement to live above reproach, to promote unity of faith and life through strong church leadership, and to keep the faith witnessed by the Pauline tradition in the midst of various distractions.

THE CONTENT OF PAUL'S GOSPEL MESSAGE

If an apocalyptic, eschatological center describes Paul's view of Messiah Jesus, what would be the content of Paul's gospel? What did Paul mean by using the word "gospel" (*euangelion*)? The term *gospel* was not a common religious term in antiquity among neither Jews nor Greeks. Paul makes special use of this term, always in the singular. He characterized the "glad tidings" of God's saving activity revealed in Jesus's life as the "gospel of God" (Rom 1:1; 15:16; 2 Cor 11:7; 1 Thess 2:2, 8, 9; 1 Tim 1:11), the "gospel of Christ" (Rom 15:19; 1 Cor 9:12; 2 Cor 2:12; 9:13; 10:14; Phil 1:27; 1 Thess 3:2; 2 Thess 1:8), "my gospel" (Rom 2:16; 16:25; 2 Tim 2:8), and "our gospel" (2 Cor 4:3; 1 Thess 1:5; 2 Thess 2:14).

Paul uses the term *gospel* more than any other NT writer (sixty of its seventy-six NT occurrences belong to Paul). For Paul, the gospel is the revelation of God's power for salvation and God's righteousness (Rom 1:16–17). The gospel announces God's eschatological action—that God is keeping the ancient promises to Israel for the sake of the whole world. It announces what God has done through the life, death, and resurrection of Jesus, which now finally make possible the completion of the creation enterprise started so long ago. It is "good news" in three tenses, announcing the *fact* of salvation (past), the *reality* of salvation (present), and the *hope* of salvation (future). It is what God is doing to make things right, as promised.

What convictions did Paul's gospel share with first-century Judaism? As an apostle to the Gentiles, Paul called his Gentile hearers "to serve a living and true God" (1 Thess 1:9), not false, destructive idols. The Pauline missionary message reveals two convictions that Paul shared with other first-century Jews: (1) Paul's gospel was *monotheistic*. Paul, like other adherents of first-century Judaism, was convinced that God is one, that God is fair, and that God is trustworthy (Rom 3:30). Therefore Paul calls his converts to abandon their allegiances to what was false, destructive, and untrue. Instead, he invites them to become identified with the one, true God of Israel. (2) Paul's gospel was *conversionist*. As a Pharisee, Paul was accustomed to inviting people to reconsider their rebellious, immoral ways and choose wholeness. Conversion from idolatry and immorality to the true and living God describes the total transformation that is the goal of Paul's preaching: deliverance from bondage to sin and death, and attachment to Messiah Jesus, the risen Lord.

Paul's gospel message, however, did differ from first-century Jewish practice and popular belief. Besides calling people to abandon idolatry and immorality in order to serve Israel's God, Paul's missionary proclamation included a key component: namely, identifying Jesus as Messiah and Lord. Not only did the Pauline witness call Gentiles "to serve a living and true God"; the second part of the witness calls converts "to wait for his Son from heaven, whom he raised from the dead—Jesus, who rescues us from the wrath that is coming" (1 Thess 1:9-10). Paul proclaimed that Jesus, the crucified one, is the risen Lord and God's Messiah, not a cursed sinner, as a cursory reading of Torah could suggest (Deut 21:22-23). The revelation he received (Gal 1:16) is that through the cross, God chose to deal with (i.e., expose and undo) sin's rebellious rule that has kept the world in its death grip for so long (1 Thess 1:9; 1 Cor 1:18, 22; 2:2; 15:3-11; Rom 3:24-26; 4:24-25; Col 2:15).

Far from being an embarrassment to Judaism, Jesus actually demonstrated God's holiness and righteous purpose, making it possible for all to escape evil's grip. Thus the identity markers of God's liberated people were no longer limited to circumcision, food laws, and Sabbath observances (Gal 2:16-17). These ethnic identity badges no longer delimit God's people, since God's kind of righteousness is now available to all by the faithfulness of Jesus, who accomplished and is accomplishing the goal of Torah (Rom 10:4).

What were the demands associated with Paul's gospel preaching? Paul called for two kinds of responses to the announcement of God's saving activity in Jesus. First, Paul expected participants to engage the gospel in a life of faith as obedience and active trust. As a first-century Jew, Paul understood that God's election of Israel (salvation by grace) was maintained by covenant responsibility (judgment by works). This basic pattern of Jewish religion ("covenantal nomism" [Sanders 1977:422]) was modified by Paul's understanding of Jesus's death and resurrection. Rather than demonstrating a faithful response to God's gift of election through Torah observance, now an active appropriation of Jesus's ongoing story measures faithful response to God's initiative.

For Paul, active trust (faith) is the sign of a positive response to the gospel proclamation. The trusting response to hearing is heeding or obeying (Rom 10:14–17). Faith is obedience (Rom 1:5; 1 Thess 1:8) since the gospel is a message that makes a claim. Trust is a response of the whole self, calling for a reconfiguration of the self in relation to family, community, and world. To trust God as proclaimed in the death and resurrection of Jesus is to challenge existing configurations and to realign them according to a newly revealed standard demonstrated by Jesus. To reject the gospel is to maintain the status quo. Because Paul saw faith as trust and the sole condition for being rightly related to God, he concluded that Gentiles need not become kosher Jews in order to be included within God's people, Israel.

Second, Paul expected converts to give witness to their realignment by being baptized. The ancient ritual symbolized the participant's attachment to Christ, the church, and the end-time form of Israel. Baptism was a key part of Paul's mission; it signaled the indicative reality (union with Christ), which in turn empowered behavioral imperatives: "Do you not know that all of us who have been baptized into Christ Jesus were baptized into his death? . . . just as Christ was raised from the dead by the glory of the Father, so we too might walk in newness of life" (Rom 6:3–4). "Anyone united to the Lord becomes one spirit with him . . . Do you not know that your body is a temple of the Holy Spirit within you, which you have from God, and that you are not your own?" (1 Cor 6:17–19).

The religious ritual of baptism, however, did not begin with Paul. It was already practiced in the early church as well as in Judaism and in other ancient religions. For Christians, it functioned as the rite of entry into the church as a symbol of identity and commission (Isaak 2004). Christians modified the ancient rite of baptism in two ways: (1) Christian baptism was not a ritual of repeated washing since it marked the eschatological life (the end-time age) into which the candidate was being initiated. As part of the end-time people of God, the candidate needed no subsequent baptisms. (2) Christian baptism was not self-administered since it marked attachment to a new collective identity within something larger than the candidate. Participation in the new-creation people animated by the Spirit of the risen Lord made self-serve baptism impossible.

Paul's contribution to the practice and theology of baptism is the understanding that baptism means incorporation into Christ: the reconstituted people of God, Israel. This is possible only if Christ is understood as a corporate person (Rom 5:12–21). He is the head or symbol of a people. Baptism into Christ means incorporation into the inclusive new people, the new Adam. It means incorporation into the domain of Christ and his power; it means incorporation into the community of which Christ is the head and power center. Baptism into Christ means baptism into the body of Christ (1 Cor 12:13). It is about participation, intimacy, and life in the Spirit (Rom 8:1–11), all of which become the collective norm for the newly reconfigured people of God (Rom 12:1–2). To be "in Christ" is to join others in becoming one in purpose, commitment, desire, and experience with Jesus and his mission in the world so that his story becomes the story of his people.

Two anthropological issues emerge from Paul's participationist view of baptism. The first issue revolves around the question: to which "body" does baptism give access? Is it the local or the universal church, the visible or the invisible church? It is unlikely that Paul and the early Christians would have understood such a distinction. Why not? Because, as George Beasley-Murray helpfully notes, "the church is the visible manifestation of the people of God, whose life is 'hidden with Christ in God' (Col 3:3). Baptism is a visible act with a spiritual meaning; it is therefore well adapted to be the means of entry into a visible community of God's people *and* the body which transcends any one place or time" (1993:64).

The second issue turns on whether baptism is about a personal commitment or about membership in a new family. Again, it is unlikely that Paul and the early Christians would have understood such a distinction. Why? Because personality in the ancient world was essentially collectivist in nature and not individualist. According to Bruce Malina, "The person in question does not think of himself or herself as an individual who acts alone regardless of what others think and say. Rather, the person is ever aware of the expectations of others, especially significant others, and strives to match those expectations. This is the group-embedded, group-oriented, collectivist personality, one who needs another simply to know who he or she is" (2001:75). This is not to say that individual psychology, individual uniqueness, and individual self-consciousness are nonexistent in the ancient world, but these traits were not central to ancient identity formation. Therefore, when we read that someone "believed and was baptized" (like the Ethiopian eunuch [Acts 8:38]), this is less a statement of personal identity and more a statement about the people with whom he or she is being identified. Baptism is linked to collective identity in the NT.

THE SOURCES OF PAUL'S GOSPEL MESSAGE

What language does Paul use to characterize the source of his gospel? Paul asserts that his gospel is of divine origin (Gal 1:11–12). For him, the regular sources of religious ideas (received as a student or learned as one self-taught) do not describe how the gospel came to him. He claims to have had an encounter with the divine. As we noted, Paul, like all the apostles, claims to have encountered the resurrected Lord. What Paul describes as God's revelation through Jesus is the risen Lord's resurrection appearance to him (1 Cor 9:1; 15:8). The revelation is that Jesus of Nazareth is alive, and that he is indeed Israel's Messiah: not just a radical prophet, wisdom teacher, miracle worker, and so on—but in fact the Messiah of God.

Through God's disclosure of the risen Christ, Paul realized that the Christian proclamation of Jesus and his resurrection was true, not a lie or a blasphemy or a hoax or wishful thinking. This is why his thinking can be called apocalyptic: it is about a surprising revelation of God, something that could not be achieved through scholastic efforts, yet discernible in Scripture—in retrospect. Plus, Paul's thinking is eschatological: it involves accessing the end-time form of creation in a preview sort of way, even though the end has not yet arrived.

How does Paul characterize this revelation? Until the revelation of Jesus Christ at the *parousia*, the gospel proclaims the *proleptic* (i.e., received-beforehand) revelation of Jesus Christ and remains a *mysterion* to many in the world. The gospel mystery, however, has been revealed ahead of time to the first disciples or apostles, including Paul. What is the content of the mystery? Paul notes three surprising aspects of the gospel mystery: (1) Messiah Jesus *is* the embodiment of God's plan of salvation. Surprise! A crucified Christ does indeed demonstrate God's righteousness (Gal 1:4; 1 Cor 1:23–25). (2) Messiah Jesus liberates humanity from powers of evil without evil's anticipating its self-inflicted demise. Surprise! The scapegoat mechanism (that evil intended to silence Jesus and secure its reign) is actually the means by which evil's power is undone. Never again would humanity be obligated to submit to its manipulative death-dealing ways: it was exposed, laid bare for anyone with eyes to see (1 Cor 2:8–9; Col 2:15). (3) God's plan of salvation includes the Gentiles as fellow heirs. Sin was gathered into one place (Israel) so that it could be dealt with and defeated by Israel's representative, Messiah Jesus, who embodies God's intention for Israel and fills out the final form of God's people in these last days (Toews 2004:215, 293). Surprise! It is not Torah observance that identifies one with Israel, but the "obedience of faith" (Rom 1:5). God's end-time people (both Jewish and Gentile) are now defined by the Spirit of the risen Christ, symbolized by their baptism into the Jesus community and empowered to carry on God's global transformational mission (Eph 3:5-6; Gal 2:19-20).

Therefore, according to Paul, the source of his theology is a revelation from God—that Jesus is the Messiah (the promised liberator), that the power of sin is broken (exposed as illegitimate, and deposed from its rule), and that Jesus is the bringer of God's eschatological (end-time) salvation, which now extends to Gentiles and all creation.

PAUL'S MODIFICATION OF TRADITIONAL JEWISH APOCALYPTIC THEOLOGY

As noted, Paul worked with the symbols available after his symbolic map shattered and lay strewn all over the floor. From traditional Jewish thought Paul was able to take certain pieces and modify others until the reconfigured map did explain his experience; still, this new-old picture he also claimed as a gift of God. How might this reconfiguration have been achieved? I will argue that Jewish apocalyptic theology provided Paul with the basic framework of his thought.

What is the nature of Jewish apocalyptic theology? Apocalyptic theology emerged during the Jewish apocalyptic period of Israel's history (from 250 BCE to the second century CE). This theology undertook the radicalization of earlier *covenant theology*. Ancient Israelites believed that God had initiated a covenant with Israel to be their divine protector, and that Israel's response was to be one of complete devotion to God, demonstrated by faithful Torah observance (Deut 6:1-9). Covenant theology taught that all God's acts of salvation and judgment, of blessing and cursing, took place in real-time history (Gen 12:1-3; 2 Kgs 21:1-16; Isa 45:1-8; Jer 32:4-5; Hab 1:5-11). Thus, the national disasters—like foreign domination/invasion by Assyrians, Babylonians, and Persians—were assumed to be God's judgment for Israel's infidelity to the covenant. The constant refrain of Israel's prophets like Isaiah, Jeremiah, Amos, and others was the oscillation between judgment and salvation (see diagram below). This theology bred the hope that in the future God would resolve the problem of evil and bring peace by raising up a righteous king in Israel, who would restore Israel to power in its own land (Isa 52:13—53:12).

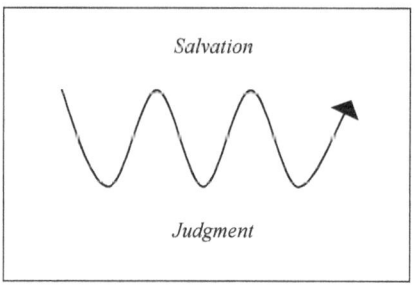

TABLE 3.2 Ancient Jewish Covenant Theology

The radicalization of Jewish apocalyptic theology (between 250 BCE. and the second century CE) involved building on covenant theology; the theological additions anticipated God's saving work in Israel through the agency of the righteous one, the "Son of Man," who enters from *outside* history ("coming with the clouds of heaven" [Dan 7:13–14]). The sense is that things have become so bad that no nation on earth can do God's saving and judging work any longer. This may be the way that God did things earlier (using the Assyrians, Babylonians, or Persians to bring corrective judgment upon Israel), but now God must intervene directly. Such apocalyptic theology is characterized by the introduction of a dualistic doctrine of two ages. Now is the "present evil age," but in the future, "the age to come" spells victory for God's people (see diagram below). There is no continuity between these two ages. At some future moment when the Son of Man comes, "the age to come" will break into the human realm by a supernatural act of God. Evil will be annihilated, and the righteous will be raised to new life.

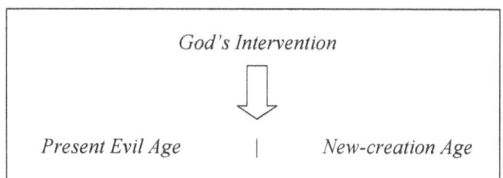

TABLE 3.3 Jewish Apocalyptic Theology

How does Paul transform the pattern of Jewish thought with which he was well acquainted as a Pharisee? Key for Paul is his identification of the risen Jesus as the "second man" and "last Adam" (Rom 5:14; 1 Cor

15:45, 47); it is his encounter with the risen Jesus and his subsequent reflection on that event that forced his traditional pattern (symbolic map) to crack and be reconfigured in a way that made sense of his new convictions. Paul's apocalyptic theology had to be modified in light of the Christ event. Paul begins with "the present evil age" (Gal 1:4; 1 Cor 2:6-8) as one ruled by the god of this world (2 Cor 4:4): namely, Satan and the elemental spirits of the universe (Gal 4:3, 9; 1 Cor 2:8; Col 2:8, 20). However, the present age must be passing away (1 Cor 7:31). Why? Because its death grip on humanity has been loosened, as Jesus is alive! Therefore, these powers/rulers must be "tottering toward their end"; they are being rendered inoperative. The second age, or the "new creation" (Gal 6:14; 2 Cor 5:17), is making its entrance as God, in Messiah Jesus, exposes the rebellious forces in opposition to God so that they are outed, deposed, and destroyed (Gal 6:14; 1 Cor 7:31; Rom 5:21; 6:1-12; Col 2:15).

Thus, the present is characterized as the overlap of the ages or as the mingling of the ages (1 Cor 10:11; 2 Cor 5:16). This is new! First Corinthians 10:11 is especially important. Here, Paul describes himself and those with him as those *eis hous ta telē tōn aiōnōn katentēken* (upon whom the ends [pl] of the ages [pl] have met). In other words, Paul and all those associated with Jesus see themselves as living during these last days, as living "on the edge" of the ages where the front end of one overlaps with the back end of the other (see diagram below). The overlap is inaugurated at the cross/resurrection of Christ (1 Cor 1:17-18) and it will conclude with the *parousia* of Christ (1 Thess 2:19; 3:13; 4:13-18; 1 Cor 15:23-28).

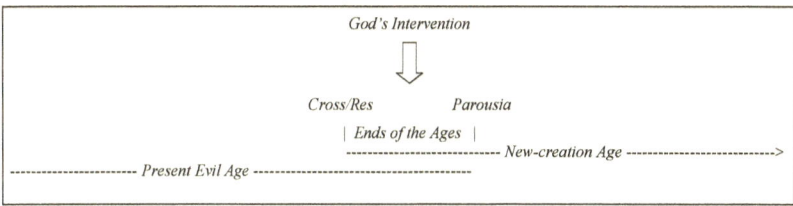

TABLE 3.4 Paul's Modification of Jewish Apocalyptic Theology

Paul believes himself to be called by God to work in God's mission during this inauguration period, celebrating now a taste of what is yet to be. Much of his pastoral care and advice to young churches is derived from his understanding of the overlapping ages—to live now out of the resources of the future. The resurrection has begun, because Jesus is alive in a powerfully new way and experienced through the power of the Holy Spirit in communities of hope—in worship, in signs and wonders, in instruction, in discernment, and so on.

Because of the cross and resurrection, the following must also be true: (1) God's sovereignty has been established and demonstrated once again (Rom 8:31–39); (2) the power of sin has been undone initially (Gal 1:4; 1 Cor 15:53; Rom 4:25); and (3) death's rule has been judged, convicted, and revoked (1 Cor 15:54–57; Rom 8:31–39). Thus, creation takes a huge step toward its completion. And yet the struggle continues in anticipation of God's final victory (Rom 8:18–25; 1 Cor 15:20–28), and creation presently awaits ("longs for") the grand judgment when all things are made right (Rom 8:18–25; 16:20; 1 Cor 6:2–3; 15:20–28; 1 Thess 5:2–11). However, this is not "plan B" that is now in effect because "plan A" failed. Rather, Paul argues that this has always been God's plan: it had just not been seen before.

Still Paul exercises a sober eschatological *reserve*. Since the kingdom of God has not yet been established in its full glory, life in the meantime must be characterized by vigilant resistance against the deceptions of the old-age empire (Rom 6:12). At the same time, this is already the messianic age in which everything (past, present, and future) is viewed from the vantage point of the cross and resurrection (2 Cor 5:16). Paul's missionary appeal amounts to an invitation to come and join the resistance movement, giving witness against all forms of religious, social, and political oppression (because their rule is no longer legitimate) and giving witness to the new possibilities of life together as God's reconfigured people gathered around Messiah Jesus, the risen Lord (even though this is but the "first fruits" of what is yet to be).

Paul uses end-time language and symbols to characterize the life of the Christian community, even if the final, "capital-E" end is still some time off. Why? Because there were only two linguistic tools in Paul's Jewish apocalyptic toolbox. It would not have been appropriate to describe the post-Easter experience of the Christian community as "the present evil age"; so only was left: "the age to come." While this one tool proved to be the most adequate for articulating the significance of Jesus's cross and resurrection, Paul's practice would later prove to be confusing to many, and his nuanced eschatological language of "the age to come" was misunderstood. Christian history records numerous unfortunate examples of communities who thought either that Paul had advocated either an imminent end of the world, or that believers lived fully victorious lives now in the Spirit, no longer threatened by the power of sin. Both of these views misconstrue Paul's eschatological language.

To sum up, Paul's use of end-time language makes two assertions: (1) *Certainty*: Paul's end-time language communicates certainty, not counting. There is no place for timetabling or calendarizing, as in some popular apocalyptic thought (e.g., three and a half weeks, seven years, or one thousand years). (2) *Engagement*: Paul's end-time language calls disciples of Jesus to live now a life of engagement with the culture in which the church finds itself, empowered by the Spirit of the risen Lord. At this point in time there is no longer a categorical opposition between "this age" and "the coming age." A two-kingdom theology of isolation or disengagement will not do. Instead, the ongoing testimony and experience of contemporary disciples of Jesus is to live now a life of engagement, "as if" or "as though" the moral center really is that of the risen Lord, who is making all things right, in spite of appearances to the contrary (1 Cor 7:29–31). Any contemporary appropriation of Paul's end-time language requires a "conversion of the imagination," revising age-old social patterns from the new perspective that Easter gave to God's reign.

For Paul, the "age to come" is already present, energizing all his ethical reflection. The Spirit of the risen Messiah is already present animating the gathered assemblies (local churches) in worship, in signs and wonders, in instruction, in discernment, and so on. Thus, the resurrection of Christ marks the beginning of the process of eschatological transformation that is ultimately to characterize all creation. Therefore, Christians can already rejoice, claim the new creation, and live in the power of the Spirit. While the final victory is not yet present, the Pauline missionary team invites all creation to live now out of those future resources. No more calendarization. No more isolationism. Instead, local faith communities live *now* as signs of the future hope.

THE BASIC COMPONENTS OF PAUL'S PROCLAMATION OF GOD'S APOCALYPTIC SALVATION

Four basic themes characterize Paul's gospel message. First, the gospel proclamation vindicates God's faithfulness (Rom 3:21–26; 1 Cor 1:9; 2 Cor 1:20). Paul's proclamation of Jesus as Messiah is anchored in a specific view of God. In the death and resurrection of Jesus, the covenant God of Israel confirmed and renewed the ancient promise of salvation to Israel and the nations. In Jesus Christ, God vindicates the honor of God's name and promises—not in the sense of *protecting* God's holiness, but in the sense of doing what is characteristic of holiness: namely, *demonstrating* God's holiness by reaching out and making things right. Christ is the manifestation and confirmation of God's faithfulness to the ancient redemptive purpose already present at the dawn of time: "For in him every one of God's promises is a 'Yes.' For this reason it is through him that we say the 'Amen,' to the glory of God" (2 Cor 1:20). Christ is the manifestation of God's Amen, as the symbol of God's faithfulness to the promises. Paul's theological thinking is God centered. It is God who triumphs in Christ (Rom 3:24-26; 1 Cor 1:9). It is God's faithfulness that is vindicated in Christ.

Second, Paul's gospel proclamation testifies to a universal, cosmic hope. In Jewish apocalyptic thought, God's faithfulness is primarily directed to the vindication of ethnic Israel and those people obedient to the law (Torah). God's activity in Christ profoundly modifies this apocalyptic thought for Paul. The division in humanity is no longer constituted by those who belong to ethnic Israel or not, but now more precisely by those choosing to associate with the victory demonstrated by Jesus or not. In Paul's gospel, the death of Jesus is the focal point of the prince of evil's death-dealing scheme, which God uses to expose evil for what it is and to disarm its grip on all people: Jew and Gentile. God used the Torah to focus and concentrate sin in Israel (no one else had the Torah), in order to expose sin's enormously destructive ways. This, Paul argues, must have been God's plan. It is not a mistake. Sin was gathered into one place (Israel) so that it could be dealt with and defeated by Israel's representative, Messiah Jesus. So the goal of Torah is realized by Jesus (Rom 10:4), by the one who embodies God's intention for Israel and fills out the final form of God's people in these last days.

The death of Jesus is paradoxical. On the one hand, Easter signifies the "wrath of God" on all humanity (Rom 1:18; 5:9)—not in the sense of God's punishing Jesus in our place, but in the sense of God's giving people what they want. The consequences of humanity's alignment with the prince of evil's scapegoating ways is made evident with the cry, "Crucify him" (Mark 15:13-14)! Jesus bears the full brunt of the power of sin's thirst for death. God allows evil to be evil, turning people over to the desires of their heart. This is the wrath of God: namely, the consequences experienced when a person rejects his or her identity as God's beloved, choosing instead to abandon life. On the other hand, Easter also signifies the "free gift" of God's salvation (Rom 5:16) now finally accessible to all humanity. God refuses to let evil have the last word. The resurrection signifies God's affirmation of Jesus's faithful life of being-for-others, which paves the way for all who are associated with Jesus's resistance movement to be included in that same resurrection at the end of this present age. Because Jesus is alive, this means that evil's death-grip on humanity has been loosened for the first time, and Jesus's victory is now accessible to all connected to him.

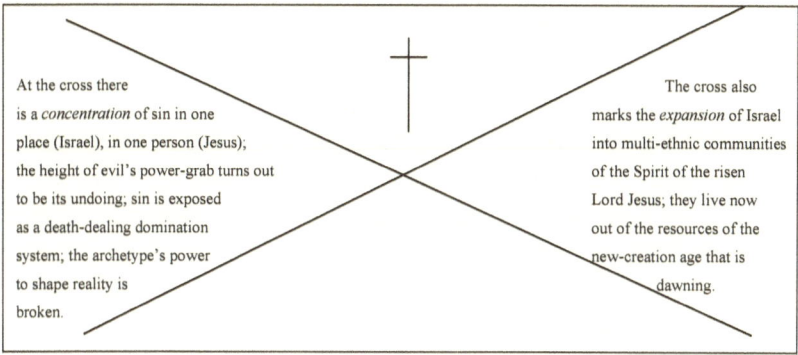

TABLE 3.5 The Concentration-Expansion Dynamic of the Cross-Resurrection

Easter underlines the conviction that there are no people groups with "favored-nation status" distinguishing them from other peoples. In Christ, all may participate in the reconfigured Israel, the end-time form of God's people. This is new, but not really new since it taps into the purpose of God from the beginning. The universal effect of God's judgment and salvation in Christ means the end of all forms of elitism. The radicalization of "wrath" and "salvation" at Easter does not lead to universalism, where all ways lead indiscriminately to God. Instead, the gospel proclamation of salvation is *extended* to all (inclusive), but it is also *restricted* to those sharing in the ongoing life of the resurrected Jesus (exclusive). Because only Jesus is victorious over death, only he can give shape to the new humanity. The time between the cross-resurrection and the close of this present age, is a time for invitation, decision, mission, vigilance, and endurance. Those who act as if the power of evil defeated by Messiah Jesus still rules over them will be granted their "desire" for darkness and death in the final judgment, even as God continues to offer life. See C. S. Lewis's insightful argument for heaven and hell in his book titled *The Great Divorce*.

The universal-cosmic nature of salvation in Christ is linked to three other cosmic themes in Paul. (1) Cosmic anthropology: for Paul, humanity was created good, but not complete; the expectation for growth and development is present from the beginning. Early on, however, humanity got itself tangled up in the worldwide conflict between the powers of evil and the lordship of God, siding with evil—even though God had invited humanity to participate with God in finishing the creation enterprise (Rom 5:12–21). Finally, in Jesus, humanity is brought to the next level (Adam #2), as Jesus demonstrates what it means to be authentically human (living in relation with God for others), as God had intended from the start. And yet the new humanity (those associated with Messiah Jesus) is still not complete until the end of time (the *eschaton*). (2) Cosmic righteousness: for Paul, since God is one and God is fair, in Jesus, God's lordship, sovereignty, and righteousness extend over all creation. All are invited to recognize their God-given identity as children of God in a world where things are being made right. Here, God's righteousness is understood as empowerment, as the gospel empowers participants in the new creation to live a transformed life (Rom 6:1–14). (3) Cosmic mission: for Paul, cosmic anthropology and righteousness have profound implications for Christian mission. It is a mission based on the global scope of God's righteousness. God's gift of righteousness is inseparable from God's claim on the world. Christians are invited and empowered to participate in God's cosmic plan of redemption. The church is the sent body, inviting people to join, to participate, and to rediscover their true identity as God's beloved. The church is expected, empowered, mandated to have a part in God's missional enterprise (2 Cor 5:16–21). The church's mission is God's mission.

Third, Paul's gospel proclamation not only vindicates God's faithfulness and testifies to a universal cosmic hope, it also warns of the intensification of "the battle" in these "last days." The confrontation in the present world between the powers of Satan and of God intensifies the crisis. The church must do battle against the old-world value system—all the more so because the cross of Christ is God's radical No to the value structures of the world. There are political implications to the gospel, and the church must challenge the powers of government to reconsider the means it uses to exercise its mandate. As a sign of the age to come, the church should anticipate challenge from all fronts. All of Paul's theological reflection aims at addressing the ecclesial and ethical challenges presented by the dawn of the end-time age.

The reality of the battle means three things. (1) The necessity of suffering: surprised by its own self-inflicted blow, evil responds with a desperate counterattack. True to its character of self-interest, evil will try to marginalize and discredit the church's resistance to the old-age values. This is predicable. Even Jesus says, "I did not come to bring peace, but a sword" (Matt 10:34). In good Semitic form, the foreseen *results* are spoken of as *purposes* in a world where God is known as the Master of the universe. It is not Jesus's purpose to bring conflict, but he is well aware that conflict will be the result if the legitimacy of old-age power structure is challenged. (2) The life of the Christian is characterized by a cruciform existence, life under the cross. The pattern of the cross is not only for Jesus but also for all those who associate with him, gather around him, are baptized into his corporate body. The faithfulness of Jesus informs and empowers others to faithfulness. (3) The church no longer gives uncritical allegiance to the state. The trump card no longer belongs to the state but to the community of Jesus, which invites and challenges the state and all the powers that be to realign themselves with the ways of God. Thus, the church can only offer nonaligned submission to the state (Rom 13:1–7), always reserving the right to resist state or institutional mandates, given its new alignment to Lord Jesus. Since the power of the new age is already at work in the church through the empowering presence of the Spirit of the risen Lord Jesus (2 Cor 5:17), Christians can (and must) resist the ways of the old, evil age wherever they may be found (Rom 6:13; 8:13).

Fourth, Paul's gospel proclamation asserts that the end of this present world has begun; the curtain has opened and the last act of the redemption drama has begun. Paul's training in Jewish apocalypticism predisposed him to believe in the imminent end of the world at the Messiah's coming. The literature expressed this belief in speculation and calendarizing. However, Paul's encounter with the risen Lord and his missionary experience caused him to modify his view of the end, as we have seen.

Two major motifs characterize Paul's eschatological hope. The first motif is the *necessity* of the end. The *parousia* of Christ is made necessary by the resurrection of Christ—the coming has only begun; it needs (or longs) to be concluded (Rom 8:1–27). Resurrection language is apocalyptic language; it denotes the resurrection of the dead, which will occur at the end of history. When Paul designates Christ as the "first fruits" (1 Cor 15:20, 23) or the "firstborn of all creation" (Col 1:15), he proclaims the necessary connection between the resurrection of Christ and the final resurrection of the dead. The Christ event is not a completed event but an event in the process of completion. As the first fruits anticipate the full harvest, so the resurrection of Christ necessitates the resurrection of the dead at the end of time. This is confirmed by Paul's view of the Spirit. The Spirit is the agent of the future glory in the present. The Spirit is the first down payment or guarantee of end-time glory (Rom 8:1–27; 2 Cor 1:22).

The second motif is the *incalculability* of the end. Paul's end-time hope is a matter of prophecy, not prediction. Paul emphasizes the unexpected, sudden, and surprising character of the *parousia* (1 Thess 5). The reality of the *parousia* is grounded in a radical faith in the faithfulness of God to the promises of God, not to historical determinism or calendarization. Paul's eschatology is not primarily temporal, but paradigmatic. It is about trust, purpose, and pattern (not chronology). This cannot be overemphasized. Paul uses "end-time" language to speak about things that he knows are not the "capital-E" end, since this is the only vocabulary he has available as an apocalyptic thinker. The eighteenth-century scholarly construct of the "delay of the *parousia*," supposedly developed in the post-Pauline era to overcome the church's embarrassment of Jesus's nonreturn, is not helpful and needs to be put to rest (Wright 1999:204). Paul's modified Jewish apocalypticism did not have a simple temporal view of the end; the view was essentially paradigmatic.

Consider Paul's counsel to the Corinthian singles to "remain as they are" in 1 Corinthians 7. Such advice is not driven by Paul's fanatical conviction that the world is going to end in his lifetime—so that getting married would be pointless. Instead, it is more that Paul is convinced that in these last days (whatever their duration), Christians should expect to live with much social pressure, because the "old regime" is cracking up and tottering to its end and yet will not just "roll over and give up." In this way, there is a present crisis. Therefore, there is no need to be clamoring for status in the old-world order; doing so would be like "rearranging the deck chairs on the *Titanic*" as it is going down (Hays 1997:123). Paul's instruction to "remain as you are" emerges from the *reprioritization* of values that comes with the dawn of the new age, disengaging from the old age's concern for power, prestige, and possessions. Thus, "remain as you are" means keep the kingdom of God central; do not put status issues like marriage, sex, career, social standing, religious ritual, and so on, in the central location. Paul's eschatology has a *decentering* or *deconstructing* character as it reorients all things from the perspective of the end, when God's creation purpose is finally realized.

Thus, according to Paul, God keeps promises and is faithful in effecting salvation for all peoples in Christ. This salvation (past fact, present reality, and future hope) is being completed in all these historical events, and they will ultimately demonstrate the complete victory of God over evil, sin, and death in real, historical time.

THE CHRISTOLOGICAL IMPLICATIONS OF PAUL'S APOCALYPTIC ESCHATOLOGICAL CENTER

Paul's inherited and learned apocalyptic theology (the old symbolic map) is profoundly modified by his encounter with the crucified and resurrected Messiah Jesus. At the same time, Paul's thinking about Jesus—his prior ministry and his engagement with the testimony of Torah—is profoundly shaped by apocalyptic categories. So while Paul's Christology is nowhere fully developed systematically or thematically, if God is triumphing in Jesus Christ to bring eschatological salvation, then all reality must be viewed through this victory. Therefore, Paul addresses every issue from a christological perspective that is profoundly apocalyptic and eschatological. It is in the process of addressing some very practical pastoral situations that Paul develops his Christology.

How does Paul's apocalyptic eschatology shape his understanding of the cross? Five pieces can be identified from his writings. First, the cross for Paul is a profound statement about God: the glory of God is seen "in the face of Jesus Christ" (2 Cor 4:6). Something so rooted in evil, like the cross, is taken up into the purpose of God and transformed into a life-giving act. While there is some tension between Paul's voice and the voice of the author of Hebrews, where Christ himself brought his offering before God as high priest (9:11, 24; 10:12–14) and John, where Jesus says, "I lay down my life in order to take it up again" (10:17),

Paul understood the life of Christ as God's eschatological intervention in the world. Paul understood the resurrection and exaltation of Christ exclusively in terms of God's activity. The critical point of God's intervention is the cross, where Christ stood at the "hinge" of history as the crucified one. Thus, Paul's statements about Christ always focus on God (1 Cor 15:3-4; 2 Cor 5:19).

Second, the cross marks the defeat of the old powers of sin, evil, and death (Col 2:15). The death of Christ marks God's victory over the powers of the old age. His use of terms like "powers," "rulers," "lordships," "thrones," "world rulers of darkness," and "the spiritual forces of darkness in the heavens" is very significant. These are allegorical and mythical ways of talking about reality, where rulers (civic, business, religious, state, military, etc.) function as representatives of spiritual "powers and principalities" (Rom 8:38; Eph 3:10; 6:12; Col 1:16; 2:15). At the cross, God exposed evil's charade for the sham that it was. At the cross, we see the lengths to which Satan goes to establish his illegitimate rule, *and* we see the lengths to which God goes to make sure that Satan does not have the last word. The cross is an apocalyptic event in that the death of Christ marks the defeat of the apocalyptic power alliance and signals the undoing of death, the last enemy (Rom 6:7-10; 7:4-6; 8:35-39; 1 Cor 2:6-8; 15:26).

The cross is not just an act of sacrificial love. The death of Christ constitutes the eschatological judgment of the powers. The rulers of this age have crucified the Lord of glory (1 Cor 2:8), reaching the zenith of their rebellion against God. By overreaching their legitimate jurisdiction, they cannot any longer hold sway over those attached to Jesus; the accuser's prosecuting days are over (Caird 1994:108, 149-50). The death of Jesus counters sin as a cosmic power and slave master, announcing the negation of the power of sin that controls the world. The death of Christ, therefore, has not only a moral meaning but also an ontological meaning (a meaning related to a new way of being): "Everything old has passed away; see, everything has become new" (2 Cor 5:17).

Third, the cross signifies the final judgment of the old age (Rom 1:18-32). The cross is a demonstration of God's cosmic-apocalyptic wrath. Romans 1:18-32 pictures wrath as the "apocalyptic harvester," which gives people what they want as a sign of the final judgment on history. All people fall under God's wrath and judgment, because all are under the power of sin (Rom 5:18-21). The death of Christ is the apocalyptic judgment of the world: "The death he died, he died to sin, once for all" (Rom 6:10). Paul uses "powers-and-principalities" language to speak of sin, evil, and death, claiming that the judgment of God is on them all in Christ. Death is turned inside out. Instead of silencing Jesus, the cross screams out for all with ears to hear, "This is not God's way, and it will no longer be able to masquerade as the norm any longer!" The single-victim mechanism—the key instrument in the age-old myth of redemptive violence where someone is forced to be the scapegoat in the name of a good cause, such as maintaining order or securing justice—is undone (Girard 2001). The single-victim mechanism that evil has used to secure its domination and to enslave humanity from the beginning is exposed at the cross for the lie that it is.

Fourth, the cross is inseparably connected with the resurrection (1 Corinthians 15). The cosmic-apocalyptic interpretation of the death of Christ is the result of its inseparable connection with the resurrection. When that connection is dropped, both the cross and the resurrection lose their significance. Without the cross, the resurrection is fantasy disconnected from history, leaving the world unchanged. Without the resurrection, the cross, however courageous, is just another sad story of crushed dreams that is repeated everywhere and at all times. Everything continues "business as usual," and nothing is changed. However, the resurrection inaugurates a new ontological reality, the new creation. While still *proleptic*, it has changed the nature of historical reality forever.

Fifth, the death of Jesus has soteriological (i.e., salvation) implications. It opens a way for all who trust in the faithfulness of Jesus to join him in the pattern of the cross, which both deconstructs the power of sin and constructs God's way of being-for-others. As a point of interest, Paul does not try to explain the machinery of how the powers were disarmed (Col 2:15). In fact, none of the NT writers claim to know. The NT writers prefer to use metaphors to talk about that which they are convinced is true: Jesus is alive (death could not hold him), and thus the new age has dawned (the old-age powers no longer have automatic jurisdiction over humanity). The NT writers chose to use what they knew something about (metaphors drawn from everyday life) in order to talk about that which they did not fully understand yet knew to be true. Paul's preferred metaphor to talk about this reality is the battleground, where Jesus triumphs over the forces of evil at the cross, using weaponry that counters the myth of redemptive violence and at the same time demonstrates God's preferred rule of engagement. Still this is not the only metaphor NT writers use for what would later be called atonement (see Green and Baker 2000:97). We will consider these other metaphors in later chapters.

How then does Paul's apocalyptic eschatology shape his understanding of the resurrection? Four points emerge. First, resurrection language is end-time language. But Paul exercises a sober "eschatological reserve," carefully reserving resurrection language for the age to come. Resurrection speaks of the transformation of the created order: something inaugurated by Jesus to be sure, but something that remains future for the rest of humanity and the created order. Yet the resurrection of Jesus has ethical implications now. According to Paul, "As Christ was raised from the dead by the glory of the Father, so we too might walk in newness of life" (Rom 6:4). Jesus's resurrection life empowers and animates the Christian community's life and witness, even though their own bodily transformation awaits the general resurrection at the end of time.

Second, the resurrection is the "bodily" exaltation of Jesus by God and his enthronement to cosmic lordship. It is a *proleptic* event that foreshadows the apocalyptic general resurrection of the dead and thus the transformation of the created order and the gift of new corporeal life to dead bodies. Resurrection is a historical category, manifesting in this world the dawning of the new age of transformation. While a bodily phenomenon, it is *not* a physical one, as "flesh and blood cannot inherit the kingdom of God, nor does the perishable inherit the imperishable" (1 Cor 15:50). However, resurrection remains a bodily reality of cosmic dimensions such that God's end-time people testify to the new-creation age (Luke 24:39) and invite all to abandon their rebellion and to reorient themselves according to God's pattern of being and behaving (Isa 45:22–23; Ps 110:1; Rom 16:20, 1 Cor 6:3; 15:25; Phil 2:6–11).

Third, the resurrection is understood apocalyptically as the preliminary manifestation of the general resurrection of the age to come, marking the final triumph of God. Therefore, Paul characterizes Christ as "the first fruits" (1 Cor 15:20) and as "the firstborn" (Rom 8:29; Col 1:16). The resurrection of Christ announces the dawn of the general resurrection still to come. In this sense the *parousia* is divided into the beginning of the coming (cross-resurrection) and the consummation of the coming, when this age is gathered up completely into the age to come, and the creation enterprise with which God launched this world is completed. Thus, the resurrection of Jesus guarantees the general resurrection of the dead and signals the liberation of the created order from "bondage" and "decay," in order to "obtain the freedom of the glory of the children of God" (Rom 8:21).

Fourth, the historicity of the resurrection and the bodily resurrection are crucial for Paul, without which there is no good news, glad tidings, or gospel. The historicity of the resurrection signifies its eschatological, real-time significance. The apostles, including Paul, speak of the resurrection as something that happened to Jesus, and that they witnessed and to which they bore witness (1 Cor 15:5–9). They did not see a resuscitated corpse or a ghostly phantom, but they identified the risen Lord as a "spiritual body" from another dimension of existence, which was nevertheless present with power and might (1 Cor 15:44–46). The resurrection of Messiah Jesus is the *proleptic* event that inaugurates the new-creation age. It looks backward, as God's vote of confidence in solidarity with Jesus's life and ministry; and it looks forward to the consummation of the *parousia* announced already at Easter. Without the resurrection, there is no gospel, and "we are of all people most to be pitied" (1 Cor 15:19). Why? Because the conviction that God is completing creation as promised would be unfounded; it would be "misrepresenting God" (1 Cor 15:15). Plus, the Easter story would be evidence of delusional thinking, since the conviction that Jesus's life and ministry truly presented a workable alternative to the status-quo ideology of redemptive violence would be false. Without the resurrection of Jesus, the ancient scapegoat mechanism that has animated cultures from the beginning continues unchallenged. Without the resurrection, there simply would be no good news, no hope, and no NT.

Thus, the cross-resurrection announces that Jesus has inaugurated both the end and the end-time process of cosmic transformation, which is the guarantee of the total transformation still to come.

This has been a long chapter. There just is no getting around Paul's significance for shaping the conversation around the NT conference table. Still, Paul's voice, significant as it is, is not the only NT voice. In the next chapter, the writers of the Synoptic Gospels take the microphone.

EXERCISES

1. What Paul wrote about faith, righteousness, participation in Christ, and the Jewish law has led to much debate. There are three problems: a) English is not able to translate Paul's key terms well; b) Paul uses "righteousness" in a typically Hebrew way, emphasizing covenantal relationship; and c) the Protestant Reformation gave Paul's righteousness language a new emphasis (judicial, forensic, transactional). Let's consider each of these three problems.

a) The problem of English-language development (Sanders 1991:46). Modern English has two parents: Norman French and Anglo-Saxon. Usually this gives English speakers a rich vocabulary for making fine distinctions and nuances. However, sometimes this creates a problem when Greek words like *dikaiosynē* and *pistis* (and their cognates) are translated into English.

As the chart below shows, the cognate verb form of *dikaiosynē* no longer has an Anglo-Saxon form; presumably the French form drove out the Anglo-Saxon form over time. This means English speakers are forced to switch to the legal translation ("to justify") even if they want to talk about righteousness in relation terms as in the proper ordering of life in community. Similarly, the cognate verb form of *pistis* no longer has a French form. This means English speakers are required to change to the more cognitive Anglo-Saxon translation, "to believe," even when talking about faith as a vital, relational trust.

	Greek	Anglo-Saxon	French
Noun	*dikaiosynē*	righteousness	justification
Adjective	*dikaios*	righteous	just
Verb	*dikaioun*	-------------	to justify
Noun	*pistis*	belief	faith
Adjective	*pistos*	believing	faithful
Verb	*pisteuein*	to believe	-------------

TABLE 3.6 English Language Development and the Translation of "Faith" and "Righteousness"

For Paul and other Jews, both *dikaiosynē* and *pistis* were primarily relational in nuance. English language development, therefore, creates a special problem when translating these terms. Suppose we want to use more relational terms to translate the Hebrew concepts of righteousness and faith. We could choose words derived from the Anglo-Saxon to translate *dikaiosynē* (i.e, "righteousness") and from the French to translate *pistis* (i.e., "faith"), but we would have a problem. In both cases, no cognate (corresponding) verbs (as in "to right" and "to faith") are available in English.

Try translating both the nouns and the verbs of Galatians 3:6–8 below using relational terms (i.e., "righteousness" *dikaiosynē* [n.] plus "righted" *dikaioun* [v.] and "faith" *pistis* [n.] plus "faithed" *pisteuein* [v.]). What do you notice?

"Just as Abraham *pisteuein* (v.) _____ God, and it was reckoned to him as *dikaiosynē* (n.) _____, you see that it is people of *pistis* (n.) _____ who are the descendants of Abraham. And the scripture, foreseeing that God would *dikaioun* (v.) _____ the Gentiles by *pistis* (n.) _____, declared the gospel beforehand to Abraham."

Discuss the translation challenges created by the development of the English language. What implications do you see for translating other Pauline texts?

b) The problem of Paul's special use of "righteousness." For Paul and other Jews, *dikaiosynē* was fundamentally concerned with the proper ordering of life and community in the world. The primary concerns were relational within the sphere of ethical-political-social language (Toews 2004:400–407). The Anglo-Saxon term "righteousness" best carries this concept. However, as Christianity became the dominant religion in the Roman world from the fourth century onward, *dikaisosynē* came to be understood in the Latin terms of the Roman legal system. Here the concerns were judicial, as in weights, measures, and the balance of crime and punishment. The French term "justification" fits best this context. The two are quite different: one is judicial ("justification") and one is relational ("righteousness").

Ernst Käsemann (1969) is credited with the landmark study aimed at recovering Paul's special use of "righteousness" language. Käsemann argued that the "righteousness of God" (Rom 1:17; 3:21, 22) is a technical term for Paul, which focuses on God's faithfulness to the covenant (the normal emphasis) and especially on God's redemptive activity in Jesus for the world (Paul's special verbal emphasis). The "righteousness of God" refers to God's righteousness, where God is the acting subject, and so does not refer to the human quest to achieve God's righteous standard, where God is the object of measure. Righteousness in Paul's writings describes how God extends lordship and power over God's people (Jew and Gentile) and all creation in order to transform it and make it right. Righteousness is both an aspect of God's being (noun) and an activity (verb) to which God is committed.

Discuss the soteriological, theological, and anthropological implications stemming from the transformation of Paul's relational understanding of *dikaiosynē* to the judicial understanding through Christian history.

c) The problem of the Protestant Reformation's new judicial, forensic, and transactional emphasis for Paul's righteousness language. During the Reformation, Martin Luther came to understand *dikaiosynē* in a largely judicial way. This is not surprising given his struggle with Catholicism in the sixteenth century. Justification by faith offered an attractive alternative to the sale of indulgences and other rituals for procuring release from purgatory. Still, for Luther, to be made "righteous" was to be "justified" or to have an alien, fictional status imputed on men and women (Luther 1961:86–88). While this view enabled him to maintain a healthy respect for the power of sin (since according to his two-kingdom theology believers always retained one foot in the old-age kingdom as well as one foot in the new age), it did create other problems. Luther's two-kingdom theology suggested that Christ followers were not really made righteous; they were only declared or proclaimed righteous. In later developments of some Protestant theology this set up a sharp distinction between justification (relegated to the cognitive level) and sanctification (relegated to the behavioral level), often making sanctification a second, additional step that could be misunderstood as unconnected or even optional—necessary only for some.

However, when Paul uses the passive verb "to be righted" or "to be made righteous" he usually is talking about the release from service to the power of sin (setting free) and the transfer to another "enslavement" in obedience to Christ: about moving from one realm or dominion to another, from rebellion to obedience, from death to life, from being under the rule of sin to being under the rule of grace. Paul's special participatory emphasis is on that which actually happens to a person in relation to a new community identity: namely, a fundamental change in reality and orientation generated by the person's incorporation into the body of the risen Lord.

Discuss the soteriological, theological, and anthropological transformations brought about by the Protestant Reformation's interpretation of Paul's use of *dikaiosynē*.

2. The soteriological language of Paul in Rom 3:21–26 has been a source of much debate through Christian history. Translators struggle with how best to translate his terms of reference like "faith" and "sacrifice of atonement" (see Gundry-Volf 1993:279–84). The chart below gives three translations of these verses with certain phrases underlined. Compare and contrast the translations. What do you notice? Below the chart are additional discussion questions.

Rom 3:21–26 (NIV)	Rom 3:21–26 (KJV)	Rom 3:21–26 (NRSV)
21 But now a righteousness from God, apart from law, has been made known, to which the Law and the Prophets testify. 22 This righteousness from God comes through <u>faith in Jesus Christ</u> to all who believe. There is no difference, 23 for all have sinned and fall short of the glory of God, 24 and are justified freely by his grace through the <u>redemption</u> that came by Christ Jesus. 25 God presented him as <u>a sacrifice of atonement, through faith in his blood</u>. He did this to demonstrate his justice, because in his forbearance he had left the sins committed beforehand unpunished— 26 he did it to demonstrate his justice at the present time, so as to be just and the one who justifies those who have <u>faith in Jesus</u>.	21 But now the righteousness of God without the law is manifested, being witnessed by the law and the prophets; 22 Even the righteousness of God [which is] by <u>faith of Jesus Christ</u> unto all and upon all them that believe: for there is no difference: 23 For all have sinned, and come short of the glory of God; 24 Being justified freely by his grace through the <u>redemption</u> that is in Christ Jesus: 25 Whom God hath set forth [to be] <u>a propitiation through faith in his blood</u>, to declare his righteousness for the remission of sins that are past, through the forbearance of God; 26 To declare, [I say], at this time his righteousness: that he might be just, and the justifier of him which <u>believeth in Jesus</u>.	21 But now, apart from law, the righteousness of God has been disclosed, and is attested by the law and the prophets, 22 the righteousness of God through <u>faith in* Jesus Christ</u> for all who believe. For there is no distinction, 23 since all have sinned and fall short of the glory of God; 24 they are now justified by his grace as a gift, through the <u>redemption</u> that is in Christ Jesus, 25 whom God put forward as <u>a sacrifice of atonement by his blood, effective through faith</u>. He did this to show his righteousness, because in his divine forbearance he had passed over the sins previously committed; 26 it was to prove at the present time that he himself is righteous and that he justifies the one who has <u>faith in* Jesus</u>. *or *faith of*

TABLE 3.7 Comparison of Three Translations of Romans 3:21–26

(a) What is the best translation of *pistis Christou* (literally, "faith of Christ"; see underlined phrases in vv. 22 and 26)? Is it "Christ's faith" (with Christ as the acting subject) or "faith in Christ" (with Christ as the object of faith)? The same phrase appears elsewhere in the Pauline corpus (Gal 2:16; 2:20; 3:22; Phil 3:9; Eph 3:12). Both are grammatically possible, but which seems most likely given the context of Paul's theological argument here? Why? What do you make of the NRSV's alternate reading, noted by the asterisk? What difference does it make if God's end-time righteousness is revealed in the world "through Christ's faithfulness" or "through the response of humanity"?

(b) What does *pistis* mean (see underlined terms in vv. 22, 25, 26)? Is it "faith(fulness)" or "belief"? What connotation does each entail? What difference does it make?

(c) What does *apolytrōsis* mean (see underlined term in v. 24)? Given Paul's theological argument, how should his "redemption" language be conceptualized? Is redemption another word for "purchase," as in a price paid to God? Or is it about "deliverance from" an oppressive power? What difference does it make?

d) How should *hilastērion* (see underlined phrase in v. 25) be understood given the Jewish framework of Paul's theological world? Is the "sacrifice of atonement" to be understood as "propitiation," as in satisfying a wrathful deity? Or is it "expiation," as in dealing successfully with the power of evil by undoing the grip it has over all humanity and creation? What difference does it make?

(e) What is the thrust of this text? Is it to prove the righteousness of God through the faithfulness of Jesus (which makes possible human faithfulness), or is it to prove the righteousness of God through human belief in Jesus (which does not compromise God's righteous demand for purity)? What is the difference?

3. After the shocking events of September 11, 2001, when a series of suicide airplane hijackings resulted in nearly three thousand deaths in New York and Washington DC, the faculty of Mennonite Brethren Biblical Seminary (MBBS) gathered later that week for prayers. Professor Elmer Martens suggested that an email be sent to Mennonite Brethren pastors on Friday. It was to be a word of encouragement, consolation, and solidarity, along with a plea for calm, prayer, and faithfulness to the gospel as these ministers prepared to

face their congregations on Sunday. Elmer wrote the letter, but he insisted on one thing; given the critical circumstances, he felt it was imperative that the letter come from the seminary president. So the letter was attributed to the president, Henry Schmidt. That letter is reproduced below.

Discuss how this not-uncommon practice of attribution to another in special circumstances might shed light on the discussion of the disputed letters of Paul.

September 14th, 2001

On this day of national mourning and prayer, we, your colleagues in ministry pray for you as you minister to your congregation Sunday, especially that you will bring the reassurance of God's comfort. We pray for you as pastor. "The Lord is my light and my salvation—whom shall I fear? The Lord is the stronghold of my life—of whom shall I be afraid? . . . when my enemies and my foes attack me, they will stumble and fall" (Ps 27:1, 26 NIV).

1. We stand with you and your congregations in calling all God's people to intercessory prayer: for the families, friends, and co-workers of victims, for our national leaders, but also for all those associated with the terrorist attacks. In dying for all of us Christ showed his love for all alike. Therefore Paul urges "that supplications, prayers, intercessions, and thanksgiving be made for everyone, for kings and all who are in high position, so that we may lead a quiet and peaceable life in all godliness and dignity. This is right and is acceptable in the sight of God our Savior, who desires everyone to be saved and to come to the knowledge of the truth" (1 Tim 2:1–3).

2. We pray with you and your congregation for peace as well as for justice. Strident voices in harsh language are calling for "an enraged America." But violence begets violence. Escalation of violence leads to further injustice. Racism blinds the eyes of even the righteous. Pray for restraint. Pray that the church's voice for peace will not be muted in these days of strong emotions and desire for revenge. Though like the Psalmist (cf. Ps 109) we will not be spared feelings of anger, let these come to expression in the recognition, "Vengeance is mine, I will repay, says the Lord" (cf. Rom 12:17–19). "When peacemakers sow seeds of peace, they will harvest justice" (James 3:18 CEV). "May the Lord give strength to his people! May the Lord bless his people with peace" (Ps 29:11 NRSV).

3. We pray with you that our nation would repent. Officials are pointing the blaming finger at various outsiders. Few seem to look inward or to the larger flow of God's providence and guidance. Joseph recognized God's hand in his brother's acts against him (Gen 45:7, 8). Daniel discerned God's activity in Babylon's attack and sack of Jerusalem (Dan 1:1, 2). As we interpret the events of the last week, the scriptures remind us that calamity may be a way to urge us to remember our own actions—Hiroshima, the 500,000 dead strewn across the sands of Iraq, our insatiable need for oil, corporate oppression in Third World countries. Our hands are not clean. Pray that we may see our role in creating the political and social conditions that drive people to such destructive acts of violence.

"Even now," declares the Lord, "return to me with all your heart, with fasting and weeping and mourning. Rend your hearts and not your garments. Return to the Lord, your God, for he is gracious and compassionate, slow to anger, and abounding in love and he relents from sending calamity" (Joel 2:13 NIV).

4. Pray for positive steps forward in the spirit of Craig Hallman's letter published this morning in the *Fresno Bee* under the caption "Endless Cycle." Hallman, our graduate, now with MBMSI writes from Karachi, Pakistan, "I strongly discourage the United States or NATO from making a counterattack on Afghanistan or Osama bin Laden. This will perpetuate an endless cycle of retribution; Israel being the prime example of this death trap. The more people killed by the U.S. guarantees more radicals and future attacks—a reality we must consider in our national debate about how to respond to Tuesday's terrorism."

"The hijackers have unwittingly created a sympathetic climate for partnership with moderate Islamic states to defuse radicalism. Diplomacy, trust, and friendship—not militancy—is our only hope for stopping future attacks."

Just yesterday Elmer Martens, President Emeritus at MBBS, received a call from his Muslim neighbor sending her condolences to his family and for America. The stunning carnage in New York has made many more Muslims sympathize with America and doubt the radicals. This goodwill will immediately evaporate when the first bomb drops.

Grace and Peace,

President Henry J. Schmidt, MBBS

TABLE 3.8 Email sent to Mennonite Brethren Pastors, Dated September 14, 2001

4

The Theological Contribution of the Synoptic Gospel Writers

IT IS TIME TO turn the microphone over to other conference participants for their interpretations of Easter, Jesus's prior ministry, and its ongoing significance. Paul has been at the podium long enough! In this chapter we hear from the writers of the Synoptic Gospels—the first three gospels in the NT, which came to be known in canonical order as Matthew, Mark, and Luke. The chapter has two objectives: (1) to clarify the distinctive character of the Synoptic Gospels and (2) to outline the theological vision of Mark, Matthew, and Luke, in their presumed order of composition, including the current debate, the structure, the articulation, and the thematic implications of the central vision that each one puts forward.

THE DISTINCTIVE CHARACTERISTICS OF THE SYNOPTIC GOSPELS

The Synoptic Gospels are distinctive writings in five ways. First, they, along with the Fourth Gospel, represent a hybrid genre that is unique to Christianity. Using the established rhetorical patterns of Greco-Roman biographies, these anonymous writers—whom we can call Evangelists—drew from the circulating memory of Jesus's life and ministry in a variety of sources and shaped the memory from the Easter perspective into a sustained narrative of Jesus's life, culminating in his suffering, the "passion" story—Jesus's crucifixion and resurrection. This particular narrative—Jesus's passion story with an introductory narrative—came to be known as the genre called gospel.

Second, the first three gospels are also unique in that they retell Jesus's story from a similar perspective, using the same symbolic world and same narrative framework. They can be studied side by side in a specially made book called a "synopsis" or "seeing together," which brings out their many parallels. It is from these comparisons that their collective title derives, the Synoptic Gospels (e.g., Aland 2006; Throckmorton 1992). For all their sameness, these gifted literary composers, whom we will identify by the shorthand titles later assigned to their compositions (Mark, Matthew, and Luke), produced gospels giving voice to particular interpretations of the significance of Jesus. While the Fourth Gospel also fits this genre, it follows a different sort of narrative framework and is best understood with the other writings of the Johannine symbolic world (see chapter 5).

Third, the Synoptic Gospels are unique in that they share a complex relationship of literary interdependence. The precise character of that literary relationship, however, is not easy to determine. On the one hand, a large amount of material is shared among the three gospels (90 percent of Mark is in Matthew, 45 percent of Mark is in Luke, 56 percent of Matthew is in Mark). Furthermore, what is shared has nearly identical Greek wording and follows nearly the same ordering of textual units or *pericopae*. The high degree of literary correspondence suggests some borrowing relationship. The literary correspondence also suggests that the Evangelists themselves were not eyewitnesses to the events they narrate but framers of the eyewitness testimony circulating in various sources.

On the other hand, striking differences occur over those same stretches of copied material, suggesting that the Evangelists either preferred to use different wording than the source text in front of them or preferred to omit certain words or phrases altogether. Then there are large blocks of narrative material completely missing from Mark that appear in both Matthew and Luke (some two hundred verses of sayings material). Is this by design, or did Mark not know of this material? Evidently, the delineation of the relationship is difficult to establish. Who copied from whom? Is one the source for the other two? Who knew which sources? What do the different orderings, wordings, omissions suggest? The term "Synoptic Problem" is used to describe this complex phenomenon.

There are several ways to explain the similarity and diversity. The hypothesis with the scholarly consensus today combines the theory of Markan Priority with the Two-Source Hypothesis to "solve" the Synoptic Problem. Why is Mark thought to be the first written gospel or at least the first known to us? First, the patterns of agreement point to the priority of Mark. When Matthew and Luke share a story that is also found in Mark, it is rarely different from Mark's wording. More specifically, when either Matthew or Luke disagrees with Mark's wording, the other agrees. In this so-called triple tradition, Mark plays the role of middle term, pointing to independent copying of Mark by Matthew and Luke. Note the agreements and disagreement in the pericope below (Jesus Foretells his Betrayal): Matthew and Mark against Luke, Luke and Mark against Mathew. Even though the comparisons are best made with the Greek text of the gospels, an English translation like the NRSV still makes plain the agreements and disagreements (note the underlined text).

Matthew 26:21–25	Mark 14:18–21	Luke 22:21–23
and while they were eating, he said, "Truly I tell you, one of you will betray me." And they became greatly distressed and began to say to him one after another, "Surely not I, Lord?" He answered, "The one who has dipped his hand into the bowl with me will betray me.	And when they had taken their places and were eating, Jesus said, "Truly I tell you, one of you will betray me, one who is eating with me." They began to be distressed and to say to him one after the another, "Surely, not I?" He said to them, "It is one of the twelve, one who is dipping bread into the bowl with me.	"But see, the one who betrays me is with me, and his hand is on the table.
The Son of Man goes as it is written of him, but woe to that one by whom the Son of Man is betrayed! It would be better for that one not to have been born."	For the Son of Man goes as it is written of him, but woe to that one by whom the Son of Man is betrayed! It would have been better for that one not to have been born.	For the Son of Man is going as has been determined, but woe to that one by whom he is betrayed!"
Judas, who betrayed him, said, "Surely not I, Rabbi?" He replied, "You have said so."	(Judas saying absent)	(Judas saying absent) Then they began to ask one another, which one of them it could be who would do this.

TABLE 4.1 Jesus Foretells His Betrayal in Synoptic Parallels

The second reason for assuming Markan priority is that the relationships between the content of the gospels suggest that Mark was first. With virtually all of Mark reproduced in Matthew and/or Luke, it is easier to imagine that Matthew and Luke copied from Mark. The reverse is more difficult to imagine. If Mark were copying from Matthew and/or Luke, why would Mark leave out so much good material (over four hundred verses from Matthew alone)?

Still, other explanations for the complex interdependence have been suggested. The Griesbach Hypothesis is that Matthew was the original gospel, which was later used by Luke, leaving Mark to copy from *both* Matthew and Luke. While theoretically possible, this scenario still requires Mark to reject many key pericopae from Matthew and Luke. For most gospel scholars today, the Markan Priority hypothesis is the most plausible explanation for most of the data. For a thorough discussion of the Synoptic Problem and arguments for and against Markan Priority in the triple tradition, see Sanders and Davies (1989:51–63).

The Two-Source Hypothesis, which goes along with Markan Priority to "solve" the Synoptic Problem, is based on two observations: (1) the existence of the so-called double tradition in Matthew and Luke and (2) the different arrangement of the double tradition in the two gospels. The double tradition is that material common to Matthew and Luke, but not in Mark. In most cases this double tradition material shows almost verbatim agreement. See the pericope below (Lament over Jerusalem).

Matthew 23:37–39	Mark	Luke 13:34–35
"Jerusalem, Jerusalem, the city that kills the prophets and stones those who are sent to it! How often have I desired to gather your children together as a hen gathers her brood under her wings, and you were not willing! See, your house is left to you desolate. For I tell you, you will not see me again until you say, 'Blessed is the one who comes in the name of the Lord.'"	(absent)	"Jerusalem, Jerusalem, the city that kills the prophets and stones those who are sent to it! How often have I desired to gather your children together as a hen gathers her brood under her wings, and you were not willing! See, your house is left to you. And I tell you, you will not see me until the time comes when you say, 'Blessed is the one who comes in the name of the Lord.'"

TABLE 4.2 Lament over Jerusalem in Synoptic Parallels

The Theological Contribution of the Synoptic Gospel Writers 107

In addition to the near-verbatim agreement, it is important to note that the placement of the pericope in Matthew differs from Luke. Matthew places the textual unit *after* Jesus's final entry into Jerusalem (Matt 21:1), while Luke places the textual unit *before* it (Luke 19:28). Why? It appears that each Evangelist is using the memory of Jesus's words for a particular purpose. For Luke, the saying is fulfilled by Jesus's entry into Jerusalem, as the crowds say, "Blessed is the king who comes in the name of the Lord" (Luke 19:38). For Matthew, however, the saying looks forward to the future eschatological return of Jesus at the *parousia* (Sanders and Davies 1989:64).

One way to account for both of these observations is to posit the existence of a sayings source that Mark did not know, and which both Matthew and Luke used independently. Gospel scholars have identified this sayings source as Q, the first letter of the German word *Quelle*, "source." While Q is not extant, it is thought to be preserved in the double tradition of Matthew and Luke. While many (though not all) imagine Q as a written text, debate still remains as to whether Q was a contiguous, ordered collection of Jesus sayings or more like a loose-leaf scrapbook of collected Jesus sayings, interchangeable and in no particular order. In any case, these two sources, Mark and Q, are thought to lie behind Matthew and Luke, suggesting a plausible solution to the Synoptic Problem. In this scenario, Matthew and Luke both copied Mark independently, following Mark's narrative framework; and they also inserted sayings from Q here and there, independently of each other, as depicted in the diagram below.

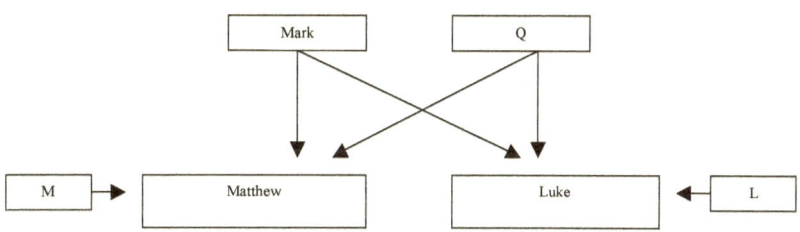

TABLE 4.3 Two- or Four-Source Hypothesis for Solving the Synoptic Problem

However, the simplicity of the Two-Source solution to the Synoptic Problem is misleading. The Two-Source Hypothesis pictured above may be more accurately called the Four-Source Hypothesis in recognition of the presence of special material unique to Matthew and unique to Luke. What could be the source of this material? Scholars posit yet two more sources to account for this unique material: M for Matthew's special source material and L for Luke's special source material. A surprising number of pericopae are thought to have come from these special sources. For example, M includes the visit of the Magi (Matt 2:1–12); the flight to Egypt (Matt 2:13–23); and Jesus's parables of hidden treasure (Matt 13:44), the pearl of great price (Matt 13:45–46), the dragnet (Matt 13:47–50), the unmerciful servant (Matt 18:23–35), and the ten virgins (Matt 25:1–12). L includes the birth of John the Baptist and the annunciation to Mary (Luke 1:5–80); the shepherds' visit to the baby Jesus; the presentation in the temple and Jesus as a twelve-year-old (Luke 2:1–52); and Jesus's parables of the good Samaritan (Luke 10:29–37), the prodigal son (Luke 15:11–32), Lazarus and the rich man (Luke 16:19–31), and the unjust judge (Luke 18:1–8).

For some scholars, the Two or Four-Source Hypothesis is not satisfactory because it still leaves a few pieces of data unexplained. Several places remain where Matthew and Luke *do* agree against Mark (e.g., the healing of the paralytic, Mark 2:1–12; Matt 9:1–8; Luke 5:17–26). This raises questions if Matthew and Luke copied Mark completely independently, as the Two- or Four-Source Hypothesis asserts. Also, in a few pericopae Mark carries a brief account of a much fuller narrative shared by Matthew and Luke's Q material (e.g., the testing or temptation of Jesus, Mark 1:12; Matt 4:1–11; Luke 4:1–13). This too raises questions if Mark did not know Q, and if Mark did not omit material (the key assumption to the priority of Mark!). Because these problems remain, it must be emphasized that the Two- or Four-Source explanation remains a *hypothesis* and that the Synoptic Problem remains far from resolved. For a thorough discussion of the views for and against the existence of Q and the Two- or Four-Source Hypothesis, as well as presentation of some alternative proposals for addressing the Synoptic Problem (i.e., hypotheses by Griesbach, Goulder, and Boismard), see Sanders and Davies (1989:64–119).

The contribution of the gospel writers at our NT conference, however, does *not* depend on solving the Synoptic Problem or on the correctness of any one of the hypotheses. We are assuming that the Evangelists are indeed authors who composed literary texts, and that our analysis of their voice is based on the final form of their texts. Still, as Johnson says, "The awareness that this final stage of composition resulted from a complex oral and written process makes us sensitive to the peculiar density of these texts, as well as more appreciative of the simplicity and coherence of their finished condition" (1999:157).

The fourth aspect of the gospels' distinctive literary character is that they (speaking now about all four, including John) combine two levels of presentation in a unique way (Fee and Stuart 2003:130–43). The first level is concerned with retelling the story of Jesus's life, which scholars usually date from 4 BCE to 30 CE (Sanders 1993:282–90). Here the aim is to preserve the memory of Jesus and his significance for the historical record, especially for use within the Christian communities. At this level, we can read the gospels "horizontally," by comparing the parallels in other gospels. Distinctive interpretive emphases of each Evangelist's account of Jesus's life are sometimes discernible. The second level is concerned with retelling the story of Jesus for the needs of later communities of faith who did not speak Aramaic but Greek. At this level, we can read the gospels "vertically," by comparing Jesus's context with that of the Evangelists' a generation later (from the late 60s to end of the century). Again, distinctive interpretive emphases of each Evangelist are sometimes discernible. While on the one hand these levels seem to be apparent in the stylized biographies composed by the Evangelists, on the other hand it is not easy (or even possible) to distinguish them with certainty. If their genre as literary products is taken seriously, it is probably best to imagine the Evangelists *always* working with both levels at the same time in each pericope—telling stories about Jesus *and* bearing witness to the ongoing significance of Jesus. In this case, separating one level from the other may not be possible.

Fifth, the second-century struggle with the heterodox movements like gnosticism and Montanism likely forced proto-orthodox Christians to attach apostolic titles or apostolic associations to the four anonymous Gospels that had been circulating for some time, in order to secure the place they had already come to enjoy within the faith communities around the Mediterranean. During the second century there was a large expansion of Christian literature. Many gospels, apocalypses, and acts of various apostles were produced, largely from the side of gnosticism and Montanism, with the aim of shaping Christianity in the direction of individualistic, mystical, and anti-institutional spirituality (Johnson 1999:602). Long before standards of orthodoxy were established, these early heterodox writings championed diverse ethical and liturgical practices and various claims for authority. They did not, however, advocate the competing theologies or Christologies (like Arianism or Docetism) that would later arise in the third and fourth centuries (Wisse 1986:189–90).

Still, while initially considered harmless or at least tolerable, by the fourth-century heterodox writings likely became a threat too great for the more institutionally-minded bishops in Alexandria and Rome to overlook. With authorities no longer willing to tolerate the inner diversity of heterodox teachers, *and* armed with the greater power and resources of the church hierarchy in the fourth century (having now added the teaching function to the bishops' own office), lists of approved texts for Christian reading were produced, distributed, and enforced (Wisse 1986:190). Recall the purging of gnostic texts, which likely caused certain monks to hide the recently named "contraband" gnostic texts near the Egyptian monasteries at Nag Hammadi. At any rate, Athanasius's list of the twenty-seven NT books endorsed for Christian reading first appeared in his thirty-ninth Easter letter (367 CE). This list served to officially ratify the texts that had already long proved useful, apostolic in derivation, and theologically consistent with the church's "rule of faith."

Besides a long record of usefulness in the early church, one key criterion for establishing a NT gospel's place in the church's approved reading list (canon) was apostolic origin or association. The use and abuse of Paul's collection of letters (2 Pet 3:15) as well as claims of certain gnostic teachers who alleged secret apostolic succession for their esoteric gospels and treatises compounded the conflict and heightened the tension over order, leadership, and authority. In response, the proto-orthodox argued that a canonical gospel could not emerge out of nowhere or only recently; there had to be a public and universally recognized line of ecclesial tradition. As Johnson notes, "The earliest church was also very conscious of having descended from 'eyewitnesses' to the work of God in Christ, and connecting tradition back to these 'eyewitnesses' made obvious sense" (1999:604–5).

For the first one hundred years, however, the gospels in the NT likely circulated without attribution to specific apostles or their associates (Sanders and Davies 1989:13). What evidence suggest such an assessment? It was not until 180 CE that the heresiologist and bishop of Lyons, Irenaeus, named all four gospels (the Synoptics plus John) and quoted passages from each in his refutation against gnostics (*Against*

Heresies 3.11.7), showing that he knew the gospels as we have them named today. This is the first evidence that gospel quotations are tagged with names Matthew, Mark, Luke, and John. Thirty years earlier, Justin Martyr, writing in 150 CE had quoted Jesus sayings from a text he called, "Memoirs of the Apostles" (*Dialogue with Trypho* 106.3). Justin did not name the authors of the gospels he quotes, though he is quoting from both Matthew and Luke; neither did he seem concerned to keep them distinct—his citations were simply run together as sayings of Jesus, which he received from the Christian tradition (*Apology* 1.19.7). Going back ten more years we come to Papias, who, writing in 140 CE, is the first one to relate a scenario linking Mark to the eyewitness Peter. He does not offer a gospel quotation but defends the authenticity of the gospel that would become known as Mark's. Eusebius, the fourth-century church historian, records the following selection from Papias's writing:

> And the presbyter [or Elder] used to say this, "Mark became Peter's interpreter and wrote accurately all that he remembered, not, indeed, in order, of the things said or done by the Lord. For he had not heard the Lord, nor had he followed him, but later on, as I said, followed Peter, who used to give teaching as necessity demanded, but who did not make, as it were, an arrangement of the Lord's oracles, so that Mark did nothing wrong in thus writing down single points as he remembered them. For to one thing he gave attention, to leave out nothing of what he had heard and to make no false statements in them." (*Eccl. Hist.* 3.39.15)

Prior to Papias, writers who made reference to the sayings of Jesus also do not assign them to a particular Evangelist but use them as if they were anonymous, or as if they went directly back to Jesus without the mediation of an author or editor with a particular perspective (e.g., *Letters of Ignatius*, the *Didache*, *The Letter of First Clement*). According to Sanders, "It is at least slightly dubious that Papias got it right when other Christians seem not even to have been interested in the question" (Sanders and Davies 1989:10). Regardless of how one assesses Papias's assertions, the attempt to tie Mark to Peter and to defend Mark's order and completeness signals a growing concern for establishing apostolic origin—something that would occupy proto-orthodox Christians a great deal at the end of the second century in their struggle with gnosticism. The conflict "raised the bar" such that what was once not important (the source of the otherwise-affirmed eyewitness, apostolic testimony) became important to ascertain or at least defend.

Thus, it came to be that all four gospels, which had already been found to be useful for teaching and training, were declared retroactively tied to a specific eyewitness apostolic testimony; so their places were secured on the approved reading list: Mark, as Peter's companion and translator, Luke, as Paul's shipmate and co-worker, and Matthew and John as apostles themselves. The oldest extant copies of the gospels (ca. 200) do record these names in the gospel titles, but it is unclear when they first became attached to the gospels. Johnson summarizes the key claims regarding apostolic origin:

> Two important claims were made against the Gnostics by this principle of apostolic origin. The first was the claim of historical priority: these were the writings that first gave expression to the Christian identity. The second is the claim of historical continuity: the church of today reads and understands—as though written to itself—the writings of Jesus' first followers. It requires no esoteric code for understanding their plain meaning; the context was given with the text, in the church's public life. The criterion of apostolic origin was important, but it was also somewhat artificial and it was certainly not decisive as many of the writings that were attributed to apostles were not accepted, such as the *Gospel of Thomas*, *Gospel of Peter*, and the *Apocalypse of Peter*. (Johnson 1999:605)

To sum up, since the attribution of the gospels to named authors (Matthew, Mark, Luke, and John) came so late, most likely these anonymous texts circulated initially without attribution. Of course, the local community to which the authors belonged knew who the authors were, but this was not deemed a vital fact and left to fade away, since each Gospel was just that, *the* Gospel of Messiah Jesus. While the authors clearly wrote with persuasive aims, they probably did not wish to call attention to their individual judgments, since they were not the subject of the story. For one hundred years the gospels were copied and circulated, giving witness to the truth of Jesus' life and ministry. By the end of the second century, the situation had changed, and given the intensified conflict, the eyewitness testimony already preserved in the four gospels needed the *further* authorization of attribution to or association with a named apostle. The apologists and heresiologists at the end of the second century found enough clues in the texts themselves to make compelling enough cases for apostolic origin, in order to secure the place that these gospels (and eventually all twenty-seven NT texts) had already occupied for as many as one hundred years.

MARK'S THEOLOGICAL VISION

For much of Christian history, Mark was neglected as inferior (tucked behind Matthew in the NT order) and thought of as merely Matthew's abbreviator—and a clumsy one at that (recall Papias's attempt to defend Mark). Today, however, Mark has been rehabilitated and is now highly regarded among gospel scholars for two reasons: (1) The so-called inferior character is thought to hold evidence of an earlier Jesus community. Instead of seeing the rough grammar as unfortunate, it is seen as evidence of its primary witness (minus the smoothing-out influences of Matthew and Luke). (2) The growing scholarly conviction that Mark ends at 16:8 ("for they were afraid") combines with other Markan features to suggest that Mark is really quite a thoughtful, provocative, and artful piece of theological literature. Instead of a literary embarrassment, Mark offers readers a profound challenge to consider their own discipleship options as they carry the gospel story forward (Geddert 2001:390–403). These two reasons have combined to catapult Mark to center stage. Once deemed the inferior Gospel, cobbled together by a clumsy editor, the Gospel of Mark now enjoys the "pride of place"—not only first but more representative of the historical Jesus.

Now, Mark's sudden promotion to fame can be read in two ways. For some, Mark is *so* artful that he is credited with being the political genius who created the Jesus we see on the pages of his gospel—a Jesus specifically intended to silence the Jesus of other communities who knew him only as a wise teacher, but not the eschatological bringer of salvation. Mark is lumped together with Paul as a great co-conspirator who changed the simple message of Jesus, augmenting it with redemption theology and judgment language, in order to secure a new basis to stabilize the Jesus movement (Kelber 1997). For others, Mark is a remarkably creative literary theologian who finds provocative ways (sometimes troubling, but always challenging) to invite believers to faithfully follow Messiah Jesus on the way of Christian discipleship (Geddert 2001).

How could such divergent views emerge? If Mark is given priority, as both contemporary views assert, how does Mark's theological vision relate to that of the other Jesus communities? Is the relation best described by continuity or discontinuity? Two issues relate to this question.

First, Mark's use of a literary device called the "messianic secret" is variously viewed, and it shapes how one understands the theological vision of Mark. Wrede (1971) argued that the frequency with which

Mark has Jesus silence the crowds with respect to his messianic identity was a literary creation of Mark (1:34; 3:12; 5:43; 7:36; 8:30). Jesus is cast as continually telling people during his ministry to "keep quiet" until after the resurrection (9:9). Wrede's solution to this puzzling situation is to propose that during Jesus's ministry, Jesus never urged secrecy at all, because he did *not* see himself as the Messiah. Instead it was Paul, the second founder of Christianity, and others like Mark, who, following Jesus's death, invented the idea that Jesus *had* proclaimed himself as Israel's Messiah.

How did Wrede come up with this? Convinced as he was that Jesus did not make any messianic claims about himself during his life, Wrede had to find a way to explain the early Christian confession that Jesus was the Messiah, when (as he assumed) Jesus himself left no such tradition. Wrede came up with an elaborate theory, suggesting that it was the early Christian community that invented a Jesus who continually tried to keep his identity a secret. This would explain why Jesus's own lack of any messianic consciousness was missed by so many. Wrede suggested that Mark used the fiction of a messianic secret in order to transform Jesus's nonmessianic history into a messianic one. The device explains why so few understood that Jesus was the Messiah prior to Easter: few got it because Jesus habitually kept his identity a secret! To make the fiction even more plausible, Mark portrayed the disciples as especially dull (compare Mark 6:52 with Matt 14:33) in order to explain further why so few really understood Jesus to be more than simply a good teacher of true morality.

Theologians who use exclusively the historical or chronological model tend to build on Wrede's view of Mark. Various scenarios are proposed for narrating the evolution of the story from Jesus to the Christ, where Jesus of Nazareth is transformed to the Christ of the church's faith. While this is a vocal group, it is certainly not the only way to assess the evidence. Mark's messianic secret may be interpreted in other ways.

Wrede's assessment is not compelling for two reasons. First, the memory of eyewitnesses remains in control. While the Evangelists (post-70) selected, edited, and elaborated their received Jesus traditions, this does not mean they were free to invent something as large as a messianic Jesus out of one who never made such claims. The model of oral transmission of Jesus sayings later framed by Evangelists presupposes that the memory of eyewitnesses remained in control (Caird 1997:215).

For example, it is hard to imagine that the disciples would agree with their portrayal in the gospel as dull if there was not some core truth to it. Wrede assumes that oral tradition would not have caught up with Mark's fabrication. What would it be like to be portrayed in the story as a dull disciple, when this was not the case at all? Surely this would have been challenged if it were not true. Wrede's reconstruction is more difficult to imagine. The burden of proof lies with Wrede, and the evidence is lacking for any tradition of a nonmessianic Jesus.

The second reason to question Wrede's reconstruction is that Mark's use of the messianic secret has a simpler explanation; it is more about God's kingdom and Jesus's messianic role than about an elaborate cover up. Jack Kingsbury (1983) argued the secret identity of Jesus in Mark concerns only the *kind* of messiah Jesus was, not whether he was the Messiah. In other words, the messianic secret in Mark is not about making Jesus something he was not, but about provoking readers to consider the way God was in fact working through Jesus, the Messiah. The point is that the kingdom of God is coming in ways not immediately obvious in Judaism; the victory over evil is coming in an unexpected and nontraditional manner. In fact, only after Easter would the kind of messiah that Jesus was all along become clear. Mark's literary device is not so much a secret as an expression of the "mystery" of the gospel, one that cannot be controlled, deciphered, or decoded, only revealed. Hence, the tradition of Jesus being misunderstood and hidden is taken up into the narrative. Mark uses the messianic secret and several other literary devices (matching sets of doublets, sets of three, apocalyptic symbolism) to encourage his audience to embrace the mystery of God, which is being revealed by Jesus. And so Mark tells an open-ended narrative, inviting listeners/readers to a life of obedience and service in the way of Jesus.

Mark's alleged merger of a Hellenistic divine man or gnostic redeemer myth with the Jewish apocalyptic Son of Man tradition is the second issue often raised when sorting out Mark's relation to other Jesus communities. Again working from a historical (chronological) model, this view asserts that Mark borrows opportunistically from Greco-Roman mythology, claiming that Jesus is indeed a heroic, superhuman figure in the Hellenistic tradition, who is endowed with divine wisdom and power to perform miracles, *and* who is the end-time Jewish Messiah soon to come for judgment and salvation: neither identity is actually true for Jesus in the historical model. Earlier, we saw how the gnostic redeemer myth was purportedly used by Paul. Here in the synoptic tradition, Bultmann argued similarly that gnostic mythology was merged with the Jewish Son of Man or the eschatological bringer of salvation; both were transferred to Jesus for the purpose of contextualizing the Christian message for a Hellenistic audience (1951:34, 164).

At issue is a key verse in Mark: "Those who are ashamed of *me* and of my words in this adulterous and sinful generation, of them the Son of Man will be ashamed when *he* comes in the glory of his Father with the holy angels" (8:38, italics added). While the third-person reference to the Son of Man is common in the synoptic tradition, usually Jesus is clearly associated with the title (see Mark 2:10; Matt 9:6; Luke 5:24). In Mark 8:38, however, Jesus appears to be referring to the Son of Man as someone other than himself (Bultmann 1951:29). Earlier we saw how Bultmann used the criterion of dissimilarity as a tool to reconstruct from the NT sources what he believed to be the profile of the "historical Jesus." In Mark 8:38 we have an example of another one of these tools: the criterion on embarrassment. Bultmann argued that it is unlikely that the early Christians would have made up such an embarrassing saying: why have Jesus speak in such a way as to leave it open to question whether he was speaking about himself or not? This means there is strong likelihood that Jesus actually uttered this saying much like it is found in Mark 8:38. It passes the criterion of embarrassment.

In Bultmann's scenario, Mark 8:38 is evidence that Mark and the early Christians syncretistically employed Hellenistic terminology to recast Jesus's ministry in conformity to their new post-Easter view of him as the cosmic, futuristic Son of Man and bringer of salvation. Bultmann explains the process as follows: "The Gnostic stock of concepts served to clarify the history of salvation. According to these concepts the redeemer appears as a cosmic figure, the pre-existent divine being, Son of the Father, who came down from heaven and assumed human form and who, after his activity on earth, was exalted to heavenly glory and wrested sovereignty over the spirit-powers to himself" (Bultmann 1951:175).

So while Jesus of Nazareth is a shadowy figure who proclaims that God's kingdom is near and that the Son of Man is coming, later the early church's proclamation projected onto Jesus their community's faith that Jesus *is* the Son of Man whose *parousia* they await. It is Mark's ingenuity that connects something not previously connected. Mark is the one who projected onto Jesus the combination of the Hellenistic divine redeemer and the Jewish eschatological Son of Man. Thus, "the proclaimer became the proclaimed" in the life of the post-Easter Jesus communities (Bultmann 1951:33).

Is there a way to understand Mark's literary project that does not attribute so much "creativity" to Mark? Two things can be said here. First, the diversity of gnostic religion does not confirm the presence of stable gnostic redeemer mythology at this early date. As argued above, the 1945 discovery of the gnostic library of spiritual writings at the Egyptian village of Nag Hammadi seriously undermined the way gnosticism had been perceived. The collection shows an amazing variety of beliefs and practices. Thus, it would be saying too much if we thought as Bultmann did, that the gnostic redeemer mythology was a well developed and common myth available for Mark to use for his own polemical purposes. To be sure, such characterizations of Jesus did develop later, emerging in the late second and third centuries. So while there is evidence of the beginnings of gnostic ideas in the NT (see 1 John), the direction of development is more likely the reverse of Bultmann's reconstruction—that is, from the historical Jesus to gnostic redeemer, and not from gnostic redeemer to the NT interpretation of the historical Jesus.

The second problem with Bultmann's gnostic reconstruction is that the Hebrew title Son of Man was historically multivalent and not limited to one referent as Bultmann thought. In Ps 8:4, "son of man" (*ben 'adam*) is a paraphrase for the whole human race that is assigned a position of dignity, sharing in the dominion of creation and the mandate to participate with God in its completion. In Dan 7:13, "son of man," here in Aramaic (*bar 'anosh*), refers to God's agent of salvation who ushers in the new age; he is pictured as one coming on the clouds, making presentation to God. The Son of Man, then, is more like a "job description" set out first for Israel and ultimately all the nations, who join God's agent in fulfilling God's creation intentions (Caird 1994:380). The tradition shows both *collective* usage (Israel) and *individual* usage (Israel's representative, the bringer of salvation).

Such a "both/and" scenario is well known as Semitic style and is even evident in Hebrew grammar, known for *parataxis* (the placing of statements one beside the other without making explicit the relation between them—whether hierarchical, temporal, causal, or other—with connecting conjunctions). In a similar way, it is very possible that Jesus used the term "Son of Man" as a self-designation precisely because of its multivalent ambiguity, which enabled him to link with the past, the present, and the future activity of God. At times, "Son of Man" referred to his own ministry (Mark 2:10) of calling Israel back to its founding story, illustrated by his words of proclamation and acts of healing. And at other times, it referred to the future day when God would vindicate the end-time people and complete the work of salvation begun during his life and looming demise (Mark 8:38; 13:26). Thus, according to Caird, "The Son of Man is an *open-ended* term which includes all who are prepared to respond to the preaching of the gospel of the Kingdom, who share with Jesus the demands the Kingdom is making on the Israel of the new age" (1994:380).

Turning to the structure of Mark's gospel, we find that the narrative has two main parts with a transition pericope known as Peter's confession (8:27–33). In the first section (1:14—8:26), Mark depicts Jesus in Galilee, active in a ministry of preaching, gathering disciples, teaching, healing, and exorcising demons. Then in the second section (8:27—16:8), he portrays Jesus on a journey to Jerusalem, where he suffers, dies, and is raised. Mark's narrative is characterized as apocalyptic with a surprising revelation about God's kingdom: the identity of who is actually *inside* and who is actually *outside* gets redefined in terms of how Jesus's interlocutors respond to the mystery of the kingdom that Jesus represents (Johnson 1999:169).

Taking the microphone, Mark gives his center or vision statement: *The crucifixion constitutes the climax of my story of Jesus. While the earthly ministry of Jesus is central to all of God's dealings with humanity, I attribute special importance to the cross. It is the cross that is the decisive event in the history of salvation—it is linked to the mystery of the coming kingdom and it is confirmed by the resurrection to be God's way. In meeting the resurrected Jesus, God offers a new chance for the world.*

THEMATIC IMPLICATIONS OF MARK'S VISION

Five themes can be traced emanating from this center. First, Jesus is the Son of God from the outset of his ministry, but only gradually is his identity revealed. While readers know who Jesus is, Mark hides Jesus's identity as Son of God from Jesus's inside group of friends: "Who then is this, that even the wind and the sea obey him" (4:41)? Gradually, over the course of the narrative, Jesus's disciples come to understand who he is. At his baptism, only Jesus is addressed by the voice from heaven:

"You are my Son, the Beloved; with you I am well pleased" (1:11). At the transfiguration the disciples are addressed: "This is my Son, the Beloved; listen to him!" (9:7). The trial of Jesus narrates the penultimate disclosure of Jesus's identity: "Are you the Messiah, the Son of the Blessed One?" (14:61); "Are you the King of the Jews" (14:2)? It is at the crucifixion, however, where the mystery of Jesus's divine sonship finally surfaces unambiguously in the mouth of a Gentile centurion: "Truly this man was God's son" (15:39)! The gospel closes with words of comfort and challenge from the heavenly messenger for those gathered at the empty tomb: "Do not be alarmed; you are looking for Jesus of Nazareth, who was crucified. He has been raised; he is not here... He is going ahead of you to Galilee; there you will see him, just as he told you" (16:6–7).

Second, Jesus is the Son of Man, from the outset without secrecy. This is the common self-designation used by Jesus, and it occurs always on the lips of Jesus. This is Jesus's favorite title for himself. However, its exact meaning is ambiguous. Characteristic of Jewish apocalyptic writers, Mark uses it to tie Jesus to the eschatological bringer of salvation (Dan 7:13): "Then they will see 'the Son of Man coming in clouds' with great power and glory. Then he will send out the angels, and gather his elect from the four winds, from the ends of the earth to the ends of heaven" (13:26–27). While this is the *parousia* of the Son of Man (on the clouds) when all people (both far and near) are compelled to acknowledge Jesus as Savior and Lord, Mark's Jesus also uses the Son of Man in reference to ministry sayings (2:10) and passion sayings (8:31; 9:31; 10:33). Thus, it is a flexible, multivalent term probably going back to Jesus's own conviction that he was bringing into existence the Israel of the new age. Therefore, "Son of Man" is also an inclusive, collective term, as Jesus invites his disciples to share in his vocation by taking up their cross with him (8:34), by taking upon themselves the struggle for the kingdom (10:39), and by exercising their own calling through service to and for others (10:44).

Third, Jesus's ministry announces that the kingdom of God is at hand (1:15). Mark's Jesus announces that the end-time age has dawned and that God's rule in the person of Jesus has drawn near. Like the multivalent term "Son of Man," the term "kingdom" is also used by Jesus in several ways. God is the King, Creator of heaven and earth, the Lord of history (4:30–32). Then too God is King of Israel by virtue of the ancient and enduring covenant relationship with Abraham and his posterity

(11:9-11). Finally, God's reign also has an eschatological future dimension (14:22-25). According to Caird, "the Kingdom in Jesus' teaching is all these, and more besides" (1999:369). In the face of the gathering storm, the turn of the ages, Jesus calls "Israel to discover what it means for God to reign over Israel; then they will know what part Israel is to play in the plan of God ... For Jesus, entering the Kingdom was synonymous with the life of discipleship—of submitting to the demands of the God who is King" (ibid.:369).

Fourth, Jesus's ministry involved healing, signs, and wonders, revealing their meaning to those who have eyes to see and ears to hear (8:18). Miracles like the feeding of five thousand reveal Jesus' identity, but they can easily be misunderstood (6:52). Mark's Jesus triumphs over storms, Satan, sickness, and death (4:35—5:43). And yet for Mark, the apologetic value of these signs is not stressed; they are not recounted so as to persuade people to believe, as in the Fourth Gospel (John 20:31). "Instead," says Geddert, "they are reported to demonstrate how fully Jesus can meet human need. They are designed to provoke reactions that lead to reflection, insight, and convictions about the arrival of God's reign. They also reveal the true nature and identity of Jesus" (2001:124). Jesus's acts of power do not aim to dazzle the crowds with shock and awe. Neither does he always exercise his power to heal or to rescue (6:45-52; 8:1-21). The miracle stories function for Mark as pointers to the nature of God's reign, that Messiah Jesus is revealing for those with eyes to see and ears to hear.

Fifth, Jesus's way of the cross deals with the powers of evil in a new way and charts the way of discipleship for all who choose to follow Jesus (8:34). For Mark, the centrality of the cross is vital to the gospel narrative that he constructs. It is precisely in a place like the cross, where God seems the most absent, remote, or impotent (15:34), that God is most fully and effectively present. In this way, the cross undoes the grip that the oppressive power of evil exercises over individuals, institutions, and societies, manifesting itself as fear, guilt, or shame. No longer must people pursue with violence and coercion the causes which they deem to be righteous or just. This is new; it is a reversal of the classic myth of redemptive violence that has funded the imagination of all people groups in some way from the dawn of time (Girard 2001).

Instead, for Mark, the way of the cross is characterized by the way of self-giving love—a love that absorbs and transforms evil, draining it of its power to dominate and oppress. The image is derived from the commercial world of redemption and ransom (Mark 10:45). Such gift-giving characterizes God's way with the world and sketches out the pattern for all God's people. At its center, the kind of cross-bearing Mark has in mind for disciples is as simple as saying yes to God's way. According to Geddert, "The cross is not a symbol of horror and should not be thought to define discipleship in negative terms. Discipleship is, at its heart, saying yes to God; thus it is participating in the reign of God, with all the related blessings and challenges, costs, and rewards. The cross is a way of *living*, not just a way of *dying*" (2001:211).

MATTHEW'S THEOLOGICAL VISION

We turn our attention now to Matthew's voice. What will we hear? Until the nineteenth century, Matthew enjoyed the "pride of place," as the first gospel in the NT. It was the church's gospel, giving the clearest and fullest instruction for the community of believers, in contrast to Mark's marginal reception. For most of Christian history Matthew is the gospel that the church turned to for worship, preaching, and teaching. As far as ecclesial use is concerned, "Matthew is the most successful edition of Mark's Gospel" (Johnson 1999:187).

Two developments in Matthean studies worked to modify the assessment of Matthew. First, the Markan-priority hypothesis unseated Matthew's comfortable first-place position, and scholars began to assess the tradition differently. Papias (140 CE) had claimed that "Matthew collected the sayings in the Hebrew language, but everyone translated them as best he could" (Eusebius, *Eccl. Hist.* 3.39.16); and then Irenaeus (180 CE) indicated that Matthew was first written in Hebrew and then translated into Greek (*Against Heresies* 3.1.1). The exact dimension of these assertions is no longer clear, and it appears they likely refer to prior versions and not to the Matthew that we know in the NT. Most scholars now agree that the Greek text of Matthew does not suggest direct translation from either Hebrew or Aramaic. Johnson contends, "When compared with Mark, for example, Matthew shows consistently clearer, more concise and correct, use of Greek . . . It remains far easier to explain the differences as Matthew's commentary on and correction of Mark than as Mark's clumsy omission of fifty percent of Matthew" (1999:188) as Augustine contended (*Harmony of the Evangelists* 1.2.4). At any rate, pre-1945 Matthean research focused on source criticism,

Markan Priority, and further refinement of the Two- or Four-Source Hypothesis to the Synoptic Problem. The interest was in determining what in Matthew came from Mark, what came from the hypothetical Q source of sayings, and what came from Matthew's special source.

Second, Matthean studies after 1945 moved beyond source criticism to a new kind of study, which also modified thinking about Matthew's gospel. Günther Bornkamm (1963) published a famous article on the pericope of the Stilling of the Storm (Matt 8:23–27). In that article, Bornkamm showed how Matthew reordered the Markan material that he copied; so he showed Matthew to be an editor and interpreter of his tradition. Attention to such editing became known as redaction criticism. In this case, the nature miracle (Stilling of the Storm) was taken out of the biographical context in Mark and moved into a series of pericopae in Matthew, where the two sayings of Jesus about discipleship that precede the Stilling of the Storm give the miracle story its meaning. Matthew, according to Bornkamm, interprets "the journey of the disciples with Jesus in the storm and the stilling of the storm with reference to discipleship, and that means with reference to the little ship of the church" (1963:55).

Instead of conceptualizing Matthew as a mindless "cut-and-paste" editor of Mark and Q, which was common in source criticism, scholars practicing redaction criticism became interested in *how* Matthew artfully used his sources. Of course, the extent of creative invention could not be attributed to Matthew as some had imagined for Mark (i.e., Wrede, Bultmann, Kelber), since Matthew's dependence on his sources is clearer than it is for Mark. Nevertheless, Matthew's adaptation of his sources gave concrete "evidence" of editorial changes and creative interpretation of the Jesus tradition passed on by Matthew's sources.

What is the structure of Matthew's theological statement? Matthew's theology takes the form of a kerygmatic story—a story told for theological purposes with a broader scope than Mark's. The theological claim set forth by this structure is established by the inclusio of 1:23 and 28:20. (An inclusio is an envelope framework created by placing similar material at the beginning and end of a section). Beginning at 1:23, the birth of Emmanuel ("God is with us") is narrated as the hope of Israel that has come to its fulfillment in Jesus, God's Son. Here, Matthew affirms that Jesus is of decisive significance for the salvation of *Israel*. Then in 28:20, the risen Jesus proclaims, "I am with you always, to the end of the age." Thus, the risen Christ commissions his followers to "make disciples of all nations." Here, Matthew affirms that Jesus is also of decisive significance for the salvation of the *Gentiles*.

The two inclusio passages set forth the broad theological claim that Matthew advances: Jesus, the Son of God is of decisive significance for the salvation of both Jews and Gentiles. Thus, Jesus is of ultimate importance for Jew and Gentile alike. Even though the gospel ends, the story goes on in the lives of those who follow.

If Mark offers an apocalyptic narrative, Matthew chooses to frame things in the rabbinic tradition. Unlike Mark, Matthew has extended teaching sections and liturgical structures. Five discourses are set off by transitional formulas: the Sermon on the Mount (chaps. 5–7), the discourse on mission and discipleship (chap. 10), the parabolic discourse (chap. 13), the discourse on life in the community (chap. 18), and the discourse on the coming kingdom (chaps. 24–25). Some see in this a deliberate allusion to the five books of the Pentateuch, the center of the Torah.

Matthew also structures his narrative with two temporal transitions at 4:17 and 16:21. This sets up a three-stage presentation of Messiah Jesus: the person of Jesus (1:1—4:16), the proclamation of God's kingdom by Messiah Jesus (4:17—16:20), and the revelation of Messiah Jesus to his disciples through his suffering, death, and resurrection (16:21—28:20).

The setting that seems to fit Matthew's catechetical and liturgical features best is the time where second-generation Christians are sorting through questions of self-definition and self-understanding as they dialogue (or debate?) with rabbinic Judaism, which is doing the very same thing after the destruction of the temple (70 CE). Likely, the debates between messianic Jews and the nonmessianic Jews grew more and more hostile, providing the background for the Matthean community's attempt to define itself with regard to the Pharisaic movement, which was becoming dominant in the post-temple reformation of Judaism. By 85 CE the formal composition of the *birkat ha-minim* (the "benedictions against heretics") finally forced the Jewish Christians out of the synagogue altogether. It became impossible for them to pray in the synagogues, because they could no longer recite the revised eighteenth benediction with its curse on Jewish believers in Yeshua or Jesus. Thus, Matthew narrates the story of Jesus, editing and interpreting his sources from the vantage point of the Matthean community sometime between the 70s and the 90s CE.

As he comes to the microphone, we now have the statement from Matthew: *My theological center is that in the person of Messiah Jesus, God has drawn near to abide to the end of time with God's people, thus inaugurating the eschatological age of salvation. This is of ultimate importance for Jew and Gentile alike as Israel is thus reconstituted to be what God had always intended it to be, a "light to the nations" in the tradition of Isa 49:6.*

THEMATIC IMPLICATIONS OF MATTHEW'S VISION

Three implications can be noted from Matthew's presentation of Jesus. First, Jesus's messianic sonship is established by citations from the OT. There are eleven such "proofs from prophecy." Matthew advances the thesis that Jesus is the messianic Son of God promised in the Hebrew Scriptures in a very specific manner, drawing on wording from the Greek translation of these Scriptures, called the Septuagint (LXX). No other gospel, and no other NT writing, points so stereotypically to the fulfillment of scriptural prophecies through Jesus's life and ministry as does Matthew. These fulfillments include:

- the virginal conception (1:23; Isa 7:14)
- birth in Bethlehem (2:6; Mic 5:2)
- flight into Egypt (2:15; Hos 11:1)
- murder of the children in Bethlehem (2:18; Jer 31:15)
- Jesus is called a Nazorean (2:23; Isa 11:1)
- Jesus's public ministry in Galilee (4:15–16; Isa 9:1–2)
- Jesus's healing and exorcism (8:17; Isa 53:4)
- Jesus's hidden work of healing (12:18–21; Isa 42:1–4)
- Jesus conceals speech in parables (13:14–15; Isa 6:9–10)
- Jesus humbly enters into Jerusalem (21:5; Isa 62:11; Zech 9:9)
- the payment to Judas (27:9–10; Zech 11:12–13; Jer 18:1–3).

For a Christian community engaged in conversation with an aggressive Pharisaic movement in a post-temple world, simply declaring Jesus as the resurrected Messiah was not enough. His credentials as a Davidic king needed demonstration.

With formulaic citations from the OT, Matthew marshals "proofs" from Israel's story to explain Jesus's dubious parentage, lowly place of origin, radical teaching, surprising fulfillment of Torah, and significance that extends beyond Judaism to include all the nations. What appears to be Matthew's aim? Brought together, specific Torah texts and specific moments in Jesus's life work to interpret one another. Johnson states it succinctly, "From seeing Jesus, we understand the real meaning of Torah; by reading Torah, we discover the full meaning of Jesus' ministry" (1999:202).

Second, Matthew is intent on emphasizing royal titles for Jesus, especially "Son of David." For Matthew, Jesus is the Davidic Messiah, the royal Son of God, who descends from Abraham. This is Matthew's fundamental christological assertion. No one in the NT is occupied more with the Davidic sonship of Jesus than Matthew. Mark and Luke employ the title Son of David four times each, but Matthew uses it eleven times (all but once in reference to Jesus). Matthew appears interested in pursuing two objectives: (1) to affirm the Davidic lineage of Jesus as proof of his messiahship; and (2) to challenge Israel to reclaim its missional mandate, given its apparent rejection of Messiah Jesus.

As the Son of David, Jesus is promised and sent specifically to Israel (1:1; 15:22–24; 21:5, 9; 22:42). But this should not be understood as exclusivism. Jesus probably found in the prophets and in the psalms the strategy for his own mission (Jeremias 1958:55). Here, God's coming salvation is described in two stages: (1) Israel is rescued and restored to the holiness that honors God; and then (2) the redeemed Israel helps the nations to see that God truly is worthy of worship and allegiance as the source of all things (Isa 2:2–4; 49:5–6; Zech 8:23; 14:8–9). Jesus likely believed that his role was restricted to stage 1, since stage 2 could be safely left to the renewed Israel (Caird 1994:52).

The church picked up Jesus's example of the two-stage mission, carrying it forward in its own missional life. Three times in his letter to the Romans, Paul says that God's salvation is "to the Jew first and also to the Greek" (1:16; 2:9–10). Matthew, too, arranges several healing miracles in order to relate Jesus's provocative ministry to the Matthean community's own interaction with rabbinic Judaism decades later. Jesus's acts of healing are intended to provoke Israel; he heals two blind men (9:27–31), a blind and mute man (12:22), the daughter of a Gentile woman, reluctantly at first (15:21–28), two more blind men (20:29–34), and the blind and lame in the temple (21:14). What is noteworthy in these healing stories is that all the people involved typically account for nothing in Israel; all are marginalized in some way. These "no-accounts" acknowledge that Jesus is the Son of David. They see and confess what the leaders of Israel and the crowds do not yet see—both in Jesus's day and in Matthew's. And so Matthew's gospel continues to issue its appeal to people everywhere to live a life befitting God's people.

Third, Matthew develops the relation between Israel and the church more explicitly than any other Evangelist. Matthew is the only Evangelist who explicitly mentions the church (16:18; 18:17). He extends Jesus's own mission through the witness and mission of the church. While the scribes and the Pharisees persist in "locking up" the kingdom, the church is given "the keys to the Kingdom" so as to make it accessible to all who decide to share in God's mission (Johnson 1999:206). The power to "bind and loose" goes along with the responsibility to extend Jesus's mission to all the nations and all creation. As in any community, there is provision for support, teaching, rebuke, correction, advocacy, and discipline—binding and loosing. However, the Christian community carries the added mandate of joining God in completing creation, helping to "loose" all still trapped in the bondage of sin. The stakes are high; for if the Christian community falters in its witness, creation continues to suffer bondage. For better or for worse, the church in its association with Israel is invested with the power to "bind and loose."

Matthew shaped Jesus's encounter with Israel's scribes and Pharisees as a unique salvation-historical time of decision. Now is the time to choose. According to the genealogy that opens the gospel (1:1–17), Jesus came as the son of Abraham and the son of David in order to "save his people from their sins" (1:21). In other words, to set Israel free from its narrow, self-centered nationalism and invite Israel to reclaim its original mandate to be a blessing and a light to the nations (Gen 12:3; Isa 49:6). However, the leadership of the narrower form of Jewish nationalism rejected Jesus and his vision for Israel. But according to Matthew, the story does not end there. The extension of Jesus's ministry to the Gentiles is not thwarted; Israel's mission carries on through the discipling mandate with which Matthew ends his gospel (28:18–20).

Matthew's theological convictions receive forceful articulation in the way that he edits and interprets two of Jesus's parables, the Evil Tenants (21:33–46) and the Royal Wedding Feast (22:1–14). The conclusions to these two parables show evidence of the Matthean community's struggle for self-understanding in a context of rabbinic Judaism. See the synopsis below that highlights each Evangelist's conclusion to Jesus's parable of the Evil Tenants. Note the underlined text.

The Theological Contribution of the Synoptic Gospel Writers 127

Matthew 21:42-45	Mark 12:10-12	Luke 20:17-19
Jesus said to them, "Have you never read in the scriptures: 'The stone that the builders rejected has become the cornerstone; this was the Lord's doing, and it is amazing in our eyes'? <u>Therefore I tell you, the kingdom of God will be taken away from you and given to a people that produces the fruits of the kingdom.</u> The one who falls on this stone will be broken to pieces; and it will crush anyone on whom it falls."	Have you not read this scripture: 'The stone that the builders rejected has become the cornerstone; this was the Lord's doing, and it is amazing in our eyes'?"	But he looked at them and said, "What then does this text mean: 'The stone that the builders rejected has become the cornerstone'? Everyone who falls on that stone will be broken to pieces; and it will crush anyone on whom it falls."
When the chief priests and the Pharisees heard his parables, they realized that he was speaking about them. They wanted to arrest him, but they feared the crowds, because they regarded him as a prophet.	When they realized that he had told this parable against them, they wanted to arrest him, but they feared the crowd. So they left him and went away.	When the scribes and chief priests realized that he had told this parable against them, they wanted to lay hands on him at that very hour, but they feared the people.

TABLE 4.4 Conclusion to Parable of the Evil Tenants in Synoptic Parallels

Extending Jesus's parable of the evil tenants, Matthew characterizes the condemnation of Jesus as the concluding act of Israel's countercovenantal conduct. The murder of the final messenger, the son, leads to a severance of the tenants' relationship with the master. The owner of the vineyard "will put those wretches to a miserable death, and lease the vineyard to other tenants" (21:41). The concluding statement is unique to Matthew: "Therefore I tell you, the kingdom of God will be taken away from you and given to a people that produces the fruits of the kingdom" (21:43). For Matthew, the severance is not between Jews and Gentiles, but between Gentile-rejecting Jews and Gentile-accepting Jews. Matthew interprets Jesus as reconstituting the old covenant people with a new covenant people—believing Jews and Gentiles gathered around Jesus, who will carry forward the mission of God to be a "light of the nations."

Consider also the way the Evangelists conclude another of Jesus's parables, called the Royal Wedding Feast in Matthew and the Great Feast in Luke.

Matthew 22:7–14	Mark	Luke 14:21–23
The king was enraged. <u>He sent his troops, destroyed those murders, and burned their city.</u> Then he said to his slaves, '<u>The wedding is ready, but those invited are not worthy.</u> Go therefore into the main streets, and invite everyone you find to the wedding banquet.' Those slaves went out into the streets and gathered all whom they found, both good and bad; so the wedding hall was filled with guests.	(absent)	Then the owner of the house became angry and said to his slave, 'Go out at ounce into the streets and lanes of the town and bring in the poor, the crippled, the blind, and the lame.' And the slave said, 'Sir, what you ordered has been done, and there is still room.' Then the master said to the slave, 'Go out into the roads and lanes, and compel people to come in, so that my house may be filled. For I tell you, none of those who were invited will taste my dinner.'"
"<u>But when the king came in to see the guests, he noticed a man there who was not wearing a wedding robe, and he said to him, 'Friend, how did you get in here without a wedding robe?' And he was speechless. Then the king said to the attendants, 'Bind him hand and foot, and throw him into outer darkness, where there will be weeping and gnashing of teeth.' For many are called, but few are chosen.</u>"		

TABLE 4.5 Parable of the Royal Wedding Feast or Great Feast in Synoptic Parallels

In Matthew's version of Jesus's parable of the feast, the king is so angered over the rejection and mistreatment of the servants that he extends his invitation to all, "both good and bad," and sends his army to destroy those murderers and burn their city (22:7). Then later, the king upbraids and casts out the guest without a wedding robe. Before exploring the particularly harsh "judgmental" conclusion, once again we see how the Matthean community was able to tap into the Jesus tradition and see their own conflict with emerging rabbinic Judaism mirrored in Jesus's parable. As Caird notes, "For Jesus, Israel was at a cross-roads; it must choose between two conceptions of its national destiny, and the time for choice was terrifyingly short" (1994:361). A storm was gathering.

Jesus called on Israel to renew its commitment to its founding narrative—to be both the *blessed* and *blessing* nation, the *gathered* and *gathering* nation, the *saved* and *saving* nation. Unfortunately, it had forgotten the second part of that mandate, and Jesus aimed to correct that. As Caird asserts, "Jesus believed that Israel was called by God to be the agent of [God's] purpose, and that he himself had been sent to bring about that reformation without which Israel could not fulfill its national destiny" (1994:366). Matthew's own community was sounding the same warning, likely seeing the events of 70 CE (the temple destruction and the fall of Jerusalem) as one more warning of the coming storm and the extreme urgency of the moment. These events were seen not as literally the end of the world but as symbols and metaphors for the final end: now was the time to decide for life or for death.

The particularly strong "judgmental" conclusions in both Matthean parables (quite different from their synoptic parallels) represent Matthew's conviction that Jesus's ministry involved reconstituting Israel in order that it might finally be what God had always intended it to be: namely, a "light to the nations." The language of "taken away," "thrown out," and "destroyed" should be read as the consistent *result* that flows from persistent rebellion against God's ways, whether by Jews or anyone else for that matter. These consequences should not be characterized as working out God's vengeance (even though within the parables the land owner and the king appear motivated by revenge), but illustrative of the way God honors even willful rejection of life, which amounts to death.

The Matthean parable conclusions do not relay punishment for killing Jesus, but the consequences associated with persistent rebellion against God's intended purpose and enmeshment with narrow nationalistic ideals. These parable endings should not be read as God's purposeful rejection or replacement of Israel with Gentiles (displacement or supersessionism). Rather, they are typical Israelite ways of expressing that since Jesus is the way God is choosing to fulfill Israel's hopes for both Jews and Gentiles, all other ways will continually "come up short." The Matthean parable framing should not be understood as a call for revenge, punishment, or destruction of Judaism; it does not justify an anti-Semitic agenda.

A close reading of the text shows this kind of expression as good Hebrew theological speech: speech about anticipated results as intended purposes, speech about God in anthropopathic terms, and speech about processes in absolute terms. This is good Hebrew form. But make no mistake; in the Israelite worldview of modified providence and dual causality (the notion that causes spring from both human and divine sources), such "purpose" statements were never thought to imply partiality, coercion, and manipulation (capriciousness) on God's part, or loss of responsibility (fatalism) on humanity's part. Now, of course, rebellion has consequences—and they are hideous: broken relations, confusion, anxiety, decay, and death. However, while these can be called "God's judgments," they are part of God's "consequential" will and cannot be identified with God's "antecedent" will. The judgments of God are restorative and educative, not retributive like judgment in the style of the old Adamic humanity. God's vengeance is not like human vengeance (Isa 55:8–9).

For instance, in Mark 4:12 we read the apparently harsh statement that for those on the outside, Jesus chooses to say everything in parables "so that" (*hina*) they may not understand (purpose statement). The parallel passage in Matthew 13:13 has Jesus speaking to the outsiders in parables "because" (*hoti*) they do not understand. Matthew then inserts a citation from Isa 6:9–10, probably to show that the rejection experienced by Isaiah is also now being experienced by Jesus—so their misunderstanding is a result of their rejection (result statement). Thus, Matthew chooses to express the people's misunderstanding as a *result* of rejection, whereas Mark expresses the same thing as Jesus's *purpose*.

What is going on here? This is another example of the dual-causation so typical of the ancient Near Eastern worldview. Everything can be explained as God's purpose since God is sovereign, *and* at the same time everything can be explained as a result of human choices since humanity is responsible for its own outcomes. The biblical writers do not seem to be bothered by this tension (is it a purpose or is it a result?) as much as Westerners, who are preoccupied with origins and single cause-effect relations. The biblical writers, in their ancient Near Eastern way, can affirm *both* to be true at the same time.

LUKE'S THEOLOGICAL VISION

Finally, we turn to the Third Evangelist, commonly known as Luke. Twentieth-century discussion of Luke's literary work can be divided into two parts. During the pre-1950 era, Luke was considered a historian, not a theologian. At that time the focus of study was on the sources used by Luke as a historian: on his use of Mark and Q, on his special material, on his prologue, on his narration of Paul's missionary voyages in Acts, and so on. The questions focused on his merits as a historian. In the post-1950 era, Luke's moniker flipped; now he was considered more a theologian rather than a historian. As redaction criticism developed, as it did in Matthean studies, Luke's own voice as a theologian who shaped, extended, and interpreted the Jesus tradition became more appreciated. The debate over Luke's center also shifted accordingly.

Two scholars in the history-of-religions school made significant impact on Lukan studies. Each of them, following in the tradition of Bultmann, suggested that Luke found creative ways to overcome some of early Christianity's "embarrassing" problems during the chaotic first decades of its quest for self-understanding. First, Ernst Käsemann (1964) argued that Luke "fixed" the problem of the fading of early Christianity's original eschatology (the imminent return of Jesus) by replacing it with salvation history, in the tradition of Hegelian dialectic. Luke's two-volume literary work, Luke-Acts, according to Käsemann, narrates a smooth development from the life of Jesus, through Pentecost, and on to the Gentile mission, leaving Judaism behind. Thus, church order replaces the original charisma and the near expectation of the kingdom is diminished or abandoned altogether. In Acts, the apostles become the guarantors of the tradition. Peter and Paul show a harmonious mission centered in and emanating out from Jerusalem. The summaries of faith and the sermons in Acts reflect concern for theological order as the institution of the church becomes the center of faith. For Käsemann, Luke-Acts should be characterized as "early catholicism," in the sense that it no longer lived in the hope of the imminent *parousia*; thus, it deviates from the gospel of the early Christians.

While Käsemann highlights the theological character of Luke, the rigid chronological development in terms of Hegelian logic (thesis-antithesis-synthesis) is unnecessary to explain Luke-Acts. Certainly Luke wants to show all of Paul's activities as relating to Israel, but then this is what Paul wants as well (see Romans 9–11). Probably a term like "promise-fulfillment" better explains Luke's strategy than Hegelian salvation history. While salvation history is central to Luke, it should be redefined as promise-fulfillment history, rather than as the machine-like Hegelian dialectic projected onto a more complex dynamic of experience and interpretation. It is harder to imagine that Luke cooked up things to cover up problems than to imagine that the early Christians saw things only later that always were present in the tradition. The Christian confession is not that this is God's Plan B, offered now because Plan A failed—as if the Gentile mission is only possible because of Jewish rejection of the gospel. No, the argument is that though bumpy at points, God's plan from the beginning of time included all nations—otherwise God is not one and God is not fair. Promise-fulfillment is a better way to frame things because it keeps the bumpiness of the unfolding developments (i.e., history) and keeps the conviction that this is God's story after all (i.e., theology).

The second history-of-religions scholar to make a significant impact in post-1950 Lukan studies was Hans Conzelmann. What Conzelmann (1982) offered was a literary hypothesis to show how Luke engineered the transition to early catholicism that Käsemann suggested. Using redaction criticism, Conzelmann noted that by comparing Luke with Mark, Luke's distinctive perspective could be determined. For example, he claimed that the redemptive significance of the cross is absent in Luke. Compare the synopsis of the pericope of Jesus's Pronouncement of True Greatness below. Note how Luke (underlined) differs from Mark (italics).

Matthew 20:25–28	Mark 10:42–45	Luke 22:25–27
But Jesus called them to him and said, "You know that the rulers of the Gentiles lord it over them, and their great ones are tyrants over them. It will not be so among you; but whoever wishes to be great among you must be your servant, and whoever wishes to be first among you must be your slave; *just as the Son of Man came not to be served but to serve, and to give his life a ransom for many."*	So Jesus called them and said to them, "You know that among the Gentiles those whom they recognize as their rulers lord it over them, and their great ones are tyrants over them. But it is not so among you; but whoever wishes to become great among you must be your servant, and whoever wishes to be first among you must be slave of all. *For the Son of Man came not to be served but to serve, and to give his life a ransom for many."*	But he said to them, "The kings of the Gentiles lord it over them; and those in authority over them are called benefactors. But not so with you; rather the greatest among you must become like the youngest, and the leader like one who serves. <u>For who is greater, the one who is at the table or the one who serves? Is it not the one at the table? But I am among you as one who serves.</u>

TABLE 4.6 Pronouncement of True Greatness in Synoptic Parallels

In addition, Conzelmann argued that the *parousia* for Luke no longer had present implications, but was projected out into the distant future. All this was to overcome the second generation's embarrassing problem with early Christianity's expectation of an imminent end of the world. In order to deal with the nonfulfillment of that early expectation, Luke recast his sources, eliminating the primitive Christian expectation. In its place, Luke built an elaborate three-stage history-of-salvation framework, spanning his two-volume literary work, Luke-Acts. For Conzelmann, the Third Evangelist wrote to address his community's shock and frustration over "the delay of the *parousia*," coming up with a schema that reshaped the primitive tradition. The three-stage development included Israel's story, Jesus's life and ministry (the center of time), and the church's story. In this scenario, the faith community responded to the delay of the *parousia* by substituting the presence of the Holy Spirit in the life of the church at the third stage and pushing the hoped-for *parousia* to the distant end of time. The result, according to Conzelmann, is the creation of a timeless message where the length of the interim period no longer constituted a problem.

Is there an alternative to this rigid chronological development of Conzelmann? Yes, indeed. The eschatological expectation of the first Christians is more complex than simply a flat-footed literal understanding of the end of time that Conzelmann presumed was so troubling for some early Christians and for the next generation as a whole. Of course a few exceptions, like the Thessalonian congregation, took Paul's end-time language literally, quitting their jobs; but even here Paul corrected their misunderstanding (1 Thess 4:13—5:11; 2 Thess 2:1–12; 3:6–13). These instances function more as the exceptions that prove the rule. According to Caird, that "rule" was this: early Christians "regularly used end-of-the-world language metaphorically to refer to that which they well knew was not the end of the world" (1997:256). Why? Because end-time language was the only vocabulary available to the early Christians, coming as they did from the Jewish apocalyptic two-age worldview. These were the only "pieces on the floor" when at Easter their symbolic map cracked, tumbling to the ground. These end-time language pieces were the only ones available from which to make meaning of their religious experience. While they employed end-time language, they did not mean for it to be understood as they once had understood it. How do we know? Because Jesus shattered their previous understanding of the end. The new age had started, *but* it was not yet in full display. The resurrection had begun, *but* the rest was still to come.

The NT writers and likely Jesus himself regularly used end-time language for things they knew were not yet the "capital-*E*" end. In Mark 13, Jesus tells his disciples that the end is "any day now," so "hurry up and wait," since "all these things need to happen first." Only God knows the final end, not even Jesus does. But Jesus knows that in the gathering storm, the coming destruction of Jerusalem prefigures the end. Why? Because the consequences of not choosing life continually pay wages of death and destruction. Jesus strikingly asserts that some people in that generation will live even to experience its destruction, as in fact was the case some forty years later. Was this the end? No. But in it the character of the end (decision, judgment, accounting, and the like) was prefigured.

Consider again Paul's three-fold exhortation to the Corinthians to "remain as you are" (1 Cor 7:20, 24, 26), since "the appointed time has grown short" (1 Cor 7:29). As we have seen, the reference to time should not be taken as flat-footed literalism (Caird 1997:270–71). For the time to be "short" does not mean there is no time for the engaged couple to marry. Instead it means, do not be tempted to put anything except the kingdom of God at the center of your life. These days are difficult with all sorts of distracting temptations to center life around (e.g., power, prestige, and possessions), each of which can lead to death.

On the one hand, suggesting that Luke used creative genius to overcome the delay of the *parousia* credits Luke too much. It is unlikely he could have cooked up such a divergent story without being challenged by the control of the remaining eyewitnesses. On the other hand, the "delay theory" does not credit Luke enough. He made good use of the only language available in his toolbox in order to carry forward the eyewitness tradition and to articulate his own religious experience with the risen Lord, where the character of the end was already giving shape to the church's present life together. The notion that Christians, out of embarrassment, cooked up an ingenious delay theory to explain Christ's nonreturn is not compelling. N. T. Wright appropriately recommends that "it is time that the old scholars' myth of the 'delay of the *parousia*' was given a decent burial. Metaphorically, of course" (1999:204).

Additionally, Luke's ending of Acts functions much like the ending of Mark, inviting readers to enter the narrative and to bear witness, as Paul did, to what God is doing now, filled with hope for what God will yet do. While Luke's apologetic aim is clear (to write an "orderly account," Luke 1:1; Acts 1:1), this does not mean that Luke gives us early catholicism, in the sense that his account silenced other, opposing Jesus movements. As we have noted, at this early stage (before the third and fourth centuries), it is more reasonable to assume that the early Jesus movements are more alike theologically than different, differing mostly in liturgical formats, community ethics, and leadership styles. These differences flourished in the chaotic period of heterodoxy through the second century, but it is not likely they extended to theological confessions. That would develop later.

Furthermore, contrary to Conzelmann's assessment, Luke does not remove the redemptive significance of Jesus's death (Luke 22:19–20; Acts 20:28). Instead, Luke's primary emphasis is to show how Jesus's death is aligned with God's ultimate purpose of forwarding the creation project. Moreover, the early church's eschatological summons to decision is not replaced by ethics. Instead, it is the Jesus community's advocacy for the least, the last, and the left out that announces God's eschatological rule. It would be incorrect to characterize Luke's theology as an ingenious invention or early catholicism. While distinctive, Luke's testimony remains in agreement with the central NT proclamation.

Turning to the structure of Luke's theological statement, we see a carefully constructed two-volume framework introduced with a prologue: "Since many have undertaken to set down an orderly account of the events that have been fulfilled among us, just as they were handed on to us by those who from the beginning were eye-witnesses and servants of the word, I too decided, after investigating everything carefully from the very first, to write an orderly account for you most excellent Theophilus, so that you may know the truth concerning the things about which you have been instructed" (Luke 1:1–4).

In the prologue, Luke refers to existing documents as well as the eyewitness testimony of the Jesus tradition that he has at his disposal for his own narrative project. Two features of his project stand out in Luke's purpose statement: (1) it will be based on a thorough examination of the Jesus tradition; and (2) it will be an "orderly account," emphasizing the succession of events that carry the ministry of Jesus from its earliest beginnings all the way to Rome. Like Matthew, Luke narrates the story of Jesus, editing and interpreting his sources from the vantage point of his community sometime between the 70s and the 90s CE.

Luke's gospel is broader in scope than are Mark's and Matthew's, situating Jesus within Israel's story, reaching all the way back to Adam (Luke 3:38) and all the way forward to the center of world power, namely, Rome (Acts 28:30–31). The metaphor that best describes the structure of Luke's theology is journey. The story of the life and ministry of Jesus in Luke's first volume (the Third Gospel) is largely a story of Jesus's journey to Jerusalem, from the edge of Judaism to its center. The first volume is divided into two parts: (1) Jesus's ministry in Galilee and departure on the journey to Jerusalem (1:1—9:51), and (2) the journey to Jerusalem with its temple as the center of Israel, the locus of power that Jesus must confront with his claims and reform message (9:51—24:53). By casting the ministry of Jesus in the form of a journey to Jerusalem, Luke brings into focus his theme that in Jesus, God is offering salvation to Israel, inviting Israel to reclaim its divine mandate.

The story of the church in volume 2 (Acts of the Apostles) is also cast in the form of a journey narrative: this time from Jerusalem to Rome, from the center of Judaism to the center of the Gentile nations. Again the story is divided into two parts: (1) the journey from Jerusalem to Antioch with the focus on Peter (1:1—12:25); and (2) the journey from Antioch to Rome, with the focus on Paul (13:1—28:31). In addition, two outpourings of the Holy Spirit occur—one Jewish and one Gentile. In Acts 2:4-11, the Jewish pilgrims who gather for Pentecost in Jerusalem are filled with the Holy Spirit and hear testimony of God's mighty acts of power in their own languages, as though the story of the tower of Babel is reversed (Gen 11:1-9). Then in Acts 10:44-48, the Gentiles who gather at Cornelius's home in Caesarea are also filled with the Holy Spirit, bearing testimony to God's mighty acts of power. These Gentiles are baptized into the body of the risen Lord Jesus. In both cases, Peter plays the decisive role. He is the instrument of God used to inaugurate the mission to the Jews and to the Gentiles, ensuring continuity between Peter's mission to the Jews and Paul's Gentile mission, which ultimately leads to Rome.

Besides employing the metaphor of journey as its framework, Luke's narrative puts the accent not on the heroic deeds of individuals but on the mighty acts of God seen in Jesus's ministry, which are linked to the movement of the Holy Spirit. The role of God's Holy Spirit is prominent in the entire story. Compare the frequency of references to the Holy Spirit in the writings of the four Evangelists: Mark (6 times), Matthew (12 times), John (14 times), but Luke (74 times: the Gospel of Luke—17 times, Acts—57 times). In Luke-Acts, all the key events in the narrative are initiated by the Holy Spirit: Jesus's birth (Luke 1:35), baptism (3:22), testing (4:1), departure to Jerusalem (10:21), disciples' commission (Acts 1:8); then the Jewish Pentecost (2:4), Peter's facing Jerusalem rulers (4:8), the selection of deacons (6:5), the call of Paul (9:17), the Gentile Pentecost (10:44), and the Jerusalem Council (15:28). Thus, it is the Spirit of God that initiates and empowers new developments in salvation history. God's faithfulness can be discerned even through the opaque events of history. Luke's point: God can be trusted to complete the salvation/creation enterprise.

The center of Luke's theology is salvation history—not in the Hegelian sense but in the theological sense of tracing the unfolding of God's purpose through time. Luke's salvation history is of promise and fulfillment. So when Luke speaks at the podium during our conference of NT writers, this is his vision statement: *It is the Spirit that initiates and empowers new developments in salvation history, all in accordance with God's plan. In this way, the eschatological promises of God are fulfilled in Jesus as the Spirit of the living Lord continues through the history of the church in two periods: (1) the time of the mission to the Jews; and (2) the time of the mission to the Gentiles, which is never disconnected from Israel.*

THEMATIC IMPLICATIONS OF LUKE'S VISION

Three themes can be traced from the Third Evangelist's vision statement. First, God's salvation extends to the poor, the marginalized, and the oppressed. Jesus saves people who recognize that they are lost within oppressive and deceitful systems of materialism, elitism, and exploitation. Luke defines the starting point of Jesus's ministry as his position toward the poor and the rich. Consider Mary's Magnificat (Luke 1:46–55). Jesus and the salvation he represents are introduced by Mary with a prayer/song drawn from Hannah's prayer (1 Sam 2:1–10), declaring the mighty acts of God's salvation: "He has brought down the powerful from their thrones, and lifted up the lowly; he has filled the hungry with good things, and sent the rich away empty" (Luke 1:52–53). The Magnificat announces that Jesus is launching God's salvation with revolutionary implications both socially and materially.

Luke's summons to abandon allegiance to materialism is seen by his rendering of the First Beatitude: "Blessed are you who are poor, for yours is the kingdom of God" (6:20). (He also includes a woe against the rich (6:24), which is found only in Luke.) Compare this to Matthew's rendering of the Jesus tradition: "Blessed are the poor *in spirit,* for yours is the kingdom of God" (Matt 5:20). Quite plainly, for Luke, sin is characterized not so much by failure in relation to Torah, as in Matthew and Mark, but by failing to rightly regard material possessions: Zacchaeus, the chief tax collector, gains wealth by fraud (19:8), the Prodigal Son squanders his father's property (15:13, 30), Ananias and Sapphira misrepresent the proceeds from the land sale (Acts 5:3). All ran from God, choosing to give primary allegiance to material possessions.

Jesus is the Savior of people who begin to recognize their lost condition, aligned as they are to systemic powers that do not deliver on their promises. Jesus effects a change in social relationships and in the people to God, as people participate in a shared life together (Acts 2:42–47; 4:32–35). Jesus ushers in a new relationship to God and also a new social reality. The new social situation frees people to place at the disposal of fellow Christians what is economically needed for the community to function better.

Second, Jesus's death is part of God's characteristic way of reversing things for the least, the lost, and left out, in order to bring about wholeness in relationships. In this way, Luke's atonement imagery functions differently from Paul's and Mark's, adding another voice to the NT choir interpreting Easter. If Paul prefers the battlefield imagery of victory over the power of sin (1 Cor 15:56; Col 2:15), and Mark uses commercial imagery of redemption and ransom (Mark 10:45), Luke uses relational imagery of friendship obligation to describe atonement.

While Luke mentions the atoning significance of Jesus's death twice (Luke 22:19; Acts 20:28), his preferred way to speak of the cross is not focused narrowly on the death of Jesus. For Luke it is the quality of Jesus's life of service for others, which is held up as a characterization of God. Jesus's life represents exactly what God is all about; Jesus's death belongs to the plan of God, not in a morbid sense of satisfying God's desire for blood or in a fatalistic sense of playing the pawn on God's global chessboard. No, Jesus's death belongs to the plan of God because it demonstrates the sacrificial love he shares with God for creation. Twice Luke cites the Isaiah 53 servant text (Luke 22:37; Acts 8:32–33), highlighting the relational self-obligation that characterizes Yahweh's servant of salvation. At the Last Supper Jesus says, "For I tell you, this scripture must be fulfilled in me, 'And he was counted among the lawless'; and indeed what is written about me is being fulfilled" (Luke 22:37). Only Luke employs this saying in his gospel.

The same "necessity" or "obligation" language characterizes the risen Lord's explanation of the events that trouble the disciples walking to Emmaus after Easter. Jesus says, "'Was it not necessary that the Messiah should suffer these things and then enter into his glory?' Then beginning with Moses and all the prophets, he interpreted to them the things about himself in all the scriptures" (Luke 24:26–27). For Luke, the death of Jesus was *necessary*—not to solve God's problem or to pay for human sin—but to demonstrate the lengths to which God will go to fulfill the relational self-obligation to reach those so lost under the power of sin that they could not find their way back home.

Third, the church of Jews and Gentiles is continuous with Israel in fulfillment of God's promise and purpose for the world. From Jesus's inaugural sermon in Nazareth (Luke 4:16–30) at the beginning of Luke's first volume to the proclamation of Paul before the Jews in Rome (Acts 28.17–28) at the end of Luke's second volume, the foundational principle is the same: God's salvation project begins with the Jews and then extends out to include the Gentiles, thus to all nations. Luke pictures the church as growing in historical continuity with all those in Israel who, like Simeon, were "looking for the consolation of Israel" (Luke 2:25).

Luke aims to shape the church's self-understanding for two reasons. First, for its own internal discussions, the church must see itself as part of God's people Israel. Since God can be trusted to keep the ancient covenantal promises to Israel, Luke's Gentile readers can be assured that God will not abandon them, as they now have come to be identified with that same people of God. In fact, Luke sees the church as helping to restore to Israel its authentic character. The election of Matthias completes the twelve tribes of Israel (Acts 1:15–26; Luke 22:29–30). Israel's ancient mandate to be a blessing to all nations (Gen 12:1–3) is made possible as Babel is reversed at Pentecost, when people from many nations hear in their own languages the mighty acts of God's salvation (Acts 2:1–11). The legitimacy of the inclusion of Gentiles within Israel's messianic community comes to a head in Peter's interaction with Cornelius and his household. "Can anyone withhold the water for baptizing these people who have received the Holy Spirit just as we have" (Acts 10:47)?

Luke takes special interest in the Jerusalem Council (Acts 15:6–29), because it clears the way for Paul and his associates to concentrate their missionary work among the Gentiles, without burdening the new converts with Jewish ethnic practices of circumcision and the observance of ritual-purity and diet laws. Only the basic and well-known covenantal norms of Israel transfer to these new converts to the restored Israel: prohibitions against idolatry and sexual immorality (Acts 15:19-21, 29; see 1 Cor 5:1-13; 10:23-33). For all those involved, this was self-evident. Even when Paul describes the meeting in his own words, he says the Jewish leaders added "nothing" to his mission except that which was already well known (Gal 2:6, 10). Finally, while Luke's presentation of Paul softens some of the tension between Peter and Paul (Gal 2:11-14), the Paul of Acts is a faithful representation of what is known from Paul's own writings: namely, that he never saw his mission apart from God's concern for Israel (Romans 9-11).

The second reason Luke hopes to shape the church's self-understanding is for its own ongoing life in the Greco-Roman world. For Luke, the church must see itself as part of God's missional people Israel. Perhaps Luke was also involved in correcting misconceptions about Christianity that were circulating in the Roman world, as the prologues to Luke and Acts show. Luke seems intent on demonstrating that Christianity is not "a new and mischievous superstition" (Suetonius *Nero* 16) but part of the ancient Israelite faith that championed the best interests of all nations. In this regard, the church ought not to be a threat to "good" government (see Rom 13:3) but to offer a constructive critique and an alternative to oppressive empires in all their manifestations (which may well be interpreted as a threat to those in power). The church's pedigree was ancient and well known. Given the church's presence as a reform movement within Israel, Luke's recipient, "Theophilus" (which means "friend of God" or "beloved by God") should know the truth of the church's origins and aspirations (Luke 1:1, Acts 1:1).

In order to demonstrate its antiquity, Luke is careful to tie all the significant moments of the growth of the Jesus movement to Jerusalem. Jerusalem is mentioned more often and with greater emphasis in Luke-Acts than in any other NT gospel: Mark (11 times), Matthew (13 times, John (13 times), Luke-Acts: 90 times—Luke, 31 times and Acts, 59 times). Jerusalem is the goal of Jesus's earthly life and the starting point for the emergence of the church. Luke is the only Evangelist to have Jesus say, "I must be on my way, because it is impossible for a prophet to be killed outside of Jerusalem" (Luke 13:33). Luke insists that after Jesus's departure, the disciples are to remain in Jerusalem in order to receive the Spirit in that city (Luke 24:49; Acts 1:4). This is unlike Mark, who sends them to Galilee (Mark 16:7). Luke restricts the Easter appearances to the region in and around Jerusalem (Luke 24:13, 18, 33, 52), unlike Matthew who also includes Galilee (Matt 28:16). Luke is careful to underline that the missionary outreach to the world must be carried out from Jerusalem (Luke 24:47; Acts 1:8), so that the church grows outward from Jerusalem in a concentric way.

Each newly founded community establishes ecclesiastical fellowship with the church in Jerusalem (Acts 8:14-25; 11:22; 12:25; 13:13; 16:4), and each of Paul's missionary campaigns around the Mediterranean world begins with a synagogue visit—at Cyprus (13:5), at Pisidia (13:14), at Iconium (14:1), at Thessalonica (17:1), at Beroea (17:10), at Corinth (18:4), at Ephesus (18:19), and at Rome (28:17). Why? Because Luke wants readers to be aware that the mission of the church is intimately connected to God's concern for Israel and for Israel's mission. Some of Paul's final words in Acts are, "It is for the sake of the hope of Israel that I am bound with this chain" (28:20). In this way, the church of Jews and Gentiles is continuous with Israel in fulfillment of God's promises.

From the three Synoptic Gospels, we turn our attention in the next chapter to a set of writings sometimes called the Johannine traditions.

EXERCISES

1. Read the noncanonical gospels usually dated to the second century but before 130 CE: *The Gospel of Thomas*, *The Gospel of Peter*, *The Infancy Gospel of Thomas*, *The Secret Gospel of Mark*, *Papyrus Egerton 2: The Unknown Gospel*, *The Gospel of the Ebionites*, *The Gospel of the Nazarenes*, and *The Gospel according to the Hebrews*. These can be found on the Internet or in Bart Ehrman's reader, *The New Testament and Other Early Christian Writings: A Reader*.

   Compare and contrast the noncanonical gospels with the canonical Gospels. What observations can you make?

2. Secure a copy of a gospel synopsis like the one edited by Burton H. Throckmorton, *Gospel Parallels: A Comparison of the Synoptic Gospels*.

   Select several pericopae and compare the ways that each Evangelist arranges the Jesus tradition. What observations can you make about the rhetorical strategies adopted by Matthew, Mark, and Luke?

3. Some years ago *Newsweek* (December 13, 2004) did a feature on Jesus's birth. It generated some controversy, and a friend of mine asked me for a response. I wrote him a letter trying to draw out the significance of the gospel genre for interpretation. Below is a copy of my letter.

Discuss the topics raised by the letter: genre, history, literature, interpretation, and so on. What areas of further exploration are raised for you?

Christmas 2004

Dear _____:

Thanks for the engaging conversation after church. I've thought some more about your question and the recent article on the birth of Jesus (*Newsweek*, December 13, 2004). Much like the differences we discussed in the narration of the crucifixion in John's Gospel and in the Synoptic Gospels, the key is to recognize the genre. While the differences may not be possible to reconcile historically, they certainly can be understood theologically as compatible.

Anyway, I'm of the opinion that the literary genre controls the kinds of questions one can ask of a biblical text (at least if you hope to get an answer!). A literary text is quite different than a documentary text in terms of yielding answers to historical questions. Documentary texts, like Paul's letters to churches, more readily yield a profile of the occasion and concerns shared by Paul and his readers. Literary texts (like the 4 Gospels—and the bulk of the Bible!), while they do yield some answers to historical questions, are simply not as transparent. And this is how it ought to be since their genre (as literary) means that they are interested in referring to historical events with an eye to persuasion, formation, and signification.

This means we should expect some creativity on the parts of these literary authors—not misleading creativity, but creativity that would admittedly still disqualify them as reporters for the *New York Times*. Then again, they were never trying to write that kind of biography of Jesus. They were interested in relating the significance of Jesus in what might, by our standards, be best termed a "stylized biography."

Here is what we find then in the two birth narratives of Jesus that we have in the NT.

Points of agreement: Jesus' mother was not married, only betrothed to Joseph; Jesus' conception was miraculous; Jesus was born in Bethlehem; Jesus grew up in Nazareth.

Points of disagreement: John the Baptist plays a role in Luke that is not in Matthew; Jesus is visited by shepherds in Luke and Magi in Matthew; Herod slaughters the children only in Matthew; the family flees to Egypt only in Matthew; Luke speaks of a temple presentation before Simeon and Anna.

There are two points that are difficult (impossible?) to reconcile between these two narratives: (1) the travel between Nazareth and Bethlehem, and (2) the genealogy of Jesus in Matthew and Luke.

Consider the problem regarding the travel between Nazareth and Bethlehem. In Luke, Joseph and Mary reside in Nazareth (Luke 2:4) and apparently only go to Bethlehem because of a census, after which they return to Nazareth in Galilee (Luke 2:39). In Matthew, Joseph and Mary seem already to reside in Bethlehem (Matt 2:1), because only after they flee to Egypt to escape Herod, do they move their home to Nazareth in Galilee, when Herod dies (Matt 2:19, 23).

While both have Jesus born in Bethlehem, some questions are raised as to how the family gets there and then to Nazareth. Take Luke: there is some external evidence of a census when Quirinius was governor in the year 6 C.E., but it was only in Judea and not during Herod's rule (Herod died in 4 B.C.E.). It is possible that Luke had some of this information and used it to get the family from Nazareth to Bethlehem and back to Nazareth.

Then consider Matthew: Herod is known through external evidence (like Josephus) to have been a ruthless man. Apparently, he killed many people—even his wife and two of his sons! However, Josephus does not mention a mass killing of children. It is possible that Matthew modeled his narrative on the story of Moses where the biblical story narrates a story of infant slaughter (Exod 1:15–22). Matthew may well have used the horrific persona of Herod to get the family from Bethlehem to Egypt and then to Nazareth.

Now, is this shoddy history? No. It is "stylized biography" or "biography plus." The two Gospel writers knew two things: (1) Jesus was from Nazareth and (2) he was the fulfillment of Israel's hope—and therefore of the house of David and born in David's city (Bethlehem). To put these two "facts" together, Luke chose to use "history" (census) and Matthew chose to use "prophecy" (OT texts) to locate Jesus' birth in Bethlehem.

By the way, I'm assuming that the Gospel writers, who are anonymous (but whom we traditionally call "Matthew" and "Luke"), are not themselves eyewitnesses, but the framers of the eyewitness tradition. They could well be Gentile converts to Christianity, fixing in a literary gospel form (*ca.* 70–85) the "nuggets" of Jesus stories that have been circulating orally, preserved by the eyewitnesses to Jesus' life and teaching.

Back to my argument. The modern biographer might ask the question, who got it right? Matthew or Luke? However, this may not be the kind of question that a literary text like the birth narratives can answer to the satisfaction of the contemporary historian.

Instead, the gospel genre yields more satisfactory answers when the questions posed to Matthew and Luke are about significance and meaning. For example, Matthew is intent on showing that Jesus is indeed the fulfillment of biblical prophecy. He works hard to show that this obscure birth has everything to do with God's salvation plans (there is a miraculous conception—see Isa 7:14; there is the slaughter of the innocent—see Jer 31:15; there is a flight to Egypt—see Hos 11:1; there are kings from the nations bearing gifts and even a guiding star—see Isa 60:1-6). And so, Matthew uses these biblical texts to cast the birth of Jesus. Now consider Luke. He focuses much more on the human drama to cast his narration of the coming of Jesus. He traces the stories of Zechariah and Elizabeth, Joseph and Mary, Simeon and Anna, as they each reflect on the birth of Jesus who is destined to be the hope of Israel and more properly, the hope of the whole world!

So, while it is virtually impossible to harmonize the two narratives without doing some violence to either Matthew's or Luke's version, the two stories are often woven together (conflated) in a composite as is evident in any Sunday School Christmas Eve pageant (or any nativity scene on Christmas Tree Lane). And this is okay because both Matthew and Luke share a number of convictions that make the conflation work, if the aim is significance and meaning. Both are in absolute agreement regarding the significance of Jesus—he is the promised savior, the Son of David, the Messiah. Both are absolutely sure of Jesus' identity as the Son of God and of his role in fulfilling the hopes and destiny of Israel. Thus, they used the "information" provided by their sources, including the Hebrew scriptures, to tell the birth of Israel's Messiah in ways that suited their aims.

So, who got it right? I would say both did—if we pay attention to the Gospel writers' aims and read their literary works as persuasive texts geared to proclaim the good news of Jesus' birth.

By the way, a similar argument can be made regarding the genealogies of Jesus in Matthew and in Luke. They are irreconcilable. Even though some harmonizers suggest that one is Mary's and the other is Joseph's, there is no evidence for this solution. I would rather suggest that they can be "reconciled" in terms of significance, if you appreciate the goal both have for situating Jesus in Israel's salvation history. Matthew aims to show Jesus' genealogical link to Abraham and David (given Matthew's concern for Jesus' royal descent), while Luke wants to show Jesus' lineage all the way to Adam (given Luke's concern for Jesus' role in reconciling all humanity and the whole world).

I would not call this creative fantasy. It is accurate (but probably not in the modern sense of the word). However, it is accurate in the ancient Near-Eastern sense where primary attention is given to persuasive speech, homiletical impact, significance, and transformation of behavior.

By the way, the birth narratives are probably the one place in Matthew and Luke where such creativity can be seen most clearly. The rest of the gospel material in Matthew and Luke is remarkably "conservative" in that both seem to stick very closely to their written sources without modifying them greatly.

At any rate, I hope this helps understand those *Newsweek* articles somewhat. They are likely only focusing on accuracy in the modern sense. While this is valid, it is not the whole story. I find it more helpful to consider the aims and purposes of the authors of these birth narratives and withhold quick judgments as to their falsehood.

If you would like to read more about these birth narratives (and see where I got most of this information), see E. P. Sanders's very helpful little book called, the *Historical Figure of Jesus*. The Hiebert Library has a copy. I use it with my advanced students.

Merry Christmas,
Jon Isaak

TABLE 4.7 Letter to a Friend in Response to the Christmas Article in *Newsweek*

5

The Theological Contribution of the Johannine Traditions

THE JOHANNINE TRADITIONS INCLUDE five NT writings composed in three distinct genres—a gospel narrative (the Gospel according to John), three letters of exhortation (1–3 John), and an apocalyptic writing (the book of Revelation). Traditionally, these writings have been held together by a common attribution to John, one of the sons of Zebedee (as author of the Fourth Gospel), later assumed also to be known as "the elder" (as author of the three letters) and "John, the seer" (as author of Revelation). While the connection is not uncontested, from the end of the second century, most church theologians like Irenaeus, Papias, and Clement made the link between John, the elder/seer *and* John, Jesus's disciple, the son of Zebedee. In this way, all five texts were tied to the Apostle John (Kümmel 1975:244, 451, 470).

This chapter has two objectives: (1) to clarify the distinctive character of the Johannine traditions; and (2) to outline the theological vision of the Fourth Gospel, the Letters, and the Revelation, including the current debate, the structure, the articulation, and the thematic implications of the central vision that each one puts forward.

SORTING OUT THE JOHANNINE TRADITIONS

Although the traditional attribution of these five writings to the apostle John is not impossible, the assertion rests only on inference. We do not know whether the tradition, on which Irenaeus and others rely, goes all the way back to the original recipients. If the Fourth Gospel had been written by the apostle, it is difficult to understand why this information did not surface earlier. Why was it not passed along? Since there is no prior evidence, however, the link holding together the Gospel, the Letters, and Revelation as compositions of John, the son of Zebedee, must remain uncertain.

Complicating the picture of the original setting of the Johannine traditions are two realities that pull in opposite directions. First, the great linguistic and stylistic differences between Revelation and the Fourth Gospel and the Letters raised for some early Christian readers (e.g., Dionysius of Alexandria, Eusebius) the probability of different authors. With respect to the Fourth Gospel, the ease with which its terms of reference were taken up in service of gnostic spirituality raised serious questions about its apostolic origin. The Valentinian gnostic Heracleon is credited with writing the first commentary on the Fourth Gospel (ca. 170). In addition, the Fourth Gospel's deviation from the Synoptic tradition raised doubts about its apostolic origin for some heresiologists (e.g., Caius, Epiphanus). With respect to Revelation, the grammatical problems within the work itself conspired to pull it away from any other NT writings (how could such grammatical problems have slipped through?), further weakening the link holding together the Johannine traditions and delaying Revelation's canonical ratification (Kümmel 1975:465).

Second, the third and fourth centuries saw increased pressure to tie useful Christian texts to apostles in order to ratify these existing texts as authoritative for Christian teaching; it is possible that this pressure may have caused the leading bishops and theologians to stretch these associations. After almost a hundred years of circulating, collecting, copying, and editing these literary texts without concern for precise details of their originating situation, now they were pressed to yield information as to their provenance. Such information could never be more than ambiguous, given the literary character of the Johannine writings (as opposed to the occasional and documentary character of Paul's letters). Nevertheless, such pressure worked to pull the Johannine traditions together, sometimes forcing or stretching the notion of apostolic association, in order to meet the new demand.

In any case, by the end of the fourth century, enough clues (e.g., the beloved disciple, the elder, John) had been found in the five texts themselves to complement the late second-century testimony of Papias, Irenaeus, and Clement and to assure most early Christian theologians and bishops that these texts could be linked to John, the disciple of Jesus, the son of Zebedee. Athanasius's Thirty-Ninth Easter festival letter (367 CE) listed all five texts as officially apostolic and canonical. As noted above, it is unlikely that this conclusion rests on reliable information, as it has more to do with finally arriving at a compelling-enough rationale for an earlier conclusion that found these writings so useful to the early church (Kümmel 1975:472).

The apostolic attribution of these five writings remained largely in place until the Reformation when Luther and others challenged again the linkage that tied the Johannine traditions to the same author, the Apostle John. Since the Reformation many scholars have continued to find the stylistic and content differences between Revelation and the Fourth Gospel too large to be accounted for simply by the different genres being employed; these differences are enough for some to rule out authorship by the same person. Nevertheless, many remain convinced that the Letters and the Fourth Gospel are authored by the same person.

It may well be that Papias's reference to "the elder John," "disciple of the Lord," "writing from Ephesus" (in Eusebius, *Eccl. Hist.* 3.39.3) is another John (not one of the twelve) who was part of a circle of elders in Ephesus (Asia Minor) charged with guarding and bearing witness to the apostolic tradition (Kümmel 1975:243, 451). If so, this could tie the traditions loosely together around a John who was not one of the twelve, but was one who interpreted a set of circulating apostolic Jesus traditions, a person known as "the elder" and/or "John, the seer," and who addressed an apocalypse to various Christian communities around Ephesus in Asia Minor (Revelation).

While the arguments regarding the authorship of or the relationship between these five writings is unlikely to be resolved definitively, still good reasons remain to continue grouping these distinct writings together as a collection, the Johannine traditions. Why? Simply because these distinct traditions have more in common with one another than with any other NT texts (Johnson 1999:522). They share a symbolic world. The Fourth Gospel narrates the story of Jesus using symbols that distinguish it from the Synoptic tradition. The Johannine letters employ a similar symbolic world that enables the church to differentiate between true and false representations of Jesus. Revelation uses related apocalyptic symbols to give witness to the victory of Jesus in the presence of opposition from the powers that remain rebellious. It is this symbolic world that holds these traditions together. There are stark symbols of good vs. evil, light vs. darkness, truth vs. falsehood, life vs. death, and us vs. them. Readers of the traditions in this collection are confronted with the necessity to make a decision for life or for death, regardless of the historical and cosmic conflicts that present themselves: Whose side are you on? According to Johnson, "In the Gospel, allegiance to [Jesus] demands separation from the synagogue but also invites identity as his friend. In Revelation, true witness to Jesus against falsehood and idolatry continues his witness to the truth, leading, perhaps, to a death like his. In the letters, the community divides precisely over proper understanding of Jesus" (1999:523).

All five writings are literary constructions, not occasional letters. While the church found them useful from the start, as already noted, the lack of situational details made their ratification as canonical Scripture more challenging in the increased tension between the various Christianities of the third and fourth centuries. Although the details of the community setting from which these five literary texts emerge are not transparent, all three genres appear to draw on traditions developed in the cut and thrust of real community life in search of self-understanding. For some scholars the allure of reconstructing these originating communities is too much to resist. Some read the Johannine traditions with "archeological" aims of discerning the shape of the community that generated these rich literary texts (e.g., Martyn 1979; Brown 1979). This is a hazardous enterprise without corroborating external evidence, given the character of literary text intent on shaping an audience rather than on documenting in an unambiguous manner their originating situation (Isaak 2002).

What is clear is that in the Johannine traditions we have five texts that share an incredibly rich fund of symbols employed by skilled literary artists (poets, preachers, and prophets). Each author interacts interpretively with the implications of the risen Lord and the memories of Jesus circulating within their communities. Their conviction is that Jesus is the living Lord of the church. The interplay between the experience of Jesus and interpretation of his significance, expressed in these three literary genres, creates a space of tension, conflict, and understanding.

It is a space that the early church and successive generations found particularly fertile for their own theological reflection, construction, and self-understanding. As Johnson helpfully notes:

> In no other NT writings do we find the ideal of peace, unity, and love so clearly expressed, and yet so evidently at odds with the community's own experiences. All of these writings make a sharp distinction between insider and outsider. In the Gospel, the historical conflict between the Jews and Jesus represents the continuing conflict between the world and Jesus' "friends." In the letters, the issue of who is an insider and who is not tragically spells out the division *within* the community, as different parties claim exclusive rights to the truth. And in Revelation, the battlefront is double: there is hostility and persecution from the world outside, as well as division and corruption from within. (1999:523)

It is to the five writings of the Johannine traditions that we now turn our attention. Leaving aside whether one author, two authors, or three authors are making their way to the podium, we are interested in hearing the three distinct genres (the Fourth Gospel, the Letters, and Revelation) within the collection of Johannine traditions state their theological vision and contribution to the NT conference.

THE FOURTH GOSPEL'S THEOLOGICAL VISION

We begin with the debate on the Fourth Gospel's theological center, especially as its voice compares with the Synoptic voices. Like the Synoptic Gospels, the Fourth Gospel is anonymous, although commonly associated in some way with the testimony of the Apostle John, as noted above. John is a gospel narrative in that it also follows the pattern of the gospel genre established by Mark: an introductory section focusing on Jesus's life and ministry, followed by a narration of Jesus's final week that culminates in the crucifixion and resurrection appearances. However, it is immediately obvious to any careful reader that John is quite different from the three Synoptic Gospels. While John follows the gospel genre for framing and elaborating on the circulating Jesus traditions, it is not clear that John has read the Synoptics. The differences are simply so great between them.

From early on, however, John's unique voice was recognized as a valued member of the gospel quartet. Second-century theologian

Clement called John the "spiritual Gospel," which aimed to "supplement" the Synoptic witness: "But, last of all, John, perceiving that the external facts had been made plain in the Gospel, being urged by his friends, and inspired by the Spirit, composed a spiritual Gospel" (in Eusebius *Eccl. Hist.* 6.14.7; 3.24.7–13). The organizers and shapers of the canonical witness inserted John between Luke's Gospel and Luke's Acts, so that John could function to fill out the theological significance of the Synoptics before leaving the Gospels and moving on to the Acts of the Apostles. Thus, most consider the composition of John to be later than the Synoptic Gospels, usually 90–100 CE (Kümmel 1975:246).

The genius of the gospel genre was that it capitalized on the popular story format to interpret the ongoing significance of Jesus's ministry and the reality of the risen Lord. The extended discourses of Jesus in the Fourth Gospel (e.g., the "I am" sayings, the Bread of Life Discourse in chapter 6, the Temple Discourse in chapters 7 and 8, the Farewell Discourse in chapters 13–17), the signs that reveal deeper truth (e.g., "living water," "bread of life"), the conflict with and separation from the synagogue (9:22) all worked to move theological reflection beyond that of the Synoptic Gospels. In this way, John became extremely popular among proto- or emerging orthodox communities in their ongoing quest for self-understanding and differentiation from competing visions of the Christian life.

Ironically, the themes and terms of reference in the Fourth Gospel were found to be equally compatible and useful for all sorts of diverse Christian groups. The best example of this is the second-century Valentinian gnostic named Heracleon, who wrote the first commentary on John (ca. 170 CE). Evidently, the themes of spirit vs. flesh, light vs. darkness, second birth, signs, mystery, Jesus's being misunderstood by others in the mainstream, and so on could all be exploited for his conception of spirituality. Such developments reinforce our growing understanding of the heterodox character of Christianity in the second century. Without resources, structures, networks, and unified teaching, there really was no choice but to tolerate a wide range of teaching during this early period (Wisse 1986:184). In addition, the gnostic appropriation of the Fourth Gospel testifies to the abiding ingenuity and creativity of religious writers in general, who have always, for better or worse, been able to make use of a wide variety of spiritual texts in order to promote their particular theological aims.

While there was much appreciation for the theological sophistication of John, its deviation from the Synoptic traditions did slow its canonical ratification in the minds of some, as noted earlier. There is simply no way to get around the fact that while John appears in the NT alongside the other three Synoptic Gospels, it is quite different from them. What are some of these differences? John opens with a cosmic setting ("in the beginning was the Word"), not with an infancy narrative as in Matthew and Luke. There are also differences of language. Several common words or phrases carry much more theological freight in John than they do in the Synoptics (e.g., "life," "light," "darkness," "true," "world," "knowing," "seeing," "the Jews," "I am"). John also presents differences in chronology from the Synoptics. The Synoptics refer to only one Passover celebration during Jesus's ministry, while John refers to three Passover celebrations (2:13; 6:4; 12:12), suggesting a ministry of over two years. The Synoptics place Jesus's temple disturbance at the *end* of his ministry to mark the height of his challenge to the religious establishment, while John places the incident at the *beginning* of his ministry to signal the character of Jesus's resistance movement from the start.

In the Synoptics, Jesus concentrates his ministry in Galilee, going to Jerusalem only at the end. In John, Jesus's focus is more on Judea, with repeated trips to Jerusalem for feasts and festivals (2:13; 5:1; 7:10; 12:12). Yet when Jesus comes to Jerusalem in John, it is to contend and argue with his opponents, "the Jews," and then to retreat to Galilee where he is more secure. "The Jews" in Jerusalem are at odds with Jesus almost from the beginning of the Fourth Gospel, and John offers clear indications that the conflict will lead to Jesus's death (2:13–22).

The portrait of Jesus in John is also different from the picture in the Synoptics. Whereas Jesus is a speaker of brief, pithy sayings and parables in the Synoptics, he is known for long discourses, speeches, and prayers in John. Several stories of Jesus's ministry are found only in John: the wedding in Cana (2:1–11), the conversation with Nicodemus (3:1–21), the encounter with the Samaritan woman (4:1–42), the raising of Lazarus (11:1–57), the washing of the disciples' feet (13:1–38), to name only a few. Some Synoptic stories are not found in John: the baptism of Jesus by John the Baptist, the testing in the wilderness, Peter's confession at Caesarea Philippi, the transfiguration, the struggle in Gethsemane, the institution of the Lord's Supper, and the cry of dereliction from the cross.

Of note is the way that John's gospel offers readers repeated clues from the start, acknowledging that greater insight into each incident of Jesus's ministry comes through the resurrection (2:17–22; 12:16; 14:25; 20:9). In this way, according to Johnson, "John is free to collapse the distance between the story of Jesus and the story of the church . . . the reality of the *now* permeates the narration of the *then* in much more explicit and conscious ways than was possible in the Synoptics" (1999:530). An example of the collapsed distance is the way that the controversy caused by Jesus's healing of the man born blind presupposes a later reality: "The Jews had already agreed that anyone who confessed Jesus to be the Messiah would be put out of the synagogue" (9:22). This situation reflects the strained nature of the Johannine community's relation with emerging rabbinic Judaism, which came to a head ca. 85 CE with the formal composition of the *birkat ha-minim* (the "benedictions against heretics"). The revised eighteenth benediction effectively banned Jewish Christians from the synagogue. In John, the *now* and the *then* are woven together in a seamless and inseparable narrative, where ongoing significance always moves to the center stage of the Gospel's drama.

Probably nothing illustrates the literary character of the Synoptic Gospels and especially the Fourth Gospel better than a comparison of how each narrates the timing of Jesus's crucifixion. In John, Jesus is crucified on the day of Preparation *before* the start of Passover (John 19:14–18), when the Passover lamb is typically slaughtered. The last meal then is not a Passover meal at all, but an occasion to talk about and to demonstrate true service: Jesus washes the disciples' feet (John 13:1–11). Later that service is demonstrated most clearly in that Jesus himself becomes the lamb shared at the Passover meal, as he is "the Lamb of God who takes away the sin of the world" (John 1:29). Jesus does not eat the Passover; he *is* the Passover! In the Synoptics (Mark 14:12–25), the disciples are instructed to prepare the Passover, and Jesus shares the meal with them after sunset when Passover begins. For the Synoptics, the Passover meal signals the significance of the crucifixion that will take place the *following* afternoon at the end of Passover.

How do these chronologies work, and what do we make of them? Let's go step by step. In John, Jesus is arrested and brought for questioning before two Jewish leaders, Annas and high priest, Caiaphas; and then he is taken to Pilate for trial early in the morning on the day before the

Passover (John 18:28). After the trial, Jesus is handed over to be crucified at noon, finally dying sometime in the afternoon before sundown (19:14, 30). Jesus's body is removed from the cross before the beginning of the Sabbath, which was also the Passover, without any need to hasten death by breaking Jesus's bones (19:31–33). In John's chronology, the Sabbath and the Passover that year fell on the same day. Notice also that there is no trial in front of the whole Sanhedrin in John, as in the Synoptics (Mark 14:53–65). Furthermore, in the Synoptics, Jesus does eat the Passover meal *before* his arrest and trial (Mark 14:12–25). Remember, the Passover begins at sunset with the evening meal.

Both the Synoptics and John use the language of "the day of Preparation." However, in John, Jesus is crucified *on* the day of Preparation, and in the Synoptics the disciples get ready for the Passover meal that will follow the day of Preparation at sunset. In fact, in the Synoptics, they meet at sunset to eat, and then there is a series of events that go through the entire night: the Gethsemane prayer and struggle, the arrest, the trial before the Jewish Sanhedrin, the trial before Pilate, the trial before Herod Antipas (Luke only), and then finally the crucifixion on the *following* afternoon at three o'clock (Matt 26:30—27:54; Mark 14:26—15:39; Luke 22:39—23:49).

In both the Synoptics and John, Jesus is crucified on Friday, the day before the Sabbath. The difference is that in John's scenario, the Passover that year fell on the Sabbath, and in the Synoptics the Passover fell on the day before the Sabbath. The celebration of Passover in the NT world is like the celebration of Christmas today: while always on the twenty-fifth of December, Christmas is not on the same day of the week from year to year. This explains how John could have Jesus crucified the day *before* the Passover and the Synoptics could have Jesus crucified *on* the Passover late in the afternoon long after the Passover meal. Even though it is Friday in both scenarios, they are each referring to a different calandarization of the year.

What is to be made of this timing discrepancy? We may be tempted to ask modern, Enlightenment questions: who got it right? Was Jesus killed on the Passover or not? Was it Nisan 14 or 15? Did Jesus share the Passover meal with his disciples or not? But are these appropriate questions to pose to a literary construction like a gospel? Apparently, the early Christians were not overly bothered with discrepancies like this one—and others are found in the gospel quartet. It seems that an early appreciation for the distinct theological voices of the Evangelists was enough to trump any unease regarding strictly historical concerns. This appreciation has not carried forward uniformly into the contemporary period. Some have tried to harmonize discrepancies in the Gospels with elaborate and complicated proposals. While such proposals may succeed in forcing all the Gospels to march in lockstep with one another, typically the harmonization requires introducing new assumptions, and in the end each Evangelist's particular theological aim and message is obscured.

John and the Synoptics are saying the same thing but in different ways. So who got it right? Could not both sets of traditions be true? Of course, on one level, it is appropriate to notice that it is *impossible* to reconcile the Synoptics and John with regard to the timing of the crucifixion; Jesus cannot have been killed on two different days! But on the level of meaning and significance, both do work. How so? Both John and the Synoptics tell the story of Jesus's crucifixion on Friday and of resurrection on Sunday. However, they tell the same story with different but compatible aims. For John, it is important that Jesus be offered up in sacrifice on the cross at the same time that the Passover lambs are slaughtered. Like a real Passover lamb (Exod 12:46), no bone of Jesus's body is broken—something that John is sure to stress with regard to Jesus's legs (John 19:32–33). From the start of the Fourth Gospel, Jesus is the pure and spotless "Lamb of God who takes away the sin of the world" (John 1:29). For Mark, followed by Matthew and Luke, it is important that Jesus celebrates a deeply meaningful Passover meal with his disciples before his arrest and crucifixion. This shows that his coming death will be like the Passover sacrifice, which the Last Supper imagery suggests. "This is my body... This is my blood of the covenant, which is poured out for many" (Mark 14:22–24).

So what could account for such differences between John and the Synoptics? One popular suggestion is that John the Evangelist had access to a sign source, which the Synoptic Evangelists did not, one that linked the timing of the crucifixion to the slaughter of the Passover lamb. Signs (Greek: *sēmeia*) play a key role for John because of their capacity to point to Jesus's glory—God's presence in him. Two specifically named signs are the preparing of the better wine at the wedding in Cana (2:1–11) and healing the official's son in Capernaum (4:46–54). The role of signs is highlighted by these concluding words: "Now Jesus did many other signs in the presence of his disciples, which are not written in this book. But these are written so that you may come to believe that Jesus is the Messiah, the Son of God, and that through believing you may have life in his name" (20:30–31).

However, even if the Fourth Evangelist depends on various sources, some known to the other Evangelists and others not (i.e., a signs source, the discourses, passion accounts, resurrection appearances), it is unlikely that he was just clumsily "stitching together" the various sources. What is more likely is that we have here a genuine literary product, where the rhetorical craft and literary skill of the Fourth Evangelist guided and shaped his sources for persuasive and theological aims. From what we now know of ancient Greco-Roman rhetorical art, it seems more plausible to imagine a compositional process of selection, shaping, and elaboration (Mack and Robbins 1989). Like their fellow students of the Synoptics, so most Johannine scholars have abandoned the image of a "cut-and-paste" editor intent on simply joining pieces of existing texts together. The Evangelists are now given much more credit as artful theologians who are writing in rhetorically persuasive ways in order to shape a community's behavior and self-understanding.

From the start, early church theologians (such as Clement) recognized John's gospel as simply more theologically bold than the Synoptic accounts. That is, John creates a narrative that makes explicit what is implicit but undeveloped in other narratives of Jesus's life; John recasts the whole story of Jesus—from beginning to end—from the perspective of the risen Messiah and Lord of the church in ongoing conflict with powers still resistant to his rule. It is unlikely that John had access to the Synoptics, but it is clear he had access to the same eyewitness tradition of Jesus's life and ministry. So while the differences are striking, it seems better to think of John as simply an extremely gifted theologian using the sources available to him in a creative way, in order to give expression to his interpretation of the significance of Jesus (e.g., scripting players with speeches that make explicit the later community's experience of the significance of Jesus). Certainly, the choir is richer for his distinctive voice. See diagram below.

The Theological Contribution of the Johannine Traditions 157

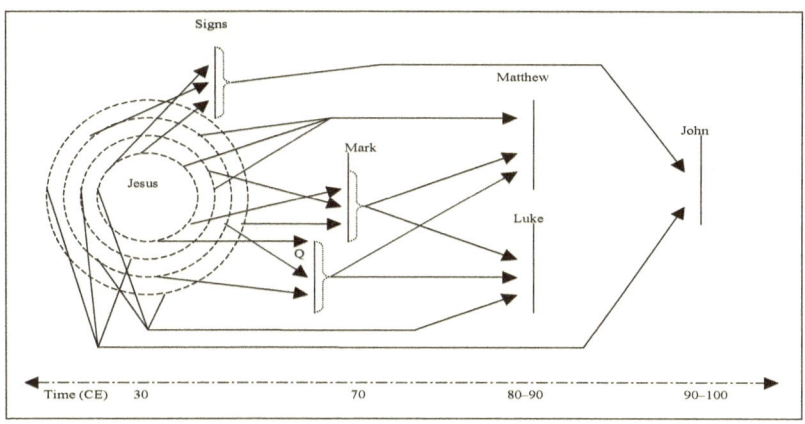

TABLE 5.1 Conceptualizing the Framing of the Jesus Tradition

What is the structure of John's theological statement? A feature of John that impacts discussion about its structure is the observation that it has gone through several stages of composition. The addition of an epilogue (21:1–25) after the Gospel's conclusion (20:30–31) indicates later editing. Then there is the well known case of the insertion of the *pericope adulterae* (7:53—8:11), which fluctuates in the textual transmission history. Some manuscripts place the pericope in Luke's gospel either after 21:38 or 24:53, and the earliest manuscripts do not have it at all. Most conclude that it was probably not part of the initial composition of John's gospel. While the precise character of this editorial activity is not clear, the most probable explanation is the one offered by Johnson: "an originally radical version was thoroughly reworked by a later 'ecclesiastical redactor,' who modified the spiritualizing tendencies of the original along more orthodox lines" (1999:525).

The structure of the final version of John has four parts (Johnson 1999:534). First, the *Prologue* (1:1–18) sets out the major themes of the gospel. Second, the *Book of Signs* (1:19—12:50) dramatizes an assertion of the Prologue (1:5) through seven mighty signs, demonstrating that the light has indeed overcome the darkness: making better wine at Cana (2:1–11), healing an official's son at Capernaum (4:46–54), healing a lame man at the pool (5:2–9), feeding the five thousand (6:1–15), walking on the sea (6:16–21), healing the man born blind (9:1–41), and raising Lazarus to life (11:1–57). Third, the *Book of Glory* (13:1—20:31) further dramatizes another assertion of the Prologue (1:12), showing how those who align themselves with Messiah Jesus are really children of God. The revelation of Jesus's glory through his teaching (13:1—17:26) and the demonstration of Jesus's glory through his death and resurrection (18:1—20:31) make up this section. Fourth, the *Epilogue* (21:1-25) narrates the restoration of Peter and the affirmation of the beloved disciple's testimony.

John 3:31-36 offers a compact treatment of the themes around which the Fourth Gospel is structured. Four motifs are evident in these verses:

> The one who comes *from above* is above all; the one who is of the earth belongs to the earth and speaks about earthly things. The one who comes from heaven is above all. He *testifies* to what he has seen and heard, yet no one accepts his testimony. Whoever has accepted his testimony has certified this, that God is true. He whom God has *sent* speaks the words of God, for he gives the Spirit without measure. The Father loves the Son and has *placed all things* in his hands. Whoever believes in the Son has eternal life; whoever disobeys the Son will not see life, but must endure God's wrath. (3:31-36)

First, Jesus comes *from above* (i.e., from heaven) and therefore speaks of the Father. The description of Jesus as the one who comes "from above" is repeated frequently throughout the gospel (3:13; 6:33, 38, 41, 42, 50, 51, 58; 7:28; 8:14, 42; 13:3). From the start, Jesus makes the most distinctive identifications about himself. There is no Markan secrecy here! Jesus identifies himself as the Son of Man who has "descended" from heaven; therefore, he is uniquely capable of revealing the things "from above." Typically, the "descent" of the Son of Man in glory is associated with the end of time (Mark 8:38), but in John the Son of Man has already descended. God's eschatological work is being realized in the present reality. Jesus is the man from heaven who, when "lifted up," returns to where he was before, in order to "draw all people to myself" (12:32).

Second, Jesus is the Son who makes the Father *known*. Jesus bears witness to what he has seen and heard. This is the motif of revelation. Jesus is the self-revelation of God—he makes known (exegetes) the Father (1:18). God's unseen power and presence are made explicit in time and place, in the person of Jesus. Jesus carries out the same function as the Father in the world—to reveal God's way of life and to dispel the darkness.

Third, the Father *sent* the Son. The phrases "he whom God has sent" and "he who sent me" are formal christological designations in John. The theme features prominently in many of the summary statements in John. At the raising of Lazarus, Jesus longs for the crowd to know that the Father has sent him (11:42). Jesus is supremely "the one whom the Father sent" (3:34; 10:36; 17:3). John's Christology is a "Father" Christology in that his Christology always points to the Father and the Father's missional passion for creation. Because the Father sent the Son, Jesus shows the glory of God most clearly and embodies God's character, which is continually turned toward the world. The missional dimension of John's Father Christology is expressed by the risen Lord's charge to his disciples: "Peace be with you. As the Father has sent me, so send I you" (20:21).

Fourth, the Father has *placed all things* into the Son's hands. Jesus is especially qualified to carry out the functions of teacher, revealer, and judge since he does what the Father does (13:3). Therefore the response human beings give to the Son represents as well their response to God. Commitment to and identification with Jesus is a decision for life, light, and truth—in other words, a decision for God. Rebellion against and rejection of Jesus is a decision against light (i.e., for darkness), against truth (i.e., for lies), against life (i.e., for death), against God (i.e., for the devil)—in other words, a decision for "the wrath of God." Jesus's pattern of "descent" and "ascent" as the Son of Man validates his dual role as revealer and judge such that the Father "has placed all things in his hands." Jesus reveals who he is, and people either accept or reject that revelation, which becomes the basis by which all are judged. The diagram below illustrates the gospel's structure.

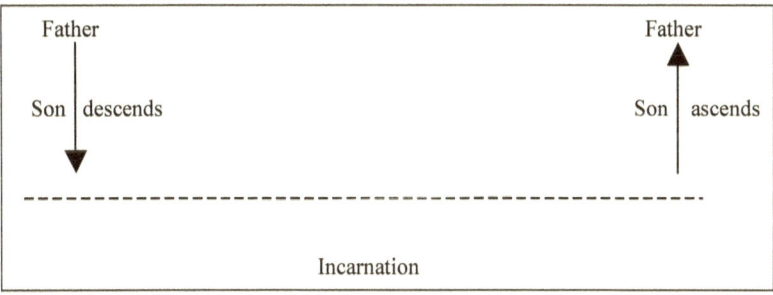

TABLE 5.2 The Structure of the Fourth Gospel's "Father" Christology/Theology

In 1903 William Wrede conjectured that the pattern of a descending and ascending divine Revealer of truth may have been drawn from gnosticism. But a textual case for a gnostic background was first made by Bultmann in 1925. He drew upon the newly accessible Mandaean writings, in addition to the half-Jewish, half-Christian gnostic Odes of Solomon and Manichaean texts (Kümmel 1975:219). Bultmann (1971) used the idea of a gnostic background for John in his major commentary on the Fourth Gospel. John's terms of reference (like "being born from above"), his use of "I am" revelation discourses, and his reliance on literary devices (irony, ambiguity, double meaning, misunderstanding) all served to ground a dualistic worldview that paralleled the gnostic spirituality found in the Mandaean literature—texts usually dated to the seventh and eighth centuries CE and found in the Euphrates region in what is today known as Iraq and Iran. For Bultmann, the existence of Mandaean literature was enough to extrapolate backward and assume that the Fourth Evangelist was influenced by "gnosticizing Judaism" already in the first century (1955:13). Of special interest to Bultmann's existential theological program is the way that John asserts that the path traversed by the "one who comes from heaven" (3:31) is the path of descent and ascent set out for all the followers of the Revealer to travel as well (14:6–7).

As we have seen, the 1945 discovery of the gnostic library of spiritual writings at the Egyptian village of Nag Hammadi greatly clarified the perception of gnosticism—previously known only from the polemical arguments against gnostics by the heresiologists. The collection shows an amazing variety of beliefs and practices (Ehrman 2008:197–201). Yes, the gnostic writings did feature cosmic dualism (e.g., the belief that souls of people are imprisoned in an evil world of the flesh and long to shed this earthly existence in order to realize their essential divine nature), and they told of a divine redeemer who opened up pathways to light and knowledge for those "in the know" (i.e., those who were "gnostic"), but the writings are not uniform about what characterized a gnostic. Ideas like a gnostic Redeemer mythology, while sometimes present, were not stable or well developed. About the only common gnostic theme in the Nag Hammadi texts was the call to an ascetic life, which, as noted earlier, may explain why some Christian monks near Nag Hammadi found aspects of these gnostic texts interesting extracurricular reading and worth hiding when church authorities began to ban such texts (Wisse

1978:440). Again, while there is evidence of the beginnings of general gnostic religiosity in the NT (see 1 John), the direction of development is more likely the reverse of Bultmann's reconstruction. Those with gnostic proclivities found the story of Jesus fascinating and a useful ally in their emerging religious program that came together as gnosticism in the second and third centuries—of this there is evidence. However, there is no evidence that early Christians found a well-developed gnostic mythology through which to read their experience of Jesus and thereby to convert their disappointment into a hope-filled spirituality.

So, what is to be made of the parallels to gnostic spirituality found in John? That various protognostic religious ideals were in circulation in the first century and earlier *is* clear; the discovery of the Qumran writings (1947) demonstrates a Jewish form of gnosis operative in sectarian Judaism. While conceptual parallels to John (ethical dualism, emphasis on the idea of creation, distinction between those of the light/truth/life and those of the darkness/falsehood/death) were found in the Qumran texts, these same parallels were also linked to other early Jewish writings as well (Kümmel 1975:221). No determining relationship has emerged; the most that could be said is that John and Qumran shared a common religious background of strongly dualistic speculation. No more than this can be said with assurance.

Thus, the fact that John relies heavily on a Jewish-gnostic thought world existing at the margins of Judaism to frame his interpretation of Jesus does *not* mean that John offers a form of Christianity conformed to gnosticism. Rather, it is more likely that John consciously employed proto-gnostic religious language in a *counter*gnostic sense (Kümmel 1975:228). A careful reading of John shows that John uses gnostic language to directly challenge proto-gnostic ideals. Consider these four examples that undercut gnostic ideals: "The Word became flesh and lived among us" (1:14), "for God so loved the world that he gave his only Son" (3:16), "I am not asking you to take them out of the world, but I ask you to protect them from the evil one" (17:15), and the risen Lord "showed them his hands and his side" (20:20).

Evidently, proto-gnostic spiritualists raised questions that the Fourth Evangelist could not ignore. Therefore his Gospel uses similar terms of reference but subverts and corrects them based on the memory of Jesus's victory over evil, and Jesus's ongoing powerful presence within the community. Put another way, the gnostic-like symbols that John uses in his gospel achieve their coherence in the life of Jesus; it is *not* that Jesus is made to fit a preformed gnostic Redeemer myth. Such a conclusion takes seriously the operative assumption with which the NT writers work: namely, that the historical events of Jesus's life, death, and resurrection lie behind all the creative selecting, editing, and elaboration being used to interpret Jesus. The Fourth Evangelist is no exception, although he is arguably the most creative of all NT writers.

What then is the interpretation of Jesus that John sets out? As he comes to the podium, we can expect John to make a statement of his driving theological conviction in these terms: *Jesus is the Lamb of God sent from God to reveal the glory of God to the world in order that his disciples can continue to fill out his body in the world as the sent ones in the power of the Lamb. Because Jesus ascends back to the Father, the Son empowers his disciples by his indwelling Spirit, to carry on through the conflict and to follow him back to the Father. Even though there is conflict with those that do not share the new symbolic world, I am convinced that Jesus's followers see the light and know what true life is.*

THEMATIC IMPLICATIONS OF JOHN'S VISION

Four themes emerge from John's central theological conviction. First, the Messiah, the Son of God, is the Revealer of the divine purpose present at the foundation of the universe. Already in the Prologue we see Messiah Jesus as the embodiment of God's purpose (*logos*), who is with the Father, who is given all things, who comes from the Father, and who makes known (exegetes) the Father (1:18). Following the Prologue, Jesus is presented as the Messiah, as the fulfiller of Jewish messianic expectations. Jesus's Messiahship is revealed to the Samaritan woman (4:25) and is linked directly to his revelation of the Father (4:21, 23). In the Passion Narrative, Messiahship is defined as coming into the world, as bearing witness to the truth (18:37), and as finishing the Father's work (19:30). The point: Jesus not only reveals and implements the divine purpose (*logos*) of God's love; he *is* the purpose of God! According to Caird, "The union of the human and divine, which he displays in all his works and words in chs. 1–12, and which through the cross he imparts to his disciples, and which they are to share with others and finally the world, is the purpose for which God set the universe in motion" (1994:51).

Second, Jesus is the sovereign and the Lord of all aspects of his life, acting much like a king organizing his own coronation: "No one takes [my life] from me, but I lay it down of my own accord. I have power to lay it down, and I have power to take it up again. I have received this command from my Father" (10:18). Jesus, the Son of God, is the Son who reveals the Father; this revelation is explicated in terms of the Father-Son relationship. While Jesus's home is in the heavenly realm with the Father (he speaks only of what he has seen and heard, 3:11–15), his whole earthly life is a continuous process of watching and listening to his Father (5:19–20). This helps explain the descent of the Spirit on Jesus (1:33). Why would the incarnate *logos* need the addition of the Spirit? According to Caird, "The incarnation established an objective union between the *logos* and the individual humanity of Jesus. But the man Jesus needed the guidance of the Spirit to lead him to a subjective awareness of this fact . . . It was true of him, as later of his disciples, that only when he came to see himself as he truly was did he also see the Father" (1994:298).

Thus Jesus is sent by the Father, and his ascent into heaven is described as his being "lifted up." Note the double meaning of "lifted up," referring to the *crucifixion* of Jesus as well as to his glorious *exaltation* (3:14; 8:28; 12:32). In the very act of crucifixion, Jesus is glorified. Crucifixion is the glorification of Jesus; it is the moment when we see the character and glory of God in the clearest way: these are the lengths to which the love of God goes! Thus, in the Johannine passion story, Jesus is not the victim; rather, Jesus is the sovereign and Lord of the proceedings, heading off to his own coronation.

Third, Jesus's death/glorification means a change in the cosmic power structures, not a sacrifice to appease God's anger or holiness. Instead, the exaltation of Jesus means the ousting of Satan. Terms like "Son of Man," "glorification," "being lifted up," "the hour," and "judgment" all carry significance in John's narrative. Glorification is spelled out as the realization of the glorious purpose shared with the Father from the foundation of the world (17:5). The hour of Jesus's death is clearly seen as the moment which begins the final act of glorification. At the cross we see two cosmic activities at the same time: both the *judgment* and the *salvation* of the world. While Satan, the prosecutor, has no claim over Jesus (14:30), Satan manages to secure Jesus's death sentence in the earthly court but loses his case in the higher court of heaven. Building on this imagery, Caird states, "From that court he is drummed out, losing his claim not only over the innocent Jesus, but over the guilty world, for the death he has engineered has drawn the whole human race into union with Jesus" (1994:149–50). As the Son of Man is glorified/lifted up, the Holy Spirit is poured out, the Scriptures are understood, God's mission bears fruit, the truth about Jesus is known, and true life becomes accessible to all.

Fourth, John's Christology is carried by the narrative structure and is characterized as both "high" and "functional." The center of the "high" affirmations of Jesus's identity with the Father are based on the "functions" that the Son does as the Father does, speaks of what he has heard, and tells of what he has seen. Thus, Jesus is the God-filled man because of his special relationship to the Father, and because of what he does. More specifically, as Caird notes, "It is the humanity of Jesus which is the perfect expression of what God intended when His *logos* created the universe. Jesus was the only one who could express and disclose the ultimate end which God has for men and women: that they should become His children (1:12)" (1994:322).

In Jesus, then, the purpose (*logos*) for which God made the world becomes a real possibility. As the Son is lifted up/glorified, the individual humanity of Jesus becomes a collective or inclusive humanity such that God's divine purpose (*logos*) from before the world's existence is now finally a real possibility. "Now, Father, glorify me in your own presence with the glory that I had in your presence before the world existed" (17:5). "And I, when I am lifted up from the earth, will draw all people to myself" (12:32).

THE JOHANNINE LETTERS' THEOLOGICAL VISION

There is little doubt that the three letters attributed to John are "occasioned" by some conflict or dispute. The exact parameters, however, are less than clear. The main reason for the ambiguity of the author's historical setting is that instead of writing an occasional letter documenting the problem, the "elder" chose to write literary texts of generic exhortations. In the end, however disappointing the letters are for the historian (given the lack of unambiguous clues for reconstructing the historical situation of the community's story), we have what we expect from a literary text—a testimony of the author's distinctive Johannine convictions regarding the shape of how things *ought* to be in the Christian community.

Apparently, particular disputes arose over the messianic character of Jesus (1 John), theological disputes emerged over appropriate teaching (2 John), and political disputes surfaced over rival leaderships (3 John). Some within the Johannine community appear to have emphasized Jesus's heavenly origin to such a degree that it overshadowed his earthly ministry and his witness to God's new-creation humanity. In contrast to the issues that precipitated the Fourth Gospel, however, these conflicts are generated from *within* the community and are not the result of hostility or persecution from outside the Johannine community. Certainly it is tempting to imagine all sorts of historical scenarios that could account for these literary texts (e.g., Brown 1979). However, the problem with all such reconstructions is that we have no way to verify them, and the hypotheses risk overtaking the text's stated theological vision. All the evidence we have for the author, setting, aim, and theological vision is found only in these three letters.

What can we say? First, the terms of reference and symbolic world are very similar to the Fourth Gospel. For example, in 1 John the same dualisms and distinctions exist between light and darkness (1:5; 2:8–10), between truth and falsehood (1:6; 2:4; 3:19; 4:6), between the community and the world (2:15; 3:1; 4:3; 5:19), and between life and death (1:2; 3:14–15; 5:11–13). All this suggests that the Letters of John and the Gospel of John share the same setting and perhaps even the same authorship.

However, unlike the gospel (with its triumphant and strident declarations), 1 John makes assertions that appear contradictory: "If we say that we have not sinned we make [God] a liar" (1:10) *and* "those who have been born of God do not sin, because God's seed abides in them; they cannot sin" (3:9). These observations are not literary seams indicating sources stitched together from different settings, but are best understood as the community elder's attempt to speak into a conflicted reality. As Johnson helpfully states, "What is granted by way of proposition ('everyone sins') in one place is taken away by way of exhortation ('do not sin') in another. The vacillation between affirmation and exhortation in 1 John derives not from multiplicity of sources and editors but from the internal tension created by the author's task: encouraging faithfulness to God in a context where many of the community have left to 'walk in darkness'" (1999:565).

Second, whereas the Fourth Gospel is marked by the hostility experienced from those outside the community, the Letters focus on conflict generated by those within the community. The trauma of such a situation is understandable. For a community that put much stock in unity, friendship, fellowship, and love (see Jesus's Farewell Discourse: John 13–17), the division, conflict, and dissention experienced was a shock to the community's self-understanding and identity. The problem for contemporary readers comes in assessing how much precision can be achieved with regard to profiling this division. Have the dissident views on Jesus's nature hardened into discernable positions and party lines, or is this more about the elder's rhetorical speech aimed at establishing coherence, unity, and identity within the community?

This question is answered differently. Raymond Brown (1979) argues that the conflict gives witness to christological positions already firmly demarcated. In his scenario, the Johannine community has split into two communities. One part has adopted an increasingly gnostic interpretation of the Fourth Gospel, well on the way to making common cause with second-century gnostics. The other part, peopled by those who produced the Letters, articulates the position of the emerging ecclesiastical orthodoxy of the second century. The two groups introduce two ways of reading the Fourth Gospel: the doecetic side championed by gnosticism, and the incarnational side championed by the Letters: the side that eventually emerged triumphant. Not only does this reconstruction fail to take seriously the inner diversity characteristic of the second-century heterodox situation, where tight party lines along christological formulations were not yet in place (Wisse 1986:189–90); it also fails to take seriously the literary character of the Letters.

What is noteworthy is that the Letters do not display any bitter polemics against those who have departed or even refute their claims with careful argumentation (Johnson 1999:566). The focus is not on the outsiders, those who have left, but on those who remain. Typical of literary texts, there is a challenge to renew their commitments to each other, their identity, and their mission. These observations suggest that the conflict is real but not defined by strict christological camps, which would emerge later in the third and fourth centuries. Instead, the exhortation is generic in outlook, aiming primarily to solidify group cohesion.

Third, the Letters were probably sent at the same time to the same destination; this would explain the preservation of such short letters (2 and 3 John)—they were the companions of the more significant writing, 1 John (Johnson 1999:561). Otherwise there would be no obvious way to account for keeping them together. Most likely 3 John functioned as a letter of recommendation from the elder to Gaius, certifying that the carrier of the Letters, Demetrius (3 John 12), is trustworthy and to be welcomed. Then 2 John functions as a cover letter from the elder to be read to the gathered assembly, introducing the themes of the attached letter of exhortation from the elder, 1 John. The three-letter package is usually dated not very long after the composition of the Fourth Gospel, close to the end of the first century (Kümmel 1975:445).

Fourth, the canonization history of the Letters suggests that they became useful later to clarify reception and authorization of the Johannine traditions. Both 2 and 3 John were only ratified as canonical with much hesitation and after some time. The problem was likely that the brief ascription to "the elder" was not traceable to any one apostle (Kümmel 1975:452). By the late fourth century, however, all three letters were ratified as authoritative for Christian instruction in Athanasius's canonical list (367 C.E.). What happened? Evidently, the link that some theologians (Papias, Irenaeus, Clement) made between the Apostle John, the beloved disciple, and the elder became especially compelling when the third- and fourth-century bishops found the Letters to be very useful for guiding the interpretation of the Fourth Gospel. While Brown's quip (1979:150) that the Letters saved the Fourth Gospel for the church is probably overstated, it does touch on the significance of the practical usefulness of the Letters in the later ratification debates. When the Letters were composed, it is unlikely that polemics about the Fourth Gospel or its interpretation were in view (Childs 1984:482–83). However, by the end of the second century, interpretation of the Fourth Gospel *had* divided into two camps: incarnational (proto-orthodox) and docetic (e.g., Heracleon's gnostic commentary on John). By the fourth century, both the ecclesiastical editing of the Fourth Gospel (revision and addition of chapter 21) and the recognition of the Letters' value in rejecting any gnosticizing interpretation of the Fourth Gospel secured the place of the Johannine traditions in the canon.

What is the structure of the Letters? Third John follows the pattern of a genuine Hellenistic personal letter. It is, however, not a private letter. Rather, it is a letter of community interest bearing an official stamp of approval for Demetrius, the letter carrier, from the elder to Gaius. Apparently, a rival leader named Diotrephes (3 John 9) has refused to accept the elder's authority, his letters, or his emissaries. Diotrephes even expels from the local assembly those who do not accept his leadership.

By contrast, the letter of recommendation exhorts Gauis to welcome Demetrius with warm hospitality and not to follow the example of Diotrephes, who does not welcome and does not show hospitality. These exhortations signal that the dispute is on the level of leadership style, worship practice, and community relations, not on the level of deeply held doctrinal divisions. In characteristic Johannine symbolism, the elder instructs Gaius and his particular community as follows: "Do not imitate what is evil but imitate what is good. Whoever does good is from God; whoever does evil has not seen God" (3 John 11).

Second John also follows the form of a Hellenistic personal letter. Again, it is not a private letter, but a letter addressed to the whole community that Gaius leads. The letter functions as a cover letter introducing the topics to be addressed in a more substantial manner by the attached exhortation (1 John). The two concerns introduced are false teaching (2 John 7) and practical directives relating to hospitality (2 John 10). Hospitality is not limited to sharing space and food—it also implies a spiritual connectedness. Johnson offers a helpful explanation to the rather sharp exhortation to withhold hospitality in some cases: "Evil behavior is thought to follow directly from wrong thinking. Thus, in this view, listening to wrong teaching about Jesus leads to evil deeds against Jesus. The refusal of hospitality in this case is therefore not an act of hostility toward individual persons but a defensive measure against error and evil by a community fighting to maintain its own identity" (1999:564).

Even though 1 John purports to be a letter, it really does not follow the structure of a letter. It is missing prescript, conclusion, greeting, and benediction. It has much more in common with a sermon, treatise, or tract; it is a general exhortation from the elder to various communities making up the Johannine family of communities. In view of the various tensions and divisions, each community is urged to renew its commitment to the fundamentals of the faith and the recognition of its past failures. In particular, they can no longer be content with the comfortable assurance of being an insider; instead, they must "not believe every spirit, but test the spirits to see whether they are from God" (4:1). They can no longer be content with claiming distinction from the world; the departure of those who were once a part of the community shows that now the world is not only outside but also within the community itself. Thus, the exhortation to faithfulness involves both an acknowledgement of the community's own sinfulness (1:8–10) and a realization that truth does not entail only an abstract confession of Jesus, the Messiah, the Son of God come in the flesh (incarnation), but also leads to appropriate behavior (3:11). "We know love by this, that he laid down his life for us—and we ought to lay down our lives for one another. How does God's love abide in anyone who has the world's goods and sees a brother or sister in need and yet refuses help? Little children, let us love, not in word or speech, but in truth and action" (3:16–18).

Thus the three-letter package from the elder functions as a remarkable piece of persuasive rhetoric aimed at reforming troubled and divided Christian communities. So while the precise occasion is unknown, it is unnecessary for meaningful interpretation; we have texts here that aim to persuade and encourage readers generally to embrace a particular orientation toward true teaching and true hospitality. They combine to form an exhortation to faithfulness.

As the elder makes his way to the podium, he carefully sets out his rendition of his guiding theological vision in these terms: *I would be the first to admit that we have had our share of conflict, disputes, and division as a network of communities of Christian faith. However, I am convinced that if we uphold the basics of the apostolic confession, and if we renew our commitment to love one another, this will prevent further divisions, and our communities will heal and flourish. So let's strengthen our grasp of the incarnational story of Jesus and embody toward one another the active love he represents. Let's abandon the reductionistic thinking that threatens the fellowship of the community and risks leading us into sin. For it is by remaining united in our fellowship that we remain in relationship with the Lord—and thus have eternal life.*

REVELATION'S THEOLOGICAL VISION

It is difficult to be neutral about the Apocalypse of John. Typically it is read either with great interest and pressed hard with enormous expectation, or it is neglected and shunned as fanciful science fiction. Its history of interpretation, however, reveals that both popular responses to Revelation are usually rooted in tragic misinterpretation, largely due to a misunderstanding of the writing's literary genre and purpose.

Martin Luther's critical assessment of Revelation was that "my spirit cannot accommodate itself to this book. For me this is reason enough not to think highly of it: Christ is neither taught nor known in it. But to teach Christ, this is the thing which an apostle is bound above all else to do; . . . Therefore I stick to the books which present Christ to me clearly and purely" (Luther 1960:399). Revelation was one of four NT writings—along with Hebrews, James, and Jude—that he relegated to the appendix of his German translation. While Luther was bothered by Revelation's content ("too many tales and pictures"), which did not portray Jesus as he expected, others have in fact seen Jesus in a powerful way. Jesus is portrayed in Revelation with beauty and glory; he is the Lord and victor over history and everything! For these interpreters, a more beautiful picture of Jesus, the lion and the lamb, is not found in the entire Bible. Wherever the church suffers, Revelation continues to be highly valued for its ringing affirmation of God's ultimate victory, regardless of appearances to the contrary.

Part of the reason for Revelation's diverse reception among contemporary readers is that it employs the ancient genre known as *apocalyptic*. The name of the genre actually comes from the book's title: "The revelation [*apokalypsis*] of Jesus Christ" (Rev 1:1). However, the origin of the apocalyptic literary genre is much earlier and is found in Judaism. While the first apocalypticists saw themselves as successors to Israel's prophets responding to questions regarding the end of the world (eschatology), the origin of their literary genre reflects Hellenistic influences on Judaism, especially concepts like dualism and demonology (Kümmel 1975:453). During the postexilic time, expectations of the end of the age, the triumph over evil, and the formation of God's kingdom—not of this world—found theological expression in the new literary genre that used vibrant images of visions, dreams, world catastrophes, cosmic battles, and fantastic beasts.

Apocalyptic material can be found in several prophetic books of the Hebrew Bible (e.g., Isaiah 24–27; Ezekiel 38–39; Daniel 7–12; Joel 2; Zechariah 9–14), and whole books of Jewish apocalyptic prophecy were composed beginning in the period of the Maccabean Wars. Examples of the apocalypses produced during the Jewish apocalyptic period (from 250 BCE to the second century CE) include *1–2 Enoch*, *The Testaments of the Twelve Patriarchs*, the Jewish *Sibylline Oracles*, the *Ascension of Moses*, *2 Esdras*, the *War Scroll* from Qumran, the *Apocalypse of Abraham*, the *Apocalypse of Baruch*, and the *Apocalypse of Elijah*. From these titles one of the key characteristics of an apocalypse becomes clear: Jewish apocalypticists concealed themselves behind the authority of ancient worthies like Enoch, Moses, Abraham, Elijah, and Baruch. The idea was to write in a revelatory form a grand history of the world, beginning with the time of the alleged author to the end of time, using revelations of dreams and ecstatic visions. The genre was a well-accepted literary form of ancient theological writing—popular for its convictions that the present godless earthly rule will come to an end and that God will intervene, making things right in the new age. Writings in this genre are also sometimes categorized as Palestinian Pseudepigrapha (composed in Hebrew or Aramaic) and Alexandrian Pseudepigrapha (composed in Greek).

The book of Revelation is a prime example of how early Christians exploited the Jewish apocalyptic genre, employing its concepts and developing them further to give expression to their interpretation of Jesus and his significance. John's Revelation addresses the fundamental theme of all theology: God and history. Attention is directed toward the one *from whom* and *to whom* all things are. "Holy, holy, holy, the Lord God the Almighty, who was and is and is to come" (4:8), and "You are worthy, our Lord and God, to receive glory and honor and power, for you created all things, and by your will they existed and were created" (4:11).

Other Christian apocalyptic writings following this pattern were also produced (e.g., the *Apocalypse of Peter*, the *Apocalypse of Paul*, and the *Shepherd of Hermas*). However, Revelation is the oldest and most important apocalyptic writing produced by Christians, typically dated toward the end of the reign of Domitian (ca. 90–95 CE). It aims to encourage Christian communities threatened by persecution at the hands of the Roman Empire with a resounding confidence in the ultimate victory of Christ over the powers of the anti-Christ (Kümmel 1975:469).

While Revelation has much in common with Jewish apocalyptic writing, two significant differences appear. First, the author does *not* conceal himself behind a pseudonym of an ancient worthy (e.g., Moses or Enoch), as in Jewish apocalyptic literature. Rather, he identifies himself simply as John four times (1:1, 4, 9; 22:8). This John, sometimes called the seer, bears prophecies for seven specific communities of faith in the Roman province of Asia Minor: Ephesus (2:1), Smyrna (2:8), Pergamum (2:12), Thyatira (2:18), Sardis (3:1), Philadelphia (3:7), and Laodicea (3:14). As was noted earlier, by the end of the second century the three Johannine traditions (the beloved disciple, the elder, and the seer) were drawn together by early theologians and heresiologists (e.g., Justin, Papias, Irenaeus, Clement) and located in John the apostle (Kümmel

1975:470). In some areas, the apostolic association was contested, as it rested on speculation. However, the arguments for apostolic linkage proved sufficiently compelling for the leading bishops of the fourth century (i.e., Athanasias et al.) to ratify Revelation as apostolic and to secure its place within the canon of authoritative Christian Scriptures. By far the most important reason for Revelation's inclusion, however, was the recognizably useful role its interpretation of salvation history played; it added a distinct voice to the emerging NT choir of voices. The alleged apostolic association helped to strengthen its case for legitimacy.

Second, unlike other Jewish apocalyptic literature, which focused on God's future victory (e.g., Dan 7:14), John's Revelation makes clear that because of the Lamb's victory (Rev 12:11), the triumph of God has *already* been realized in heaven! As in all of the NT writings, the expectations of the *future* are shaped by God's *present* power demonstrated by the cross and resurrection of Jesus and the gift of the Holy Spirit. Notably the victory of the angel Michael and the ouster of the dragon from the heavenly court (Rev 12:7-12) is located not in some precosmic fall of Lucifer or limited to some future battle of Armageddon but is realized in the victory of the Lamb at the *cross* where his lifeblood (12:11) and the testimony of all his followers (19:13) confirm the defeat of the evil one. According to Caird, "The victory in heaven is the symbolic counterpart of Christ's victory on the cross, which carries with it the guarantee of victory for his martyred followers" (1997:55).

The conviction that Jesus has risen from the dead transforms the apocalyptic symbols so that they not only point to Jesus, the Son of Man; they *come from him* (Johnson 1999:578). The voice of the one who addresses the seven churches through the seer is the risen Lord; he is not only the Son of Man who *will come* as judge (Rev 14:14), but the Son of Man who *now lives* (1:13) and speaks words of judgment already. The classic Christian dynamic of "already" but "not yet" is in play. Messiah Jesus is already the bridegroom of the new Jerusalem that is not yet (21:9). As the waves of apocalyptic visions pass (seals, trumpets, and bowls), readers know that the essential victory has already been won. Rome's imperial cult with its demand for total and complete allegiance not only must be resisted, but *can* now be resisted with confidence. Why? Because the outcome is clear, appearances to the contrary notwithstanding. The visions of the future simply portray the assured results of the victory already achieved by Jesus.

Furthermore, Revelation describes the earthly drama in light of the reality of the reign of God that has already dawned, reshaping the apocalyptic framework. Note that when the sealed book (5:6-9) is presented to the Lamb, it signifies the establishment and accomplishment of God's purpose, God's reign. This reign is well on its way to triumph in history, confirming the proclamation: "Hallelujah! For the Lord our God the Almighty reigns" (19:6). Thus, the *eschaton* (the end) is both present and future for Revelation.

Revelation does not portray the course of history, but history's encounter with the *eschaton*. This portrayal of history is fundamentally different from Jewish apocalyptic. For example, the four apocalyptic horsemen (Rev 6:1-8) likely do not represent singular events following upon one another sequentially. Rather, they are essential moments or expressions of the same thing—history's climax: world conquest, war, plunder, and pestilence. Thus, Revelation differs from Jewish apocalypses by not simply portraying the course of history, but by proclaiming the essential character of the historical drama from the perspective of the exalted Christ.

What is the debate concerning Revelation's theological center? In spite of Revelation's certainty with regard to the victory of the Lamb, its history of interpretation reveals little certainty and much wide-ranging diversity. Two kinds of problems typically emerge (Johnson 1999:574). (1) The term "prophecy" is often reduced to its narrowest meaning: namely, "prediction." Here the significance of contemporary world events is probed, based on the constellation of the signs and symbols of the seer's visions in Revelation. (2) The symbols of the apocalypticist are pressed like an ancient magical code to reveal details of contemporary significance. Both these reductionistic interpretations have led to much misinterpretation, many disappointments, and even disaster. Failure to appreciate the purpose and function of the apocalyptic genre has resulted in both of these unfortunate scenarios. Johnson asserts, "Rather than telling people something about how Christian existence might be lived in the face of evil and apparent hopelessness, the text becomes something of a train schedule" (1999:574).

The issue revolves around hermeneutics. Few disagree on what the text says, at the level of the meaning of "the words on the page" (exegesis). The problem is on the hermeneutical level: that is, determining the contemporary significance of the meaning of "the words on the page."

Typically, four hermeneutical approaches have been used by contemporary faith communities. First, the *Preterist* approach reads Revelation as an apocalyptic tract limited to its own time in the first century. The ancient church, threatened by growing demands of the Roman imperial cult, drew courage from the apocalyptic vision of ultimate victory. The symbols picturing the end of the world refer to either the fall of Jerusalem 70 CE or the fall of Rome 476 CE, and no more. The contemporary church draws encouragement from the fulfillment of those predictions *back then*, assuring its own ultimate victory.

Second, the *Timeline* approach transposes the apocalyptic symbols into a description of world history from the time of the author to the end of the world. Revelation prophesies the entire course of world history. Revelation is thought to trace the major periods of Western civilization: the various popes, the Reformation, the French Revolution, and on to the present with different world leaders foretold and plotted on the timeline. Some contemporary faith communities may find this interpretation of history useful in their self-definition; however, its validity must be questioned since the situation of the initial readers is given little importance (not to mention the non-Western world) is given little importance!

Third, the *Futuristic* approach translates the apocalyptic symbols into a schematic that describes the future that lies before contemporary readers. Chapters 2–3 outline world history up to the present; the seven churches represent the seven successive ages of Christian history. The rest of Revelation from chapter 4 to the end predicts the future, as symbols are decoded with specific referents (e.g., locusts become attack helicopters, 666 and the "mark of the beast" are associated with terrorists or world leaders hostile to the West). Future events are charted either through to the time leading up to the "rapture" or to the time after the "rapture," depending on the version being promoted. This is probably the most well-known approach in America, popularized by the Left Behind series of novels.

Fourth, the *Symbolic* approach reads the apocalyptic visions metaphorically. No one specific historical referent is intended, but the representative power of the apocalyptic symbols addresses the historical situation of the church in every age. Certainly this would include, but not be limited to, the Roman imperial cult and its far-reaching and oppressive demands on first-century Christians. Revelation is appreciated as a theological poem or drama that gives expression to the ancient struggle between the kingdom of light and the kingdom of darkness, but with one huge key feature. Readers of Revelation in the first century all the way through to the present have found deeply meaningful the assurance that God's ultimate victory over evil is guaranteed by the exaltation of Jesus at the cross. Why? Because he is alive, and his ongoing presence animates the church's experience. Even though all the effects of the victory have yet to be realized, the impact of the victory is experienced now and continues to be played out until it is fully realized in the "new heaven and new earth" (21:1).

While the first three models do some things well, each fails to take seriously the language and imagery of John, the apocalypticist. The Preterist, Timeline, and Futuristic approaches all freeze the apocalyptic symbols, assigning them to concrete referents in the first century, western civilization, or the future. Two problems result: (1) The hermeneutical result of freezing the point of reference is that the symbols lose much of their power to transform and to shape the faith community today in significant ways—the assigned referents exhaust the meaning potential. (2) All three approaches also neglect one of the key features championed by the proto-orthodox shapers of the canonical witness. Johnson states it like this, "The contemporary significance of any NT writing does not derive from the fact that it was written expressly for our age but from the conviction that a truth spoken to the first age of Christians can and does remain a truth for every age of believers" (1999:574). The Christian confession is that God's Word speaks directly to the contemporary church; and it does so precisely as mediated through its original historical expression.

The advantage of the fourth approach (Symbolic) is that it takes both of these problems seriously; it offers an alternative that recognizes both the form and function of Revelation's apocalyptic genre *and* the potential for hearing a fresh, contemporary message from the ancient text. In particular, the symbolic view appreciates the significance of the way that the NT writers use end-time language (eschatology) to describe what is already current, in view of their conviction that what is yet to come has already been set in motion by the Lamb of God. This is reasonable since the only adequate "tools" for the job were a set of end-time-language symbols from Jewish apocalypticism (mythological dragons and beasts); they had no choice but to use these tools, as they were the best to talk about things that are not the final end but nevertheless end-like in their certainty, reality, and ultimate consequences. Caird puts it well: "Wherever in the course of time men and women come face to face, whether for judgment or salvation, with him who is the beginning and the end, that event can be adequately viewed only through the lenses of myth and eschatology" (1997:271).

What then is the structure of Revelation's theological statement? The outline of John's apocalypse is clear from the start. "Write what you have seen, what is, and what is to take place after this" (1:19). Thus, there are two parts: (1) prophecy for the present ("what is") in the letters to the seven churches (chapters 2–3); and (2) revelation regarding the future ("what is to take place after this") through a series of vision cycles (chapters 4–22).

In part 2, the revelation for the future is introduced by a vision of God, the "one seated on the throne" (4:2), with angelic courtiers calling out, "Holy, holy, holy, the Lord God the Almighty, who was and is and is to come . . . You are worthy, our Lord and God, to receive glory and honor and power, for you created all things, and by your will they existed and were created" (4:8, 11). It quickly becomes evident, however, that the task of carrying out God's purpose has been committed to the exalted Messiah Jesus; it is he who directs God's creation project, for he is the only one worthy "to open the scroll" (5:5) and accomplish God's purpose of ransoming "saints from every tribe and language" (5:9) and making "them to be a kingdom and priests," serving God forever (5:10).

A chain of vision cycles follows the opening throne room scene—seven seals (6:1—8:1), seven trumpets (8:2—11:19), and seven bowls (15:1—16:21). Each new cycle comes forth out of the previous cycle (8:1; 11:15; 15:5; 16:1), giving the drama a wave-like, growing intensity as the cycles build on one another. A further principle of division is that there are interludes between the sixth and seventh seals (7:1–17), and between the sixth and seventh trumpets (10:1—11:14). In each interlude, attention turns from the unfolding of world events to the destiny of God's people, assuring them that they are secure, that the purpose for which God made the universe will not fail, and that the victory is not in doubt, as it may sometimes appear.

Throughout the narration of the vision cycles, Revelation uses a standard set of apocalyptic symbols. Numbers are important for communicating precision, order, and design. The number seven appears often (e.g., there are seven lampstands, stars, spirits, seals, horns, trumpets, heads, bowls, and plagues). There are four living creatures, horsemen, and angels at the corners of the world. The number twelve and its multiples are used extensively: twelve gates and twelve foundation stones of the new Jerusalem correspond to the twelve tribes and twelve apostles (21:12–14); the tree of life bears twelve kinds of fruit (22:2), the woman's crown has twelve stars (12:1); twenty-four elders and twenty-four thrones are featured (4:4); and the number of the elect is one hundred forty-four thousand, twelve thousand from each tribe (7:4; 14:1–5). In addition to these numbers are fantastic images of beasts and cosmic phenomena. However, Johnson cautions, "No particular number, beast, or star is significant in and of itself; it is the cumulative effect that creates the sense of mystery and transcendence essential for the dramatic impact of the revelation" (1999:576).

Near the end of John's apocalyptic vision is a curious six-verse section revealing a provocative image of a thousand-year period, called the millennium (20:1–6). Already in the second century, early-church theologians argued about these six verses. Millenarians or Chiliasts appealed to these verses to substantiate their view that the elapsed time from the victory of Christ to the end of the world was to be exactly one thousand years. Those who opposed the Chiliast view tried to discredit it by challenging its foundation in these six verses. Dionysius of Alexandria, for example, argued that Revelation was not apostolic in origin since it differed so much from the Gospel of John, and therefore was not authoritative in its portrayal of the millennium (Kümmel 1975:471). Such disputes worked to delay Revelation's canonical ratification, as noted above.

Today there are three ways that Revelation's millennium language is interpreted. First, the *Postmillennialist* view imagines the kingdom of God spreading through a gradual christianizing of the world until Jesus returns at the end of time to celebrate the conclusion of the "millennial" project. This view was strong in the eighteenth and nineteenth centuries and included a heavy dose of Western optimism that the world could be transformed through good social policies, Western civilization, and political reform. The colonial and missionary imperialism of this period was thought to be bringing heaven to earth. However, the horrors of world wars, genocide, and disease have dampened the enthusiasm for trusting in "political" solutions alone.

Second, the *Premillennialist* view takes these six verses more literally in that they provide the framework for inserting key OT promises into a coherent map spanning both testaments. Briefly put, at some point the elect are "raptured" either before or after a period of catastrophic tribulation (depending on which view is being promoted), and finally Christ returns to judge the living and the dead, establishing the glorious, new-millennium world. This view tends to be rather pessimistic with regard to humanity, ecology, and history, since the earth will be destroyed anyway before Christ comes to usher in the new heaven and new earth. This view takes various forms, but the most common has been popularized in America through the bestselling adventure novels of the Left Behind series.

Third, the *Amillennialist* view reads the millenarian language symbolically. A thousand years describes both the certainty of the end *and* the length of God's patient resolve to work with creation toward the end (purpose) for which God made the world in the first place. A glimpse of that end was achieved at the cross where Jesus challenged evil and won, rising victorious over death and initiating the shape of the final stage of creation. Thus, in these last days before the final end (*eschaton*), however many thousands of years this may be, the church bears witness to the victory of God and invites all creation to abandon its rebellion against God's design. The challenge is to live fully and wholly by rediscovering the prior and true identity essential to each one's humanity and to all creation. In other words, the invitation is to *embrace* our true human identity as God's image bearers and then to *engage* God's design in order to become what God always intended.

In the amillennial view there is no golden age of freedom on earth prior to *eschaton*; in fact, things are likely to get worse as the deceiver tries valiantly to distract as many as possible before the end. However, neither is the end predicated on a complete destruction of the created order; there is continuity between this world and the world to come, as the new heaven and new earth grow out of this world. This view has little concern for dates and details about how this mystery will be accomplished; the "soon" language simply means, "count on it." For some, the amillennial view does not provide sufficient detail of the Lord's victory over evil, detail that they argue is warranted by the text. Nevertheless, the strength of the amillennial view is that it resonates most with the key features of the apocalyptic genre. It keeps the accent on the power of symbols: the assurance of God's triumph over evil; the coming of the new heaven, the new earth, and the new Jerusalem; and the ongoing challenge to resist the status quo. Plus, it refuses to allow these six verses to trump the rest of the biblical witness.

Although the three millennial views illustrate disagreement on how to read the millennial language (20:1–6), agreement exists on the basic message of Revelation. Watching as John the seer makes his way slowly to the podium, we can imagine him proclaim with much boldness his basic theological conviction in these terms: *What is and what is to take place hereafter is the triumph of God in history through the exalted Jesus Christ. Jesus is alive; he is "the faithful witness, the firstborn of the dead, and the ruler of the kings of the earth" (1:5). Because he reigns, Christians have reason to hope, even in the most difficult of circumstances. Regardless of how successful those who rebel against God seem to be in their resistance to Jesus, the gospel, the church, and so on, they cannot win, because God is on the throne. Based on what God has already done, I am certain that God will fulfill all that is promised, bringing history and creation to the goal for which it was made in the first place. Jesus is saying, "Surely I am coming soon"; and I say, "Amen. Come, Lord Jesus" (22:20)!*

THEMATIC IMPLICATIONS OF REVELATION'S VISION

From Revelation's theological center four implications emerge. First, the dominion of the Lamb is central to John's apocalyptic vision, reshaping the traditional apocalyptic symbols on account of Jesus's crucifixion and resurrection. Messiah Jesus is presented as the one who alone is able to turn around the apparently hopeless situation of the world. "'Who is worthy to open the scroll and break its seals?' . . . I began to weep bitterly because no one was found worthy . . . One of the elders said to me, 'Do not weep. See, the Lion of the tribe of Judah, the Root of David, has conquered, so that he can open the scroll and its seven seals.' Then I saw . . . a Lamb standing as if it had been slaughtered . . . He went and took the scroll" (5:1–7). In true apocalyptic form, someone must *reveal* the meaning and significance of history, especially its outcome. However, for John, it is the unexpected Lamb, the crucified one, who lives to take the scroll from the one seated on the throne and reveal its contents.

The image of the Lamb appears twenty-eight times in Revelation as the special symbol for the exalted Christ. The seer's use of the Lamb is striking. The Lamb is the one *sacrificed* for us—not to change God's mind about humanity, but to rescue us from the grip of sin's rule. "You are worthy . . . for you were slaughtered and by your blood you ransomed for

God saints from every tribe" (5:9). "Worthy is the Lamb that was slaughtered" (5:12). "They have washed their robes and made them white in the blood of the Lamb" (7:14). The Lamb, the exalted one, stands before God as the one who died, demonstrating both the lengths to which evil will go to victimize others to maintain its grip, *and* the lengths to which God's love will go to absorb and upend the death-dealing ways of evil. Evil is not permitted the last word; God's love is longer, deeper, and wider. Jesus is alive and now rules in heaven as the exalted one; he is fully qualified to complete the creation task, purposed by the one on the throne from the beginning.

In addition, the Lamb characterizes the one who is also *powerful*. Through the power of the Lamb, the eschatological reign of God is established. Revelation emphasizes this role to a greater extent than any other NT book. The Lamb before the throne is both the one who died once for all *and* the powerful ruler, drawing together humanity and divinity like no one had before. The Lamb reveals the divine purpose "fully" *and* completes "fully" humanity's creation destiny. Thus, the Lamb is now at the center of all those liberated from sin's grip; now they may be what they were meant to be in the first place (7:9, 17; 14:1, 4; 19:7, 9; 21:9, 22–27; 22:1–5). The power of the Lamb defines their identity, for their names "are written in the Lamb's book of life" (21:27). "Now have come the salvation and the power and the kingdom of our God and the authority of his Messiah, for the accuser of our comrades has been thrown down, who accuses them day and night before our God. But they have conquered him by the blood of the Lamb and the word of their testimony, for they did not cling to life even in the face of death" (12:10–11).

Second, the turning-point event in Revelation (and in world history) is the moment that the Lamb receives from the one on the throne the book of the seven seals (5:7). God's glory, only partially visible heretofore, is now clarified. The task of carrying out God's purpose for history and all creation is turned over to the Lamb who was slaughtered. The Lamb is portrayed as "worthy" to carry out the purpose of history, because proleptically he has already realized that which was of decisive and positive importance for all nations and all creation—the defeat of death and the beginning of life everlasting: "You are worthy to take the scroll and to open its seals, for you were slaughtered and by your blood you ransomed for God saints from every tribe and language and people and nation; you have made them to be a kingdom and priests serving our God, and they will reign on earth" (5:9-10). This is the most central statement in Revelation. It states that the exalted one, by his sacrifice and nonviolent resistance, has won for God a people out of every people group and has transferred them into God's kingdom. Therefore the Lamb is worthy and able to direct the rest of history.

Third, the judging role of Christ is part of the discerning and exposing character of God's kingdom rule. Since humanity is invited to participate in God's creation project, and humanity is necessary for its completion, that participation must be consequential, leading either to life or death. The gracious dominion of the Lamb includes the final judgment at the end of time. When God's rule is consummated and God's purpose for creation is complete, nothing can be admitted to the new Jerusalem that contradicts God's holy and life-filled character (21:27); whatever remains recalcitrant to God's will can only be destroyed (Caird 1994:78). However, the final judgment should not be understood as God's condemnation of some people or some part of creation. It is not so much about handing out rewards to some and punishing others, but more about a process of discerning (judging) each one's true commitment. At the "great white throne" of final judgment, each one's primary allegiance is clarified, as all are "judged according to their works" (20:12) and only those aligned with the "book of life" escape death (20:15).

Neither is the final judgment about God's exacting revenge on God's enemies—the blood that stains the robes of the Lamb and the Horseman is not that of his enemies (12:11; 19:13) but his own and those of the martyrs (Caird 1994:154). The power of their spilt blood is that it is gathered into the one inclusive act of self-consecration by which the Lamb exposes, reveals, discerns, clarifies, names, and destroys sin's deathly rule, judging it to be broken and without jurisdiction for all who share in the Lamb's collective, new-creation life.

Still, from Revelation 6 on there is an unrelenting chain of judgments. The negative consequences of persisting in rebellion are emphasized with greater breadth and intensity in Revelation than anywhere else in the NT. While God's face remains turned toward creation, it is firmly set against evil; it will be judged and not allowed to carry on forever, even though it often appears to do so. While the kingdom of God gathers representatives from all nations (Rev 5:9), the nations of the world and particularly their political representatives continue to reject the kingdom. The situation looks grim. In the unfolding vision narrated by Revelation, the exalted one directs history toward its goal, even though the nations and their political representatives are lined up against the people shaped by the gospel.

The heart of the apocalyptic drama is developed in Revelation 13. Two beast figures emerge: each represents systems, powers, and rulers that rebel against the victory of the Lamb. The powers, though mortally wounded, do not simply "roll over and give up." Instead, they resist as long as possible and are more vicious in these last days, trying to take as many down with them in their desperate campaign of destruction, dysfunction, and distraction. They know their time is "short." The manifestations of such ideological attacks upon the church likely resonated with the experience of John and his community in Asia Minor near the end of the first century—something that numerous subsequent faith communities living under threat also experience. Not surprisingly, the hostile reaction of the world in rebellion against the people of the Lamb is powered by Satan (12:9; 20:2, 7) and continues to the end when Satan's culture of death finally succeeds in exhausting itself of all possibilities. At the presentation of the bridegroom in the new Jerusalem (21:9), nothing evil is present, since having spurned life to the end, Satan's name is not found in the "Lamb's book of life" (20:15; 21:27), and he is "thrown into the lake of fire" (21:10).

The end-time character of judgment was set in motion at the cross where something truly amazing happened. The tools that evil has used from the dawn of civilization (the cycle of victimization, the scapegoat mechanism, the myth of redemptive violence) to keep all in its service, were finally broken. According to René Girard, "Only Satan could have set in motion the process of his own destruction without suspecting anything was wrong" (2001:151). Evidently, Satan was genuinely surprised by God's identification with the victim (Lamb) and by the fact that Satan was unable to get the disciples to abandon their conviction of Jesus's resurrection and their newfound concern for victims everywhere.

Thus, the rule of death and the cycle of victimization were effectively broken at the cross—they no longer have power over those associated with the Lamb. The Lamb's disclosure (judgment) of Satan's manipulative domination system set evil on the path toward self-destruction. Without the death-dealing lie by which it props itself up, its rule is drained of its power until one day it will no longer exist. The graphic image John uses to describe this is the "second death," in which all that refuses to abandon rebellion against God, all that refuses to give up deadly behaviors, and all refuses life in effect chooses the "second death" and is consumed in the "lake of fire" (20:14; 21:8).

As evil is eliminated, John pictures the new heaven and the new earth emerge with the holy city, the new Jerusalem at the center. This is the goal to which all of God's judgments ultimately lead: the realization of the new Jerusalem where all nations are welcome (the gates remain open), where humanity's creation mandate is fulfilled (the people bring their contributions), and where God's presence is visible everywhere (no temple is needed).

> And in the spirit he carried me away to a great, high mountain and showed me the holy city Jerusalem coming down out of heaven from God . . . I saw no temple in the city, for its temple is the Lord God the Almighty and the Lamb. And the city has no need of sun or moon to shine on it, for the glory of God is its light, and its lamp is the Lamb. The nations will walk by its light, and the kings of the earth will bring their glory into it. Its gates will never be shut by day—and there will be no night there. People will bring into it the glory and the honor of the nations . . . On either side of the river is the tree of life with its twelve kinds of fruit, producing its fruit each month; and the leaves of the tree are for the healing of the nations . . . But the throne of God and of the Lamb will be in it, and his servants will worship him; they will see his face, and his name will be on their foreheads. And there will be no more night; they need no light of lamp or sun, for the Lord God will be their light, and they will reign forever and ever. (21:10, 22–26; 22:2–5)

Fourth, the central issue in Revelation is not the interpretation of history but the issue of power (Schüssler Fiorenza 1989:419). The apocalypticist's burning question is: Who is Lord over the world? Revelation explicates the power of God and of the Lamb not only over the lives of individuals but over the whole world and its political powers. Therefore the imperial cult with its demand for total and complete allegiance must be resisted, because offering ultimate honor to the emperor would mean ratifying Rome's dominion over all people and thus denying the end-time power of God manifested in Christ. Still, as representatives of God's rule and partners in the mission of the Lamb on earth, Christians remain "subject" to the political powers and realities of their time without giving them automatic or uncritical allegiance.

The refusal to give ultimate allegiance to the political powers and the outright rejection of those elements of the political process that are contrary to the rule of the Lamb are sure to cause Christians a measure of exclusion from the social and community life of their time, possibly even captivity or death (13:11–18). Evidently, while allegiance to the power of the Lamb and to his nonviolent peacemaking ways is "right," this does not mean it necessarily "works" in the short term—one is likely to get hurt along the way. No wonder the martyrs call out, "How long will it be before you judge and avenge our blood on the inhabitants of the earth?" And this is the assurance received: "They were each given a white robe and told to rest a little longer" (6:10–11). According to John, the seer, nonviolent resistance of evil remains "right" in the deepest sense and "works" in the long term, because it is the way that God's people anticipate the ultimate triumph of the Lamb (Yoder 1971:61).

In its deepest sense, evil cannot really ever be killed; of course, it must still be challenged, but how? With a larger arsenal? No. For John the seer, evil must not be met on its own violent terms. Evil, as well as all creation, must be free to be evil, free to separate itself from God and life, but also free to abandon rebellion and choose life. This is not apathy, isolationism, or fatalism. The seer calls the church to lifelong resistance to and condemnation of evil (7:14; 12:11; 19:13). Yet the power of the Lamb is different from the way that cultures have typically manifested power and authority—usually to make people do certain things, even if they do not want to do them. Instead, the power of the Lamb is the very expression of God's creative love and purpose, which makes possible—consequentially and not coercively—the creation design for which the world was made. By God's liberation of creation from sin's deceptive lie (19:20–21; 20:14–15), people at last by the power of the Lamb can be truly and fully human as God intended from the start. Thus the power of the Lamb gives voice to the divine purpose: "It is done! I am the Alpha and the Omega, the beginning and the end. To the thirsty I will give water as a gift from the spring of the water of life. Those who conquer will inherit these things, and I will be their God and they will be my children" (21:6–7).

The last voices to speak at the NT conference are those representing the General Letters; they are the subjects of the next chapter.

EXERCISES

1. Many artists have attempted to portray the significance of Jesus in the contemporary medium of film. The impact of these attempts varies from the provocative to the disturbing and points in between. Some of these Jesus movies include *Jesus Christ Superstar, The Passion of the Christ, Jesus of Montreal, Monty Python's Life of Brian, The Last Temptation of Christ,* and others.

   View one or more of these movies with some friends and discuss the screenwriter's project. What portrait of Jesus is being conveyed? How compelling is the image for you? Why?

2. Read the noncanonical apocalypses usually dated before 130 CE: the *Shepherd of Hermas* and the *Apocalypse of Peter*. These can be found on the Internet or in Bart Ehrman's reader, *The New Testament and Other Early Christian Writings: A Reader*.

   Compare and contrast the noncanonical Apocalypses with John's Revelation. What observations can you make?

6

The Theological Contribution of the Remaining Canonical Witnesses

So far we have heard from Paul, the Synoptic Evangelists, and the Johannine traditions. It is time to turn over the microphone to the writers of the remaining canonical witnesses—Hebrews, James, 1–2 Peter, and Jude. While these writings are often neglected or marginalized in some way, they are not inferior; they simply represent expressions of the church's framing of the Jesus tradition that differ from Paul, the Synoptics, and the Johannine traditions. They have a rightful place at the table! In this chapter we listen to the voices of these final canonical witnesses, sometimes called the General or Catholic Letters.

The chapter has two objectives: (1) to clarify the distinctive character of the Catholic Letters and (2) to outline the theological vision of Hebrews, James, 1–2 Peter, and Jude, including the current debate, the structure, the articulation, and the thematic implications of the central vision that each one puts forward.

THE DISTINCTIVE CHARACTER OF THE CATHOLIC LETTERS

Eventually the bishops in centers like Rome and Alexandria designated seven NT writings as the Catholic Letters—two letters of Peter, three letters of John, Jude, and James. The anonymous Letter to the Hebrews, which we will also consider in this chapter, came to be seen as one of Paul's letters, an association that many in the ancient church made, though not all. The seven Catholic Letters plus Hebrews are now sometimes termed the General Letters.

What is distinctive about these letters? It is plain from a quick reading of these letters that they are unlike the occasional letters in the Pauline collection. If there ever were occasioning situations driving the composition of these letters, they are no longer self-evident. They are catholic or generic in the sense that they are useful to the church everywhere or in general. They share three key features.

First, the Catholic Letters are fashioned as letters. The fact that these writings are framed as letters (sometimes artificially, as we will see below) shows early Christianity's high regard for Paul and his custom of writing or sponsoring pastoral letters of exhortation and of encouragement to Christian communities. By the end of the first century, the standard form of written teaching for ecclesial communities was the pastoral letter, following the pattern of Paul's practice (Gamble 1995:107).

Even though Paul's letters were not initially written for general or universal utilization, they quickly became appreciated as useful for Christians everywhere—that is, catholic. By circulating, copying, collecting, and editing Paul's letters for use in communities outside those initially addressed, Paul's missionary associates during his life and probably shortly after his death, helped to generalize the particularity of a Pauline letter. Plus, the tradition that Paul had written to seven churches (the number symbolizing totality and universality) strengthened the perception of catholicity for the Pauline collection of letters (Gamble 1995:59–60). Traces of such collection values remain in our NT, where Paul's letters are ordered and arranged by decreasing length and by association with the same community.

While the number of letters in the Pauline corpus appears to fluctuate in the history of transmission—first ten, then thirteen (counting the Pastorals), and even fourteen (counting Hebrews)—the number of ecclesial communities addressed by Paul does not—there are *exactly* seven: Corinth, Rome, Ephesus, Thessalonica, Galatia, Philippi, and Colossae. As a collection of letters to seven churches, Paul's occasional letters to particular communities were transformed into catholic letters, useful for instruction in churches anywhere and everywhere. Probably the seven letters at the beginning of Revelation (2:1—3:22) and the seven letters of Ignatius of Antioch reflect appreciation for an early edition of Pauline letters circulating as a collection of letters to seven churches (Gamble 1995:61).

Second Peter 3:15 clearly mentions a collection of Paul's letters already circulating (earliest reference) and acknowledges its esteemed role (as Scripture) in shaping and guiding early Christian communities in their discernment and struggle for self-understanding.

> Therefore, beloved, while you are waiting for these things, strive to be found by him at peace, without spot or blemish; and regard the patience of our Lord as salvation. So also our beloved brother Paul wrote to you according to the wisdom given him, speaking of this as he does in all his letters. There are some things in them hard to understand, which the ignorant and unstable twist to their own destruction, as they do the other scriptures. You therefore, beloved, since you are forewarned, beware that you are not carried away with the error of lawlessness and lose your own stability. (2 Pet 3:14–17)

However, besides the strong affirmation of Paul, the Catholic Letters also signal the church's willingness to recognize other "framers" of the memory of Jesus's life, the significance of Easter, and the Christian experience. While the voices of the Catholic Letters may not be as strong as Paul's and the Evangelists', their inclusion in the Christian Bible signals their value as equal contributors to the NT choir and the NT conference.

Second, the Catholic Letters offer general teaching and exhortation not obviously linked to a specific congregation. Their story of provenance is different from the Pauline collection. Postapostolic editors worked to arrange, edit, and supplement the Pauline corpus for canonical use, transforming Paul's occasional letters into letters of general Christian interest. By contrast, the seven Catholic Letters (or eight with Hebrews) began their lives as generic addresses, where the audience or author's community was not self-evident and no longer retrievable. This consequence of genre and history meant that the road to canonical ratification proved to be *more* difficult for these generic letters than for Paul's occasional letters.

The four gospels, with their eyewitness testimony to the words/deeds of Messiah Jesus and Paul's collection of letters, with its apostolic witness to the message of the risen Lord for specific communities, were easily ratified as canonical for the authoritative role they played from the start among the early churches. Such was not the case for the General Letters. There is little doubt that these texts were written sometime

The Theological Contribution of the Remaining Canonical Witnesses 189

between the early decades of the Jesus movement and the end of the first century. However, their composition dates are hard to pin down or even to estimate, because of the generic character of their exhortation and the lack of detail relating to the author or to the church being addressed.

Apparently, the ambiguity of the Catholic Letters in terms of origination and destination proved to be problematic for the fourth-century bishops, theologians, and heresiologists, as they began to set out the approved canonical lists of texts for reading and instruction in the churches. What was it that helped prod church leaders to finish the task of ratifying the Catholic Letters for liturgical and catechetical use in the church?

One explanation is that the passage of time worked to heighten the pressure to settle on the parameters of the church's guiding Scripture or canon. The apostles and those who knew them were no longer alive. Thus, the witness of those close to the apostolic tradition was also fading. This was a new situation. The passage of time following the apostolic period required the early Christian movement to complete work on an authorized collection of writings that could serve as a theological norm for the ongoing life of the church globally.

In addition, the increased conflict between various Christian groups in the second and third centuries proved to be another motivating factor for establishing a canonical norm. Some groups offered individually orientated spiritual expressions (Montanism, gnosticism, and the like); others advocated severing all connections with Israel (Marcion). The increased internal conflict raised the bar for selecting which writings could be ratified as apostolic and serve as the church's canonical norm. It was no longer enough to point to widespread usage, early reception, or theological consistency.

By the fourth century, in order to ward off further fragmentation from gnostic appeals to new and equally authoritative spiritual writings, clear historical justification of apostolic origin had to be made in order to establish a writing's place among the collection of texts functioning as the ongoing "rule of faith" or scriptural norm for the church (Johnson 1999:602). However, the originating details for the General Letters were no longer available or remembered, having been lost already early in the second century, after years of circulating, collecting, and copying. This meant that initially there were gaps and uneven affirmation of these texts in the various centers of Christianity around the Mediterranean.

For example, three church theologians of the second century—Clement of Alexandria, Irenaeus, and Tertullian—recognized a NT that had four gospels and an apostolic section including thirteen letters of Paul, Acts, 1 Peter, 1 John, and Revelation (Kümmel 1975:491). The other Catholic Letters and Hebrews were known, but their justification as apostolic witnesses was disputed. Furthermore, in some communities other writings were treated as canonical (e.g., the *Letter of Barnabas*, the *Shepherd of Hermas*, the *Apocalypse of Peter*, and the *Didache*). These assessments are derived from the texts that the second- and third-century theologians and heresiologists (e.g., Origen, Eusebius) quote in their tracts and homilies, and from the early lists (canons, e.g., the Muratorian canon) authorizing certain writings as acceptable (and those which were unacceptable) for public reading in the churches.

The writings approved for ecclesiastical use in the Muratorian canon (often dated to the second century, though sometimes also the fourth century) include four gospels, Acts, thirteen letters of Paul, two letters of John (1 and 2), Jude, and Revelation; missing are Hebrews, 3 John, James, and two letters of Peter (Sundberg 1973). Origen (ca. 253 CE) included the following writings in his canon of approved Scriptures: four gospels, thirteen letters of Paul, 1 Peter, 1 John, and Revelation; he noted that 2 Peter, 2–3 John, Hebrews, Jude, and James were "doubtful writings" (quoted in Eusebius, *Eccl. Hist.* 6.25.3). Eusebius of Caesarea (*ca.* 303 CE) listed four gospels, fourteen letters of Paul (including Hebrews), 1 Peter, 1 John, and Revelation (with some hesitation) as unanimously approved, noting that James, Jude, 2 Peter, and 2–3 John were still disputed by some, although recognized by the majority (Eusebius *Eccl. Hist.* 3.25).

While acceptance of the Catholic Letters was not quite unanimous yet, by the beginning of the fourth century church leaders were getting past their ambiguous origination and destination and recognizing them as authoritative and useful for Christian instruction. But it was the next feature in our summary of traits that proved decisive for overcoming the lingering questions of Catholic Letters' provenance and for securing their ratification as canonical.

Third, the Catholic Letters eventually achieved ratification as canonical when their association with an apostle or a brother of Jesus (1 Cor 9:5) could be established to the satisfaction of the various bishops and the Christian communities they represented around the Mediterranean. Apparently, by the fourth century, it was clear that if the emerging orthodoxy was to survive the repeated threat of the *expansion* of the NT canon from Montanism and gnosticism, or the threat of *contraction* of the NT canon from Marcion, an approved list of writings for ecclesial use needed to be established. In other words, "if Christian identity was to avoid being fragmented in diverse directions, limits needed to be set" (Johnson 1999:602).

The threat of the heterodox writings became too great to overlook. No longer willing to tolerate the inner diversity of heterodox teachers, *and* armed with the greater power and resources of the church hierarchy in the fourth century, the bishops in Alexandria and Rome began to produce, distribute, and enforce lists of approved texts for Christian reading (Wisse 1986:190). The motivations driving this collection were largely pragmatic in orientation, and the criteria were simple enough: demonstrated usefulness in the churches in all its locations, compelling argument for apostolic derivation, and well-recognized theological consistency.

The issue holding up the ratification of disputed texts like Hebrews, Revelation, the Letters of Peter, the Letters of John, Jude, and James was not that they were of questionable use or that they were theologically inconsistent. That they clearly were useful for instruction and exhortation was evidenced by their circulation and collection from the beginning. The problem was how to ratify these texts, given the fact that their originating setting in the first century had not been passed on along with these texts as they were collected and copied. Convincing arguments for apostolic derivation had not been made.

The Catholic Letters presented one peculiar problem that Paul's letters did not. How can a generic composition function as normative, when so little certainty surrounds its originating historical situation? This was precisely the opposite problem encountered by the collectors of the Pauline letters and the early shapers of the canon. The problem for the postapostolic Christian community was how to make Pauline writings addressed to particular churches applicable to a general Christian audience in the generations that followed.

The postapostolic shapers of the canon employed several means to extend a text's particularity to a general setting. They rearranged, edited, and supplemented the collection so that the NT could function more easily as a generic guide for churches everywhere. For example, the Pastoral Letters were added to the Pauline corpus to guide the church's reading of Paul; Acts was separated from Luke and made to introduce Paul and to track the expansion of the gospel to include Gentiles; the four Gospels were put in front of Paul's letters to ground Paul's witness in the story of Jesus, even though the Gospels were composed later (Childs 1984:52–53).

No one doubted the usefulness of the Catholic Letters; the problem was how to justify or ratify the position or place they had come to occupy in churches. Arguments continued among the bishops and theologians for another couple hundred years. Eventually, most agreed on the rationalizations, taken from clues internal to the texts themselves, that tied Hebrews, James, 2 Peter, and 2–3 John to an apostolic witness in some way. In the Eastern church, Athanasius's 39th Easter letter of 367 CE listed 27 writings as the NT, which along the OT writings, could be read (used legitimately and profitably) in the church. He was first to call this ecclesiastically fixed collection of scriptures the "canon" (Kümmel 1975:498). In the Roman church, Pope Innocent I named the canon of Athanasius in 405 CE as officially endorsed for use in the Western church as well. The list served to officially ratify the texts that had already long proved useful, apostolic in derivation, and theologically consistent with the church's "rule of faith."

Interestingly, Pope Innocent I described the NT canon as including fourteen Pauline Letters Paul (with Hebrews) and seven Catholic Letters; these numbers show again how the issue was one of justification and ratification. Apparently the symbolic number seven (and its multiple, fourteen) appears to have been the trump card. It was just the evidence for which the leading bishops were looking. Now they had a means by which to ratify the twenty-seven texts that had already come to be useful throughout the federation of churches around the Mediterranean.

While the highly charged heterodox atmosphere of the third and fourth centuries made the canonical ratification of the Catholic Letters more challenging, their lack of historical particularity is not really surprising. The writers of these literary texts were not interested in showcasing themselves. They were interested, instead, in persuading readers and listeners of their vision of God's ongoing activity in Jesus and of their convictions for the shape of the church's witness in the world. Once again these developments testify to one of the key features of the Christian Bible: namely, that for the canonical shapers, theological concerns took precedence over historical concerns. However, when they were required, enough clues could be "found" in the texts themselves to make a compelling-enough case for apostolic derivation. In the end, the church overcame its concern to historically locate its apostolic writings only in relation to Paul. The Catholic Letters were recognized as giving expressions to other apostolic voices that were equally important witnesses to the significance of Jesus and that were deserving of the church's attention, even if the full details of their historical situations were now lost. It is to their voices that we now give our attention.

HEBREWS

Theological Vision

During the third and fourth centuries, when bishops, theologians, and heresiologists began to marshal evidence for the ratification of early Christian writings like Hebrews, they stumbled into a problem. For over a hundred years the Letter to the Hebrews had circulated in many Christian communities as an extremely successful "word of encouragement" (13:22). The argument was compelling, and the exhortation was appropriate, even if the author, the setting, and the rhetorical situation were no longer known. However, as the threat of heterodoxy increased, so did the pressure to authenticate valued texts like Hebrews. Thus, the quest for its apostolic pedigree began. This was the beginning of the riddle of Hebrews.

Hebrews presented a riddle for some Christians in three ways. First, who was the author? The text was anonymous; this was odd, given that most ancient letters were not anonymous. All sorts of proposals for author were made over the centuries. Was it Paul? The reference to "our brother Timothy" (13:23) could suggest that Paul was the author. For some this was evidence enough; for others it was not. Was it Barnabas? Was it Apollos? Was it Priscilla? Was it Epaphras? Was it someone else?

The contemporary view is that no one claim to authorship is conclusive. We simply do not know who the author was. By the fourth century, however, Eusebius reports the then-consensus view that attributed Hebrews to Paul—thus assuring Hebrews of the place in the canon that it had occupied from the start in many communities. As the fourteenth letter of Paul (2 x 7), it rounded out the Pauline corpus as the complete and universal apostolic vision for ongoing church life. Some manuscripts even employed the superscription "The Letter of Paul to the Hebrews" (e.g., codex 0285). Today, however, few would contend that Paul is the author—the writing style and theological perspective is just so different from what we know of Paul in his letters (Attridge 1989:1–3). In the end, the riddle of who authored Hebrews remains unanswered.

The second riddle centers on questions like, who were the addressees, and what were the occasioning circumstances? Early on, the assumed destination was a group of Hebrews, either Hebrew Christians or Hebrews in general. This is probably because the text often refers to the Jewish sacrificial system and to the heroes and heroines of faith from the OT (3:1-6; 4:14—5:14; 7:1-28; 9:11—10:18; 11:1-40). However, these are hardly conclusive indicators of Hebrew recipients. Paul's letters addressed to largely Gentile congregations also contain many references to Jewish faith and practice. In view of the lack of direct evidence, these textual details were read as indirect clues that the original recipients were Hebrew people. While this may have been compelling for many in the ancient church, there is not the same consensus today as to the target audience of Hebrews (Hurst 1990). Some continue to advocate a Jewish setting and audience—former members of desert communities at Qumran or of Hellenistic Judaism in general. Others advocate for Gentile Christians struggling with syncretistic gnosticism. In any case, the riddle of the intended audience and setting of Hebrews remains unanswered.

The third riddle circles around accounting for the strange form of Hebrews. Wrede (1906) noted this additional version of the riddle of Hebrews. His concern was for the literary form of Hebrews. Wrede challenged the genre of Hebrews as a letter. On the one hand, the text entered directly into its argument without any introductory greeting—hardly like a letter. On the other hand, the text concluded with a personal postscript that resembled an epistolary closing, yet the thirteen preceding chapters had more in common with a homily or a treatise: Hebrews makes one of the longest sustained arguments in the NT. No explanation for its strange form has achieved consensus. Was the introductory greeting omitted, lost, or delivered orally? Perhaps Hebrews started as a treatise and was transformed into a letter by the addition of a postscript (13:22-25) in order to conform to the emerging standard for a Christian writing, a pastoral letter like those in the Pauline collection. At any rate, the riddle of the form of Hebrews remains unanswered.

It may well be, however, that the riddle of Hebrews—in its three versions—is based on inappropriate expectations. If the expectations were changed, the riddle would vanish. For example, if the essentially literary character of Hebrews were taken seriously, then it would not be unusual to situate Hebrews as a persuasive literary effort written by a gifted exegete and aimed at a general Christian audience (Isaak 2002). In other words, it is not surprising that the author or his community is no longer remembered, since these details were not the focus of the discourse. Furthermore, it is not surprising that the letter form feels forced and artificial. There is a good, plausible explanation for such a development, given the high estimation of the letter form in the history of canon formation, and given the struggle to ratify authoritative texts during the heterodox period of early Christianity, as noted above. Finally, it is not surprising that the target audience is not named, since the aim of any literary product, unlike the goal of an occasional letter, is to address a general audience with the persuasive rhetoric of its argument.

What we have then in Hebrews is a literary product of such power and significance that the Christian community worked hard to secure its place in the NT canon, finding just enough in the reference to "our brother Timothy" (13:23) to rationalize a Pauline connection. While few would doubt the grandeur of the argument, Samuel Sandmel's famous quip points out what is now the consensus view: the so-called Letter of Paul to the Hebrews is not by Paul, not to the Hebrews, and not a letter (1974:235).

What is the structure of Hebrews's theological statement? While Paul is intent to show that Scripture did *not* bring him to Christ (rather God, in Christ, opened his eyes to see the true meaning of Scripture), the author of Hebrews takes a different tack. Hebrews is a sustained theological argument making Christian *exegetical* use of the OT to show that what God spoke in fragmentary ways through the prophets (1:1), has now been fully revealed in Jesus, the Son who achieves God's purpose for humanity (Caird 1994:63).

Four OT texts get thorough exegetical treatment in Hebrews, each one showing how Jesus fulfils the OT intention (Caird 1959:44–51). Psalm 8 holds out the vision for human destiny in the economy of God's creation purpose, which remained unfulfilled until Jesus entered the promised glory as the leader and representative of all God's children (2:5–18). Psalm 95 contains the prospect of entering God's "rest," which the old order could not make effective, because it did not have the power to make possible a response of faith: something Jesus's faithfulness achieved (3:1—4:16). Psalm 110 introduces a new and eternal priesthood: the order of Melchizedek. It is to this priesthood that Jesus is appointed, completing what the Levitical order was unable to deliver (5:1—7:28). Jeremiah 31, in view of the new covenant, explicitly states that the old order has become "obsolete" (8:13) since Jesus now mediates the new covenant accessing "once for all" the promised eternal inheritance (8:1—9:28). As if to underline the point, Hebrews notes that even the OT saints, by faith, trusted God to make good someday on the ancient promises, confessing that they were seeking a city that would not become accessible until the coming of Messiah Jesus (11:1—12:29).

Besides the sustained exegetical argument, Hebrews employs a structural pattern of alternating blocks of *exposition* on the pioneering work of Jesus's ministry (e.g., 1:5—2:18) with blocks of *exhortations*, calling fellow pilgrims to a corresponding life of faithfulness and endurance (e.g., 3:1—4:14). Albert Vanhoye (1963:59) identified this pattern and proposed a series of concentric cycles or *chiastic* rings based on literary clues like catchwords, inclusions, thematic announcements, vocabulary, and alternation. See chart below. Note how the blocks of text build from the Introduction to climax at the central exposition (g) and also correspond to parallel blocks moving from the center to the Conclusion (a // a'; b // b', etc.).

a (1:1–4) Introduction	
b (1:5–2:18) The name superior to the angels	Exposition
c (3:1–4:14) Jesus, the faithful one	Exhortation
d (4:15 5:10) Jesus, the compassionate High Priest	Exposition
e (5:11–6:20) Preliminary Exhortation	Exhortation
f (7:1–28) Jesus, the High Priest according to the order of Melchizedek	Exposition
g (8:1–9:28) Jesus, the High Priest perfected	Exposition
f' (10:1–18) Jesus, the High Priest and cause of eternal salvation	Exposition
e' (10:19–39) Final Exhortation	Exhortation
d' (11:1–40) The faith of the ancestors	Exposition
c' (12:1–13) The necessary endurance	Exhortation
b' (12:14–13:19) The peaceful fruit of justice	Exhortation
a' (13:20–21) Conclusion	

TABLE 6.1 General Schema of the Letter to the Hebrews according to Vanhoye

The writer of Hebrews steps up to the lectern to give his vision statement. Like so many of the Catholic Letters, Hebrews seems to be involved in helping the Christian community establish appropriate boundaries of self-definition, so that they understand themselves as true participants in Israel's tradition. No doubt at this time non-Christian Jews outnumbered Christians, and they would have found it ludicrous for non-Jews to claim to understand the Jewish religion better than they did—but this is precisely the audacious claim that the author of Hebrews argues.

The author's opening statement would be something like the following. *Key aspects within Judaism (prophets, angels, Moses, and Torah) foreshadow the salvation that God promised, and that has now become a reality in Jesus, the pioneer and perfecter of God's people. Jesus's faithful life of sacrificial giving opens access to the sanctuary of God in a better way than traditional sacrificial systems, such that his followers more truly characterize the people of God. Nevertheless, just as the desert wanderers failed to enter the land of Canaan, so too God's people are encouraged now not to falter, but to persevere with faithful obedience and thus confirm their identity.*

Thematic Implications of Hebrews's Vision

Three themes emerge from Hebrews's central conviction. First, Hebrews offers a carefully developed Christology. The author uses numerous titles to express and to illustrate the central significance of Jesus's person and work. For Hebrews, Jesus is unique for two reasons (Johnson 1999:470). (1) Jesus is the one who brings salvation from God to humanity. Besides traditional designations like "Lord," "Son of God," "Son of man," and "Christ," Hebrews uses many other titles to speak of Jesus's messianic role as agent of God's salvation enterprise. He is called: "the one who sanctifies" (2:11), "the apostle" (3:1), "the builder of a house" (3:3), "the source of eternal salvation" (5:9), "the guarantee" (7:22), "minister in the sanctuary" (8:2), "perfecter" (12:2), and "the great shepherd of the sheep" (13:20). (2) Jesus is also the human being who first reaches what is the plan of God for all human beings. Here too Hebrews employs several titles to give expression to Jesus's messianic role of representing the new humanity. He is called "heir" (1:2), "the firstborn" (1:6), "the pioneer" (2:10; 12:2), and "forerunner" (6:20).

Both these aspects of Jesus's identity are brought together in another favorite title utilized by Hebrews: namely, "the mediator" (8:6; 9:15; 12:24) par excellence, the one who bridges humanity and divinity. As "priest" or "high priest" (2:17; 3:1; 4:14; 5:5, 10; 6:20; 7:26; 8:1; 9:11; 10:21), Jesus can uniquely say yes both for God (since he is the visible image of the invisible God) and for humanity (since he is the firstborn of the new or completed creation). Proto-orthodox Christians conceptualized this reality by saying Jesus was "fully God" (demonstrating fully God's character and desire for creation) and "fully human" (demonstrating fully humanity's true character as intended by God from the beginning). In later discussions things often got bogged down in ontological arguments over the very substance or essence of Jesus: Was he half divine and half human? Was he mostly God or mostly human? In the end, none of the partition options championed by some early Christian groups was found to be compelling, and the definition of "fully divine and fully human" was affirmed as the one that best accounted for Jesus's life and ministry (the Chalcedonian Creed, 451 CE).

When speaking of Jesus's work of atonement, Hebrews prefers to use metaphors of sacrifice. This is another indication of the different voices singing in the NT choir. We have seen that Paul prefers the battlefield imagery of victory over the power of sin (1 Cor 15:56; Col 2:15), Mark uses commercial imagery of redemption and ransom (Mark 10:45), and Luke uses relational imagery of friendship obligation to describe atonement. The contribution of Hebrews is still different: contrast and reversal are keys to the sacrifice imagery of Hebrews.

Jesus's priestly order was not of the order of Aaron but of Melchizedek (4:14—5:14; 7:1-28). In other words, it is more ancient and more effectual. Hebrews stresses that Jesus's sacrifice is of a different order from the traditional sacrifices of sheep, goats, calves, or bulls used in Israel's worship ritual—practices that tap into some of the most basic characteristics of all human cultures: namely, the redemptive violence of the single-victim, scapegoat mechanism, where group solidarity is achieved by the exclusion, expulsion, or sacrifice of another (Girard 2001). In Jesus's sacrificial offering, however, God opens access to life by absorbing the sting of death once for all and reversing its effects. According to the old order, "Without the shedding of blood there is no forgiveness" (9:22). By contrast, Jesus's sacrifice makes the old-order system obsolete (8:13)—not by a difference of *magnitude* (his blood is a better quality) but by a difference in *kind*. Instead of covering human shame or guilt year after year (Israel's religious practice) or satisfying the deity by repeated sacrifices (pagan religious practice), Jesus's sacrifice demonstrates God's own self-giving offering, exposing the whole scapegoat mechanism to be a sham, an empty scheme of victimization and domination (9:11–28). Now that evil's power to condemn is drained, all who identify with God's self-offering activity in Jesus can also experience liberation from the grip of sin (10:11–14) and open access to the sanctuary of God (10:19).

Second, Hebrews narrates the journey of discipleship as one of gradually learning and becoming the one whom God always intended, through a series of educational choices and decisions. Hebrews's Christology develops the exhortation to Christian discipleship. The human experience of learning, suffering, and growing shapes Christians in the pattern of Jesus, the one who confirmed his identity as God's Son, the Messiah, by faithfully reaching out to others—by being made "perfect" in the sense of completing or filling out what was his identity from the start (5:8–9). Without this reality of his own faithfulness, how can Jesus be any encouragement to others? Special about Jesus are his identity and relationship with God, which are unique and more than what other human beings possess. The way he confirmed his identity is not unique, however.

Thus, just as Jesus "learned" what it meant to be God's Son, confirming his identity as God's agent and bringer of salvation (5:8–9), in the same way, Jesus's disciples confirm their identity as God's children by living a life of faithful dependence on God, carrying on in their pilgrim journey (6:1). While Jesus's identity *differs* from his disciples', they like him, confirm their identity in the *same* way—by faithful obedience to God's call. Jesus is, therefore, both the "pioneer" who blazes the trail once for all and also the "perfecter" who gives those who follow him the power to complete the journey toward perfection and maturity, a destination only to be realized at the end of time (6:1; 9:27–28; 10:14, 19–25; 12:1–2).

Third, Hebrews stresses the urgent call to faithful obedience and endurance, even through testing; and this remains the identifying characteristic of God's people from the beginning. A long list of ancestors in the faith gives testimony to this kind of faith (11:1–40). Abraham, for example, represents the kind of faith that perseveres through hardship and testing (11:9, 17) and the kind of faith that lives grounded in the conviction that while things in this world may "look as good as dead" (11:12), the promised city's "architect and builder is God" (11:10). Therefore, God can be trusted to bring the creation project to completion.

Like Paul, Hebrews also conceives of faith as a response to God's initiative that involves active trust and obedience; faith is not limited to the acceptance of certain points of doctrine at the cognitive level. Instead, faith has to do with the practical confidence that God will actually do as promised. However, Hebrews puts the accent on endurance: "Do not, therefore, abandon that confidence of yours; it brings great reward. For you need endurance, so that when you have done the will of God, you may receive what was promised" (10:35-36).

The heroes and heroines of Israel's faith listed in 11:1-40 exemplify two dimensions of faith. First, faith has a vertical dimension. It is "the assurance of things hoped for, the conviction of things not seen" (11:1). That is, people of Israel's faith engage life here *below*, but live out of the reality of what is *above*. Not to be misunderstood as isolationism or dualism, it is more accurately conceptualized as an *additional* perspective that energizes participation with vital engagement: "All of these died in faith without having received the promises, but from a distance they saw and greeted them . . . They were strangers and foreigners on the earth" (11:13).

Faith also has a second dimension, a horizontal reality. It persists now in the meantime, drawing mutual encouragement from fellow pilgrims who also have "become partners of Christ," counting on God to carry forward the creation enterprise, and eventually to bring it to completion and perfection (3:14). The memory of those who have gone before and the companionship of co-travelers combine to encourage pilgrims to carry on the discipleship journey. And so Hebrews cheers on fellow travelers with these words: "Therefore, since we are surrounded by so great a cloud of witnesses, let us also lay aside every weight and the sin which clings so closely, and let us run with perseverance the race that is set before us, looking to Jesus the pioneer and perfecter of our faith" (12:1-2).

JAMES

Theological Vision

Since the Protestant Reformation, Martin Luther's misgivings about the book of James have overshadowed the question of James's theological contribution. For Luther, the problem was the content of the letter itself.

He would have preferred to leave James out of the canon, and only reluctantly included it along with three other writings (Jude, Hebrews, and Revelation) in the appendix to his 1522 German Bible translation. What were his concerns? In his preface to James, Luther writes:

> Though this epistle of St. James was rejected by the ancients, I praise it and consider it a good book, because it sets up no [human] doctrines but vigorously promulgates the law of God. However, to state my own opinion about it, though without prejudice to anyone, I do not regard it as a writing of an apostle; and my reasons follow. In the first place it is flatly against St. Paul and all the rest of scripture in ascribing justification to works ... St. Paul teaches to the contrary that Abraham was justified apart from works, by his faith alone ... In the second place its purpose is to teach Christians, but in all this long teaching it does not once mention the Passion, the resurrection, or the Spirit of Christ. He names Christ several times; however he teaches nothing about him . . . . Whatever does not teach Christ is not yet apostolic, even though St. Peter or St. Paul does the teaching. Again, whatever preaches Christ would be apostolic, even if Judas, Annas, Pilate, and Herod were doing it. But this James does nothing more than drive to the law and to its works. Besides, he throws things together so chaotically that it seems to me he must have been some good, pious man, who took a few sayings from the disciples of the apostles and thus tossed them off on paper ... St. James' epistle is really an epistle of straw, compared to these others, for it has nothing of the nature of the gospel about it ... Therefore I cannot include him among the chief books, though I would not thereby prevent anyone from including or extolling him as he pleases, for there are otherwise many good sayings in him. (Luther 1960:395–97, 362)

Luther called James an epistle of "straw," likely referring to Paul's encouragement that the church ought to build on the foundation of the risen Lord, but also ought to be aware that its constructions would be subject to assessment. "The work of each builder will become visible, for the Day will disclose it, because it will be revealed with fire" (1 Cor 3:13). Evidently, Paul is well aware that these constructions will be of varying quality—some more durable than others (e.g., "gold, silver, precious stones") and some rather combustible (e.g., "wood, hay, or straw"). In Luther's assessment, the Letter of James fits into the combustible category.

Luther's assessment of James is unfortunate for two reasons (Johnson 1999:507). First, it makes Paul the only criterion for canonical acceptance. More precisely, it makes Luther's view of Paul's central concern for "justification by faith" to be the only criterion for canonical acceptance. As we have seen already, Luther's view of Paul was skewed by his polemical relations with the Catholic Church. Luther's forensic translation of *dikaiosynē* (where justice is primarily about scales, weights, and measures) took in a different direction the Hebrew, relational understanding of Paul himself—that justice was primarily restorative in orientation. The result was that at one level, Luther overplayed "justification by faith," making it the polar opposite of Torah. (It is not anti-Torah but fulfills the goal of Torah.) At another level, Luther underplayed the concept of justification by faith, making it an abstraction separate from a life of engaged discipleship. (It is not about merely imputed righteousness but about an invitation to vital participation God's righteousness through the Spirit of the risen Lord.) In any case, that the whole of the Bible became subject to Luther's skewed criterion is an unfortunate consequence of history.

Second, Luther's assessment has also distracted readers from what James does have to say with regard to faith and has dulled James's significant theological contribution to Christian community life. Johnson is again helpful here, arguing that, contrary to popular opinion, James and Paul are *not* addressing the same topic (1999:508). Paul is describing an inner-Jewish debate. Paul contrasts faith and "works of law" (not Torah itself), because he wants to show that "faith in" the ethnic identity symbols of circumcision, food laws, and holy-day rituals have been "de-centered" by the faithfulness of Jesus (Gal 2:16). The Torah's promise of life has been achieved by the "faith of Jesus" (Rom 3:22; 10:4), as Jesus's life of faithful obedience to God's call unmasked sin's rule and undid its death-grip on creation (Rom 3:21–26), making peace and life real possibilities for all (Rom 5:1). Jewish ethnic "identity badges" (i.e., "works") are simply unable to deliver the promised life (Rom 5:18–21); they were not bad, just incapable of delivery, because of sin's corrupting God's good gift of the law (Rom 7:7–12).

James's faith language, by contrast, describes an inner-Hellenistic debate common among Greek moral thinkers: namely, the difference between speech and action, and how these two should relate (e.g., Seneca, Dio Chrysostom). James speaks a strong word against verbal professions of faith that are not lived out in real life. For James, the faithful are to "be doers of the word, and not merely hearers who deceive themselves" (1:22). "Religion that is pure and undefiled before God, the Father, is this: to care for orphans and widows in their distress, and to keep oneself unstained by the world" (1:27). For "faith by itself, if it has no works, is dead" (2:17). This is precisely the same argument that Paul makes elsewhere when he says, "In Christ Jesus neither circumcision nor uncircumcision counts for anything; the only thing that counts is faith working through love" (Gal 5:6). In fact, both Paul and James agree on the classical Jewish understanding that human beings are judged by God on the basis of their works; "for he will repay according to each one's deeds" (Rom 2:6). This is not salvation by works, as Luther supposed; it is classical Judaism, where salvation is by grace, and judgment is by works (Sanders 1977:422). Thus for James, as for Paul, "it is faith itself that works, not faith that is abandoned in favor of human achievement" (Johnson 1999:508).

Such recognition of the character and context of Paul's and James's argument goes a long way to eliminate the apparent contradiction between the two writers as seen in the diagram below.

Romans 4:3–5	James 2:21–23
"Abram believed God, and it was reckoned to him as righteousness." Now to one who works, wages are not reckoned as a gift but as something due. But to one who <u>without works</u> trusts him who justifies the ungodly, such faith is reckoned as righteousness.	Was not our ancestor Abraham justified by works when he offered his son Isaac on the altar? You see that faith was active along <u>with his works</u>, and faith was brought to completion by the works. Thus the scripture was fulfilled that says, "Abraham believed God, and it was reckoned to him as righteousness."

TABLE 6.2 Comparing the Rhetoric of Paul and James regarding Faith

For James, the fact that "Abraham believed God" means that Abraham's faith worked itself out in taking real steps of obedience in keeping with God's character of righteousness. These are the "works" of Abraham that James commends. Thus, Abraham shared in God's righteousness, according to James. For Paul, the fact that "Abraham believed God" means that he trusted God to keep the ancient promise, which culminated in the ministry of Jesus, the embodiment of God's character of righteousness. Paul commends Abraham, because his trust was *not* dependent on "works," which is shorthand for Jewish ethnic-identity symbols. Dependence on these identity symbols was not even possible, since the sign of circumcision came *after* God had established the covenant with Abraham (Gen 17:24; Rom 4:10–12). Thus, Abraham shared in God's righteousness, according to Paul. Once both writers are allowed to speak for themselves, the contradiction disappears and the theological richness of the NT collection of voices is enhanced. We hear two testimonies: one on the soteriological significance of faith (Paul) and one on the consistent praxis of faith (James).

While Luther challenged the legitimacy of James as a canonical witness because he mistakenly found James incompatible with the Pauline gospel, this was not the case for the ancient church. It also ran into problems ratifying James as a canonical text, but not because of the character of James's moral exhortation, which the church actually found to be quite valuable. The problem was the text's ambiguous form and authorship. James purports to be a letter, but it is not an occasional letter where the historical situation of the author, the letter's recipients, or the presenting problem are particularly transparent. In addition, it is not clear which "James" is the author or who the "twelve tribes" are being addressed (1:1).

While not an occasional letter, some of the ambiguity of the letter's form vanishes when the text's genre is recognized for what it is. James fits well the profile of a general or catholic letter intended as a general exhortation to sound faith and practice for God's people everywhere (i.e., the "twelve tribes"). What about the authorship? The attribution to James, likely an intended reference to James the brother of Jesus and one of the pillars of the early church, was probably not planned as a sales gimmick or as a manipulative ruse (Wisse 1986:185). Rather, the attribution was a function of the early Christian missionary practice of circulating letters of general instruction from noteworthy leaders in the apostolic community (Gamble 1995:107).

As with the book of Hebrews, little is to be gained in trying to figure out who actually wrote the Letter of James. The riddle vanishes if the literary character of a catholic letter is taken seriously. We have here a text of such singular value in its moral exhortation and instruction for Christian community development that its original situation quickly faded from view and fell away as it was copied and circulated around the Mediterranean world. Again, this should not be surprising since unlike the audience for Paul's letters, James's community setting was never in focus, given the fact that it did not come into play within the genre of generic moral exhortation employed by the text.

Evidently the ambiguity of the author's identity was tolerable for the first hundred years of circulation, but by the third and fourth centuries this was no longer the case. In the increasingly polemical character of heterodox Christianity, heresiologists likely felt compelled to track down and specify the apostolic pedigree of all the useful texts of instruction. Eventually, doubts about which James this was, and how he could have written in such refined Greek, became a problem. The absence of the text from some of the early approved reading lists (e.g., Muratorian) and from the writings of Tertullian, Cyprian, Irenaeus, or Hippolytus has more to do with doubts of its apostolic origin than with concerns about its content. By the late fourth century, however, under the influence of Eusebius, Augustine, and Jerome, a compelling-enough case was made to link James to the Lord's brother such that Athanasius could ratify James's canonical status (Kümmel 1975:405). This functioned to authorize a text that had already established itself as valuable for Christian instruction.

What is the structure of James's theological statement? The literary form used by James resembles Israelite Wisdom literature (e.g., Proverbs, Ecclesiastes, Sirach) in that James is not driven by a particular logic or by a sustained argument or a rhetorical device. Instead the whole text, like Wisdom literature in general, is driven by short, pithy sayings offering practical, ethical instruction dealing with the observable realities of life. "Let everyone be quick to listen, slow to speak, slow to anger; for your anger does not produce God's righteousness" (1:19-20). "How great a forest is set ablaze by a small fire! And the tongue is a fire" (3:5-6). "Who is wise and understanding among you? Show by your good life that your works are done with gentleness born of wisdom" (3:13). "Resist the devil, and he will flee from you. Draw near to God, and he will draw near to you" (4:7-8).

It is within real life, argues James, that the identity and character of the faith community becomes evident, both as it engages members of the covenant community and as it engages the watching world. James offers some of the most powerful moral exhortation in the NT. Although James does not attribute his exhortations to Jesus or the gospel traditions, the linkage is unmistakably present. Compare the calls to pray (James 1:5-6 with Mark 11:23-24 and Matt 7:7-8), to love neighbor (James 2:8 with Mark 12:31 // Matt 22:39 // Luke 10:27), to prepare for judgment

(James 5:9 with Matt 24:33), to speak without oaths (James 5:12 with Matt 5:34-73), and to stop oppressing the poor (James 5:12 with Luke 6:24). In many ways, the Letter of James is comparable with the second part of most Pauline letters, where the exposition of theology turns to *parenesis*, the exhortation to virtue and the well-lived life. James calls the faithful to live out what they already know to be theologically true.

As he reaches for the microphone, we could expect James to summarize his theological vision as follows: *Christian theology is not a matter of setting out statements that have internal coherence, but a matter of setting out theological statements that correspond to reality in everyday life. In this sense, Christian ethics and theology emerge from the larger framework of Torah (instruction for life) which is demonstrated practically in the law of love, as ratified by the teaching and ministry of Jesus.*

Thematic Implications of James's Vision

Two themes derive from this center and flow through the Letter of James. First, James provides a basis for a comprehensive social ethic. More than any other NT writing it makes a concerted effort to show that faith and mercy are not extended only to those inside, but also to the neighbor in the larger community outside the church. Of course, those in the church have responsibilities to love and care for those inside the assembly: to respect one another without favoritism (2:1-7), to show mercy and not condemnation (2:8-13), to keep actions consistent with speech (2:14-17), to eliminate cursing and slander from speech (3:5-12; 4:11-12), and to pray and care for the sick (5:13-16). However, according to James this kind of care for others, where "one's walk matches one's talk," extends beyond the confines of the church community and reaches out into the world in general. No statement is a more famous rendition of this conviction than James's assertion that true religion is proved by care for those typically marginalized in patriarchal societies: "Religion that is pure and undefiled before God, the Father, is this: to care for orphans and widows in their distress, and to keep oneself unstained by the world" (1:27).

Second, James gives witness to a profound theological ethic that grounds all his exhortation. In the clearest possible terms, James expresses the Judeo-Christian conviction that Israel's God is the Master of the universe and source of all life and of all that is good: "Every generous act of giving, with every perfect gift, is from above, coming down from the Father of lights, with whom there is no variation or shadow due to change" (1:17). Certainly this is not the only cosmological worldview, but it is the one that distinguishes Israel from its neighbors. In remarkably stark terms, James emphasizes that while God may be the source of all, nothing is automatic; human beings must choose with whom they will align themselves: "Do you not know that friendship with the world is enmity with God? Therefore, whoever wishes to be a friend of the world becomes an enemy of God" (4:4). War and murder are traced to the rebellious human desire for power, prestige, and possessions (4:1–2). Put another way, to reject God or to presume to act autonomously is to reject life and to choose death, as all human beings and all things are dependent on God's ongoing creation for their ongoing existence (4:13–17).

FIRST PETER

Theological Vision

As with the other Catholic Letters, the debate surrounding 1 Peter often has to do with its background and authorship. These concerns, however, do not appear to be the concerns of 1 Peter. With regard to background little in the letter suggests a particular background setting. In addition to its being generic, it shares common traditions with James (compare 1 Pet 5:5–9 with Jas 4:6–10) and Paul (compare 1 Pet 2:4–10 with Rom 9:25–33). Both of these observations are not surprising if the literary genre of 1 Peter is recognized for what it is: namely, a general letter of Christian exhortation and encouragement.

With regard to authorship, some doubt that the Peter referred to as the author (1:1) is the same Apostle Peter whom we meet in the gospels, traveling with Jesus. The Greek used by the author of 1 Peter is of a high standard. Could such a letter be written by a man whom Luke described as "uneducated and ordinary" (Acts 4:13)? Then there is the matter of audience. The assertion that "once you were not a people but now you are God's people" (1 Pet 2:10) makes clear that the audience includes Gentile converts from paganism to Christianity. How does this square with Paul's account of the division of labor that had him work with Gentiles and Peter with Jews? Paul writes, "I had been entrusted with the gospel for the uncircumcised, just as Peter had been entrusted with the gospel for the circumcised" (Gal 2:8).

However, neither the literary style nor the apparently Gentile audience automatically precludes naming the Peter that we meet in the gospels as the author. The letter may well have been written by an *amanuensis* (someone employed to take dictation or to copy manuscripts). Note the reference to Silvanus (1 Pet 5:12). If the actual writing was done by someone else, based on the testimony of Peter, this could explain the fine Greek and the unusual focus. Then again, the allusion to an *amanuensis* and the reference to "my son Mark" (1 Pet 5:13) could be artificial and part of creating the author's authoritative persona necessary for promoting reception during the heterodox period of early Christianity. This possibility cannot be ruled out, as numerous early Christian texts were also attributed to Peter (e.g., *Gospel of Peter*, *Apocalypse of Peter*).

In the end, there is no way to say anything conclusive on the questions of background setting or authorship. However, much like with Hebrews and James, the riddle of 1 Peter vanishes if our expectations are recalibrated away from those we have for an occasional letter of Paul. It is best to take seriously the literary genre of 1 Peter, which suggests it is a general letter written for a general audience aimed at persuading readers to adopt appropriate Christian behaviors. In this case, the importance of the author and the background setting recede. Not surprisingly, these situational details probably fell from memory. Since they were not deemed important for the functioning of the text, they were neglected and not transferred along with the text as it was copied, collected, and circulated. As with the other Catholic Letters, the primary reason for the selection and eventual ratification of 1 Peter as Scripture (i.e., usefulness for Christian instruction) is simply the intrinsic merit of the letter's exhortation itself (Johnson 1999:479). The attribution to Peter, Jesus's close friend, was enough to convince the early bishops of the text's apostolic association and thus to ratify its usefulness within the churches.

Part of the reason 1 Peter found such a receptive audience is that it presupposes an environment of suffering, social ostracism, and stressful self-definition within the larger and more hostile Greco-Roman world. This was a perspective that many struggling Gentile house churches could appreciate in the first century as they tried to make sense of their new identity as now part of Israel's tradition. While the author's counsel to "accept the authority of every human institution" and to "honor the emperor" (1 Pet 2:13, 17) does not fit a situation of organized and systematic state persecution, it does fit a community's quest to find a home for its new identity in a hostile environment—"rejecting but also accepting key elements of the dominant culture" (Johnson 1999:483).

It is important to recall the cosmologies with which the early Christians worked. The pagan worldview was quite different from the Judeo-Christian worldview to which these former pagans now belonged. It required a significant conversion of the imagination to embrace this new identity. How so? The pagan worldview usually involved two parallel worlds where everything on earth had a heavenly counterpart; events on the earth mirrored those in heaven. Every material reality had a corresponding spiritual reality. Chaos ruled and the gods fought among themselves trying to manage the chaos. Humanity was obligated to one national god or another and in some way carried on the celestial conflict in a parallel manner on earth against fellow human beings (Hiebert 2000:117–18). Each tribe bartered, petitioned, and appeased its national god in order to procure various benefits on earth: victory, harvest, fertility, and so on. This had been the religious landscape of Israel's neighbors in the OT times and now also informed the first-century Greco-Roman world of the imperial cult within which communities, like the one addressed by 1 Peter, were looking for a home.

By way of contrast, the Judeo-Christian worldview of the NT writers begins prior to the chaos, with God bringing order to the indeterminate matter (Gen 1:1—2:3), separating the sky from the water, differentiating the night from the day, and assigning distinguishing and productive functions to all creatures. In this way, God's creation project of heaven and earth, the cosmos, is launched. In particular, God orders humanity to carry out God's purpose and creation mandate (Gen 1:27–31), working with "the powers" (variously described as angels, principalities, spirits, host of heaven, sons of God, and the like) to accomplish God's design (Gen 28:12; Josh 5:13–15; 1 Kgs 22:19; Gal 3:19; 1 Cor 6:3; Rev 22:6). Humanity, however, by rejecting God's order and by preferring autonomy, becomes mired in alienation. The powers, thus fortified by human allegiance, rebel against God's purpose, spurning their divine mandate to serve the Lord, drawing all creation into their deadly grip (Gen 3:1–24; 6:1–6; Rom 3:9–20; 8:22). And yet, this rebellion is not seen as the last word (Wink 1998:31–36).

Essential to the Judeo-Christian worldview of the NT writers is God's persistent, indefatigable invitation extended to humanity. They are invited to participate in God's ongoing creation by witnessing of God's way to the powers, inviting the errant ones and the rest of creation to abandon rebellion against the creator and return home (1 Cor 4:9; Eph 3:9). The agents of God's creation project are a long line of people (dotted, curved arrow in the diagram below), starting with Abraham and Sarah, Isaac and Rebekah, Jacob and Rachel, Moses and Miriam, David, the prophets, John the Baptist, and Jesus, along with the many other men and women who faithfully respond to God's call.

However, it is the life of Jesus that finally made possible the original creation mandate for humanity by defeating the rebellious rule of the power of sin at the cross: a life validated as victorious when God raised Jesus from the dead (1 Pet 3:21-22). Thus the people of God are part of a long line of witnesses to a process (1 Pet 2:9; Heb 12:1) that comes to a climax in Jesus—a process that is only completed at the end of the age (1 Pet 2:21). In the meantime, all those who remain vitally attached to the risen Lord Jesus, symbolized by baptism (1 Pet 3:21-22), are no longer obligated to the realm of the rebellious powers, even though they continue to live in that realm (Rom 6:1-12). Instead, they live now as part of a new people oriented to God's righteousness (1 Pet 2:24), anticipating the full realization of their identity in Jesus at the end of time (1 Pet 5:10). See diagrams below. Note the stark contrasts between the two worldviews.

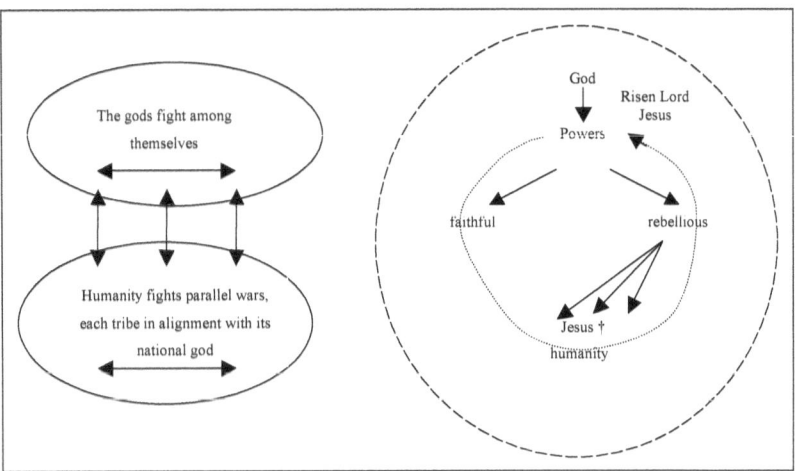

TABLE 6.3 Comparing the Pagan Worldview (left) with the NT Writers' Judeo-Christian Worldview (right)

For biblical texts like 1 Peter, the whole world belongs to God. The powers, as well as human beings, are created by God and given a mandate and a jurisdiction. Yes, a battle goes on between good and evil, but the outcome is never in doubt: the whole universe depends on God's ongoing creation for its continued existence. Thus, unlike the good-vs.-evil dualism of the pagan world, the Judeo-Christian worldview is a *modified* dualism. This is why the biblical writers can speak of God's sovereignty *and* human responsibility at the same time without contradiction. Recall Pharaoh's story: God hardened Pharaoh's heart (Exod 9:12), and Pharaoh hardened his own heart (Exod 9:34). Or consider Joseph's testimony: "Even though you intended to do harm to me, God intended it for good" (Gen 50:20). So if the battle is not about power or about who will win, then what is it about? Quite simply, it is about the establishment of God's reign on earth as it is in heaven (Hiebert 2000:119). How will it be accomplished? Who will be involved? What will it look like?

Texts like 1 Peter, along with those of the rest of the NT, testify to the conviction that by virtue of Jesus' life of faithful obedience to God's call, Jesus confirmed his calling and identity as God's Son and God raised him from death to new life above the powers, acknowledging his rule on behalf of the Master of the Universe (Rom 5:18–21; 16:20; 1 Cor 6:3; 15:45–49; 2 Cor 5:16–21; Col 2:15; Heb 5:7–9; 8:1–7; 9:23–28; 1 Pet 3:18–22). Thus the worldview imagery here involves several key pieces: a picture of God who is consistently *for* creation; a high regard for humanity and its role in the creation enterprise; a sober view of the pervasive reach of sin's death-dealing empire; a conceptualization of creation as incomplete, anticipating the Messiah's leadership to complete creation; a robust view of the powers as created, but where some have fallen; and an image of the church as a people that functions as God's outpost community, inviting one and all to abandon their rebellion and regain their true identity and vocation in God's economy. Walter Wink summarizes in particular the role of powers and the role of the people "stamped" by the Messiah's new-creation image (1 Pet 2:21) as follows: "When a particular Power becomes idolatrous—that is, when it pursues a vocation other than the one for which God created it and makes its own interests the highest good—then that Power becomes demonic. The spiritual task is to unmask this idolatry and recall the Powers to their created purposes in the world. But this can scarcely be accomplished by individuals. A group is needed—what the New Testament calls an *ekklēsia* (assembly)—one that exists specifically for the task of recalling these Powers to their divine vocation" (Wink 1998:29).

Into this worldview mix the letter that came to be known as 1 Peter made its entry. It is a letter of general instruction to churches everywhere who are on a quest to make a home within an alien context of the Greco-Roman imperial cult (1 Pet 2:11). The reeducation of former pagans is accomplished through a reminder of the basis of their hope, a reminder of the implications of their baptism, and a reminder of the prototype pattern to be found in the life of Jesus.

So, unlike Paul's occasional letters that were transformed by collection to function as general letters, 1 Peter begins its life as a general letter that quickly became a valued member of the growing collection of texts useful for Christian instruction. It appears in almost all the early lists (i.e., Tertullian, Clement of Alexandria, Irenaeus, Origen, and Eusebius).

At the lectern we can imagine the author of 1 Peter giving his theological statement in words something like these: *God is forming a new people (reconfiguring Israel) through Messiah Jesus and all those who are identified with him, whether Jew or Gentile, are part of God's "chosen race" who are now living as "aliens and exiles" in our respective cultures. Therefore, let us not grow too comfortable within the structures of our particular cultures but orient ourselves by our primary identification as a "royal priesthood" of God. However, life as resident aliens does not mean becoming dangerous or a threat to the social fabric, but living as a sign of authentic life in contrast to the culture of death, dysfunction, and destruction, wherever it may be found.*

THEMATIC IMPLICATIONS OF FIRST PETER'S VISION

Two themes dominate 1 Peter and emerge directly from its theological center. Both of them, not surprisingly, have to do with identity and self-definition. First, baptism is used to signal the believer's transfer from the old life into the new life stamped by the shape of Jesus's life (1 Pet 2:21). What began with Jesus now continues through baptism to them, as they carry forward Jesus's life. As God has raised Jesus, so God can be trusted to bring life out of death, dysfunction, and destruction. For the author, an analogy from the Christian experience of baptism to the flood in Noah's story does just this (1 Pet 3:18-22). "And baptism, which this [i.e., the flood] prefigured, now saves you—not as a removal of dirt from the body, but as an appeal to God for a good conscience, through the resurrection of Jesus Christ" (v. 21).

In the allusion to Noah, the author brings together several ideas. (1) A word of *salvation*: the mass of unredeemed people ("the spirits in prison") who rejected God's salvation plan (as "in the days of Noah"), before its ultimate manifestation in the life of Jesus, now receive the announcement of God's victory. (2) A word of *judgment*: "Just as Noah was separated from the wicked people of his day, through 'water,' so Baptism now separates the believers from the world around them" (Johnson 1999:486). The baptismal language highlights both the *extensive reach* of the salvation accomplished by Jesus and the *irrevocable impact* on history accomplished by God through the resurrection of Jesus from the dead. In this way, the occasion of baptism functions to remind Christians everywhere and at all times of the basics of Christian living (1 Pet 1:22—2:3; 2:11—3:17), especially their founding call to imitate Jesus in all things.

Second, in addition to the theme of baptism, 1 Peter uses the theme of the imitation of Christ to ground all of the exhortation to practical Christian living. In particular it is Christ's sufferings that are central. Christ is portrayed as one who suffers because of his calling (1:11, 19; 3:18; 4:1). When Christians suffer innocently for their faith (i.e., not for actual wrongdoing), they share in his sufferings (1 Pet 4:14-15). This is, however, not some sort of martyr piety; it is not a call to seek death for oneself or others. Christians are not called to replicate his death, rather they are "to imitate the *manner of his endurance* before his death" (Johnson 1999:488).

In addition to innocent suffering for the faith (which does not preclude civil disobedience), the author of 1 Peter makes an assertion that may seem surprising: not all suffering is commendable: "If you endure when you are beaten for doing wrong, what credit is that? But if you endure when you do right and suffer for it, you have God's approval" (1 Pet 2:20). This is not because of some masochist fantasy of self-mutilation, but is key to the way of Jesus that breaks into and upends the cycle of violence. The next sentence clarifies the strange expectation. "For to this you have been called, because Christ also suffered for you, leaving you an example, so that you should follow in his steps" (1 Pet 2:21). Why must this be so? Because as Caird stresses: "Resentment or retaliation is inimical to God's grand strategy for the defeat of evil. To this extent it must be said that those who share Christ's sufferings share also this redemptive quality" (1994:201).

Anthropologist René Girard (2001:15) argues that human beings are unique in their capacity and need to desire and to imitate. In fact, without desire or the drive to mimic others, human beings could not grow, develop, thrive or be open to the divine. The problem is that by rebellion, human cultures allow the power of sin to make an ally of what is intended for good (i.e., desire), bringing about alienation and death. Sin uses desire to enslave humanity in the death-dealing lie that one needs what the other has in order to live happily. This contagion spreads sin's power through humanity, manifesting itself in the cycle of violence, which is used to secure the all-consuming concern for power, possessions, and prestige. The lie remains hidden behind the temporary realization of happiness at someone else's expense, but the feeling proves to be fleeting and requires more violence to secure the same effect. Girard calls this systemic violence, a single-victim or scapegoat mechanism characteristic of all human cultures. It works because human beings are normally unaware they are trapped within this circular process of using violence to rebalance their system, even if it is only for a short time. It is this cycle that Jesus exposed as fraudulent and evil at the cross. Thus 1 Peter offers a stunning analysis of the old-age, single-victim, scapegoat mechanism and replaces it with a better model to imitate: namely, Jesus, the prototype of the new age.

However, this call to share with Jesus the undoing of the cycle of violence by innocent suffering should not be understood as quietism, isolationism, or fatalistic resignation. There are no winners when the church, the body of the risen Lord, fails to critique the domination systems that oppress the orphan, widow, alien, victim, and powerless. The church fails not only to realize its new-age identity; it fails to realize its vocation as having a share in Jesus's call to announce the victory of God that will eventually result in the cessation of evil's rebellion (1 Pet 2:11–12; 4:12–19). The church begins to fulfill its job description as it joins Jesus in challenging the domination systems that control many institutions. Such domination manifests itself in unjust economic arrangements, oppressive political relations, biased race provisions, and sexist gender dealings, wherever they are found (e.g., office, school, church, neighborhood, municipality, state, nation).

While the rebellious powers will *not* be able to hear the church's critique fully as long as they are blinded by self-preservation and self-interest, this does not release the church from its obligation to stand up and unmask the powers. With a good dose of realism, however, 1 Peter notes that even though good behavior should lessen hostility toward the cause of Christ, it is not automatic and it is often not the case (3:16). Just because something is the right thing to do, does not mean it will "work" in the short term. Instead, the moral integrity of the believer's baptismal identity places the Christian community in the exact situation occupied by Jesus with the real possibility of unmerited suffering (4:12–17). Nevertheless, the guiding desire remains that the rebel system will stop persecution (i.e., will give up allegiance to the corrupting domination system) because of the faith community's exemplary conduct, firm resistance, and direct exposure of deceit (5:9). Thus, regardless of the immediate outcome, the resistance community is reassured by the ultimate outcome: "And after you have suffered for a little while, the God of all grace, who has called you to his eternal glory in Christ, will himself restore, support, strengthen, and establish you" (5:10).

JUDE AND 2 PETER

Theological Vision

We turn now to the final pair of letters in the category of the Catholic Letters. What the other Catholic Letters suffer in debates about authorship and authenticity these two letters suffer even more. Why? Because the profile of the setting that generated these texts is even fuzzier. Three features are notable. (1) Their situational origin is obscure, and little is known about the authors outside the letters' attribution to Peter, "apostle of Jesus Christ" (2 Pet 1:1) and to Jude, "brother of James" (Jude 1). Whatever additional information about the authors and their situation that might have been known by the initial recipients is now lost. (2) Jude and 2 Peter have so much material in common that their independence is questionable, complicating even more the reconstruction of their historical setting. For example, Jude 4–16 appears to be the source of 2 Peter 2:1–22. (3) The character of faith represented in these two letters is reduced from a dynamic trust in God ("faith" as a verb) to an adherence to the received tradition (the "faith" as a noun): namely, the teaching of the apostles (2 Pet 1:1, 5; Jude 3, 20) and of the inspired

Scripture (2 Pet 1:20–21). These developments push these two letters to the outer fringes of the apostolic witness.

Second Peter is considered by some scholars to be the latest writing in the NT for three reasons (Kümmel 1975:431). (1) It is a second-generation writing by its own admission. "You should remember the words spoken in the past by the holy prophets, and the commandment of the Lord and Savior spoken through your apostles" (2 Pet 3:2). (2) It makes a clear reference to a collection of Paul's letters already in place and to their status as "scriptures" (2 Pet 3:15–16). (3) In comparison with Jude, 2 Peter appears to expand on Jude's rhetoric, suggesting its literary dependence on Jude. These clues suggest dating the composition of 2 Peter to the end of the first century, perhaps even as late as 120 CE (Ehrman 2004:1).

Jude purports to be the "brother of James," and 2 Peter is attributed to an "apostle of Jesus Christ." However, we know so little about Peter or Jude as writers and church leaders that we cannot say much about what these two wrote or did not write. Further complicating matters are the great linguistic and thematic differences between 1 Peter and 2 Peter. Whereas 1 Peter offers comfort to believers and exhorts them to be open to outsiders, 2 Peter combats deviance within the community and exhorts community members to be wary of teachers who deceive the unsteady. These discrepancies raise questions about whether 1 Peter and 2 Peter were written by the same author. In the end, it is better to conceptualize both 2 Peter and Jude as truly catholic letters. They are "testaments" of encouragement and challenge not directed primarily to or from one community but to a general Christian audience, and they are tied to an apostolic association through Jesus's disciple (2 Peter) and brother (Jude). In this way, the riddle of their provenance vanishes, as expectations for detailing the author, setting, and audience of either letter are rendered unnecessary for literary texts such as these.

About all that can be said for these texts is that they proved to be quite useful in the chaotic heterodox period as the emerging orthodox groups worked at questions of identity and self-understanding in the midst of competing views of what the community of the risen Lord should look like and act like. Their usefulness is what "tipped the scale" in favor of their ratification as Christian Scripture. In the end, the brief, cryptic allusions to the apostolic witness were enough to confirm the place that these short letters had come to enjoy for their usefulness in the debates over inner diversity within earliest Christianity.

What dominates the structure of these two tractates of warning, judgment, and exhortation is a great deal of polemical language. For motivational and rhetorical purposes there are threatening allusions to unscrupulous characters from the past (e.g., Cain, Balaam, and Korah [Jude 11]) and to deviant behaviors (2 Pet 2:12–22): "These are grumblers and malcontents; they indulge their own lusts; they are bombastic in speech, flattering people to their own advantage" (2 Pet 2:18; Jude 16). For contemporary readers this kind of encouragement to faithful Christian living through negative counterexample and ridicule may seem inappropriate. However, such language is standard fare for ancient polemical tracts both Jewish and Greco-Roman.

Some have also wondered if specific opponents are in view, or if these allusions are simply generic motivational warnings and exhortations without any specific referent. There are different views on this question. It is unnecessary, however, to project a major theological controversy or the christological battles of third- or fourth-century vintage at this early stage. More likely, these authors are addressing the inner-Christian debates regarding the practical matters of leadership, authority, ethics, and liturgy during the rough-and-tumble heterodox period of earliest Christianity. Much like the range of activities Paul and his missionary associates found as they worked among the Corinthians, the variety of behaviors exhibited by new believers was great, and some of it undermined their new identity in Christ (e.g., partisan rivalry, refusal to share food, sexual immorality, competition for status during worship, trivialization of the body, idolatry). At this early point, controversy among the young churches had more to do with differences of leadership style and worship practices.

Given this situation, how is the polemical language of Jude and 2 Peter to be understood? It seems most likely that these two authors are employing a favorite ancient rhetorical tactic known as *ad hominem* (or personal attack) in order to shape behavior *away* from those being ridiculed. It is probably more accurate to frame this choice of strategy as a necessity, not as a preference. Why? Because there could not be polemics based on doctrine (*ad doctrinam*). In this early heterodox period "there was no comprehensive and widely accepted rule of faith which could function as a standard for truth and falsehood" (Wisse 1986:184). Given these rhetorical aims and the historical situation, contemporary readers should not press these personal attacks to reveal some particular opponent group with a distinct doctrine (Wisse 1972). Without any external information to confirm such reconstructions, the most plausible expectation is to read these ad hominem attacks as part of the rhetorical pattern of persuasive speech used by heresiologists to strengthen allegiance to the preferred behaviors.

At the same time, it is important to note that for all their similarity, the polemic functions differently in Jude and 2 Peter. Their voices are distinct. In Jude the ridicule is stereotypical—not directed at specific opponents but used to galvanize commitment from insiders. It functions much like traditional parental warnings that use references to unsavory characters to strengthen their appeals to good behavior. "Listen children, do not be like so-and-so, that good-for-nothing" (e.g., Cain, Balaam, Korah).

In 2 Peter the ridicule is directed against disturbing and troubling ideas that are circulating and have the potential of distracting the Christian community from its primary mandate. The author asserts, "False prophets also arose among the people, just as there will be false teachers among you, who will secretly bring in destructive opinions" (2 Pet 2:1). Promoters of these destructive opinions are aligned with the "licentiousness of the lawless" during Lot's day (2:7). They are described as "ignorant" and "unstable" (3:16), peddling "cleverly devised myths" (1:16). But even these charges should not be seen as directed at a specific community, but rather as part of the same motivational strategy necessitated by the inner diversity, charismatic beginnings, and chaotic development of earliest Christianity. Ridicule of outsiders is used to solidify the faith commitments of those inside the church to adhere to the emerging proto-orthodox faith. By projecting vivid images that mock the behaviors and views of opponents, the writer creates "the motivation for obedience and, through contrast with the opponents, establishes the basic substance of faithfulness for the believer (Johnson 1999:499).

While it takes some imagination to read this ancient rhetoric and refrain from reading too much into its ad hominem rhetorical strategy, when Jude and 2 Peter rise and take their turn at the microphone, we can expect them to articulate their theological vision something like this: *We aim to remind readers of the truth that they already have received from the prophetic and apostolic witnesses and to motivate readers* by way of negative counterexamples. Either indirectly (Jude) or directly (2 Peter), our literary texts argue passionately for the defense of the Christian community's identity in the face of deviance and defiance. We warn opponents within the community of the consequences of rebelling against God—which already has been experienced as destruction by some. Our aim is to motivate believers to adhere to the integrity of their Christian identity and not to be sidetracked by distracting behaviors and practices.

With this speech our first go around of the NT conference table comes to a close. It is time for a break. The next chapter represents a pause in the conference proceedings—a brief period of reflection before beginning the second round of deliberations.

EXERCISES

1. Luke Timothy Johnson suggests that the historical process involved in the formation of the NT canon included five separate but interconnected stages ("The New Testament as the Church's Book," in *The Writings of the New Testament: An Interpretation* (rev. ed.). Review these five and discuss their significance:

    a. ***Composition***: Christian communities existed before the NT. Thus, the early Christian writings (letters, gospels, histories, apocalypses) emerged as the crystallizations of the Jesus traditions circulating in the churches in Corinth, Ephesus, Jerusalem, Rome, Antioch, and elsewhere. They aimed to give new shape to the Scriptures that Christians shared with Judaism (OT) in light of Easter and the memories of Jesus's life.

    b. ***Use***: The early Christian writings do not appear to be composed for private devotion, but for public reading and liturgical use alongside readings from the Law and the Prophets. With time, they were increasingly read as also Scripture, as an extension of and commentary on the Torah. In addition, they were quickly recognized as useful in communities other than those initially addressed. As they were copied and circulated, many of the particularities of their generating situation were lost, because their usefulness for exhortation and encouragement took precedence.

    c. ***Collection***: By exchanging, copying, and circulating the early Christian writings, churches began to build local collections. First, Paul's letters (40s–60s) were collected and later Gospels (late 60s–90s) were added, eventually forming a collection or a book of sewn-together writings. The small far-flung Christian communities found they were joined to the larger communion by sharing common texts. The growing collection spoke of identity, unity, and universal pertinence.

d. *Selection:* The Christian movement produced many more texts than the ones that found their way into the NT. The second century was especially fruitful. There was much conflict over the shape of the emerging church: some wanted to expand it individualistically (gnosticism), and others wanted to sever the link to Judaism (Marcionism). It became clear that a canon or standard of authorized texts by which to discern truth from falsehood in the ongoing life the church was needed.

e. *Ratification:* Various "recommended reading lists" emerged in order to respond to these conflicts and to nurture the life of Christian communities. To keep a spot on the list, even long-recognized texts needed ratification—especially when community conflict "raised the bar" for identifying a text's attribution. Since many of the details of a text's provenance were now long forgotten, a compelling case had to be made for each writing. Three criteria for ratification emerged: use in the church, apostolic derivation, and theological consistency. By the end of the fourth century, this organic process had found compelling enough ways to ratify all twenty-seven books now found in the NT.

Discuss what it might have been like to be an early Christian before the NT canon was ratified. What factors do you think went into negotiating the competing voices?

2. Read the remaining noncanonical Christian texts (the ones that are not Gospels or Apocalypses) usually dated before 130 CE: the *Third Letter to the Corinthians*, the *Letter of First Clement*, the *Didache*, the seven *Letters of Ignatius*, the *Letter of Polycarp to the Philippians*, the *Letter of Barnabas*, the *Preaching of Peter*, and the *Fragments of Papias*. These can be found on the Internet or in Bart Ehrman's reader, *The New Testament and Other Early Christian Writings: A Reader*.

Compare and contrast the noncanonical writings with the Catholic Letters selected and ratified for inclusion in the church's canon. What observations can you make?

3. The diversity within earliest Christianity is hard to dispute. However, the important question is how to conceptualize this diversity. We

know that by the third and fourth centuries the church in cities like Rome and Alexandria had the resources to begin networking, organizing, and censoring Christian teachers, writers, and communities. This was not possible during the preceding centuries. In fact, there are few if any monuments, inscriptions, artifacts, or texts that survive from this period, probably because the early Christian movement was too insignificant, disconnected, and scattered to produce this kind of enduring evidence. Furthermore, the threat of persecution during the first couple centuries meant that early Christians gathered in private homes and did not develop monuments, church buildings, and symbols until the Constantinian period (fourth century) when state resources and power were first allocated for these structures.

The only evidence for the first hundred years or so (from 30 to 130 CE) of earliest Christianity that remains are later copies or translations of fifty Christian writings (the twenty-seven NT texts, the *Gospel of Thomas*, the *Gospel of Peter*, the *Infancy Gospel of Mark*, *Papyrus Egerton 2: The Unknown Gospel*, the *Gospel of the Ebionites*, the *Gospel of the Nazareans*, *The Gospel according to the Hebrews*, the *Third Letter to the Corinthians*, the *Letter of First Clement*, the *Didache*, the seven *Letters of Ignatius*, the *Letter of Polycarp to the Philippians*, the *Letter of Barnabas*, the *Preaching of Peter*, the *Fragments of Papias*, the *Shepherd of Hermas*, and the *Apocalypse of Peter*) and four non-Christian references in historical books (Josephus, Pliny, Suetonius, and Tacitus).

By the end of the second century, the Christian movement was comprised at least four strands (Ehrman 2008:3–7): (1) *Jewish-Christian Adoptionists* (JCA), who saw Jesus as the most righteous Jewish man, as adopted by God at baptism, but not in any way divine; (2) *Marcionite Christians* (MC), who saw Jesus as the true God, having nothing to do with the wrathful Jewish God of the OT; Jesus only seemed to be human; (3) *Gnostic Christians* (GC), who saw Christ as one of the deities that make up the divine realm who had been imprisoned for a time in Jesus's body but who had been released or had escaped just prior to Jesus's death; the secret knowledge necessary for liberation was meant only for the chosen, and was passed on through teaching, careful study of meaning hidden beneath the text, ascetic practice, and separation from the world; and (4) *Proto-Orthodox Christians* (POC), who, in contrast to each of the above early Christian groups (*ca.* 200), saw Jesus as both divine and human; he is one being not two, and he taught his disciples the truth openly. This is the strand that would eventually define orthodox Christianity, preserving the apostolic witness and giving shape to the emerging canon of Scripture for liturgical and catechetical use in Christian churches through to today.

The pressing question, however, is, how should the first two centuries of Christian history (up to 200 CE) be conceptualized, given the meager evidence that remains? Three models typically explain the development of Christianity during the first two centuries. The three models are described and illustrated in the diagrams below. No longer does one view enjoy the consensus among historians and theologians of early Christianity, although I find much that commends the third model.

Compare and contrast the three models of Christian development during the first two centuries. Each model recognizes the presence of four types of Christianity by the end of the second century: *Jewish-Christian Adoptionists* (JCA), *Marcionite Christians* (MC), *Gnostic Christians* (GC), and *Proto-Orthodox Christians* (POC). However, how each model accounts for the development of Christianity—the triumph of the Proto-Orthodox and the demise of the others—is different. How so? Which do you find most compelling and why?

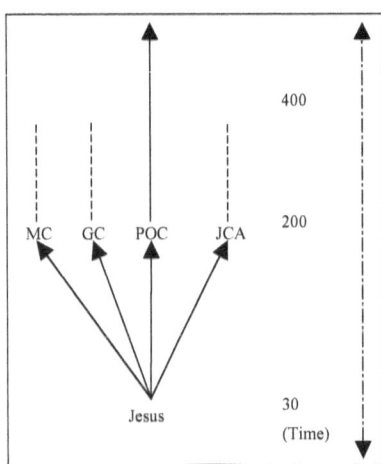

TABLE 6.4 Traditional View: Orthodoxy Precedes Heresy

This view takes seriously the probability that the earliest Christian confession was that Messiah Jesus is Lord. However, this view also tends to minimize the heterodox nature of earliest Christianity. It imagines Christianity beginning with a unified start (orthodoxy) and then splintering into heretical groups. By the 4th century, the heretical groups had fallen away to leave only the Orthodox groups.

This model depends almost exclusively on Eusebius's 4th century account of early Christian history, which portrays the expansion of Orthodox Christianity from Acts to Constantine as inevitable, always dominant, and unbroken. For many historians, these claims are suspect and questionable.

The Theological Contribution of the Remaining Canonical Witnesses 223

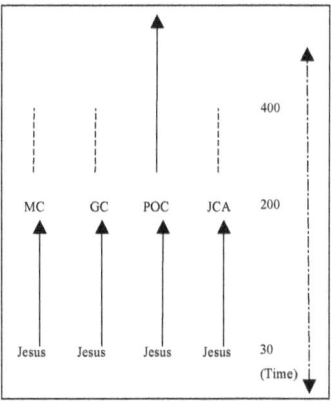

TABLE 6.5 Critical Response to the Traditional View: Heresy Precedes Orthodoxy

This view takes seriously the diversity of forms of early Christianity. However, it exaggerates the heterodox character of earliest Christianity. It argues, without evidence, that the mutually exclusive christological claims of the 3rd and 4th centuries were present within the Christian movement from the start. In effect, the Proto-Orthodox form is just one of four early forms, but it survives to define Orthodox Christianity by silencing the others.

This model is based on a conspiracy theory. It has gained a large following in some circles and is seen as a corrective to the sweeping claims and abuse that sometimes characterize holders of the traditional model. However, the burden of proof remains with the proponents of this view. At this point it is subject to charges of anachronism and argument from silence.

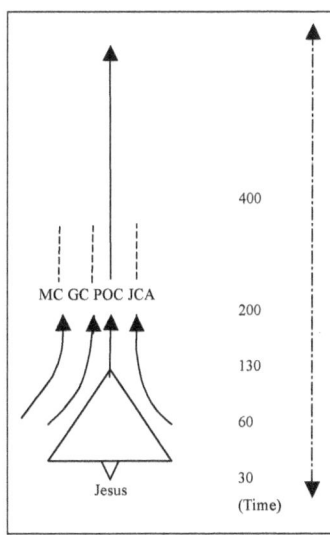

TABLE 6.5 Alternative View: Heterodoxy Precedes Orthodoxy

This view takes seriously both the strengths of the traditional model and the critical response to its oversimplification. It recognizes the heterodox character of earliest Christianity which is not surprising given the movement's leader-oriented, charismatic beginnings. Christianity moved rapidly around the Mediterranean, but remained largely insignificant, disconnected, and spread out prior to the 4th century. Worship practices and leadership styles varied greatly, creating much diversity and some controversy, but presumably the confession that "Messiah Jesus is Lord" remained constant. There is no evidence for alternate christological views or conspiracy plots during the first 100 years. However, other groups likely found the emerging Christianity favorable in some ways and exploited it for their own religious ideals, while at the same time constructing alternate views of Jesus.

This model contends that by the end of the 2nd century, the alternate christologies were countered by heresiological arguments from the Proto-Orthodox and most found the alternate visions of Christianity to be wanting. The result was that by the 4th century their numbers had fallen until they were no longer a threat to the emerging Orthodox church leadership in Rome and Alexandria, which had just come into new resources and power for organizing, managing, and networking the church.

7

Conference Intermission

IN THE FIRST ROUND of discussion, we gave each NT contributor an opportunity to give voice to driving theological convictions. What have we heard? What is the sense of the meeting so far? In the intermission, we pause for some analysis before resuming the conference with round 2. What is the corridor conversation like? Two observations are clear to all. From the presentations that we have heard so far, the problem is real, and the solution is taking shape. A brief discussion of these two observations forms the objective of this chapter.

THE PROBLEM IS SIN'S DECEPTIVE RULE

All the NT contributors are convinced that things are not as they should be; while God's creation project got off to an excellent start, things have gone horribly wrong. The basic symbolic world out of which these writers work begins with a deep theological conviction that the world created by God is good (or better), that the world God *is* creating is one that is characterized by life, light, and peace. However, it is clear to all the NT writers that the purpose for which God made the world is not yet a reality. In fact, there is much that is evil, working to counter God's good purpose for creation and making life miserable for all. However, the NT writers are also convinced that the problem is not rooted in God's creation. As Caird states, "In a world created by God evil must derive its existence and power from the corruption and distortion of original goodness; and this is the deception which underlies all sin" (1994:94).

Sin's deceptive death-dealing lie has compromised God's good creation purpose. Sin is the problem. The NT writers use four metaphors to describe the palpable experience of sin (Caird 1994:87-90). These are not four different experiences, but four ways sin is experienced, depending on the individual, group, or social setting. (1) *Guilt*: Sin is experienced as the acceptance of responsibility for an action that is wrong. Paul says not only that "all have sinned" (Rom 3:23), but that all are "without excuse" (Rom 1:20; 2:1; 3:9). All have refused to acknowledge God as God, preferring autonomy rather than the covenantal relationship that God intends for creation. (2) *Stain*: Sin is experienced as that which evokes emotions of disgust and repulsion, feelings common in all societies, deeply rooted in the instinctive aversion to dirt, disease, and death. John the seer champions the work of the Lamb as the removal of the barrier and stain so that "nothing unclean will enter" the new Jerusalem (Rev 21:27). (3) *Alienation*: Sin is also experienced as the disruption in and disloyalty to the fellowship between humanity and God with which the world began. James gives expression to the *Two Ways* worldview common to Judaism: the way of life and the way of death. "Do you not know that friendship with the world is enmity with God" (Jas 4:4)? The hyperbolic language of extremes—all or nothing, truth or falsehood, good or evil, love or hate—is used by the NT writers to give expression to their understanding of the absolute demand of God on creation for an exclusive covenantal relationship of love and allegiance. (4) *Slavery*: Sin is also experienced as bondage to the death-dealing lie that enslaves human imagination, desire, and bodies. Paul's exasperated plea to God ("Wretched man that I am! Who will rescue me from this body of death" [Rom 7:24]?) gives voice not to Paul's introspective consciousness but his profound conviction that sin has co-opted God's good creation gifts for its own deathly purposes.

THE SOLUTION RESTS WITH GOD, WHO IS STILL WORKING TO COMPLETE CREATION

The biblical writers are also convinced that sin does not have the last word—"the Lord's hand is not too short to save" (Isa 59:1). The grim, cancerous situation that has disrupted God's good purpose for creation is not terminal. The ringing affirmation that accompanies the sober expression of frustration with sin's capacity to cause destruction is the pronouncement that God has not abandoned the creation enterprise.

God is still at work! Do not give up hope. After the gut-wrenching cry that accompanied Paul's realization of the magnitude and extent of the deadly viral infection threatening all creation (sin), he shouts even louder, "Thanks be to God through Jesus Christ our Lord" (Rom 7:25)! Indeed, the solution that the NT writers proclaim is that God must be on the move again, because Jesus is alive, and therefore the reign of sin, evil, and death has been broken (1 Cor 15:55–57). The ancient creation project is renewed, taking a giant step forward as Jesus gives definition to the new-creation community taking shape around him for the transformation of all things everywhere.

The reality of salvation is central to all the NT writings. However, none of the participants at the NT conference attempt to explain the inner workings of God's salvation act of liberation. No schematic diagrams or architectural blueprints are presented at the conference. Instead, as we have seen, the NT writers use a variety of metaphors and images drawn from their own experience to give expression to their interpretation of what they experienced as wonderful, powerful, and liberating—the mysterious power of God continually at work in their midst through the Spirit of the risen Lord.

The NT writers frame their interpretations of the Easter salvation event and what it means for creation in several images. From their testimony what becomes clear are the three tenses of salvation that Caird outlines as "a threefold act of God: an accomplished fact, an experience continuing in the present, and a consummation still to come" (1994:118). A particular tense may receive different emphases depending on the NT writer, but all the writers give witness to the threefold pattern. However, they also leave ambiguous the relationship between the three tenses, which cautions against forcing too much temporal precision on these terms. For example, we have noted how several NT writings (Mark 13; 1 Corinthians 7) speak about the present using end-time terms of the prophetic hope of the *eschaton*, so that one timeframe helps to interpret another (e.g., the past shapes the future, and the future shapes the present).

Consider the four NT images for salvation in these summaries, paying particular attention to the diversity of metaphors and the time references to all three tenses—past, present, and future (Caird 1994:119–20):

(1) *Law court*: Those associated with the triumphant Christ have been vindicated, sharing his court victory (Rom 8:24; 10:10); but they are

also being vindicated as they join in and "work out" their salvation (1 Cor 1:18; Phil 2:12), looking forward to a salvation yet to come (Rom 13:11; Phil 3:20).

(2) *Slave trade*: The redeemed have been set free (John 8:36; Rom 6:22; Heb 9:12; 1 Pet 1:18); but they are to live as free people as they hold fast to their new freedom (Gal 5:1; 1 Pet 2:16), actively waiting for their final liberation (Mark 13:32–36; Luke 21:28; Eph 1:14; 4:30).

(3) *Purification practices*: The purified have been washed clean (Eph 5:26; Rev 7:14), but the cleansing process continues (2 Cor 7:1; 1 John 1:7–10; Jas 4:8) until complete purity is realized (Rev 19:8).

(4) *Battleground*: Those associated with the conquering Christ have decisively defeated the powers of sin, evil, and death at the cross (John 16:33; Col 2:15; 1 Pet 3:22; Rev 3:21), but the war goes on (Eph 6:12; Phil 1:20; 1 Pet 5:8–9; 1 John 5:3–5; Rev 12:10–11) until no enemies are left to challenge the sovereignty of God (Rom 16:20; 1 Cor 15:25; Heb 1:13; 10:13; Rev 17:14; 19:19; 20:14–15).

Both sin's pandemic destruction of God's creation purpose, and the good news of God's salvation are at the heart of NT writings. The central conviction that calls all the NT writers to the conference table is this: *God's people-gathering activity has now taken final shape around Messiah Jesus in communities of the Spirit of the risen Lord, through whom God's mission to disarm the powers and to move all creation forward toward completion is being accomplished.*

THE WAY FORWARD: CONSTRUCTIVE BIBLICAL THEOLOGY

In the remaining chapters the implications of this central NT conviction will be explored. How so? Now that we have passed the microphone around the table and have listened to the NT writers give their vision of what God did and is doing in the world through the risen Lord, it is time to hear them speak with one another about the topics or themes they themselves raise. This is part 2 of our conference and will occupy us for the remainder of the book.

A word of protocol is necessary at this point. For some, the task of biblical theology is finished; we have heard from the twenty-seven witnesses. Now all that remains is to hand over the transcripts from the twenty-seven speeches of the NT conference to the theologians meeting around a different table at the systematic-theology conference convening down the hall. In this view, the systematic theologians take it upon themselves to sift, organize, amend, revise, and reduce the biblical witness into a coherent and consistent theological vision suitable for consumption in a given faith community. While such a protocol may seem self-evidently appropriate, unfortunately it tends to diminish the impact of the NT writers' testimony and its transformative power. Of course, well-meaning systematic theologians do not start out trying to drain the power from the biblical witness. Nevertheless, the effort to simplify, manage, and organize the twenty-seven NT voices in a tight theological system, tends to domesticate their testimony and dull their transformative impact.

More specifically, two problems constantly threaten the systematic theologian's project: it is dangerous and sometimes ill conceived. First, it is dangerous because it typically presumes that the theological product (i.e., the secondary abstraction) resulting from the second conference is balanced, representative, and relatively bias free. However, the history of Christianity, and the history of interpretation show that this assumption is not valid, and that the danger is real. Too often philosophical, political, or social preferences have been allowed to shape the NT testimony so that its witness is skewed, muted, or even reversed. (For example, consider the history of biblical interpretation regarding slavery, discrimination, nationalism, and war.)

Second, the systematic project can be ill conceived, because it typically fails to recognize that the NT itself is *already* a secondary abstraction; it is itself a theological product, a collection of interpretations of Jesus's significance that the church found especially useful in its struggle for self-definition and ongoing existence. Too often the multivalent character of the collection of the apostolic testimony is not appreciated for its thickness and diversity. Instead, the witness is intentionally reduced to a single voice. (For example, consider the history of biblical interpretation regarding dispensationalism, fundamentalism, liberalism, and nationalism.) Usually, dissonant voices are silenced through elaborate (and often forced) synchronization or through simple exclusion, such that a coherent but sterile biblical construct emerges as the authoritative source for doctrine. Unfortunately, this confuses the witness with the source. By not appreciating the thickness and texture of the interpretations that make up the biblical witness, not only does the systematic theologian lose an opportunity to make an ally of the rich texture for guiding contemporary appropriation, but the text's dynamic theological witness is also transformed into something iconic, inert, and lifeless.

Is there an alternative to the protocol of systematic theology, with its long history of reductionism and domestication noted above? Yes indeed! Biblical theology sets out a different protocol for facilitating the reception of the invitation to biblical imagination issued by the rich and diverse testimony from the NT conference. The key to biblical theology lies in discerning *how* the many voices, images, and theologies represented by each writer sing together in chorus. In the practice of biblical theology, the Bible functions like a symphonic orchestra or a mass choir. As interpreters attend to each writer's voice, a *resonance space* is created by the symphonic effect of multiple voices. In this space the tension between the voices (bass, tenor, alto, and soprano) enables successive generations of God's people to resonate with and to be shaped by the voices within the same theological vision of the risen Lord (the source) that first moved these writers to give voice to God's activity in the world (the witness). Thus the biblical-theology protocol helps to lessen the confusion of witness with source.

Unlike the goal of some systematic theologies, the aim of biblical theology is not to force all the voices to sing in unison, even though this may seem at first to be simpler and more straightforward. Instead, while the tensions between the diverse biblical voices may sound disturbing and even dissonant, it is precisely the interplay between the points of tension in the biblical witness that creates the *theological space* within which successive faith communities are authorized to do their theological reflection and appropriation. The confession God's people have made from the start is that authentic life is only really discovered by resonating with the way God's people have always heard, experienced, and participated in the life of God. Greater appreciation of the biblical text's character as witness puts the faith community in touch with a network of witnesses reaching back to the dawn of time and forward to the end of time. While biblical theology is not immune to the dangers of cultural bias, its protocol for doing theological reflection within the parameters of the biblical witness provides it some measure of protection from those concerns that can easily take over and skew the witness.

The biblical theology protocol resists the image of "baton passing," where the theologian *does* systematic theology *on* biblical theology. Instead, the faith community's task is to do biblical theology systematically. That is, after completing the *descriptive* task, biblical theology is not finished. Now, the *constructive* task begins. Contemporary faith communities join the long list of faithful pilgrims who have gone before in attending to the theological chorus sung by the twenty-seven-voice NT choir, and in constructing contextually appropriate extensions. Thus, present-day faith communities locate themselves *within* the parameters (on the spectrum) of the diverse voices so as to resonate with and be shaped by the impact of the witness, extending this witness in contemporary and transformative ways.

In the seven chapters that follow, we engage with the NT writers on seven themes that they themselves raise either directly or indirectly in their testimony. The Christian confession made by faith communities from the start is that even though they may live in times and cultures far removed from the first Christians, they can still hear and be shaped by the voice of the risen Lord to which these ancient texts give ongoing witness.

EXERCISES

1. Paul's use of the ancient mythological language of the "powers and principalities" (Rom 3:9; 8:38; Eph 3:10; Col 2:15) enables him to talk about sin in a way that is often missed in Western civilization. For Paul, sin as transgression and offence is the symptom of a much deeper malady: humanity's self-inflicted enslavement to the death-dealing domination power of sin. While Western peoples may be desensitized to the powers as heavenly representatives of civil, religious, and natural law, the world of the powers and principalities is the world that Paul inhabited.

    Discuss what difference it might make for you to consider sin in Paul's terms, as a magnetic field that draws all into its sphere of influence. Why do you think it is difficult for Westerners to think of sin and slavery in the same context? How might the ancient insights into "powers and principalities" contribute to the way you think about freedom? Identity? The authorities? Where do you think sin gets its power?

2. Read Craig Bartholemew's essay "Biblical Theology" (84–90) and Kevin Vanhoozer's essay "Systematic Theology" in *Dictionary for Theological Interpretation of the Bible* (773–79).

    Review the main points of concern for both biblical theology and systematic theology. What are their points of overlap, and what are their points of divergence? Each author attempts to trace the development of his respective ways of doing theology and then to chart out prospects and challenges for the future. Compare and contrast these visions. Which aspects of each of these visions can you affirm? Why?

3. Visit a theological library and browse the systematic theology section (BT75). Pull from the shelves several texts and review their introductions and tables of contents.

    What do the introductory comments and the topics under discussion reveal about the assumptions of these theologians?

4. Occasionally the question arises: how reliable are the NT manuscripts anyway? If the NT voices that we have spent so many pages reconstructing are based completely on the manuscript evidence, some discussion of the reliability of these manuscripts is in order. After all, since the original documents, as composed by Paul, the Evangelists, or any other NT writer, are no longer available, we are obligated to work with hand-transcribed copies. So how reliable are these copies? Have they been corrupted in the process? What is the history of the transmission of these manuscripts? Four pieces make up a response to this question:

    a. Manuscript composition in earliest Christianity. In the first century, at about the time the text of Hebrew Bible had assumed a fairly standardized form, the earliest Christians were gathering and shaping their recollections and elaborations—both oral and written—of Jesus's life, teaching, and ministry (40s–90s CE). As we have seen, they addressed their local faith communities by composing gospels, letters of various kinds, histories, and apocalypses—all for the purpose of encouraging and challenging one another in their faith commitments.

    b. Manuscript transmission up to the sixteenth century. Unlike the stability achieved by the Hebrew Bible in the first century (and its Greek translation called the Septuagint [LXX]), these early Christian writings did not yet share the same stability. During the first two centuries, thousands of variant readings "crept" into the manuscript tradition of the texts that would eventually be called the NT. As texts were copied and circulated from one house church to another in the creative, charismatic, and sometimes chaotic times before the church had standardized its practices, many variant readings entered the manuscript tradition. This was partly due to the fact that texts needed to be copied by hand up to the sixteenth century, when the advent of the printing press made copying by hand unnecessary. Most variants were the result of copying errors and were unintentional (slips of the eye or ear), especially during the first few centuries, before professional ecclesiastical scribes took over the copying in the fourth century. The Roman Empire's adoption of Christianity in the fourth century brought, among other things, more stability to the copying process; the empire infused the process with resources, expertise, oversight, and power.

While most errors were unintentional, copyists made some intentional or deliberate "interpolations" to "improve" the theology, harmony, or grammar of the manuscript they were copying. Look, for example, at 1 John 5:7–8 in a contemporary study Bible, and note the footnote at this verse. What do you see? Evidently some early copyist of the Latin text found the phrase "there are three that testify" too great an opportunity to be missed. Hoping to "help the text along," a scribe apparently inserted a marginal comment linking the three witnesses to "the Father, the Word, and the Holy Spirit." Eventually, this marginal gloss "migrated" into the body of the text as a subsequent and well-meaning copyist integrated the comment into what would later be called verse 7, so as not to lose the insight. Having entered the manuscript tradition, this comment secured a place in the Latin Vulgate. (For a discussion of this later interpolation, commonly know as the *Comma Johanneum*, see Metzger & Ehrman 2005:146–48). So the question remains: If there is evidence of such textual corruption, is the transmitted text trustworthy? Is it reliable?

c. Recent manuscript discoveries. Four manuscript "discoveries" in the nineteenth and twentieth centuries have strengthened the case for the reliability of the manuscript copies to represent the original NT compositions (see Metzger & Ehrman 2005:52–94). First, a fourth-century parchment manuscript of a Bible in Greek—with the whole NT complete, and only some parts of the OT missing—found in a monastery near Mount Sinai (1859) caused much excitement in the nineteenth century. At that time, the only Greek NT readily available was the one published by Desiderius Erasmus (1516), which was based mostly on twelfth-century manuscripts. Erasmus's Greek NT later came to be known as the *Textus Receptus* and was used as the basis for the King James Version of the NT. The fourth-century parchment codex found near Mount Sinai is called Sinaiticus and is housed today in the British Museum, in London. Its significance is that it gave scholars access to the biblical text circulating in the Christian community eight centuries earlier than the biblical text available in the manuscripts used by Erasmus!

Second, another fourth-century parchment manuscript of a Greek Bible was released by the Vatican for scholarly study in 1889. It became known as Vaticanus. It has three *lacunae*, or gaps: the first forty-six chapters of Genesis are missing; some thirty psalms are lost; and the concluding pages from Heb 9:14 until the end of the NT are gone (including 1–2 Timothy, Titus, Philemon, and Revelation). Both Vaticanus and Sinaiticus are printed in professional book hand, and while not identical, they are remarkably similar. However, the significance of these two manuscripts is that when compared with the *Textus Receptus*, they shared a surprising number of small differences (word spellings and shorter readings—by a phrase or by no more than a sentence). Look at the footnotes in a contemporary study Bible that correspond to the following verses: Matt 6:13, 17:21, 18:11, 23:14, 27:35; Mark 7:16, 9:44, 9:46, 11:26, 15:28; Luke 1:28, 9:55–56, 17:36; John 5:3–4; Acts 8:37, 15:34, 24:6–8, 28:29; Rom 16:24; Eph 5:30; and 1 Pet 4:14 (only a partial list). But by far the largest surprise, in addition to the numerous shorter readings, was the absence of two large blocks of text from both Vaticanus and Sinaiticus (Mark 16:9–20 and John 7:53—8:11). What is the obvious question? Did these two fourth-century manuscripts preserve a text closer to the original than the twelfth-century text represented by *Textus Receptus*? Or was the opposite the case? Perhaps the *Textus Receptus* actually preserved a text closer to the original. In other words, were Vaticanus and Sinaiticus deficient or superior?

Third, twentieth-century manuscript discoveries brought new light to the question of establishing merit of the text represented by Vaticanus and Sinaiticus. Numerous papyri manuscripts dating to the second and third centuries were found in Egypt in the twentieth century. While these papyri—now housed in various libraries and museums around the world—were fragmentary (some as small as a credit card, and all missing some pages of text), they were met with great anticipation by scholars. Could they function to "break the tie"? Conceivably, they would either confirm the fourth-century parchment manuscripts (like Vaticanus and Siniticus) as basically preserving a text closer to the original of the NT, or they would show the fourth-century parchment codices to be corruptions. None of the papyri fragments were complete enough to allow direct verification of the two large lacunae: Mark 16:9–20 and John 7:53—8:11, or of many of the smaller lacunae such as 1 John 5:7–8 and those noted in the partial list of the previous paragraph. All the papyri are damaged, with many of these particular sections missing. However, these earlier papyri manuscript fragments were more similar to Vaticanus and Sinaiticus than to *Textus Receptus* at the more than a thousand other places where these two textual traditions differed. Thus, for many scholars, the earlier papyri confirmed the merit of the fourth-century manuscripts for preserving a closer representation of the original NT writings.

Fourth, the discovery in 1947 of the Dead Sea Scrolls near the village of Qumran, comprising most of the Hebrew Bible (among many other works) and dated from the mid-third century BCE to the early first century CE, was greeted with much anticipation by biblical scholars. Could these scrolls confirm the accuracy of the Hebrew Bible? At that time, the oldest complete copy of the Hebrew Bible was the eleventh-century Leningrad Codex; the Masoretic scholars introduced vowel pointing in this manuscript in the ninth century in order to better preserve the pronunciation of the consonantal Hebrew text. The Lenigrad Codex is housed in the Russian National Library in St. Petersburg. The obvious question was, how would the Dead Sea Scrolls compare to the Leningrad Codex? The analysis showed that the Dead Sea Scrolls were, in fact, remarkably similar to the Leningrad Codex and exhibited the stability achieved by the Hebrew Bible over the thirteen centuries of hand copying—a testimony to the dedication and devotion of the Hebrew scribal tradition.

These recent finds—the parchment manuscripts from the fourth century, the papyri manuscripts from the second and third centuries, and numerous other hand-copied manuscripts dated through to the sixteenth century (a total of about 5,700 Greek NT manuscripts) together with the Dead Sea Scrolls of Hebrew OT texts—combine to make the Christian Bible one of the best attested ancient texts. But not only is the biblical text well attested, but these recent discoveries have given access to a text that is both remarkably stable and extremely useful for reconstructing the NT into a form much closer to the way it was composed by the NT writers themselves than was previously possible. While there are a few cases among the thousands of variant readings where there is evidence that copyists intentionally added significant chunks of material (Mark 16:9–20 and John 7:53—8:11), these instances appear to be "the exceptions that prove the rule": namely, that generally the text was copied and passed on with remarkable care and with no evidence of systematic or heavy-handed editing.

d. Textual criticism. Still, if no two of the 5,700 Greek NT manuscripts now available are exactly the same, and if the original text is likely preserved somewhere among the 5,700 manuscripts, how do scholars sort through manuscript tradition in order to establish the most likely original text from among the thousands of variants, both unintentional and intentional? Textual criticism (sometimes called lower criticism) is the oldest and most widely accepted form of biblical criticism and is devoted to precisely this task. Like a crime-scene detective trying to reconstruct the chronology of the events leading up to a crime from the evidence that remains strewn about the room, textual critics use deductive reasoning to sort out the relationship between differing manuscripts of the same text (Which reading is older? Which reading is dependent on another? Why? How?), and to establish which reading is most likely the earliest, and therefore probably the "original" reading.

Most textual critics work with three basic assumptions (see Metzger & Ehrman 2005:300–315). (1) Earlier manuscripts are generally superior to later copies. This explains why most contemporary Bible translations (e.g., NIV, TNIV, RSV, NRSV, NLT, NASB, and others) have abandoned the *Textus Receptus* used by the KJV. (2) The more difficult a reading is, the more likely it is earlier. Difficulties (grammatical, theological, and the like) tend to be smoothed out by copyists. The reading that explains the emergence of other variations is likely the earlier reading: Similarly, on a family tree, the genealogical relations can be traced out. (3) The shorter reading is likely the earlier reading. The tendency of well-meaning copyists would be to add explanations and lengthen texts rather than reducing them—recall 1 John 5:7–8.

e. Exercise. Below are examples of textual variants that have been transmitted through the manuscript tradition. As note above, only relatively few textual variants are reproduced in contemporary English Bibles; most of the thousands of NT variant readings are not visible to the reader of an English Bible. However, the textual variants are recorded in the critical editions of the NT, such as the *Nestle-Aland* editions or the United Bible Society's *Greek New Testament*, which are identical and only differ in how the variants are presented. In these editions, committees of textual critics work to record their decisions about which reading most likely represents the original text; this reading is put in the main body of the text. The other readings of the text (i.e., textual variants) are then put in the apparatus at the bottom of the page. Thus the reading judged to be "stronger" (i.e., most likely the "original") is incorporated into the main text. It is from this reconstructed text that contemporary English Bible translations are made (e.g., NIV, TNIV, RSV, NRSV, NASB, NLT, and others).

Read and compare the variant readings below; they are italicized. Each one is an actual reading that appears among the manuscripts of one of Paul's letters. Taking into account the three basic assumptions of textual criticism (the better reading is usually the earlier, more difficult, and shorter), answer the questions below. Ultimately, the goal is to decide which reading is most likely "original," identifying the others as secondary variants. Let's see how we compare with the scholars.

Variant A: We sent Timothy, our brother and *God's servant* in the gospel of Christ, to establish you in your faith ... (supported by some of the earliest manuscripts available: namely, Sinaiticus, and some later ones).

Variant B: We sent Timothy, our brother and *God's fellow-worker* in the gospel of Christ, to establish you in your faith ... (supported by some early manuscripts and some later ones).

Variant C: We sent Timothy, our brother and *fellow-worker* in the gospel of Christ, to establish you in your faith ... (supported by some of the earliest manuscripts available: namely, Vaticanus, and some later ones).

Variant D: We sent Timothy, our brother and *God's servant and our fellow-worker* in the gospel of Christ, to establish you in your faith ... (supported by some early manuscripts and the majority of manuscripts; taken up in the *Textus Receptus* and carried into the KJV).

(i) What are the differences in meaning between the variants? By what do the copyists appear to be bothered?

(ii) Which variant has stronger manuscript support? What is the basis for your assessment?
(iii) How significant is it that Variant D has the largest number of manuscripts supporting it? Why?
(iv) Which variant has the more "difficult" reading (grammatically, theologically, etc.)? Why?
(v) Which variant best explains the origin of the others? How so? This is the reading that you would recommend be included in the main text, leaving the other three at the bottom of the page in the apparatus of variant readings.

Open a NT to 1 Thessalonians 3:2, and see how your decision compares with the "experts."

It is clear that some copyists struggled with the use of "fellow-worker" (which implies equality), finding "servant" (which implies subordination) to be easier in the context. While the first three readings all have strong manuscript support, no manuscript is automatically assumed to contain the best reading; each reading must be assessed for the strength of its manuscript support. The large number of manuscripts reading Variant D does not necessarily make it stronger—the *quality* of manuscript support is more important than the *quantity*. Variant B is deemed most "difficult"—implying that Timothy is God's equal—because the other variants each find a way to overcome the difficulty (substitute "servant" for "fellow-worker," delete "God," or conflate readings). If B is seen as original, then the emergence of the other three is explainable. Thus, the B reading should be moved to the main body of the NT text, and the other three readings identified as "variants" and placed in the apparatus at the bottom of the page in the critical edition of the NT (for a complete analysis of this text, see Metzger & Ehrman 2005:337–39).

After several centuries of textual criticism (variant discovery, collation, assessment, and ranking), most textual critics are fairly confident that the critically reconstructed NT text (*Nestle-Aland* and United Bible Society's *Greek NT*) reliably represents the texts as they were first composed by the NT writers.

8

Christology

The Person and Work of Messiah Jesus

THIS IS THE FIRST of seven discussions that make up round 2 of the NT conference. The NT writers are back in their seats around the table after the intermission, and now we listen in to their deliberations on seven topics. The aim of this chapter is to address the topic of Christology. Usually, Christology is divided into two sections: (1) the person of Jesus (identity), and (2) the work of Jesus (atonement). These are also the two objectives of this chapter. What do the NT writings have to say on these two topics?

THE PERSON OF JESUS: IDENTITY

After listening to the NT writers tell their stories and make their presentations, we note that at least three issues have sometimes come up for discussion in the subsequent centuries regarding Jesus's identity. First, debate surrounds whether Jesus's identity should be understood in terms of *evolution* or *development*. Some hear the NT writers and wonder if their assessment of Jesus evolved by stages from a Palestinian rabbi through a variety of experiences until he came to be worshiped as the divine Lord, someone whom he was not. Others hear a more developmental approach being witnessed by the NT writers. In this understanding, the various NT descriptions of Jesus's identity are attempts to make explicit what was always implicit and always true, even if not immediately perceived.

The developmental explanation pays closer attention to what the panelists at the NT conference are actually saying. Even though many of Jesus's contemporaries did not correctly perceive Jesus's identity initially, they claim that their experience of the risen Jesus clarified that his identity as God's beloved Son, the bringer of salvation, was present from the beginning (Luke 24:44–45). Jesus's life of continuing to choose faithfulness to God's way and of tirelessly calling Israel back to its original mandate, worked to confirm his identity as God's Messiah, which he had from the start. According to Caird, "The incarnation established an objective union between the *logos* and the individual humanity of Jesus. But the man Jesus needed the guidance of the Spirit to lead him to a subjective awareness of this fact" (1994:298). Worthy of note is that what was true of Jesus became also true for his disciples. Not that they became what he was, but that they learned their true identity as he did his. The pattern of requiring a *subjective affirmation* in order to confirm the *objective reality* is the same dynamic that the NT writers use to describe Christian discipleship and the appropriation of the new-creation identity initiated by Jesus (John 12:32; Heb 3:6; 6:4; 10:23).

Second, debate centers on whether discussion about Jesus's identity should start *from above* or *from below*. Christological discussions beginning in the fourth century typically start from above: Jesus is identified with God as the second person of the Trinity, who travels down from heaven by incarnation to live on earth, completing his salvation mandate before returning to heaven. This approach can tend toward *Docetism*, according to which Jesus is thought of as only appearing to be human but not really human at all. By contrast, some christological discussions start from below: Jesus is identified as a human being who through the choices he makes for God, becomes thought of as divine. This view can tend toward *Arianism*, where traditional affirmations of Jesus's divinity and the Trinity are undermined.

Is there a way through this impasse, a way that avoids Docetism and Arianism? Are not the traditional alternatives of stressing either Jesus's humanity or divinity a false dichotomy? A close reading of the NT writers reveals that they did not choose between one or the other; they were able to affirm both Jesus's divinity and his humanity. Paul can say both without difficulty: "When the fullness of time had come, God sent his

Son, born of a woman" (Gal 4:4). They witness that from the beginning, Jesus is known as a human being "born of a woman" (from below), but also as God's divine Son (from above), the preexistent "Word" (John 1:1) in whose "face" we see God most clearly (2 Cor 4:6).

The NT writers do not seem to have much of a problem with the two natures of Jesus as did later theologians. In fact, the NT writers make their most elevated statements about Jesus precisely by taking seriously his true humanity. Paul claims in Romans 5 that God created the human race for just that union of the human and the divine that Adam failed to achieve, but which was achieved by Jesus (Caird 1994:320). Yet, Jesus was *more* than just a human being, in that "in him the whole fullness of the deity dwells bodily" (Col 2:9) and that by uniting with him, people put on "the new self, which is being renewed in knowledge according to the image of the creator" (Col 3:10).

All the NT writers are convinced that Jesus was a real human being, but *more* than that, the perfect human being. Jesus is the God-man, who lived in a way unlike any other human being, in a way that showed most clearly what God is like, and what humanity is to be like. By his faithful life, Jesus confirms his prior identity as the divine Son of God, living out the kind of humanity that God intended from the start—humanity tasked with completing the creation project. Thus, it is Jesus's kind of humanity that finally makes it possible for others to join him in filling out the dimensions of the new-creation age. Since Jesus does not conform to the old humanity with its rebellion against God and its preference for autonomous living, all peoples are invited to be attached to Jesus's perfect humanity and thus to participate with God in making "all things new" (Rev 21:5).

Third, debate arose about whether Jesus's identity should be understood in *functional* terms (what he does) or in *ontological* terms (who he is). Making such a choice would likely have seemed strange for the NT writers; they understood who Jesus was by what he did and, conversely, understood what he did as rooted in who he was. Nevertheless, by the fourth century, christological discussions became dominated by ontological terms. The new focus was on the "substance" or "essence" of Jesus, and how this material could be related to God. The ontological focus became important for Greco-Roman Christians in the fourth century, because their social standing changed rapidly when Christianity suddenly moved from a loose network of diverse, marginalized groups to the dominant religion of the Roman Empire. Proto-orthodox Christians found ontological terms more useful in the larger Greco-Roman context for pressing their vision of Christianity in the debates with other forms of Christianity (Jewish-Christian Adoptionists, gnostic Christianity, and Marcionite Christianity), which held alternative Christologies, and supported more individualistic spirituality.

By contrast, functional christology pays closer attention to what we learn about Jesus's identity from his words and actions. It is less concerned with speculation about Jesus's bodily substance or fundamental essence, and more concerned with how Jesus's actions functioned like God's. Functional Christology, however, should not be viewed as a recent reaction to orthodoxy or ontological Christology. Why? Because it is easily the earliest Christology.

All the NT writers are convinced that Jesus was a real human being; but *more* than that, he was the perfect human being, the divine Son of God, who lived in such a way as to show most clearly what God is like, and what humanity is to be like. Later, this conviction was enshrined in the ontological language of the proto-orthodox creeds, confessing that Jesus was fully divine and fully human (The Chalcedonian Creed, 451 CE). Such "fully"-"fully" terminology was designed to rule out the *half-and-half* terminology (half divine and half human) and the *either-or* terminology (either divine or human) that some early Christian groups promoted. However, the fully-fully terminology should not be seen as an intrusion on the biblical text. Why? Because it picks up the consistent NT witness both to who Jesus *is* and to what he *does*; he both initiates and empowers God's creation. Jesus is both "pioneer and perfecter" (Heb 12:2). By virtue of his obedience, Jesus confirms his identity as God's Messiah, the divine Son of God, and opens access to God so that freed from sin's grip, humanity is finally able to join Jesus in accomplishing humanity's mandate of partnering with God to complete the creation enterprise (Heb 5:8–10).

Of course, such functional language raises ontological questions about Jesus's identity, but these are not resolved in the NT in any modern sense of the word. The NT writers never question whether Jesus is God, and how that might be possible. (This later became the question of Greco-Roman Christianity.) Instead, the NT writers' ontological question is this: Is God really present in the life of Jesus? On this they all answer in the affirmative, giving witness to Jesus's remarkable life as a prophet, miracle worker, healer, and teacher, as well as to his unique character as sinless (Heb 4:15) and perfect (Heb 5:9). It seems that more problems are introduced than solved by trying to "update" the NT witness to Jesus.

For example, sometimes theologians argue that various aspects of Jesus's remarkable life are the *result* of the special circumstances of his birth. And yet no NT writer does this. In fact, only two of the four Evangelists, Matthew and Luke, even speak of his birth, and they do so for other reasons. They speak of his mother, Mary, found to be with child by the Holy Spirit while she was a virgin (Matt 1:18; Luke 1:35). Matthew and Luke use the virgin birth to make two large theological statements. In Matthew, Jesus's miraculous birth is tied to prophecy and fulfillment (Matt 1:22–23). Jesus's birth is living proof that "God is with us" (Emmanuel) and that God's ancient promise to Abraham is being fulfilled (Gen 12:1–3). These affirmations resonate with the gospel's concluding promise: "I am with you always, to the end of the age" (Matt 28:20). In Luke, Mary's virginal conception links Jesus to the creation story in Genesis. Jesus's birth is a new creation story; it is God's miraculous intervention, moving creation to the final stage of its completion. The Holy Spirit that overshadows Mary (Luke 1:35) is the same Holy Spirit that broods over the waters of chaos generating light and life (Gen 1:2).

Unfortunately, in later centuries the Evangelists' theological affirmations have been pressed for more details than they could provide, with the result that the NT witness is distorted. In popular usage the virginal conception has typically been either *overplayed* or *underplayed*. Already during the ancient period, Augustine (354–430 CE) was one who overplayed the virgin birth. He viewed the infancy narratives in Matthew and Luke as "proof" that Jesus was sinless; Jesus's sinlessness is something the NT writers do affirm, but in other ways (2 Cor 5:21; Heb 4:15). Since Jesus was presumed to be without a human father, Augustine reasoned that Jesus's conception was therefore untainted by semen (*Against Julian* 5.54). Augustine thought sin was passed from generation to generation through the semen (based on a faulty reading of the Latin text in Rom 5:12). His view of semen transfer became instrumental in his formulation of the doctrine of original sin and in his justification for infant baptism (*On Marriage and Concupiscence* 2.29.51). In any case, the story of the virginal conception of Jesus was transformed from an assertion of God's miraculous intervention to an assertion about Jesus and his essence, substance, or physiological makeup. On the other extreme, during the modern period when the historical model eclipsed other ways of reading biblical literature, the virginal-conception stories were underplayed and dismissed as a mythological cover-up for Mary's irregular pregnancy. Both such attempts to update the infancy narratives (overplaying or underplaying the virgin birth) unfortunately mute and distort the theological witness to the virgin birth by Matthew (that Jesus is God with us, Emmanuel) and by Luke (that Jesus is God's making creation as God always intended).

So what then are some of the ways that the NT writers do speak about Jesus? How do they speak about his person or fundamental identity? The NT lists at least twelve different ways that Jesus's identity is described, and these can be briefly summarized as follows.

(1) *Title* Christology: Jesus is identified by titles like Messiah, Son of God, and Son of David.
(2) *Pre-Existent* Christology (John 1:1-18): Jesus is the embodiment of the divine *logos*, the purpose of God, which existed with God before the creation of the world.
(3) *Humiliation/exaltation* Christology (Phil 2:5-11; 1 Pet 3:18): Jesus is humbled (crucified), then vindicated by God (resurrected), thus becoming a model (norm) for disciples.
(4) *Eschatological* Christology (Col 1:15-19): Jesus represents the full presence of God revealed now in history's last days.
(5) *Fulfillment* Christology (Heb 1:1-3; 7:11-28): Jesus fulfills God's promises and intentions.
(6) *Triumphant* Christology (Col 2:15): Jesus triumphs over the powers of Satan (sin, evil, death), and thus Jesus is and will be king.
(7) *Solidarity* Christology (2 Cor 5:18-21; Rom 5:12-21): Jesus is one with humanity in order that people might become what God intended from the beginning, truly human.
(8) *Liberation* Christology (Rom 3:21-26): Jesus deals decisively with the power of sin, undoing it and liberating humanity from its grip.
(9) *Peoplehood* Christology (Mark 3:31-35; Rom 9-11): Jesus is the bringer of salvation, who gathers a renewed people of God, fulfilling Israel's mission mandate to the nations.

(10) *Spirit* Christology (Rom 8): Jesus is the fullness or empowerment of the Spirit; thus, the Spirit is the Spirit of Christ.
(11) *Mission* Christology (John 17): Jesus is the sent one, who in turn sends his followers to complete God's mission.
(12) *Jesus-as-self-revelation-of-God* Christology (1 Cor 8:6): Jesus is Lord, the creative and redemptive self-revelation of the one true God.

Thus, by virtue of their experience of what happened to Jesus, the early Christians affirmed that the one God of Jewish faith was now present in history in and through Jesus. This affirmation forced a redefinition of Jewish monotheism without abandoning it. The Christian doctrine of the Trinity is the result of this restatement of Jewish monotheism. While the NT writers did not use ontological categories of "essence" or "substance" to talk about Jesus, they did make statements about Jesus's identity. Based on their experience of Jesus's life and resurrection, they were convinced that they saw "the glory of God in the face of Jesus Christ" (2 Cor 4:6). Furthermore, they were persuaded that, in Caird's words, "the man Jesus already possessed, during his earthly career, a life over which death had no power, an indestructible, eternal life, because he lived in such a close union with God that, without loss of identity, his human personality was taken up into the divine" (1994:298).

THE WORK OF JESUS: ATONEMENT

The NT writers are clear that the "work" of Jesus had everything to do with the demonstration of the love of God; it was about freeing human beings from the power of sin and restoring them to a right relationship with God; it was about Jesus's doing something that humanity so entangled in the web of sin could not do for itself—in this sense, the saving work of Jesus is substitutionary. Actually, the English word *atonement* was invented to give expression to God's saving activity of liberation and reconciliation (the term *atonement* derives from "to make at one" or "at one-ment"). Yet the NT writers do not offer an account of the mechanism by which Jesus's death and resurrection became effective for the salvation of humanity and all creation. Were the evil powers tricked, paid off, decommissioned, dismissed, or annihilated? Was it something else? Instead, the NT writers prefer to use metaphors to explain that which they were convinced was true: namely, that Jesus is alive. Death could not hold him down. Thus, the powers of the old age no longer have jurisdiction over those associated with the risen Lord, and the new age has dawned for all creation!

The NT writers chose to use what they knew something about in order to talk about the mystery of atonement, whose inner workings they did not understand, yet that they knew to be true. They use five metaphors to portray Jesus's substitutionary work of atonement (Green & Baker 2000:97).

(1) *Law court*: God condemns evil, and people are freed from its grip in order to be truly human: humanity is justified (John 14:30–31; Gal 2:15–21; Rev 12:10–12).
(2) *Commerce*: God steps up to secure the release or purchase of humanity and all creation that is stuck in the power of sin: humanity is redeemed (Mark 10:45; Rom 3:21–26; Gal 4:1–7).
(3) *Personal Relationships*: God addresses the deep alienation and rebellion that scars all creation and takes a personal interest in working to restore right relations between God, humanity, and creation: humanity is reconciled (Luke 24:26–27; 2 Cor 5:14–21).
(4) *Worship*: God's character of being-for-others is embodied in Jesus's ministry and self-giving sacrifice for the world: humanity is moved and empowered to worship God truly because of Jesus's sacrificial demonstration of God's love (Phil 2:6–11; Heb 9:11–14, 23–28; 10:1–25; Rev 5:6–14; 12:10–12).
(5) *Battleground*: God, the mighty warrior, fights uncompromisingly against evil and secures the victory in a manner true to God's character such that humanity and all creation are rescued and liberated from sin's death spell: humanity is included in God's victory over sin, evil, and death (1 Cor 15:50–57; Col 2:15; Rev 12:7–12; 19:11–21; 20:11–14).

In addition to these five overarching metaphors, there are eighteen specific words are found in the NT to express atonement: (1) "salvation" (*sōtēria*): restoration to wholeness (Luke 19:19; Acts 4:12; Rom 1:16), (2) "mercy seat" (*hilastērion/hilasmon*): the place were sin is dealt with and undone (Rom 3:25; Heb 9:5; 1 John 2:2; 4:10), (3) "ransom" or "redemption" (*apolytrōsis*): setting free, deliverance (Luke 21:28; Rom 3:24; Heb 9:15), (4) "sanctification" (*hagiasmos*): dedication, consecration, holiness (Rom 6:22; Heb 12:14; 1 Pet 1:2), (5) "freedom" (*eleutheria*);

liberty, emancipation (Rom 8:21; 2 Cor 3:17; 1 Pet 2:16), (6) "righteousness" (*dikaiosynē*): true to God's character, what is right (Matt 5:10; Rom 1:17; 2 Tim 3:16; Heb 12:11; Jas 3:18), (7) undergoing transformation (*metamorphoō*): to be changed in form (2 Cor 3:18) (8) "new creation" (*kainē ktisis*): the goal of the created order (Rom 8:18-25; 2 Cor 5:17; Gal 6:15), (9) "reconciliation" (*katallagē*): restoration of relationship (Rom 5:11; 2 Cor 5:18-19), (10) "forgiveness" (*aphesis*): cancellation of debt, transfer from the rule of death to the rule of life (Luke 24:47; Acts 26:18; Col 1:14; Heb 10:18), (11) "adoption" (*huiothesia*): naming as children and heirs (Rom 8:15, 23; Gal 4:5; Eph 1:5), (12) "victory" (*apekdysis*): putting off, setting free from, triumphing over the power of sin (Col 2:11), (13) for humanity; "he died for our sins" (*apethanen hyper tōn hamartiōn hēmōn*): Jesus dies on behalf of humanity and all creation, which is stuck in sin (John 11:51; 1 Cor 15:3; 1 Thess 5:10), (14) revelation of "love" (*agapē / agapaō*): demonstration and disclosure of God's kind of love (John 3:16; Rom 5:8; Eph 2:4-7; 1 John 3:16; 4:7, 12; 5:3; Jude 21), (15) "eternal life" (*aiōnios zōē*): the gift of true life now with full realization in the age to come (Mark 10:17; John 17:3; Rom 6:22; 1 Tim 6:12; 1 John 5:13), (16) "kingdom of God" (*basileia tou theou*): the presence and rule of God in beginning ways with full manifestation in the age to come (Mark 1:15; 4:11; 10:13-27; Rom 14:17; 1 Cor 15:50; Rev 12:20), (17) "identification with Christ" (*en Christō / eis Christon*): participation in, attachment to, association with Christ, symbolized by baptism into Christ (Rom 6:3; 8:1; 1 Cor 1:30; 2 Cor 5:17; Gal 3:27; Eph 2:10), and (18) "election" (*eklogē*): belonging to God's chosen people (Rom 9:11; 11:28; 1 Thess 1:4; 2 Pet 1:10).

What can we say about the diversity of NT salvation and atonement language? It seems clear that no single term is capable of completely capturing the meaning of Christ's substitutionary death. The multiplicity of salvation and atonement terms suggests that the point of salvation is that it rescues humanity from whatever predicament plagues humanity. Christian salvation answers people's immediate and everyday concern for liberation, which may be expressed in various ways depending on the cultural location (fear, shame, guilt, alienation, and the like).

The early Christians invited the people that they encountered in their everyday experiences to also experience liberation. They challenged their contacts to repent, to cast off their former alienated identity, and to adopt a new pattern of living as demonstrated by Jesus—and thus to discover their true identity and purpose. These missionaries introduced people to the Jesus community, which meant the *abandonment* of their former corporate and social loyalties (to sin, evil, and death) and the *embrace* of God's reconfigured, end-time people now gathered around Jesus, the prototype of the new humanity.

But how can the reality of atonement be explained? This is what a theology of the atonement must address. It talks about how the death of Jesus is "for" people; it shows how it is substitutionary. A doctrine explains something. The doctrine of the atonement has to explain why Jesus's death was necessary. It must explain how it makes sense that it was this way that God chose to save humanity. Was it primarily about *protecting* God's holiness or *demonstrating* God's holiness? If the atonement solves a problem, with whom does that problem lie? God? Satan? Humanity? Then important subquestions include, What is the relationship between Jesus's life and the death he experienced? How does the death of Jesus deal with human alienation and the sense of brokenness? How does the cross/resurrection event change the world? the universe? Why did it have to be this way? Could it have been accomplished otherwise?

A doctrine of the atonement must answer these questions *and* do justice to all the biblical language—all the atonement metaphors used in the NT choir (i.e., the law court, commerce, personal relationships, worship, and battleground). Selecting only one metaphor to carry all the saving significance of the cross leads to two problems. (1) The confusion of categories: a metaphor is *not* the thing itself, but points beyond itself to the reality it is attempting to clarify. Atonement metaphors are illustrative signs of the reality of God's saving activity. (2) The reduction of interpretive space: some metaphors work better in some cultures than in others. By insisting on only one particular metaphor, some cultures may be hindered from hearing the significance of God's saving activity in ways that speak best to them.

Typically Western Christians have pictured the redemption drama as a transaction between two players (i.e., God and Jesus) with the cross providing the means of exchange (payment for sin) that allows God to once again welcome humanity back into God's presence. While this schema may explain the court-of-law metaphor to some degree, how well does it integrate the others (commerce, worship, relationship, and battle)? What does it say about God, Jesus, humanity, and sin? Consider the following diagram.

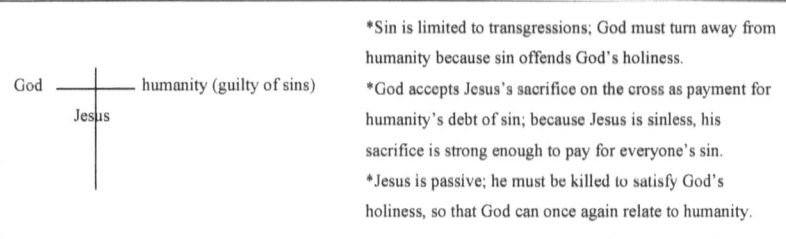

TABLE 8.1 Two-Player Salvation Model

- *Sin is limited to transgressions; God must turn away from humanity because sin offends God's holiness.
- *God accepts Jesus's sacrifice on the cross as payment for humanity's debt of sin; because Jesus is sinless, his sacrifice is strong enough to pay for everyone's sin.
- *Jesus is passive; he must be killed to satisfy God's holiness, so that God can once again relate to humanity.

How does inserting a third player, the power of sin, change the schema? How might it look now? The third player picks up on the ancient biblical language used to represent those spiritual powers created by God and mandated to help in God's creation work. While initially loyal, some act in defiance of God's purpose, drawing energy from human loyalty and siphoning away original human allegiance to God. The rebellious power of sin responds by enslaving all humankind and all creation in its death-dealing grip. God's saving activity is relentless and progressive, culminating in the person of Jesus, who upends the power of sin, making possible the release of all that is captive to sin's reign. Using the ancient schema of three players (God, the powers, and Jesus), consider what a three-player redemption-drama model offers. Like the two-player model, it explains the court-of-law metaphor, although differently. What about the other metaphors (commerce, worship, relationship, and battle)? Can it account for them as well? How so? What does it say about God, Jesus, humanity, and sin? Consider the following diagram.

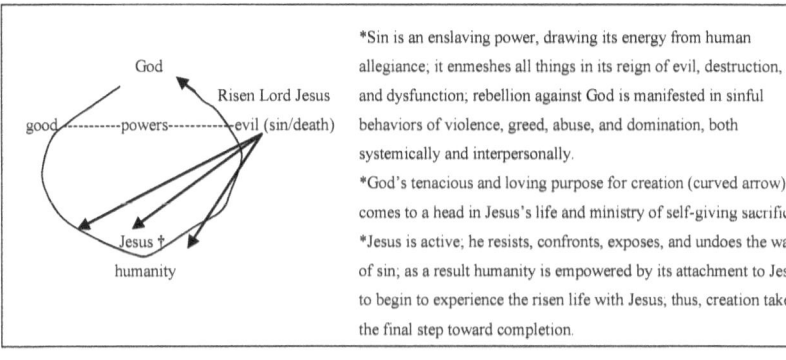

- *Sin is an enslaving power, drawing its energy from human allegiance; it enmeshes all things in its reign of evil, destruction, and dysfunction; rebellion against God is manifested in sinful behaviors of violence, greed, abuse, and domination, both systemically and interpersonally.
- *God's tenacious and loving purpose for creation (curved arrow) comes to a head in Jesus's life and ministry of self-giving sacrifice
- *Jesus is active; he resists, confronts, exposes, and undoes the way of sin; as a result humanity is empowered by its attachment to Jesus to begin to experience the risen life with Jesus; thus, creation takes the final step toward completion.

TABLE 8.2 Three-Player Salvation Model

Both the two-player and the three-player models attempt to imagine how God's saving activity works. However, the models differ largely on the image of God with which they work. Is God forced to step in (as in the two-player model) and offer or take Jesus's life in exchange for humanity's, in order to appease God's own holiness, which was compromised by human sin? In other words, is God's holiness something that is *satisfied* by Jesus's death in our place? Or is God's nature characterized by continually reaching out to creation (as in the three-player model), even to the point of being killed, if that is what it will take to rescue creation from itself and bring it to its goal? Is God the relentless giver who creates a way for humanity to step out from under its self-inflicted rebellion against God, with its allegiance to sin's power? In other words, is God's holiness something that is *demonstrated* in self-giving love?

Of course, the issue is not settled by what our preferred image of God happens to be! In biblical theology the question is, what best resonates with the truth to which the NT writers give witness? As we have seen, the picture of demonstrated holiness rather than of protected holiness is one that resonates with the early Christians' conceptualization of the roles of all three players in the redemption drama—God, Jesus, and the power of sin. However, the picture of satisfied or protected holiness, which became popular during the medieval period, continues to be widely held today. Then (as now), there were political, social, and theological reasons for promoting satisfaction theories of atonement, which limited the players in the redemption drama to two—God and Jesus (Green and Baker 2000:126–36). By silencing the role of the power of sin, the Christian gospel could more easily align to the concerns of the state: namely, the popular leadership patterns of authority and retributive judicial structures of Roman law. Unfortunately, the theological silencing of sin's role as a power has made sin even *more* able to continue unchallenged, enmeshing people, institutions, and cultures in its reckless death-dealing ways, even as it careens headlong down the path to its own self-destruction.

The NT witness to the saving activity of God (atonement) is not that God found an innovative way to deal with humanity's offensive behavior by making Jesus take humanity's penalty. No, as we have seen, the NT writers proclaim that God did something much more radical. In the person of Jesus, God entered into humanity's flawed scapegoat mechanism—the only rule of engagement that humanity, blinded by sin's rule, knew how to use—in order to bring about its collapse, its undoing. God effected this rescue operation through Jesus, in order to bring an end to the very scapegoat mechanism that Satan *thought* would secure his rule forever (1 Cor 2:8). Instead, the single-victim mechanism was reversed, as God drained sin of its power to lie about its death-dealing ways. Satan was fooled by his own thirst for power, and he set in motion his own destruction. Death was transformed from being sin's ally to becoming the path by which sin's own defeat and destiny were achieved. See J. K. Rowling's Harry Potter book series for a tale exploiting a similar dynamic where evil ultimately destroys itself in the face of uncompromising love.

At the cross sin was drawn into overstepping its jurisdiction with an act of aggression that unleashed its own destruction. Sin was no longer able to hide behind the lie, and sin's grip on humanity was loosened: the way was opened for all who identify with the way of Jesus to be included in Jesus's victory over sin. Thus the old-age power structure (the flesh) was rendered inoperative, and displaced by a new power structure (the Spirit) with ethical implications for all who now "walk not according to the flesh but according to the Spirit" (Rom 8:4). In this way, God made a way for humanity to abandon its age-old rebellion and to leave its allegiance to sin's archetypal ideal of redemptive violence so that it could rediscover its true and prior identity as God's chosen and beloved.

While the christological starting point informs all that the NT writers are talking about (it is the very center of their interpretation of the significance of Jesus's life and ministry), they do talk about other topics as well. In the next chapter, we turn to the topic of revelation.

EXERCISES

1. Historians of Christianity have debated which model best illuminates Jesus's character and ministry. Review the models that are advocated in contemporary scholarship. Visit a theological library and browse the BT198–BT205 section or do an internet search. Among the many contenders for conceptualizing the person of Jesus are Jesus as cynic sage, as wonder-working magician, as traveling healer, as apocalyptic suffering servant, as visionary teacher, as political revolutionary, as social reformer, and as doomsday prophet.

   Discuss what it is about the memory of Jesus's life that suggests each of these portraits. How well does each deal with your assessment of the evidence? What aspects of Jesus's life and ministry would you want to highlight for contemporary Christian communities that choose to be shaped by them?

2. Review the three topics often raised by NT interpreters when speaking about Jesus's identity: evolutionary or developmental, from above or from below, and functional or ontological. Which arguments seem most compelling to you? Why?

Sometimes it proves to be a good but challenging exercise to try to make a theological statement using as little theological jargon as possible. Recently I was assigned such a task. Below is my attempt to talk about Jesus's identity as forthrightly as I possibly could.

Discuss how successful you think my construction is. What questions does it address? What areas of further exploration are raised for you? Try writing your own account of who Jesus is, and why it matters, without theological jargon.

I like telling people what I do for a living—and watching their reaction. Whether in conversation with the parent sitting next to me at my son's water-polo match or my daughter's soccer game, I am sure to get an interesting response. When I tell them I teach at a local seminary, they invariably ask, "What do you teach?" I say, "Jesus."

In the conversation that follows I can elaborate on Jesus in several ways. I can respond as a professional historian and recite a list of statements about Jesus's life that are almost beyond dispute and acknowledged by virtually all Jesus scholars regardless of political or religious persuasion. These include: born near the time of the death of Herod the Great; spent his childhood and early adult years in Nazareth, a Galilean village; baptized by John the Baptist; called disciples; taught and ministered in Galilee; preached "the Kingdom of God"; went to Jerusalem for the Passover; created a disturbance in the Temple area; ate a final meal with his disciples; arrested and interrogated by Jewish authorities; executed on the orders of the Roman prefect, Pontius Pilate; after his death, his followers experienced what they described as the "resurrection"; convinced that he would return to found the Kingdom, they formed communities to win others to faith in Jesus as God's Messiah.

Sometimes, however, it is also appropriate to elaborate on my neighbor's query by filling out the significance of Jesus's life and ministry, because I am also a confessing Christian and a biblical theologian. There are three things I would highlight.

1. *Jesus's identity is unique.* The NT writers use various ways to identify Jesus. They call him the anointed one, the son of David, the Son of God, the preexistent Word (John 1:1). In addition, they are uniform in their testimony to Jesus's remarkable life as a prophet, miracle worker, healer, and teacher, as well as his unique character as sinless (Heb 4:15) and perfect (Heb 5:9).

Two writers, Matthew and Luke, underline the special circumstances surrounding his birth. They speak of his mother, Mary, conceiving him by the Holy Spirit while she was a virgin (Matt 1:18; Luke 1:35). Matthew and Luke use the Virgin Birth to make two large theological statements. In Matthew, Jesus's miraculous birth is tied to prophecy and fulfillment (Matt 1:22-23). Jesus's birth is living proof that "God is with us" (Emmanuel) and that God's ancient promise to Abraham is being fulfilled (Gen 12:1-3). These affirmations resonate with the Gospel's concluding promise: "I am with you always, to the end of the age" (Matt 28:20). In Luke, Mary's virginal conception is used to link Jesus to the creation story in Genesis. Jesus's birth is a new creation story; it is God's miraculous intervention, moving creation to the final stage of its completion. The Holy Spirit that overshadows Mary (Luke 1:35) is the same Holy Spirit that broods over the waters of chaos generating light and life (Gen 1:2).

2. *Jesus's mission is unique.* The NT writers show how Jesus linked the "Son of Man" expressions (Dan 7:13) with Isaiah's "servant" texts (Isa 42, 49, 52, 53, 61), finding in these ancient texts words to characterize his own mission. Jesus responds to God's call on Israel, a call flexible enough to include Israel, a remnant within Israel, and a representative individual, the Messiah. Likely, Jesus saw the title, Son of Man, as a "job description" for the New Israel. He saw his mission as inviting others to join him in filling out God's purpose, first for Israel, and then for all the nations of the world. By raising Jesus from the dead to new life, God showed approval for the way that Jesus chose to embrace God's mission, to defeat the power of sin, and to embody the purpose for which God set the universe in motion.

3. *Jesus's contribution is unique.* All the NT writers are convinced that Jesus was a real human being, but *more* than that, the perfect human being. Jesus is the God-man who lived in a way unlike any other human being, a way that showed most clearly what God is like and what humanity is to be like. Later, this conviction was enshrined in the creedal language, confessing that Jesus was fully divine and fully human. Such

fully-fully terminology was designed to rule out the *half-and-half* terminology (half divine and half human) and the *either-or* terminology (either divine or human) that some early Christian groups promoted.

The fully-fully terminology picks up the consistent NT witness to both of Jesus's functions; he initiates and completes God's creation. Jesus is both "pioneer and perfecter" (Heb 12:2). By virtue of his obedience, Jesus confirms his identity as God's Messiah, the divine Son of God, and opens access to God so that, freed from sin's grip, we are finally able to join Jesus in accomplishing humanity's mandate of partnering with God to complete the creation enterprise (Heb 5:8–10).

I enjoy telling people what I do. What can I say? I love Jesus; he helps me understand better who we are as human beings and what God really desires. Jesus finally makes it possible for human beings to realize their God-given potential.

TABLE 8.3 Short Essay on Who Jesus Is, and Why It Matters

3. G. B. Caird was convinced that a correct perception of Jesus's identity must be grounded in his Jewishness. Caird went on to assert, "We shall not find Jesus even indirectly relevant to our age unless we first find him directly relevant to his own" (1994:351).

   Discuss the merits of Caird's assertion and its significance for Christian self-understanding today. One particularly helpful book that explores Jesus's Jewishness in order to come to a fuller understanding of who Jesus was and how he matters, is Thomas Yoder Neufeld's book, *Recovering Jesus: The Witness of the New Testament* (2007).

4. Review the five metaphor clusters used by the NT writers to illustrate the saving significance of Jesus's death and resurrection: court of law, commerce, personal relationships, worship, and battleground. Each of these metaphors represents an attempt by a NT writer to explain how God, through Jesus of Nazareth, moved creation a huge step forward toward wholeness and completion at the cross.

   Discuss how you could explain the paradox of the cross to a group of junior-high students without theological jargon. How could the cross, an instrument of execution and something not obviously associated with salvation, still fit the thrust of the Hebrew Bible? How does the cross fit the messianic goal of bringing salvation to Israel and to the world by undoing evil's grip on creation?

5. Through the course of Christian theological reflection, thinkers have tried to explain in various ways how Jesus's death achieved salvation. The three classic explanations are *Christus Victor* (Jesus triumphs over sin's rule: Irenaeus, second century), *Penal Satisfaction* (Jesus satisfies God's honor in place of our violation against it: Anselm, eleventh century), and *Moral Influence* (Jesus provides an example for living free of sin's obligation: Abélard, twelfth century). Each of the classic atonement models conceptualizes the character and mission of God, Jesus, sin, and humanity in a different way.

   Discuss the strengths and weaknesses of each of these classic models. How do these models relate to the two models presented in this chapter (two-player and three-player salvation models)? Why do you think Jesus had to die? What aspect(s) of atonement would you want to highlight for contemporary Christian communities that choose to be shaped by the founding narrative that the atonement represents? If you could offer some other metaphor to communicate the saving significance of the cross, what would it be?

9

Revelation

God's Self-Disclosure to Humanity and all Creation

THE THEOLOGICAL THEME OF revelation concerns itself with the ways God uses to communicate to humanity and the world. It is based on the assumption that it is impossible to know anything about God unless God chooses to self-disclose. However, Christianity is not the only religion that claims divine revelation. The distinctive claim that the NT writers make is that Israel's God has always been involved in self-disclosure, but that in these last days God has been revealed most fully in a personal self-disclosure through Jesus of Nazareth (Heb 1:1–2).

This chapter has three objectives: (1) to clarify the terms *general revelation* and *special revelation*, (2) to review the different ways that the Christian Bible is conceptualized, and (3) to chart the interpretive reading strategies used by faith communities to bridge the temporal and cultural gaps between the world of the NT writers and the world of today.

GENERAL AND SPECIAL REVELATION

Usually the topic of revelation is divided into two sections in Christian theology: *general* revelation and *special* revelation. Traditionally, general revelation refers to God's self-disclosure, which is available to all humanity, and special revelation refers to the Christian Bible. However, too stark a contrast between these two aspects of revelation should not be made, because they are related. For example, we could say that general revelation refers to God's self-disclosure that comes to humanity from outside human history and reaches its climax over time in the person of Jesus; this self-disclosure of God in Jesus is recorded in the Christian Bible as special revelation; thus, the two are linked.

What do the NT writings have to say on these two topics? The NT writers are convinced that God has indeed chosen to be known by human beings in some sense throughout the course of human history (John 1:1–10; 3:16–17; Acts 14:15–17; 17:14–27; Rom 1:19–21; 2:14–16; Heb 1:1–4). Their working assumption is that God's genuine intention in revelation is to provide the real possibility of wholeness and salvation wherever God is disclosed to humanity. However, it is apparent that God respects human capacities and desires. Therefore, these general and universal self-disclosures of God are limited by the alienation caused by sin's rule, which holds all creation in its deathly grip (Rom 5:12–21). Nevertheless, God has been actively involved in self-disclosure over time (Heb 11:1—12:2). Even if these divine overtures were only partially perceived and often misconstrued by humanity enmeshed in its allegiance to evil, God's pursuit of the covenantal relationship with which the creation project was launched is relentless and never without some witness to God's preferred way of living together.

The diagram below attempts to conceptualize God's self-disclosing enterprise, beginning with creation's launch and carried forward through witnesses like Adam and Eve, Abraham and Sarah, Moses and Miriam, the Israelite monarchs, the Israelite prophets, numerous others, and finally Jesus. The good news that the early Christians proclaim and that the NT writers record is that in these last days, God has chosen to self-disclose in the clearest and most complete terms through the person of Jesus. In Jesus we have both the *full* revelation of God's character (2 Cor 4:6) and the *full* expression of God's goal for humanity (Rom 5:18). Later, this conviction was enshrined in the ontological language of the proto-orthodox creeds, confessing Jesus as fully divine and fully human (the Chalcedonian Creed, 451 CE).

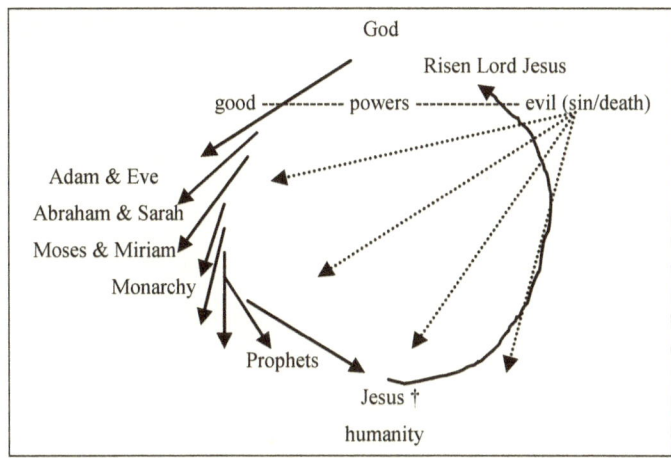

TABLE 9.1 The NT Writers' Model of God's Self-Disclosure over Time

Therefore, in Messiah Jesus, the preexistent Word of God (John 1:1) is finally and normatively revealed, so that there is true salvation in no other name (Acts 4:12), as he is the true and living way (John 14:6). A careful distinction needs to be made here. The conviction shared by the NT writers was not that Jesus is the *exclusive* revelation of God but rather the *normative* revelation of God: the one who came at a particular time in history (Gal 4:1–7) to fulfill and complete all other previous revelations.

What is clear from the NT writers is their conviction that in Christ, God finally and fully revealed to the world just what the character and identity of God really are like. This includes God's intention for human history, how God is at work in the world, and what God expects of humanity.

THE CHRISTIAN BIBLE: ITS IDENTITY AND FUNCTION

Since the revelation of God in Christ is mediated textually for members of the Christian tradition, they have generally understood that the Christian Bible plays a unique and significant role by giving witness to Jesus, the self-disclosure of God, in a way that is accessible to all succeeding generations. The Christian Bible plays the role of canon or measuring stick, enabling future generations of God's people, regardless of time or culture, to hear God's Word within the parameters set by the Christian Bible's final canonical form. While as we have seen, the canon's formation process was a historical one not without debate and conflict, with remarkable insight, the early Christians recognized the value of a canon for theological discernment. It functioned with flexibility *and* unity. Like a set of goalposts, the canon marked out an area—an area within which any number of diverse theological constructions could score a point; and those same goalposts also made it clear when a theological construction was wide of the goal.

Still, it must be said that there is not agreement on how to view the text of the Christian Bible (that space marked out between the goalposts), and as a result the disagreement raises significant hermeneutical implications, with corresponding challenges. The diagram below shows three common views of the Christian Bible operative within contemporary Christian communities. Note how each one plays out along nine continua.

Christian Bible =	The words of God	The Word of God	Some words about God
character:	←divine	divine & human	human→
mode:	←dictation	revelation through history	creative writing→
relation to culture:	←timeless deposit	time conditioned witness	cultural product→
source:	←God	human words animated by God	human words→
form:	←untranslatable	translatable & re-expressible	ancient text→
aim:	←prescriptive	prescriptive & descriptive	descriptive→
function:	←code	norm	novelty of history→
metaphor:	←box	window	fossil→
reality:	←objective	subjective & objective	subjective→

TABLE 9.2 Three Views on Conceptualizing the Christian Bible

What do you notice about each view? The views on both the left and the right illustrate what could be called biblicism, but in different ways. In these forms of biblicism, the text is frozen in time and essentially stationary—either to be followed as a rigid code always and everywhere, without any consideration of contextual particularities (left column) or to be valued as an interesting piece of memorabilia from the past, but with little ongoing significance or claim on humanity (right column).

The view in the middle column, however, sees the reality of the Christian Bible as something that is both subjective *and* objective. It is subjective not in the sense of leading to wishy-washy relativism where anything goes, "willy-nilly." It is subjective in the sense that the text functions as a window through which the acting subject of God can be accessed as continually present. According to this approach, God is viewed through the Christian Bible as God wants to be seen. But the window metaphor facilitates vision in the other direction too. Through the window of Scripture, reading communities see themselves as they truly are, as acting subjects participating in God's worldwide mission to transform creation. According to this approach, people see themselves through the Christian Bible as they truly are and as the people they are called to become. Thus, both the subjective and the objective dimensions play a role. The Christian Bible is objective in the sense that it records the testimony of real people's encounters with the divine in real-time history, inviting all who hear its testimony to enter as acting subjects and to find their places in its unfolding narrative.

The relationship between the objective and subjective character of the Christian Bible can be described in another way as well. My colleague Tim Geddert makes the distinction between the Christian Bible as a frozen deposit (static) and the Christian Bible as a compelling vision (dynamic). Both views may hold the Bible in high regard, even as infallible and authoritative for life and practice; however, the outcomes of the two views are not the same. Consider how each view approaches and uses the Bible.

The first view holds that biblical revelation is a *static deposit*. In this view, the Bible is considered to be a static witness and guide. The assumptions here are that each text, regardless of context, contributes a piece to the larger puzzle of God's special revelation. Therefore, proponents of this view arrange texts topically and set them alongside one another, combining them to make the theological whole. When all the texts on a given topic are synthesized into a coherent and consistent whole, the biblical answer emerges. The net result of this kind of harmonization is more important than the reason each specific text was written, more important than the larger context of the specific texts, and even more important than the perspective of the author. History, theology, ethics, and other topics are located within the harmonized version of the texts. Where harmonization is difficult, elaborate solutions are postulated, or difficult texts are silently ignored or forced to fit. For example, to explain the discrepancy between the two accounts of Jesus's "cleansing of the temple" (John places the story at the beginning of Jesus's ministry [John 2:13–22], and the Synoptic Gospels place it during Jesus's last week [Mark 11:15–19]), harmonizers suggest that Jesus must have cleared out the money changers two times. Little if any attention is given to the real possibility that the Evangelists had a particular theological aim for placing this unit from the Jesus tradition in their gospels as they have.

Instead the responsibility of biblical interpreters, working with the view of Bible as a static deposit, is to find biblical answers within the encyclopedic collection of harmonized biblical texts, accepting and proclaiming them as self-evident, propositional truths. Not only does this approach give little attention to the literary and theological aims of the biblical writers, but this approach offers little recognition of a cultural gap that needs to be bridged. Interpretation is immediate; the exhortation is simply to "read it off the page."

Consider this exercise: Given three spheres (the Truth, the Bible, and the church), how would someone advocating the Bible as static deposit arrange them? Typically, the spheres would be arranged in an overlapping fashion, since the Bible *carries* God's truth and *sets out* the blueprint for the church. See the diagram below for an example of the static-deposit model. What are some of the implications for this kind of reading strategy? What are its strengths? What challenges might it face?

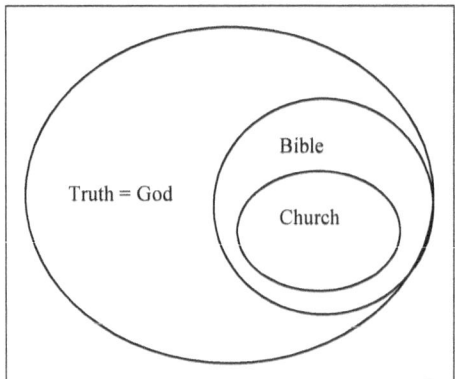

TABLE 9.3 Biblical Revelation as a Static Deposit

Second is the view of biblical revelation as a *compelling vision*. In this view, the Bible is considered to be a dynamic witness and guide. The assumptions here are that each text emerged out of a particular situation, speaking authoritatively as it gives witness to God's self-disclosure through history, which culminates in Jesus. Therefore, the biblical witness helps gathered faith communities discern what an authoritative word for their situation would be. In this view, the Bible provides the parameters for theological reflection and appropriation, guiding the construction of analogous metaphorical bridges. Biblical answers in this perspective are found in the interplay between the theological convictions that drive the texts and the insights that emerge when all the texts, even the differing ones, are taken seriously. In the middle of this tension between the diverse voices, the church discerns its next move. It is in this interpretive space that it is guided by the ongoing presence of the Spirit of the risen Lord. Thus, the canon sets out the parameters *within which* the church does its theological reflection, discerning an appropriate extension of its compelling vision for a particular context.

According to biblical revelation as a compelling vision, the purpose of specific texts, their literary and historical contexts, and the larger perspective of the authors are all important in determining what is driving the text. The Bible then represents the result of the *experience-interpretation* cycle where biblical writers give witness to their encounter with God, recording their diverse reflections on that encounter in diverse genres. The goal of biblical interpreters then is to locate their faith communities within the full "chorus of voices," so that the original theological reflection that occasioned the texts can continue to shape them in their contemporary cultural situations. The task is one of re-expressing the living Word of God in present-day ways. Theology and ethics are sought not only within the biblical text and behind it, but also in front of the biblical text, as the interpretive quest centers on what is driving a particular biblical text and where it is going. In other words, the *meaning center* is located between the Bible and the reading community in such a way that both contribute. The reading community hears what is behind and what is within the text, and then considers the ways that this meaning can shape or call into being contemporary meanings for God's reconfigured, end-time people. Thus, meaning determined completely neither by the text nor by the reading community; it resides between them.

Consider the same exercise: Given the three spheres (the Truth, the Bible, and the church), how would someone advocating the Bible as a compelling vision arrange these three spheres? Typically, the spheres are arranged to illustrate the Bible as a *witness* to the Truth (experience-interpretation model) and as a *shaper* of an interpretive space between the Bible and the church (meaning center). See the diagram that follows. What are some implications for this kind of reading strategy? What are its strengths? What challenges might it face?

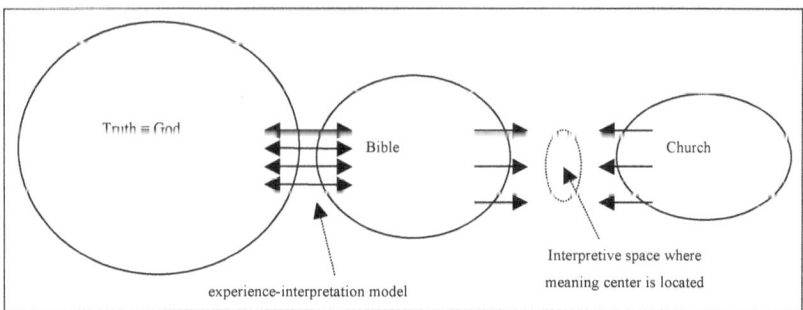

TABLE 9.4 Biblical Revelation as a Compelling Vision

Ultimately, the choice between these two fundamentally different approaches must be based on more than a matter of preference. A biblical theology must seriously ask which approach is consistent with what is actually observed in the theological work done by the NT writers themselves as they respond to their encounter with God's saving activity. According to the Christian confession, faith communities are committed to the conclusions of the biblical writers. However, learning how to practice a dynamic reading so that successive faith communities can resonate with what the NT authors were themselves doing is key to a biblical theology of revelation. As we have seen, the way that the early Christians and NT writers retold the stories of Jesus and reread their Hebrew Bible, in the new light of their surprising experience of the risen Lord, suggests that they subscribed to a more dynamic view of biblical revelation. The experience-interpretation model resonates with the common Jewish reading strategy (called *midrash*) employed by the early Christians and the NT writers. It is both objective and subjective; it reads the ancient text (objective) from the perspective of a new experience (subjective) in such a way that the ancient text is heard once again to speak in contemporary ways, shaping the church's praxis.

ECCLESIAL HERMENEUTICS: BRIDGING THE TEMPORAL AND CULTURAL GAPS

The question that contemporary faith communities face is whether they too are authorized to continue the NT writers' intertextual reading strategy. If the NT is essentially intertextual midrash of the OT, then does the church compose a midrash on the NT for contemporary consumption? The answer is, yes and no. In one sense, the church in every generation *does* practice a form of intertextual midrash as it preaches and appropriates God's Word in new contexts, finding contemporary ways to re-express the text's driving theology; the church is always contextualizing the NT message. However, in another sense, the church *does not* practice intertextual midrash as the NT writers did. Why? Because the NT witness is the formative witness to the revelatory experience of Jesus as the normative and final self-revelation of God in these last days. Thus, there can be no other formative experience for the church, since the "resurrection light from the empty tomb" continues to reach forward with the significance of Jesus, shaping God's people in each culture and each time period; the NT witness remains normative for the church.

By the end of the second century, under threat of *reduction* (Marcion) and under threat of *expansion* (Montanism, gnosticism), the church confessed that the witness of the prophets (as foundational for locating Jesus's life and ministry) and the apostles (as interpreting the memory of Jesus's life and ministry) set out the scriptural norm. It took until the end of the fourth century to confirm and ratify the collection, but the proto-orthodox conviction was that the OT and NT witnesses created the interpretive space within which God's Word could continue to be heard in the successive generations of God's people. The Christian Bible, therefore, functions as the rule or norm (canon) for faithful Christian discipleship in all contexts and in all times. Thus, the ongoing theological reflection of the Christian community remains both *rooted* in the grand story and yet *open* to the future as the church gathers to embody the witness of the Christian Bible, both reaching back to it and re-expressing it in contemporary ways.

So, how do faith communities today both appreciate the canonical norm (prophetic/apostolic witness) as authoritative *and* continue the prophetic/apostolic practice of embodying God's living Word in contemporary ways? Both are important and necessary. However, only a hermeneutical community has the resources for these vital tasks. The hermeneutical community is charged with producing new contextual readings that are consistent with the prophetic/apostolic witness, *and* it is charged with testing these new readings for bias, self-interest, and blind spots. This is a large mandate; but there is some consolation in that it is God who judges the worthiness of the construction in the end (1 Cor 3:10–15). Since contemporary faith communities confess that they live, as the first apostolic community did, in the "resurrection light of

Jesus" that proceeds from the empty tomb of God's Easter self-disclosure event, the NT apostolic witness remains normative; it cannot be set aside. However, since the light from the empty tomb (the Spirit of the risen Lord) continues to illuminate the path of God's people, faith communities find ways through preaching, teaching, worship, and community discernment to bridge the temporal and cultural gaps that exist between the ancient world and today so that the ancient text continues to shape the church's praxis.

Faith communities have always been engaged in doing the hermeneutical work of locating contemporary meaning in ways shaped by the ancient prophetic/apostolic witness. Since the dawn of time, God's people have been propelled and energized by the task of relating their vision for God's world to the world in which they live, work, and play. For the last two thousand years, Christian communities have confessed the biblical witness to God's reign, which culminated in Jesus, as authoritative and normative. But how so? The temporal gap between the ancient world of the biblical writers and the contemporary world is large and growing. How is this distance to be negotiated? Christian communities generally choose one of four interpretive reading strategies to deal with the gap between then and now.

First is the *literal approach*. This strategy seeks to appropriate the biblical text literally, regardless of context. Christians following this approach recognize a temporal gap but dismiss its significance for biblical interpretation. Typically, biblical texts that refer to various aspects of social and community life receive the greatest emphasis (e.g., leadership practices, human identity, marriage, sexual practices, family patterns, slavery, community organization, judgment, warfare, poverty, evangelism, interfaith dialogue). These texts are applied literally in each and every context in which the church finds itself. The temporal gap is recognized but not credited with any value, since the biblical text is a timeless written code.

The literal reading strategy is favored by those many call fundamentalists. For these interpreters, the fear of accommodation to variable cultural realities strengthens the commitment to a literal interpretation; it is deemed the best approach to avoid straying from the biblical vision. A literal reading strategy, however, tends to be selective and arbitrary, because only certain texts are followed literally. Ways are found to leave out biblical injunctions not deemed significant (e.g., the prohibition against planting fields with two kinds of seed or wearing clothing woven of two kinds of material). Reflection is rarely given to discerning why some biblical exhortations are carried forward and why some are dropped. Furthermore, these interpreters downplay the basic Christian practice of discerning the living Word within the community of the Spirit gathered around Jesus, the living Lord.

Second is the *principlizing approach*. This strategy constructs a set of principles drawn from biblical texts and then applies these principles directly to the contemporary scene. It claims to be more sophisticated than the literal reading strategy used by fundamentalists in that the temporal gap is given more consideration. Taking this approach, Christians look for the biblical principles that can be reduced from a survey of all the various biblical genres (narratives, letters, poetry, etc.) and then applied to each and every context in ways that are contextually appropriate. This view would not argue, for example, to stone or execute those found to be in noncompliance with Israel's holiness or purity code; that would be too literalistic.

These interpreters search instead to extract and collate a set of principles from the biblical narratives and exhortations to help the church bridge the temporal gap between then and now. Working with an additional level of abstraction, this reading strategy usually works toward making the biblical principles behind the sometimes culturally controversial biblical exhortations true for its faith community and if possible even for government policy (e.g., various social, family, national, and military policies). The guiding aim is that the reduced principle drawn from the biblical text (not necessarily the literal commands) must be applied directly to the church without giving too much weight to cultural developments. Many evangelicals would fit in this category, and many of the pitfalls of the literalist reading strategy also apply here. However, the principlizing approach is subject to one new problem: Once the biblical text is reduced to a set of principles, the biblical text tends to be left behind; there is almost no need to read the Bible any longer, because it is the set of extracted principles that carries the normative value for the church.

Third is the *transcendental approach*. This strategy seeks to transcend the biblical text toward its presumed ultimate goal. It recognizes the temporal gap and interprets it as evidence of the ongoing development of humankind. Christians taking this approach see the task of interpretation as one of following the direction of the text. The initial hints found in the text are developed further by moving forward in ongoing transcendence toward what is perceived as the ultimate goal, even if the affirmations, assumptions, or prohibitions of the text are abandoned.

So, if the text speaks strongly about certain behaviors, (be they ethical, moral, social, familial, national, or military), then a transcendental reading filters out the inherent biases and cultural taboos deemed no longer appropriate in the Western world, in order to achieve something considered relevant and contemporary. Typically, the values promoted as the biblical text's ultimate goal have to do with personal self-determination and self-actualization, which is interpreted as justice. In other words, the church ought to move beyond culturally located texts of the ancient world; they may well be interesting museum pieces testifying to an age now obsolete, but they must either remain on the museum shelf or be radically updated in order to be relevant. They no longer carry a normative bearing on contemporary Christian living. Many theologically liberal Christians could argue along these lines.

Transcendental interpreters aim to help the church by removing cultural taboos and inhibitions embedded in the biblical texts in order to promote the ongoing development of humankind toward liberation, maturity, tolerance, and freedom. However, besides severing the theological link between the church and the biblical witness, a transcendental reading tends to put the focus of human identity on self-determination and autonomy, rather than on the covenantal relationship within the community of God the Creator. In the Christian community, how individuals live really is the business of God's people.

Are these the only three reading strategies available for negotiating a bridge from the prophetic/apostolic witness to the present? Must Christian communities select from reading strategies often noted for freezing (literal approach), reducing (principlizing approach), or improving (transcendental approach) the biblical witness in the church's journey forward with God? No, there is yet a fourth reading strategy that uses metaphorical and analogical ways to *extend* the prophetic/apostolic witness, so that faith communities, in various and diverse contexts, can continue to be shaped by its witness. Instead of freezing, reducing, or improving the witness, the fourth reading strategy *extends* the biblical witness.

The *analogical approach* seeks to construct an analogical extension of the biblical text. Such an extension allows the text to continue to norm contemporary practice. Interpreters following this appoach take seriously the shaping influence of the biblical tradition, finding ways to extend its witness in culturally appropriate forms. Not only do *extenders* value the link to the "cloud of witnesses" (Heb 12:1), but they courageously and creatively find analogous ways to extend the various culturally controversial biblical exhortations in ways that are appropriate for the times.

The analogical reading strategy also recognizes the temporal gap but confesses that the impact of God's reign witnessed in the ancient text is reproducible analogously within contemporary reading communities. These Christian communities are not limited by literal readings; they are not persuaded by a set of reductionistic principles; neither are they disconnected from the "cloud of witnesses" reaching back to the dawn of time and forward to the completion of all things. Instead, these interpretive communities look for imaginative ways to carry on the *effect* or *impact* embedded within the biblical witness, so that contemporary faith communities can continue to be shaped by God's kingdom rule for the glory and purposes of God.

An analysis of these four reading strategies shows that the first three (literal, principlizing, and transcendental readings) are really very *objective*. The biblical text is treated as an object to be applied directly to another context, or as an object to be left behind. The fourth strategy (extension reading) has an additional *subjective* component. Here, the biblical text is still an object; yes, it does record the impact of God's self-disclosure in a particular time and space. However, the biblical text is more than this—it is also a living subject, shaping reading communities in the successive generations of God's people, as they find analogous ways to reproduce its impact/effect.

While reading communities across time may not discern identical extensions of the biblical text, there ought to be a recognizable "familial" similarity that "genetically" links these interpretations. Sometimes an extension reading may even go against the apparent textual expression while still tapping into the deeper structure of the text in order to carry forward its theological norm. For example, it is possible to extend a restrictive text like, "it is shameful for a woman to speak in church" (1 Cor 14:35) in a nonrestrictive way without abandoning the text. This particular text can be read as continuing to give witness to the dual character of what it means to be human as male *and* female by blessing women to share church-leadership roles with men according to their uniquely "other" perspective (see Isaak 1995). Or it is possible to extend a categorical text such as "Be subject to the governing authorities . . . [they] have been instituted by God" (Rom 13:1) in a more reflective way, without abandoning the text. The conviction that God has charged governments with the task of leading well does not eliminate the need for discernment by the Christian community; Christ followers do not simply comply with government laws unreflectively but measure them against their primary loyalty to God's reign. It is conceivable that situations where confrontation (and not acquiescence), or civil disobedience (and not compliance) would in fact also resonate with the deep structure of Romans 13:1–7 (see Isaak 2003).

Talk of extending the impact of the biblical text does not suggest that today's interpreters are in the business of renovating previous interpretations, as if the previous ones were deficient in some way. Rather, talk of extending the impact reminds us that while God's creation enterprise is not yet complete, a glimpse of its final form is visible in the body of the risen Lord: namely, local Christian communities from the first century through the present and to the end of time. The Christian Bible narrates God's ongoing relation with creation, where God's purpose remains to bring the whole enterprise to completion. In this way, the impact of the biblical text is continually present to God's people no matter which century of these last days they occupy.

Jesus's invitational message is the same for all people interested in negotiating the bridge from the ancient world to the present: seek first the kingdom of God, and then all the other concerns of life will find their appropriate significance in relation to this theological center (Matt 6:33). This is the task of biblical interpretation that has occupied all of God's people across the millennia—to move from an anthropological center to a theological center. The gospel continues to encourage and challenge humanity's "natural" desires on all issues with glimpses of what is only visible in beginning ways in the community of Jesus, as it represents what is yet to be.

The journey toward creation completion is long, even lifelong, but it is one that people should not need to travel alone. When working well, the Christian community offers support, acceptance, love, discipline, accountability, counsel, teaching, and discernment with regard to all the controversial social challenges that occupy our worlds (e.g., the numerous social, ecological, economic, national, and military challenges). The conviction that animates and nourishes such faith communities as they "stumble" forward is the powerful and transformative presence of the Spirit of the risen Lord, continuing to draw God's people into the world that is taking shape for the glory of God, even as we speak.

What then is God like? In the next chapter we explore the many provocative images used by the NT writers to talk about God.

EXERCISES

1. Review the diagrams in this chapter relating to the Bible: ways of conceptualizing the Christian Bible, revelation as a static deposit, and revelation as a compelling vision.

    Discuss the different ways the Bible is conceptualized. Compare and contrast them. What assumptions regarding God, Jesus, the Holy Spirit, humanity, the world, and so on are behind each view of the Bible? Toward which model do you feel yourself leaning? Why? What areas of further exploration are raised for you?

2. The NT writers give witness to a conviction that God's Word has not failed. In addition, they refuse to stray from the religious conviction that God's good purpose must be at work, even if they do not yet understand it. Their use of OT Scriptures, however, raises questions for Christian interpretation and proclamation today. It is clear, for example, that Paul used his Jewish interpretive method (*midrash*) to read old texts from his new vantage point "in Christ" (a look backward), so that these old texts continued to give new insights to Paul's understanding of God's world (a look forward). Notice the two-way traffic.

    Discuss the following questions: Are the interpretive outcomes of the NT writers' reflection normative for believing communities today? Or is it their interpretive reading strategy that is normative for Christian communities today? Or are both true? There is much debate on these questions. Give examples of what happens when only one of these two options is affirmed. What would need to happen to ensure that both the biblical writers' outcomes and their strategy could be affirmed and upheld as normative?

3. Christian communities have always gathered around a shared commitment to the Lord Jesus and his way of being in the world. This

does not mean that faith communities have always seen eye to eye on points of doctrine, biblical interpretation, or behavior. Even within a particular faith community there may be divergent views. Still, faith communities continue to gather as interpretive communities in the presence of the Spirit of the risen Lord as they have done from the start (Acts 6:3; 15:6–29), in order to discern next steps and to decide on a course of action. Often the particulars of the presenting issue are not the same as those of ancient Israel or of the early Christian communities recorded in the Christian Bible. Some interpretive strategy is needed in order to bridge the temporal and culture gaps that exists between the world within which the biblical writers wrote and the world of the contemporary faith community that chooses to be shaped by that same biblical vision.

Review the four hermeneutical strategies outlined in this chapter. Select a controversial contemporary issue (e.g., stem-cell research, assisted suicide, abortion, same-sex marriage, premarital sex, preemptive military strikes, global warming, free trade) and construct four interpretations, each one consistent with one of the four hermeneutical approaches for bridging the gap between the ancient world and today.

Compare and contrast your constructions. Assess the relative merits of each. What was attractive? Off-putting? Compelling? Disturbing? Were you conscious of distinguishing between the church's response to the particular issue and the state's national or foreign policy? Or were these responses the same? What do you learn from an exercise like this?

One particularly helpful book that offers concrete help to Christian communities as they struggle with ethical questions is Timothy J. Geddert's book, *All Right Now: Finding Consensus on Ethical Questions* (2008). Geddert promotes a "middle way" between "rule-oriented" approach and an "irresponsible freedom"; he sets out the various considerations necessary for community discernment in order to take seriously both human culture and the biblical witness. To demonstrate how the discerning faith community can work toward consensus, Geddert explores five controversial issues: 1) love toward enemies (nonviolence), 2) sexuality, 3) divorce and remarriage, 4) homosexuality, and 5) money and possessions.

10

Theology

God-Talk and Imagination

THE BIBLICAL WRITERS USE numerous images to represent God and to shape the imagination of God's people for faithful action. Starting with the OT, we see that these ancient writers did the same thing that the NT writers after them would do—used what they knew something about to describe that which they knew to be true but did not fully grasp. Moved by their experience of the self-involving God, these ancient writers used the only language adequate for this experience: namely, metaphor (e.g., "shepherd," Ps 23:1; "warrior," Exod 15:3; "fortress," Jer 16:19; "father," Ps 89:26; "mother," Ps 131:2; "king," Ps 95:3; "judge," Ps 75:7). This chapter has two objectives: (1) to make a case for imagination and theological thinking, and (2) to review seven metaphors used by the NT writers to talk about Yahweh, the God of Israel.

IN DEFENSE OF IMAGINATION AND THEOLOGICAL THINKING

Imagination is a quality that we praise in our youngsters. And yet as we age, our imagination often gets less exercise and is less valued. It may even be held with some suspicion. By contrast, the biblical writers use much imagination and many provocative images as they give witness to their encounter with God. This should not be surprising, because whenever people come face-to-face with the one who is Alpha and Omega, that encounter can only be adequately viewed through the lens of metaphor and image (Caird 1997:271). Using what they knew something about, the biblical writers described what they were convinced of but did not fully grasp. Moved instead by the Spirit of God, they used their own words—metaphors, images, and word pictures—to give witness to God's activity among them.

Unfortunately our Western world tends to reduce the impact of the biblical writers' God-talk imagery and its power to transform. Of course, no one starts out trying to drain the power of these metaphors. Nevertheless, the efforts to simplify, manage, and organize biblical God-talk imagery in tight theological systems tend to domesticate them and dull their transformative impact. This need not be the case.

The OT writers seem to do everything possible in order to keep God's people from falling into the reductionistic trap. For example, the biblical writers show no interest in speculating on the inner workings of God or in getting tangled up in metaphysical or philosophical arguments. Instead they choose to concentrate on identifying the living God as the one who is before all (Gen 1:1), and who discloses the very self of God to humanity in the historical process (in patriarchal families, Genesis 12-50; in deliverance from Egypt, Exodus 3-15; in covenantal and legal systems, Exodus 19-40; in sacrificial systems, Leviticus 1-7; and in monarchy, 1 Samuel 8-12). The invitation is to find resonance places and imagination stations where God's people can grow and be nudged forward, carried by evocative metaphors that illuminate God's character and purpose.

So how do the NT writers themselves talk about God? One noteworthy observation is that the proper name of the Hebrew God, Yahweh, appears to be absent from the NT even though other Hebrew or Aramaic transliterations were taken into the Greek used by the NT writers (e.g., *Abba, rabbi, hosanna, amen, Sabbath, Satan, Mammon, maranatha,* and *Emmanuel*). It is likely that a severe reading of Exod 20:7 ("You shall not make wrongful use of the name of the LORD") caused the Israelites to eventually abandon the pronunciation of Yahweh long before the Christian movement began. It is thought that the divine name, Yahweh, was some form of (or sounded like) the "I am" statement in Exod 3:14 ("Thus you [Moses] shall say to the Israelites, 'I AM has sent me to you'"). In any case, to avoid any chance of misusing the divine name the Israelites identified their God as "the Lord" and even read *Adonai* (which means "Lord") every time the four-letter Tetragram (YHWH) appeared in the Hebrew text. In spite of the NT writers' not using *Yahweh*, nevertheless it is interesting that NT writers appear to make oblique reference to the divine name in association with Jesus. For example, Jesus says to the disciples frightened by his appearance on the raging sea, "Take heart, *it is I*; do not be afraid" (Mark 6:50). The English affirmation "it is I" translates the Greek text *egō eimi*, which can also be rendered, "I am," likely an allusion to the divine name, *Yahweh*.

Furthermore, the early Christians used the term "Lord," a typical stand-in for the divine name, in reference to Jesus. The explanation for this development is rooted in the early Christian experience of Jesus, which caused major dissonance for the first disciples. How could they understand Jesus's crucifixion and his resurrection, given their inherited Jewish religious symbols for how God works in the world? Their memory of Jesus's remarkable life and their experience of his crucifixion and then of his resurrection flew in the face of their reading of Torah ("anyone hung on a tree is under God's curse," Deut 21:22-23). Yet they were convinced that God had vindicated the crucified Jesus, and that God had raised Jesus from the dead, indicating that the new age was dawning (1 Cor 10:11). For God to be involved with such an event in the first place took some reconfiguration. How is God dealing with evil here in this horrific event? How is God being faithful to the covenant promises to Israel through all this? Could this really be the way that God's Spirit is being poured out "on all flesh" (Joel 2:28)? Is the new age actually upon us?

Sorting out their convictions of God's justice and faithfulness with their own lived experience (that is, dealing with questions of theodicy) sent the early Christians back to the Torah. There they found what they were looking for. In the *old* text they found *new* ways to understand their experience of Jesus. Texts like Ps 110:1; 118:22; and Zech 9:9 were heard for the first time as also messianic texts (Johnson 1999:147). In the interplay between text and experience, mediated by interpretation, the confession of a crucified and risen Messiah resulted in new language with which to talk about God.

In this way, the early Jesus movement introduced yet another shift in Jewish theism. Their ancestors long before them had first abandoned belief in many gods (*polytheism*, Gen 31:19-35; 35:2-4), then belief in one god among many (*henotheism*, Exod 20:1-7; Deut 32:8-9) before finally by the end of the exile, understanding Yahweh as the only God (*monotheism*, Isaiah 40). Just as their ancestors continued to understand God in new ways depending on their contexts, so the early Christians came to recognize most clearly "the glory of God in the face of Jesus" (2 Cor 4:6). Based on their experience of the resurrection, the memory of Jesus's remarkable life, teaching, and ministry among them was transformed with new understanding. Now, in the post-Easter period; the signs and wonders that animated their times of worship further nurtured their conviction that the risen Lord was among them as they gathered for prayer, discernment, encouragement, meals, and study. Using the familiar patterns from within Judaism, they gave expression to their new experience. Thus, they worshiped God's agent, Messiah Jesus, as though he were God; he was their Lord and one with God. Not to worship Jesus in this way would have been to reject God, for God was surely behind all that they had experienced of the divine presence among them in Jesus (Hurtado 1998:122).

The early Christian rereading of Torah helped these groups to see that God was indeed faithful to the covenant promises, and that the dominion of evil was actually being broken; death could not keep Jesus in its grip. The mutation this caused within Jewish monotheism was not surprising. Since the Master of the universe was most clearly present and represented in the life, death, and resurrection of Jesus of Nazareth, it was not a great leap to expand the language of Lord, associated with Yahweh (OT) to include now also Messiah Jesus (NT).

SEVEN NT METAPHORS USED TO TALK ABOUT GOD

So, what do the NT writers actually say about the God that they have come to know in Jesus? What God-talk images do they use? Can these ancient metaphors continue to shape God's people? We begin our quest by exploring seven such images used by the NT writers to give expression to their conception of God.

First, *God is the self-existent one*. This is the most basic Judeo-Christian confession. The picture of what it means to be "one" describes God's character with adjectives like "inclusive" (all encompassing), "exclusive" (unrivaled), "unique" (like no other), "primary" (first and foremost), "immanent" (present everywhere), and "transcendent" (above all). Furthermore, the early Christian confessions—that God is one, and that Jesus is Lord (1 Cor 8:6)—were never seen as contradictory or in any conflict with each other. Instead, they were heard together as the proclamation of God's salvation for the world. For example, Paul uses God's "oneness" to ground his argument that the Gentiles are now to be included in God's global *shalom* project, whose goal is the salvation of "all Israel," as in, representatives from all tribes and nations (Rom 3:29–31; 11:25–26).

The early Christians confessed without apparent difficulty "one God" and "one Lord" (1 Cor 8:6) since they were convinced that in Jesus's life, death, and resurrection, God had chosen to be fully disclosed in these last days. Their experience of the risen Lord in corporate worship (signs, wonders, healing, sharing of possessions, and the like) reminded them of Jesus's life and teaching, convincing them that Jesus was indeed the Christ, God's promised agent for the world's salvation. They never thought of themselves as talking about two gods (or three, for that matter, when discussions included the Holy Spirit).

The corollary that accompanies the confession that God is the self-existent one is that lesser enemy powers also exist (1 Cor 10:19–22). However, unlike the capricious and competitive dualism within the pantheon of gods familiar to Israel's pagan neighbors, these enemy powers are not in a dualistic conflict with God (Hiebert 2000:114–24) since God is the All Powerful One who reigns above all (Deut 32:8–9; Ps 8:5–6). Still, Paul reminds the early Christians that they should not kid themselves: evil's death-dealing ways have become increasingly sophisticated during these "last days," especially after being exposed at the cross (Rom 6:4, 12). Evil ought not to be trivialized, even as it is being brought under the "heel of God's reign" (Rom 16:20; 1 Cor 6:3) through its own unsuspecting self-destruction (1 Cor 2:8).

To confess that God is one is to confess the unity of God's will and purpose. God's desire is to complete creation and bring the global *shalom* project to fulfillment on God's own terms. No doubt such a confession could be dismissed in our pluralistic Western world as intolerant, totalizing, and politically incorrect. However, to these detractors Christians can say that such a confession need not equate God's "oneness" with the absolute correctness of a particular religious system—even if it is called Christianity! All religious systems are human constructs, and each one must answer to God for its construction and its behavior (1 Cor 3:13). An open but centered confession of God's oneness has enormous potential for promoting healthy God-talk among family, friends, colleagues, and even detractors.

Second, *God is the Creator and giver of life.* The affirmation that God is the one who launches the creation project (Genesis 1–2), who invites humanity's participation carrying it forward (Pss 8; 110; 1 Cor 6:2–3), who makes the dead alive (Ezek 37:3–6), and specifically who raises Jesus from the dead (1 Cor 15:3–4) reaffirms the more general concept of God as the giver of all life. God does not deal in death. Sin always pays out its wages: namely, death (Rom 6:23). In contrast, God's goal is to give life (John 10:10).

God spares no expense to undo the dominion of sin, evil, and death; this is made clear by God's own self-giving love offered at Calvary. At the cross we see both the lengths to which Satan will go to eliminate all challengers to evil's death-dealing ways, and the lengths to which God will go to make sure that death does not have the last word and that life prevails. Unknown to Satan, the divine purpose is forwarded, ironically, in Satan's very act of resisting it (1 Cor 2:8; Col 2:15). From the divine perspective, God's purpose to establish life is described as being "destined before the foundation of the world" (1 Pet 1:20).

God's life-giving mission will one day come to completion for all those who choose to join God (Heb 9:27–28). Just exactly how the end will happen is not spelled out in the biblical witness (whether in historical time, in post-mortem, or in some other way). What is certain is the victory of the final transformation of creation, but even this is depicted in metaphor and image. John's Revelation portrays God's final *shalom* as a place where all the nations are represented creatively engaged in God's work of glory, without tears, without sin and death—with only light and life (Rev 21:22—22:7).

The NT writers articulate with great resolve God's mission in the "now time," inviting all to abandon their rebellion against God and to choose life—there is so much more to life than death! The way of Jesus remains the only way to deal with and undo the power of evil and to break the cycle of violence. Such a vision for God as the real life-giver is capable of capturing the imagination of today's generation, just as it did those of previous generations (Gen 12:1–4; John 6:68).

Third, *God is the sovereign ruler.* The NT writers specifically assert God's sovereignty with reference to Jesus's life. In the resurrection and exaltation of Jesus, God proved to be the one who overcomes the mighty and exalts the humble. The cross was not some accident or mistake; neither was it orchestrated to change God's mind about humanity. It was a willful act of aggression on the part of Satan, the evil one. However, God, the sovereign and "knower of all things," was able to absorb even this horrific event and to use it to undo evil's power over the world. Ironically, the act that Satan intended to use for Jesus's destruction turned out to be the cause of Satan's own self-destruction. Caird argues persuasively that unlike John Milton's view in *Paradise Lost*, the biblical narrative shows Satan's ouster from the heavenly court and fall from grace as occurring at the cross, not as the result of a precosmic rebellion before the dawn of time (1994:97). Thus, Jesus's ministry is about reversing Adam's failure (Rom 5:12–21; Phil 2:5–11) and undoing Satan's grip in order to take creation to its intended goal.

Satan's cover was blown at that first Easter; it was the scandal that rocked the world. The Jesus saying that captures it best and foreshadows the turn of the ages is this: "I watched Satan fall from heaven like a flash of lightning" (Luke 10:18). Never again would evil's ploys be masked and hidden in the same way, for they are being rendered inoperative (1 Cor 2:6). From now on anyone associating with Jesus's way would also be free of evil's grip, actually empowered to see the evil one and to say, no! Of course, this will not eliminate death, disease, and destruction just yet. In fact, Jesus predicted these would intensify (Matt 10:34–36; Luke 12:51–53), given that we are in the last days of Satan's defrocked rule. Nevertheless, Satan's ultimate power over humanity is broken because death no longer has the last word: Jesus is alive!

And so the confession that God is sovereign means that God will eventually overcome all opposition. Yet this affirmation is never read as fatalism or as depreciation of human freedom or of creation's responsibility. Neither is God's sovereignty thought of as some kind of game where God orchestrates events based on God's foreknowledge of our choices so that all things always turn out a certain way.

In good non-Western fashion, *both* the sovereignty of God *and* human freedom are affirmed without an attempt to resolve at any particular moment the tension between them (Caird 1997:117–21). The tension provides the space within which the faithful have always found life and authentic existence. Why pray to God if all is preprogrammed? Conversely, why pray to God, if all is up to human choices? Instead, the faithful find strength in prayer because in prayer itself both God's sovereignty and human freedom are affirmed at the same time, even though many Westerners would see these as contradictory affirmations.

Some have tried to take sides in the old Calvin vs. Arminius debate: Calvin highlighted God's determination of events while Arminius highlighted human responsibility in shaping these same events. But this is not an either/or situation; we do not need to choose between Calvin and Arminius. The biblical writers, without embarrassment, were able to hold both God's sovereignty and human free will together. They did not see these two views as contradictory or incompatible. Without difficulty they could affirm that Pharaoh "hardened his heart" (Exod 9:34), and that "the LORD hardened the heart of Pharaoh" (Exod 9:12).

The point is that Calvin and Arminius made God's sovereignty and human free will a riddle to be solved one way or another, whereas both affirmations need to stand side by side. The NT writers do not view God's foreknowledge as reducing or eliminating human freedom and responsibility. God has given humanity freedom to respond. God knows people as free creatures. Both the purposes for humanity and God's plan for their accomplishment are designed according to that knowledge (Kraus 1991:84; see also Geddert 2000; Gilbert 2001).

While the task is certainly challenging, the NT writers follow their predecessors in the OT and invite contemporary listeners to develop a both/and biblical imagination in order to worship and serve a God who is ultimately in control, willing good for the entire universe. This way of speaking about God's control is not to be confused with domination or fatalism or malicious coercion; God's kind of control is participatory. God created the universe without violent means (unlike the gods of the pagan creation myths of Israel's neighbors), caring for it, governing it, and working for its good in the long run—also without violent means. While God has all the power potential, God chooses to invite humanity's participation in completing God's goal for creation (i.e., *shalom*). For example, Israel's request for a king so that they can be "like other nations" is supported, even though it was theologically questionable; but once chosen, it is factored into Israel's story of redemption (1 Sam 8:1–22; 12:14–15; 2 Sam 7:16). Human freedom and responsibility are built in and respected within the biblical writers' articulation of God's control.

Fourth, *God is the righteous judge*. The two aspects that the NT writers affirm about God's judgments are that God is impartial (Rom 3:9–20), and that God does and will set things right (Rom 11:25–36;

Rev 20:11–15). The early Christians' experience of the salvation of the Gentiles was seen as evidence that God is impartial, and that God is demonstrating righteousness in the world by including them within God's newly reconfigured people.

Still, several critical observations about God's judgment are in order. Unlike most human types of judgments, God's judgments are not about vindictive punishment, or motivated by resentment or retaliation (Kraus 1991:210). Certainly the biblical writers do use "vengeance" images (Exod 32:12; Deut 29:28; 2 Kgs 22:13; Col 3:6). However, even the biblical writers realize that this anthropopathic imagery cannot be pushed too far, because they also stress that God's vengeance is different from human vengeance (Isa 55:8–9; Deut 32:35; Rom 12:17–19). By definition, human vengeance is based on the withdrawal of previous good will or a change in attitude toward the one causing harm. God's kind of vengeance is not about withdrawal: God does not "leave the table" (see Jeremiah 3). Rather God's vengeance is based on "the public righting of wrong." The attitude God has toward creation and the purpose God has for creation cannot change—that would be a "self-contradiction of God's essential goodness" (Kraus 1991:210; see 2 Tim 2:11–13).

Therefore, the judgment of God appears to be more about honoring the free choices that people make. God does not want our harm (God's *antecedent will* arising from God's nature is for life); however, when human beings choose to deny their identity or choose to remove themselves from God, that choice is granted (God's *consequent will* arises from the acts of human beings). Like the father of the parable of the prodigal in Luke 15, it is as if God says, "If you reject your true self, if you leave your true home, your suffering will be very profound, because away from my love you cannot live." See Henri Nouwen's masterly exploration of Jesus's parable in *The Return of the Prodigal Son*.

However, there is more to this homecoming story. God's respect for human choice is coupled with the father's indefatigable longing for the restoration of his relationship with his child. The father never gives up on his son; he continues to watch and wait for his son. While he would never force his son to receive his love, neither would he abandon the son. Instead, the father "outwaits" the son! So it is with God's judgment; it is not so much about God's handing out punishments and rewards, but more about a *discernment process* where we come to know who we were created to be as God's beloved children. This may be a painful experience, and it may take a long time, because the choices we make have real and long-lasting consequences. However, God's judgments can be counted on to bring the righting of wrong and the restoration of relationship for all willing to participate.

While many details of the working out of God's judgment are not yet clear, three affirmations can be made based on the biblical witness.

(1) However God's judgment is imagined, it must be shaped by the self-disclosure of God in Jesus. It seems theologically inconsistent to say that God will abandon God's character of *agape* love at some point in the future and condemn people to death. Likewise, it seems equally inconsistent to imagine that God could "wink" at evil, as if it did not matter.

(2) However God's judgment is imagined, it must not let human cooperation or human freedom be trivialized, manipulated, or eliminated. Both double predestination (the notion that some are elected to salvation while others are elected to damnation) and universalism (the notion that all are saved regardless of their will) trample on the fundamental characteristic of God and of humanity created in God's image: namely, freedom.

(3) However God's judgment is imagined, it must keep the church's mandate clearly focused on God's mission to invite all creation and every individual to return home to authentic life and to unalienated relationship.

The gospel invitation is to come along now and begin to experience authentic living; if one persists in rebellion, it will only get more difficult to come along. See C. S. Lewis's insightful and provocative argument for heaven and hell in *The Great Divorce*.

Fifth, *God is the faithful one*. God keeps promises. God does not divorce (Jer 3:8–14; Hos 2:19). For Paul this characteristic of God is what guides his whole argument in Romans. The inclusion of the Gentiles and the eventual salvation of all God's children are predicated on the conviction that God is faithful. Romans 9–11 gives witness to Paul's attempt to reconcile his experience of God's Spirit now among the Gentiles with what he knows to be true as a good Jew. Paul is convinced that God is faithful to the promise of election; "the gifts and the calling of God are irrevocable" (11:29).

Yet how can Paul explain the fact that his brothers and sisters in Judaism are not responding to Jesus as Messiah? Is God playing fair? Is God taking back the gift of election from the Jews? God's reputation is on the line. If God has actually given up on the Jews, then what assurance is there that God will not cast anyone aside in preference for yet another people? This idea is unthinkable, and Paul backs away from it, asserting rather that the Jewish rejection must be a "temporary" reality. He calls this a "hardening" that has the redemptive purpose of giving access to the Gentiles so that ultimately "all Israel will be saved" (11:26) as promised long ago (Gen 12:1–3).

In good Semitic form, the biblical writers often express as a "purpose" what is foreseen as a "result" (Ewert 2000:167). For example, Mark frames the Jesus tradition in a surprisingly harsh way by asserting that Jesus chose to say everything in parables to those on the "outside," *so that* they may not understand (4:12). Their misunderstanding appears to be Jesus's purpose. In the parallel passage, Matthew frames the tradition differently, with Jesus's speaking to the "outsiders" in parables *because* they do not understand (13:13). Matthew then inserts a citation from Isa 6:9–10, probably to show that the rejection experienced by Isaiah is also now being experienced by Jesus. So, here, the "outsider's" misunderstanding is a result of their rejection. Thus, Matthew chooses to express the people's misunderstanding as a "result" of rejection, whereas Mark expresses the same thing as Jesus's "purpose."

What is going on here? This is yet another example of the *dual causation* so typical of the ancient Near Eastern worldview (Caird 1997:203). Joseph can say to his brothers without any problem, "Even though *you* intended to do harm to me, *God* intended it for good" (Gen 50:20). For the biblical writers everything can be explained as God's faithful purpose *and*, at the same time, everything can be explained as a result of human choices, since humanity is responsible for its own outcomes. The biblical writers do not seem to be bothered by this tension as much as Westerners are. (Westerns ask: Who is to blame? Is it a purpose, or is it a result?) The biblical writers in their ancient Near Eastern way can affirm both result and purpose to be true at the same time. For example, God absorbs human choices and works with the "results," so that they can be thought of as part of God's "purpose." In this way human actions are expressed within a larger providential framework. The bottom line is that in everything, God is absolutely faithful to God's people-gathering purpose and promise.

Nothing better illustrates God's faithfulness than the faithfulness of Jesus (Rom 3:21–26). This is the core of the good news that the early Christians proclaimed: namely, their experience of Jesus's faithful life, which led to his death and resurrection (1 Cor 15:3–4). They experienced Jesus not only as the one who, on God's behalf, called Israel again to be and to do what had always been intended for God's people (to be "a light to the nations," Isa 49:6). But early Christians also experienced Jesus as the one who actualized the potential for being truly human as no one else had. Jesus fulfilled adamic humanity (Rom 5:12–21) and therefore became the primary source and paradigm for the new humanity: "the last Adam" (1 Cor 15:45) and the "firstborn of all creation" (Col 1:15).

Thus, Jesus embodied the climax and culmination of what it means to be human. As human beings are identified with Jesus (i.e., "baptized into Christ," Gal 3:27), they can finally access the truth of who they are as God's beloved. In this way, the imprint of God's image that all share is liberated to emerge and flourish as God had always intended. Jesus's faithful life and ministry is not about solving God's problem but about taking creation that final step forward to being what humanity was intended to be in the first place. Jesus's faithful life has its origin in the unchanging purpose and love of God (John 1:1–5). For this reason later theologians described Jesus as fully divine and fully human, in that Jesus revealed *fully* the character of God and completed *fully* God's goal for humanity. Framed in this way, the image of God's faithfulness in Jesus remains intact.

Sixth, *God is the forgiving and merciful one.* The heart of God is *agape* love, which is purposeful, tough, consequential, and unrelenting. It is not that God has two faces—a loving one and a judging one—as if God needs to choose which of these needs doing. Neither should the mercy and love of God be confused with indulgent love. Instead, it is a tough love: love that aims at transformation, growth, and reconciliation. God remains resolute in the condemnation of evil; however, God does not condemn people (John 3:16–17). God does not punish people, as if to pay them back for their rebellion. God does, however, allow people to experience the full consequences of their choices (Rom 1:18–31), because God's mercy is pure and noncoercive.

So, what about the biblical images of "wrath" in the OT and the NT? As we have seen with so much of the language and imagery of the Bible, these images often say more about the limitations of our human linguistic expression than about the heart of God. A careful distinction needs to be made here (Caird 1994:87). God's wrath is not an emotional outburst of revenge or of punishment designed to stop sinners from sinning, but rather it is the *impersonal* process that attaches to sinners the consequences of their error. These death-dealing and destructive consequences are not fundamentally part of God's life-giving purpose for humanity as described above. This is likely what Paul meant when he said, "Beloved, never avenge yourselves, but leave room for the wrath of God" (Rom 12:19). Now, does this mean God "winks at evil"? No, the face of God is set uncompromisingly against evil, and God will do all that it takes to make things right. God does *personally* resist evil; after all, God is called a "warrior" (Exod 15:3). However, God does not use violence or coercion to overcome evil. Instead God's ultimate "weapon" is the persuasive power of self-giving love (Rom 12:9–21). The cross is the clearest expression of God's kind of wrath, and it is called the "wrath of the Lamb" (Rev 6:16–17).

The NT writers are clear that Jesus's ministry had everything to do with the demonstration of the love of God. Yet they do not try to explain the mechanism by which the death and resurrection of Jesus became effective for our salvation. Instead, the NT writers prefer to use metaphors, drawn from worlds they knew something about (the courtroom, the realm of commerce, the realm of worship, the dynamic of relationships, and the battleground) in order to talk about something they did not fully understand, but of which they were convinced: namely, that sin's rule had been undone, and that Jesus was alive (Green & Baker 2000:97). Death could not hold him down. The new age had dawned. The powers of the old age no longer had jurisdiction over those associated with the risen Lord (1 Cor 2:6).

It is precisely here that the invitation to biblical imagination can be heard the loudest in the Western world. By embracing the full sound of NT choir giving voice to the redemption drama involving God, Jesus, and the power of sin, we are enabled to reread old texts of salvation in ways that challenge our Western penchant to minimize spiritual powers, to promote personal autonomy, and to fixate on guilt and punishment. Western thought is being reshaped in the twenty-first century, especially through the ways that non-Western Christians explain God's salvation. For example, teaching NT theology in Africa has given me more insight into Paul's articulation of the significance of Jesus's death in Col 2:15. There Paul describes Jesus's death in ways rarely utilized in Western theology, with its preference for personal forgiveness and retributive justice. However, my African students intuitively understand Paul's graphic portrayal of Jesus's death on the cross as one that "disarmed the rulers and authorities and made a public example of them, triumphing over them" (Col 2:15). In much of the non-Western world, the way Paul makes sense of that first Easter resonates with common worldview assumptions. For instance, non-Westerners share with Paul a high regard for evil as a spiritual power, an appreciation for the collective nature of human identity, a great respect for authority and status, a high view of relationship and restorative justice, and a concern for honor and shame. Thus for non-Westerners as for Paul, the cross is the place where God triumphed over evil in order to liberate from sin's grip all those choosing to live in association with Jesus. This is just one example of how Western Christians can benefit from hearing how non-Western Christians explain God's salvation in Christ. While it may seem novel to Western interpreters, the non-Western interpretive framework taps into a way of understanding that is often as ancient as the biblical writers themselves.

Seventh, *God is like a father*. The NT writers also use the parental image of a father to describe God, because Jesus himself called God his father: the one who faithfully saves and cares for all in the household (Mark 8:38; 11:25; 13:32; 14:36). This metaphor is rooted in the patriarchal household system in which families were identified and characterized by the leading father figure. Paul says that believers can now cry out to *abba*, father (Rom 8:15; Gal 4:6), because of their adoption into the "household" of God, the "family" of God. The image is associated with liberation from bondage: liberation from a family system of alienation. It means leaving our rebellion behind and accepting at last our true identity as God's beloved. Such adoption underlines the assertion that membership in God's family is not based on DNA, ethnicity, wealth, gender, or anything else. Instead, it involves leaving "old-family" loyalties in order to be baptized into a "new family" (Mark 3:31–35). In this case, water is thicker than blood. The Christian community is a family of brothers, sisters, and mothers; that is, of all those who have left one dominion for another dominion: namely, for the reign of God, where there is but one father, God (Mark 10:29-30; Matt 23:9).

Unfortunately some have used the masculine imagery of God to justify the suppression of women in the church and in society. This is a direct reversal of the way the early Christians understood the gospel message. Paul is well known for inviting women (e.g., Lydia, Acts 16:11-15; and other women, Rom 16:1-16) to join God's mission, which also included exploring a new way of being male and female within the new humanity that Jesus embodied (Gal 3:28; 1 Cor 11:11). However, these initial advances in being truly human were reversed within a generation after Paul's ministry; this reversal was perpetuated through the following centuries. Male church leaders have often exploited Paul's temporary and situational restriction of women from their share in church leadership (1 Cor 14:34-35; 1 Tim 2:11-12) as if it were timeless and universal. Such views adversely affect our image of God and of women. Ontologically, we must define God as "beyond gender," just as we recognize God as personal, but "beyond personality" (Kraus 1991:96).

Today in many communities, the word *man* no longer means "men and women," and masculine pronouns like *him* no longer automatically include both genders. So which pronoun would be appropriate for God, who is beyond gender? An obvious solution to this linguistic problem in English has not yet appeared. However, it is vital that the search continue to find ways to recontextualize the metaphor of God as father in such a way that it can continue to stir the imagination of today's generation without losing the intimacy and the respect that this parental image conveys.

These seven NT God-talk images taken together are not exhaustive, for God is always more. However, when the voices singing these images are heard together, they create a profoundly moving invitation for any generation or any culture to reimagine its participation in the life of God. By singing along, the church joins "the cloud of witnesses" (Heb 12:1-2) from previous generations in continuing to be shaped by the multivoice biblical choir—all the members of which witness to God's people-gathering activities that aim to bring global transformation and thus complete God's work of creation.

What do the NT writers have to say about being human? This is the subject of the next chapter.

EXERCISES

1. The Western world places much emphasis on tolerance. Judgment tends to be seen in a negative light. This is probably for good reason, given the history of abusing privilege, position, and power in the Western world. Our wariness about judgment is a helpful corrective to the discrimination and oppression that have often characterized Western societies. However, along with this corrective sometimes comes an unwillingness to engage in discernment, assessment, or critique. There is a big difference between judgment as discernment and judgment as condemnation.

    Discuss the following questions: Why is it sometimes awkward to assert that God is judge? What kind of judgment is God involved in with regard to people, according to the NT writers? How is condemnation different from discernment? Could you reframe God's judgment to have the liberating sense that the NT writers associate with God's righteous judgment? If so, how?

2. The metaphors that express the reality of God in the ancient world are often challenging for contemporary societies. The biblical writers draw heavily on a worldview that uses the language of "dominions": ancient mythical language to talk about their lived experiences. Concepts like dual causation, sovereignty, predestination, powers and principalities, foreknowledge, and wrath are tough for people to fathom or appreciate, shaped as we are by the materialistic and individualistic tendencies of the Enlightenment and by the emerging postmodernity. The seven images for God outlined in this chapter are understood differently depending on how an individual or community understands God and God's interaction with humanity and creation. At the center of these differences is worldview.

    Consider the two diagrams below. The biblical writers' worldview differs significantly from the Western worldview. In contemporary Western democracies, elected officials derive their power and authority from the people who elect them. God's involvement (or even that of the powers) is unnecessary for the logic of the Western worldview, although some do still make claims about God's involvement. By contrast, as we have seen already, the Judeo-Christian worldview of the NT writers begins prior to the chaos with God, the one who creates the cosmos and orders the powers to carry out God's creation purpose. Key to the Judeo-Christian worldview is that God invites humanity from the start to participate in God's creation work, seeing it through to completion (Ps 8; Ps 110; Rom 16:20; Heb 2:5–18). And it is Jesus who finally makes possible the original creation mandate for humanity by defeating the rebellious rule of the power of sin at the cross.

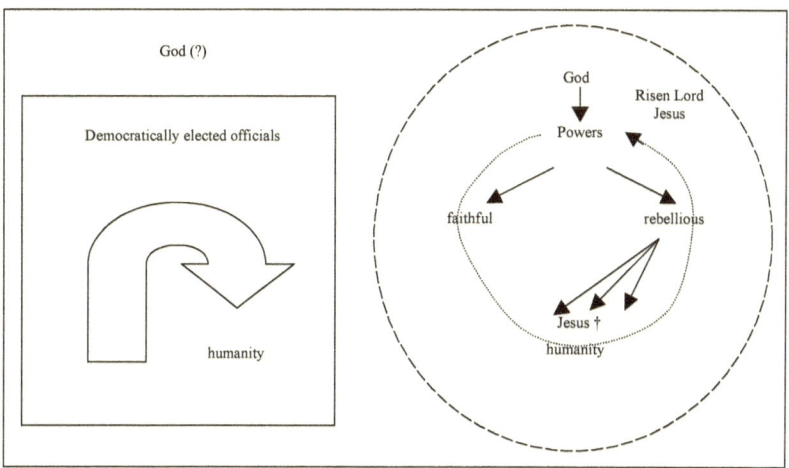

TABLE 10.1 Comparing the Western Worldview (left) with the NT Writers' Judeo-Christian Worldview (right)

Discuss the following questions: Why do you think it is difficult for Westerners to conceptualize some of the God-talk images used by the NT writers? What is lost by the Western world's apparent willingness to talk only about what can be seen or controlled by the individual? Without our giving up the gains achieved by Western civilization, what correctives do we recognize in the ancient metaphors for God used by the NT writers? How could you reframe the sovereignty cluster of concepts (i.e., powers, dominion, slavery, and reign) so that contemporary Western faith communities, choosing to be shaped by them, might be able to hear them? What other metaphors might help Westerners understand the royalty images used by the biblical writers to conceptualize God?

11

Anthropology

What It Means to Be Human

WHAT DOES IT MEAN to be human? This topic continues to capture the imagination of people, given the technological advances relating to gene therapy and medical care. We marvel at the creative ingenuity of our species. However, terrorist activity, genocide, and environmental degradation remind us how fragile human life really is. This chapter has two anthropological objectives: (1) to investigate the character of the image of God (*imago dei*) with which all human beings begin life and (2) to explore the implications of setting Jesus as the anthropological norm.

HUMANITY IN THE IMAGE OF GOD

All the NT writers agree that human beings are not what they should be. Each one has chosen to go his or her own way, which means giving allegiance to the way of death, decay, and destruction (Rom 3:19; 5:12; 8:22–25; 1 Pet 1:18–19). Yet, a deeper longing remains for something better, for something more whole, healthier, and authentic. This reality gives expression to the *imago dei* that characterizes all human beings (Gen 1:27). While language like the "image of God" has multiple layers, it speaks primarily of the God-given potential or capacity for relationships in varying degrees of commitment, something which distinguishes human beings from animals. Each person, no matter how badly "messed up"—whether by their own doing, the abuse of others, or some combination—bears the image of God, the capacity for relationships, which tenaciously refuses to be obliterated.

The NT writers testify to the gospel invitation that God extends to all: namely, to abandon allegiance to the deceptive, death-dealing spell that sin has managed to cast over creation at humanity's initiative (Gen 3; 6:5–6) and to be reconnected with God, others, ourselves, and creation. The painful truth is that humanity has chosen rebellion (sin) and is in need of forgiveness and ongoing transformation (Rom 3:9, 23). The foundational assumption of the NT writers is that humanity needs God's forgiveness as well as the follow-up practice of forgiving others (Matt 6:12; Luke 11:4), in order to rebuild the multiple levels of damaged relationships (2 Cor 3:18).

Still, what is the nature of forgiveness? According to Johnson (2003:284), we learn the true nature of forgiveness from the way that God forgives. The biblical writers testify to a conviction that God knows human beings completely, and, therefore, is able to see that they are *not* totally identified with their sinful behavior, even if they think of themselves as defined by sin. In other words, God is able to see and to summon a self that people may not be able to see. As Johnson states, "God calls into being that which is as yet only potential within us, namely a self that is not a sinner. In this sense, God forgives *us* rather than the sin. The sinful self is allowed to die. The self that can live to righteousness is raised by God. When we are able to trust that God forgives us, we are able to 'turn' or 'convert' to the self that God sees and calls into being" (2003:284). As people cultivate the habit of seeing in others a self not defined by sin, they learn how to forgive each other as well—they learn how to be *truly* human.

The transformational dynamic of becoming truly human picks up the ancient Israelite contribution to understanding creation. Genesis 1:1 reads, "In the beginning when God created the heavens and the earth, the earth was a formless void." Israel's relational understanding of creation, which differed from Israel's neighbors', in which creation emerged as an almost-unintended byproduct of violence and warfare between the gods (see the Akkadian Creation Epic), affirms that Israel's God does the most difficult thing! God, the master of the universe and mightiest of all warriors, triumphs over the primeval chaos-dragon (Isa 51:9–11), by taking that which is chaotic, useless, disorganized, indistinct, and good for nothing ("a formless void"), and actively calling into being a world that is good, fruitful, beautiful, and new. How? By taking the pre-existent chaotic matter, God gathered, separated, and ordered the world, creating differentiated, distinguishable, and productive beings.

Yet, even this classic understanding of the Israelite creation story has another dynamic in play: namely, that God is known as the creating God, from the beginning and through to the end. In the Israelite understanding of things, creation is always relational and organic. Creation is launched but not yet finished; good but not yet perfected; fully present but not yet ultimately realized; now, yet deferred. From the start humanity is chosen and mandated to work with God, participating as co-creators in God's creation project, helping to bring creation step-by-step closer to completion, wholeness, and perfection. This is a huge *affirmation* of what it means to be human; and at the same time, it comes with a huge *responsibility* for taking seriously humanity's mandate as stewards, managers, organizers, and co-creators—to make something out of what we have been given. There may not be much, but there is always just enough to make something beautiful. The ongoing challenge remains; humanity is invited to step up and do its part in taking creation forward, affirmed in who we *are* and challenged with who we are *becoming*.

JESUS AS THE ANTHROPOLOGICAL NORM

At the heart of NT anthropology is the *kerygma* that the early Christians proclaimed—their experience of Jesus's life, death, and resurrection. They experienced Jesus not only as the one who, on God's behalf recalled Israel to be and to do what had always been intended for God's people (to be "a light to the nations," Isa 49:6), but also as the one who actualized the potential for being truly human, like no one else had. Jesus fulfilled Adamic humanity (Rom 5), and therefore became the primary source and paradigm for the new humanity: "the last Adam" (1 Cor 15:45), the "firstborn of all creation" (Col 1:15). In Jesus, creation is not returned to Eden, but creation is taken up and moved forward from where Adam left off; Jesus brings the whole creation enterprise to its goal of *shalom*, life, and wholeness: the goal for which creation was launched in the first place.

Still, the ministry of Jesus and how it relates to other human beings is not viewed the same by all. At least three different ways exist to view the relationship between Jesus's life and his crucifixion.

(1) For some, Jesus lived an exemplary life, and his death amounts to a horrible accident, but it does little more than move one to pity Jesus and his unfortunate circumstances.
(2) For others, Jesus's life is important, but his death outweighs everything. Why? Because the crucifixion provides the payment required by God to deal with humanity's debt of sin. Here, the emotions are a mix of fear of God's retaliation and gratefulness for the good fortune humanity experiences at Jesus's expense.
(3) For others, Jesus's death flows out of the life he lived for others; the crucifixion illustrates the lengths to which evil will go to silence all challengers (i.e., evil orchestrates the death of Jesus only to find that it has outed itself and lost), and it demonstrates the lengths to which God will go to reverse the effects of evil, so that death does not have the last word (i.e., Jesus's victory over death opens access to God's salvation for all). Here, the emotions move toward resolve, hope, and empowerment.

The view one takes on the life and ministry of Messiah Jesus and its significance will shape the way creation, humanity, and life as a disciple of Christ is understood. Because of our having paid close attention to the NT conference deliberations, it should be clear that the third view better represents how the early Christians understood the events leading to Jesus's execution and their interpretation of that experience. "Whatever meaning atonement might have, it would be a grave error to imagine that it focused on assuaging God's anger or winning God's merciful attention . . . The scriptures as a whole provide no ground for a portrait of an angry God needing to be appeased in atoning sacrifice" (Green and Baker 2000:51).

In other words, Jesus aimed to re-gather God's people so that they could do and be what God had always intended. The NT conference participants repeatedly assert the significance of Jesus's ministry, showing how he comes to take up into himself the traditional Israelite religious symbols: Jesus is the temple (Mark 14:58; John 7–8; Eph 2:20; Rev 21:22), Jesus is the Torah (Rom 10:4; Heb 10:1–18), and Jesus is Israel (Heb 8:6). Furthermore, Jesus actualized the potential for being truly human, like no one else had. As we have seen, the NT witness is that Jesus revealed *fully* the character of God and completed *fully* the goal for humanity, intended by God all along. This is why later proto-orthodox theologians came to describe Jesus as fully divine and fully human (the Chalcedonian Creed, 451 CE). Such "fully"-"fully" language attempted to articulate the new anthropological and theological reality accomplished by Jesus, the one who helped people understand who they really are as human beings *and* what God really desires.

Thus, Jesus embodied the climax and culmination of what God means for humanity to be. As individuals are identified with and attached to the community of Jesus, they can finally access the truth of who they are as God's beloved. In this way, the imprint of God's image that all share is liberated from sin's grip to emerge and to flourish as God had always intended. In other words, Jesus's life and ministry are not about solving God's problem, but about taking God's creation that final step forward to being what God intended for creation in the first place. In this way, atonement in the NT has its origin in the unchanging purpose and love of God. Rejecting any notion of a transactional payment made between the Father and the Son, Caird asserts, "If we are to be true to New Testament evidence, we shall not frame any sentence about atonement or salvation with Jesus as its subject which could not equally have God as subject" (1994:137).

A word of caution is in order here. Sometimes putting forward Jesus as the norm for Christian living is criticized because it rests, some say, on an eschatological or timetabling mistake (Finger 1989:68–72). The argument goes like this: Jesus's rigorous teaching regarding forgiveness, nonviolence, and *agape* love could never have been practiced as long as the social institutions of this world continue to be in effect. Therefore, Jesus must have expected these behaviors for another time in the future, or he must have expected this age to come to an end shortly, and these were just "interim ethics." However, since Jesus and the earliest Christians were mistaken about the timetable for the end of the world, the church quickly filled in the available standards of normative social behavior common to contemporary Greco-Roman society. Since this happened early on (some say even within the NT), the church in every generation ought to be free to incorporate the norms of present culture, regardless of whether they cohere with Jesus's life and teaching.

People from both the so-called conservative and liberal theological perspectives can sometimes be heard to argue in this way, for different reasons, of course. Jesus's teaching known as the Sermon on the Mount (e.g., truth telling, care for marginalized, love for enemies, marital faithfulness, etc.) provides a good measure for how seriously the anthropological norm of Jesus is understood. Some dismiss Jesus's teaching as an ethic unworkable for public use, as perhaps operative in the age to come, but not now. After all, so the rationalization goes, the way of nonretaliation that led him to the cross may have been fine for Jesus, but it has little significance for guiding personal and public human behavior today.

From what we have heard so far from our NT conference speakers, there should be a great deal of skepticism regarding any view that trivializes the anthropological norm of Jesus for the Christian community today. All of the NT writers expected the cruciform life of Jesus to shape each Christian community's interactions with the world, even though they expected the broken, old-age world order to continue for some indefinite time as the dominant system. Given their Jewish apocalyptic worldview, they only had end-time vocabulary in their toolbox to talk about the defeat of sin and the birth of the new age. Jesus's resurrection and the recollections of his life and ministry gave rise to this new language. They had little choice but to use end-time language to talk about what is truly representative of the end, even though the end was not in sight. They had no other terms of reference available. As it turns out, it was not the scarcity of options, but the accuracy of the strange "already/ not yet" language that made these images stick; such language proved to be the best way to characterize the reality out of which God's end-time people were now living.

The history of the church, however, shows that this new end-time language has not always been well understood. Listen again to Jesus's "hurry-up-and-wait" speech: "Nation will rise against nation . . . This is the beginning of the birth pangs . . . This generation will not pass away until all these things have taken place . . . But about the day or the hour, no one knows . . . only the Father . . . Beware, keep alert" (Mark 13:8, 30–37). Or consider Paul's instruction regarding sex and marriage at the turn of the ages: "In view of the impending crisis, it is well for you to remain as you are . . . The appointed time has grown short . . . The present form of this world is passing away" (1 Cor 7:26–31). Some misunderstood Jesus and Paul to be promoting end-of-the-world date setting; others have chosen to explain away the NT language of the inbreaking new age as wishful thinking or as mistaken. Neither of these explanations will do.

While the new age did dawn (1 Cor 10:11) and is dawning, it did *not* consist of the abolition of history ("let them marry," says Paul, 1 Cor 7:36) but in the defeat of sin's power to oppress humankind and in the formation of resistance communities of faith (Finger 1989:80). These new communities of "resident aliens" were indwelt by the Spirit of the risen Lord and now, for the first time, had the power and the potential to resist the evil one and say no. Why? Because Jesus said no. Since they were attached now to Jesus, what was true of him could be true of them— his story became theirs. And so, Christian communities have aspired to live by the real cruciform love of Jesus and thereby to demonstrate the good news of the transformation of all creation that is still to come.

The bottom line is that the NT writers never assume an anthropological norm other than Jesus. Their writings give witness to the church's active engagement with cultural norms in order to de-center them and bring their communities into realignment according to the norms of Jesus. Remember, for example, the way Paul taught that there is no longer Jew or Gentile, slave or free, male or female (Gal 3:28). These traditional institutions (earthly representations of the "powers and principalities") are being rendered inoperative during this time when the "ends of the ages have come together" (1 Cor 10:11).

However, these old-age powers still need to be "respected" in the meantime, without our giving them primary allegiance any longer (Rom 6:12). The Corinthian correspondence records this kind of subversive "de-centering" being launched "in the Lord" (1 Cor 11:11). So, while Paul's "eschatological reserve" kept him from affirming the Corinthians' enthusiastic trivialization of the powers (see his warnings regarding their greed, pride, sexual immorality, idolatry, and so on in his correspondence with them), he along with other early Christians shamelessly held up Jesus as the firstborn and prototype of the new creation ("Jesus the pioneer and perfecter of our faith," Heb 12:2; "the firstborn of all creation . . . In him all things in heaven and on earth were created," Col 1:15–16).

But how effective or practical is such an anthropology, really? It seems that a people that claims Jesus as its norm could end up killed as he was, or misunderstood as aiding evil by refusing to use violence to stop evil. This is true. There is just no getting around the "conversion of the imagination" required to embrace the Jesus norm. Yet, the victory of the Lamb at the cross sets in motion both the *end* of evil and the *goal* for creation. Now, during these last days, when God is exercising great patience, God's people are expected to live out of the resources of what is yet to be completed. This is not about being passive, but about being active in our resistance to evil in all its forms, knowing all along that evil too must be free to be evil and to carry on hell-bent toward separation from God and destruction.

The NT writers regularly use the image of Satan to sum up all there is to say about evil. Satan is sometimes thought of as an individual evil spirit (1 Cor 10:19–20) and sometimes as a personification of the power of evil (1 Cor 8:4–7). In any case, the NT writers employ ancient mythological language to give expression to the deeply felt reality of evil experienced by all people. Caird (1994:111) lists six helpful observations emerging from the NT conference as the various writers speak about the presence of evil in the world.

(1) Evil is a real and virulent power; it cannot be explained away as simply the adolescent growing pains of human societies.
(2) "Evil is personal, and can exist only where there is a personal will in rebellion against God. In this respect the New Testament never uses Satan either to explain the origins of sin or to absolve human beings of responsibility for their sinfulness. It would be quite wrong to say that, if there had been no Satan, there would have been no sin. It would be true to say that, if there had been no sin, there could have been no Satan" (1994:111).
(3) While evil is rooted in human desire for prestige, power, and possessions, it becomes superhuman in its cumulative operation—holding all human life and creation in the grip of its power (Rom 3:9).
(4) Evil is a perversion of goodness; it is a power created by God that has abandoned its God-given purpose. Satan is one of the Sons of God holding his authority from God ("the power of sin is law," 1 Cor 15:56; Gal 3:19).
(5) Evil wins human allegiance by masquerading as good: "Satan disguises himself as an angel of light," (2 Cor 11:14).
(6) Evil is always the enemy (Matt 13:28) against which God's people must always be prepared to resist wherever it turns up (Eph 6:10–17).

The freedom with which God allows evil to carry on headlong to its self-destruction is characteristic of God's kind of *agape* love witnessed in Israel's own creation stories. God did not create evil but allowed people to rebel against God's way, giving evil the allegiance it needed to become the dominating superpower that it has become. In Israel's primal temptation stories (Gen 3:1–19), the sin of Adam and Eve according to Kraus (1991:128) is in "grasping," taking and eating; that is, appropriating the fruit of the tree for one's own selfish enjoyment and advantage without God's direction. The prohibition ("of the tree of the knowledge of good and evil you shall not eat" Gen 2:17) does not suggest that human beings should not acquire the knowledge of good and evil. In fact, the command to "fill the earth and subdue it" implies the need of such knowledge for discernment (see 2 Sam 14:17; 1 Kgs 3:9). At issue is the *way* such knowledge is to be developed. Is this knowledge achieved autonomously (in a self-directed process) or theonomously (in a God-directed process)? "It is the tempter who implied that the only way to realize the full potential of the image [*imago dei*] was to grasp for the knowledge which would enable them to control their own destiny" (Kraus 1991:128). Again, this schema is in direct contrast to the pagan creation stories of Israel's neighbors, which are rooted in violence, deception, and warfare (see, for instance, the Akkadian *Creation Epic*). For Israel, God exists before the chaos (Gen 1:1–2) with the loving purpose to create a world of mutual, authentic, and theonomous relationships.

So it makes sense for God's people to hold up Jesus as the norm for humanity. Why? Because he is the truly perfect human who refused to live autonomously like Adam and Eve, but who instead chose to live theonomously: to live the completely God-filled life in response to God's call. However, the NT affirmation of the normative character of Jesus is not based on the illusion that Jesus's life and ministry of nonviolent resistance to evil will necessarily "work" in the short term. No, Jesus is the anthropological norm because his life and pattern of resistance to evil is rooted in God's creation purpose, *and* it anticipates the triumph of the Lamb that was slain (Yoder 1971:61).

Of course, this kind of "gracious divine patience" is not the complete answer to evil. Just as the doctrine of creation affirms that God made humanity free; and the doctrine of redemption says that sin's freedom led the God-man, Jesus, to the cross; so also "the doctrine of hell lets sin free, finally and irrevocably, to choose separation from God" (Yoder 1971:62). At the final judgment, the old age, dominated by evil, achieves its goal as it is finally left to itself along with all that is loyal to it. Having chosen to have nothing to do with God's life, it excludes itself from "the new heaven and new earth," the consummation of God's creation which began in Christ (Rev 20:14–15).

The anthropological norm of Jesus remains the only effective way to deal with and undo the power of evil. This is what Paul meant when he said, "Christ fulfills the goal of Torah" (Rom 10:4), and when he said that Christ is the "firstborn of all creation" (Col 1:15). In Jesus, we see both the normative self-disclosure of God and the consummation of the *imago dei* in humanity.

In the next chapter, our attention turns to the character and role of the Spirit of the risen Lord that animates God's new creation enterprise.

EXERCISES

1. Since the beginning of time, people have exercised what has been called the single-victim mechanism: someone is forced to be the scapegoat in the name of a good cause, such as maintaining order or securing justice (see Shirley Jackson's classic short story "The Lottery"). The painful fact is that violence plays a key role in all human cultures. In popular literary works and movies, violence is used in various ways. Some protagonists use it to reclaim lost honor. Others see it as an oppressive force to dismantle and challenge. For still others, it is just the way things are, and the real story is how one schemes and manipulates events in order to survive in spite of it.

    Discuss the following questions: How does the scapegoat or single-victim mechanism (the notion that someone must pay in order to keep the order of things intact for the rest of us) or the myth of redemptive violence (the notion that violence can be used redemptively if it is in defense of justice) operate in popular movies, family dynamics, workplace interactions, educational institutions, church politics, governments, and foreign policy? In what single-victim mechanisms have you participated? What was that like? Why does the single-victim mechanism appear to be so prolific and seem to be the preferred way to deal with problems for most societies? In what ways does it or does it not bring justice? Can it bring peace? Explain.

    How could confessing Jesus as the anthropological norm challenge the single-victim mechanism and the myth of redemptive violence at work in human cultures? What does confessing Jesus as the anthropological norm say about God's preferred pattern of operation?

2. The sixteenth-century Protestant Reformation brought many changes to the theological landscape of the Western church—especially with regard to ecclesiology, revelation, and anthropology. This makes sense, given the social shifts taking place in Western civilization (in the Renaissance, during the Enlightenment, in modernity, and beyond). The diagram below focuses on the anthropological emphases of four Christian traditions in the sixteenth century. Note the differences and similarities in the ways that human experience is described in each of these traditions.

	Traditional Catholicism	Protestant Reformation (Lutheranism)	Protestant Reformation (Calvinism)	Radical Reformers (Anabaptism)
Humanity made in God's Image	mental capacity by which people control their bodies and rule the rest of creation	all power and capacities are divine; knowable in Christ	humanity as a "whole" reflects God who is sovereign	moral response and capacity for relationship in varying degrees of commitment
Fall	image compromised as the body rebels against the mind	image totally lost	image totally perverted, but not entirely lost	image is not lost, but powerless to bring about obedience
Original Sin	inherited disharmony between mind and body	inherited fallenness	inherited depravity	inherited freedom with inclination for misuse (fear, alienation, sin, rebellion)
Sin as such	misdirection and distortion of what is good	lack of perfect obedience with joy	disobedience	disobedience after choosing between good and evil as a responsible adult
Salvation	God's perfecting grace is infused gradually through study, prayer, service, and sacrament	justification by faith, but one remains a sinner; a fictional or alien righteousness (imputed)	beginning step and progress toward holiness, but never perfection	new birth brings new knowledge of true identity, new knowledge of good and evil; larger capacity to choose life and be obedient

	Traditional Catholicism	Protestant Reformation (Lutheranism)	Protestant Reformation (Calvinism)	Radical Reformers (Anabaptism)
Free Will	naturally directed to good (but may be mistaken)	free in relation to things, not God	no freedom at all for things below, theocracy	free to embrace or to separate from God
Major Mood	emphasis on attaining "the good"	emphasis on grace and visible election	emphasis on sovereignty of God visible in election	emphasis on obedience which confirms identity

TABLE 11.1 The Sixteenth Century Marks a Divergence of Anthropological Views in the Western Church

Discuss the following questions: What are the contemporary manifestations of these sixteenth-century anthropological traditions? What challenges and possibilities does each tradition hold? Which of these traditions have most strongly influenced your church or the churches with which you are familiar?

3. Any theological discussion about what it means to be human must wrestle with the biblical creation stories that have shaped the Judeo-Christian tradition (Genesis 1–3). How does thinking of Adam and Eve's disobedience as "failed potential" compare to thinking about their disobedience as a "fall from perfection"? Can you see how Adam and Eve's disobedience (grasping for autonomy) can represent all the various ways human beings have willfully rebelled against God's invitation to a theonomous relationship of growing into the potential with which God created the world?

Consider the following diagram. In what ways does it help communicate both the prospect or mandate of being human and the reality or problem of what human beings have done with the "image of God"? What areas of further exploration are raised for you?

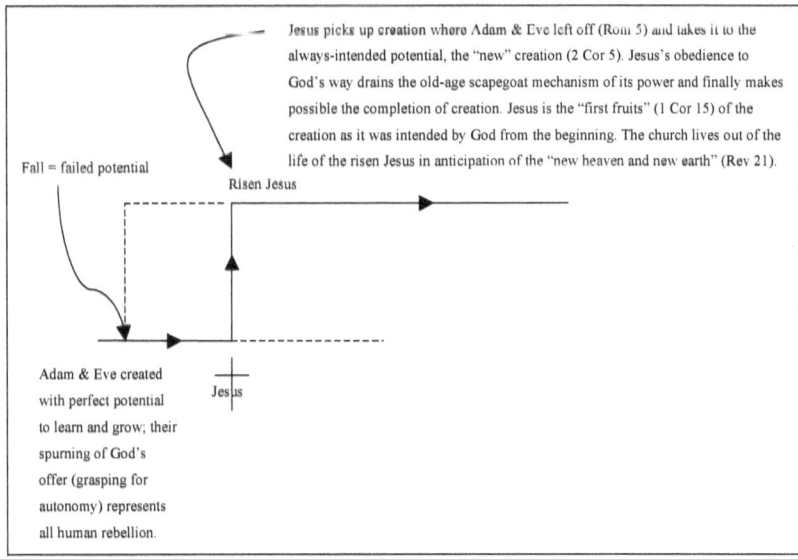

TABLE 11.2 Jesus as the Anthropological Norm and "First Fruits" of the "New" Creation

12

Pneumatology

God's Living Presence through the Resurrected Lord

THE HOLY SPIRIT IS the link between the risen Messiah Jesus and the church, the means by which the Christian community experiences the power of the resurrected one and is being transformed into his likeness "from one degree of glory to another" (2 Cor 3:18). This chapter has three objectives: (1) to explore the mutation within Jewish monotheism that generated Christian Trinitarian language, (2) to list the characteristics that the NT writers associate with the Holy Spirit, and (3) to identify the "gifts of the Spirit" given to help the church in its growth.

THE CHURCH'S TRINITARIAN LANGUAGE

What do the NT writers say about the Holy Spirit? Here again, as we have repeatedly seen, an aspect of theology—in this case, pneumatology—is closely linked to the new self-disclosure of God that came in and through Jesus. Before Jesus, the Spirit was known among the Israelite people as the "Spirit of God" (Gen 1:2; Job 27:3) or the "Spirit of Yahweh" (Judg 6:34; Isa 61:1). After the resurrection, however, the first disciples recognized Jesus in the worship experience as the Lord of God's people and recognized the deeper significance of their memories of Jesus's earthly life and ministry; it was only natural that all this activity be identified as the moving of the "Spirit of the Lord" (1 Cor 15:45). Not to identify this activity with the Spirit's action would have seemed inappropriate to the first Christians since they had no other than Hebrew categories to make sense of their experience. For example, in Rom 8:9, Paul uses "Spirit of God" and "Spirit of Christ" to identify the rule of the "Spirit" in which believers now participate; notice the interchangeable use of the designations, Father, Son, and Holy Spirit, in the unified expression of God's gracious reconciling presence; all three share a seamless identity.

The same seamlessness comes through when Paul explains that the diverse spiritual gifts energizing the church in God's mission are held together by the reality of "the same Spirit . . . the same Lord . . . the same God who activates all of them in everyone" (1 Cor 12:4–6). The varied yet unified expression for God is regularly found in the Pauline tradition and among the other NT writers. For example, "there is one body and one Spirit, just as you were called to the one hope of your calling, one Lord, one faith, one baptism, one God and Father of all, who is above all and through all and in all" (Eph 4:4–6; see also 1 Cor 6:11 and Heb 9:14).

Later, in the third and fourth centuries, Greek rational thought influenced proto-orthodox church theologians to individualize or isolate the unified expression of God's presence into "three distinct persons" or "three masks," but of the *same* "substance" or "essence" (*homoousios*); it was not enough to say they are *similar* in essence (*homoiousios*), as did Arian theologians. Only one letter distinguished the two Greek terms, but that letter made a big difference for the proto-orthodox theologians arguing the divinity of Jesus, against Arianism. In the end, the language of "same substance" (*homoousios*) emerged as the orthodox confession (First Council of Nicea, 325 CE).

Well-meaning and constructive, the Trinitarian debates in the history of the church have, however, sometimes led to division and misunderstanding. The theological rationalizations have tended to introduce more problems than they solve. Is God like the three states of matter: solid, liquid, and gas, suggesting God's evolution from state to state? Or is God like the three parts of an egg: the shell, the white, and the yolk, suggesting categorically distinct roles within God? For example, is it the Son's role to satisfy the Father's wrath by paying the penalty for sin? Often such abstractions in some Trinitarian thinking have isolated the members of the Godhead (from themselves and from the world), compromising the unity and oneness of God's "being-in-relation." See the diagram below.

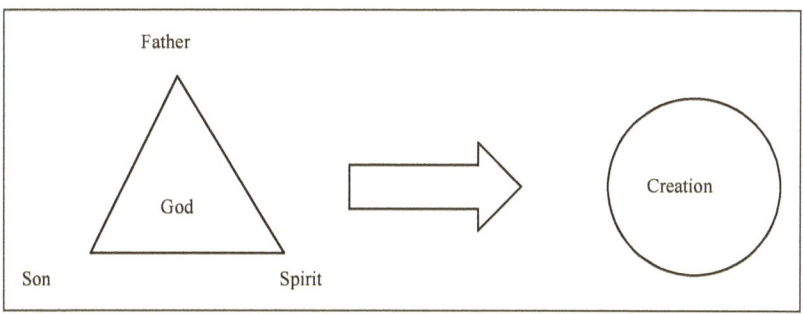

TABLE 12.1 Traditional "Isolated" View of the Trinity

While later theologians proposed an isolated view of the Trinity,"] the NT writers give no evidence of ever imagining God to have three parts or of God's evolving from one form to another. Fundamentally, the orthodox articulation of the Trinity at the First Council of Nicea in the year 325 was aimed at ruling out both of these notions: that God had three parts, or that God had evolved from one form to another, abandoning the previous form. The doctrine of the Trinity that finally emerged was an attempt to recognize the multiplex character of God's "being-in-relation," without suggesting three individual deities or some sort of transactional exchanges between them.

Trinitarian language continues to be difficult for Western "either/or" thinking. However, instead of focusing on "substance" or "persons," more promise may come in describing the Trinity in terms of relationship or as a community-of-being. Thus, the basic Trinitarian confession remains: God, as revealed in Jesus, is fully personal within God's own mode of existence as Spirit (i.e., relational and therefore necessarily plural), and God, as Creator, wills to give God's very self to the creatures of the world in loving relationship (Kraus 1991:93). In this way, there is a dynamic and relational unity within God's being.

The diagram below attempts to illustrate a relational understanding of the Trinity. In this view, as creation is launched, God makes space within the very self of God for the universe, carrying forward God's desire for intimate relationship with creation. The arrows in the diagram show the different ways that God's community-of-being relates to creation, helping it to understand both God and itself better over time. God as revealed by the Son shows God's desire to relate intimately to humanity. God as revealed by the Spirit shows God's being true to God's very character of breathing life into the world and moving all of creation forward to its goal of *shalom*. God as revealed by the Father shows God's parental desire to give God's very self for creation in loving relationship, so that ultimately it may recognize who it is, and who it is becoming. In this way, the Trinity is not so much a metaphysical problem to solve but an invitation to share the life of God together (González 1990:113–14).

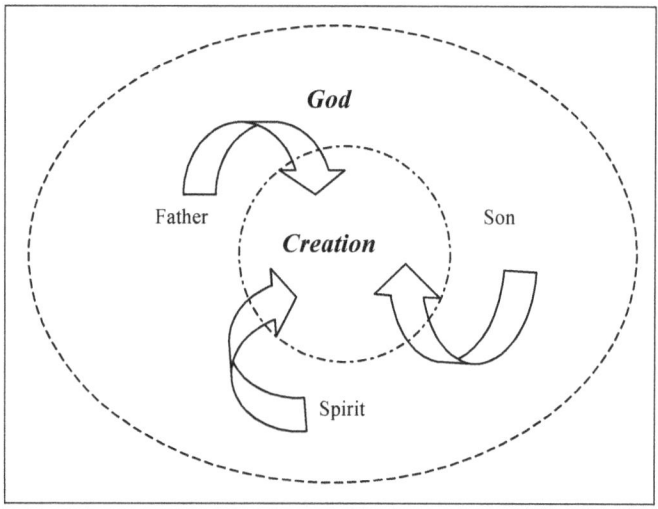

TABLE 12.2 Relational Understanding of the Trinity

With a relational understanding of the Trinity (Kraus 1991:149), we hear the NT chorus saying that the Holy Spirit is God's living presence among God's people, carrying out the mission of the risen Lord Jesus, which is the creation of a new humanity. The Spirit is the way in which God's presence is made known to us in these last days through Messiah Jesus. The Spirit motivates, empowers, and guides God's people, enabling them to go beyond previous possibilities in the formation of open, sharing, and true communities of Jesus.

The mutation within Jewish monotheism that the early Christian disciples enacted was in response to their encounter with the risen and exalted Lord Jesus. Their experience of his powerful presence among them in worship, guidance, healing, and discernment, as they gathered in Jesus's name, could only be accounted for if God were truly behind it. Thus, the monotheistic category of singleness mutated to one of *relational unity* as well, for the Christians who followed that first generation. Not to understand the experience of Jesus as an experience of God would be to reject God, for God was surely behind all that they had experienced of the divine presence among them in Jesus (Hurtado 1998:122). Nevertheless, Christian monotheism is different from Jewish or Islamic monotheism. Johnson offers a helpful clarification:

> Christians believe that God has revealed a richer inner life that enables us to think of the one God in a new way. In light of what they consider God's own self-disclosure, Christians think of the oneness of God not only in terms of singleness (as do Judaism and Islam) but also in terms of unity. What the mystery of the Trinity discloses is not a mathematical problem (how can one be three?) but the mystery of life given and shared. The Trinity is the mystery of God's own life as life given and received and shared in a never-diminished abundance of being. The Trinity shows us God as community. (2003:251)

Such developments in theism are not new, however. As we have seen already, the Christian mutation of Jewish monotheism was yet another shift in the development in Jewish theism. Like their Israelite ancestors long before them, who had abandoned belief in many gods (*polytheism*, Gen 31:19-35; 35:2-4), then belief in one god among many (*henotheism*, Exod 20:1-7; Deut 32:8-9), and who, finally by the end of the exile came to understand Yahweh as the only God (*monotheism*, Isaiah 40), the early Christians also came to recognize most clearly "the glory of God in the face of Jesus" (2 Cor 4:6) through the Holy Spirit, who animated their gatherings. Since the Master of the universe was most clearly present and represented in the life, death, and resurrection of Jesus of Nazareth, it was not a great leap to expand the language of "Lord" to refer to him. Now, in the post-Easter period, the unity of Yahweh included the Holy Sprit, who touched and continues to touch members of the faith community personally with the personal presence of God through the risen Lord Jesus.

CHARACTERISTICS OF THE HOLY SPIRIT ACCORDING TO THE NT WRITERS

What then do the NT writers actually say about the Holy Spirit? My colleague Tim Geddert notes at least twelve characteristics or activities of the Spirit that can be identified.

(1) The Spirit is both preserver and initiator of God's living presence within creation, which is why the Spirit can be further characterized as holy (1 Cor 12:3; Rom 8:9).

(2) The outpouring of the Spirit is a sign that the end-time has begun (Acts 2:16–17; 10:44–48; John 20:22).

(3) Receiving the Spirit is simultaneously a call to ministry and an equipping for ministry (Acts 1:8).

(4) The Spirit is a sign of and the effective cause of humanity's participation in God's salvation—the deposit or first installment (*arrabōn*, 2 Cor 1:22; 5:5; Eph 1:14) and the "first fruits" or "guarantee" (*aparchē*, Rom 8:23) of the promised creation inheritance.

(5) The Spirit facilitates a range of experiences, both individual and collective, in which God's people share (Acts; Gal 3:5; Heb 2:4).

(6) The Spirit facilitates moral and ethical growth (Rom 5:5; 1 Cor 6:9–11; Gal 5:22–26).

(7) The Spirit brings about a loving, trusting relationship with God (Rom 8:15–16; Gal 4:6).

(8) The Spirit is the source of the "overflowing life" that God gives the people of God (John 7:38; 1 John 3:24; 4:13).

(9) The Spirit is the mediator of the presence of the resurrected Jesus in the life of the believer and the church (John 14:18–26; Rom 8:3, 9–11; 1 Cor 15:45; Col 2:11).

(10) The Spirit who gathered the church as the end-time expression of God's kingdom is constantly about the task of preserving and renewing the church in God's mission (1 John 4:1–6; 1 Cor 2:6–16).

(11) The Spirit speaks to the church through Scripture (as it is interpreted in a discerning Christian community) in ways that invite the church in every culture and time to ongoing transformation, and that animate its witness to the world (John 16:13; 2 Cor 3:6; Gal 5:1, 13–14).

(12) The Spirit gives spiritual gifts for the "building up" of the body of Christ (1 Cor 12–14).

Given this list of characteristics of the Holy Spirit, two stand out. The Spirit is known as the power of God's presence active within human beings, *and* as the personal presence of God initiating conversion, transformation, and discernment among God's people. And yet the NT writers do not spell out the distinct personal identity of the Holy Spirit. As we have seen, the language is ambiguous—at one place, "Spirit of Christ," then at another, "Spirit of God." Why? Ambiguous language occurs because, as Johnson notes, "the distinct personal identity of the Holy Spirit in these early writings could hardly have been clear, precisely because the Spirit's role in mediating God's presence through the resurrection of Jesus could be—had to be—described in so many ways. The Spirit was the spirit of the Son *and* of the Father ... What is important to them is that the Spirit touches us personally with the personal presence of God through the resurrection of Jesus" (2003:223).

THE GIFTS OF THE SPIRIT ANIMATE THE CHURCH

The personal presence of God is brokered by the Spirit through the power of the risen Messiah Jesus, and animates the community gathered around the Lord with gifts of service and mutual encouragement. However, throughout Christian history the instruction regarding spiritual gifts has often proved controversial and divisive. Typically one or other instruction is taken in isolation from the other NT teaching. Attending to all the voices in the choir and locating one's community within the interpretive matrix are the keys to developing a biblical theology of spiritual gifts.

In outlining what the NT has to say about spiritual gifts Tim Geddert again helps steer a path through some of the contention by drawing out a number of assertions and implications.

(1) The church is the main context for the discovery and exercise of spiritual gifts (1 Cor 12:7; 14:12, 26).

(2) The church is the body that discerns what gift is genuine and what is not (1 Cor 14:29). The tests of authority remain the same as they always have been in the church: the gift promotes clear affirmation of Jesus as Lord, the gift is exercised in freedom from ulterior motivation or of personal gain, and in coherence with the memory of Jesus's life and ministry. Given these parameters, a wide variety of customs, explanations, and practices is acceptable.

(3) Spiritual *fruit* is more crucial than are spiritual *gifts*, and fruit helps the church to make sure that the exercise of gifts is proper and helpful (1 Cor 12:3; Gal 5:22).

(4) Every member of the body has at least one gift (1 Cor 12:7, 11, 18, 27; Eph 4:7).
(5) No member of the body has all the gifts (1 Cor 12:11, 14, 18, 24, 28).
(6) Each member needs the gifts of the others (1 Cor 12:21).
(7) No gift is given to *all* members (1 Cor 12:8–10, 18–21).
(8) God decides who gets which spiritual gifts (1 Cor 12:11, 18, 24, 28).
(9) Members of the body are not be ranked as important or not important based on which gifts they have (1 Cor 12:24–25).
(10) A person who has a spiritual gift is responsible before God to use that gift in ways that are helpful to the church (1 Cor 14:26–28).
(11) Spiritual gifts were not meant just for the first century. There is no biblical evidence for the cessation of gifts. (Note that 1 Cor 13:10 refers to the *eschaton*, when salvation will be completed.)

Based on what the NT writers say about spiritual gifts, several implications can be delineated for the church's exercise of spiritual gifts.

(1) No gift should be pushed onto a church that is not open to it. This would not build up the church.
(2) Spiritual gifts can be exercised in home fellowship groups, even if the whole church is not present to benefit. Early house churches are similar to home fellowship groups.
(3) There are genuine spiritual gifts that are not mentioned in the Bible. The New Testament presents no complete list.
(4) There is no clear division between spiritual gifts and human capabilities or talents.
(5) Spiritual gifts are not permanent or personal possessions, but enable God's people for specific ministries in specific contexts within the mission of God.

From the list of the Holy Spirit's gifts it is clear that the Spirit's primary purpose is to bring glory to God—to help all acknowledge God's presence, power, and claim upon human beings (Mark 2:12; Rom 1:21; 1 Pet 2:12). As believers continue to exercise the spiritual gifts within the faith community, they steadily grow in their recognition of their partnership with God. As Johnson puts it, they grow in appreciation "that the grace that comes to them in the gift of the Holy Spirit is in reality a share in the divine life, and therefore a participation in God's glory . . .

To recognize the Holy Spirit through worship, therefore, and to give the Holy Spirit glory is to acknowledge that in the work of the Holy Spirit in Christ and in us, we see the work of God" (2003:235).

Paul's affirmation offers an excellent summary of the character and function of God's Spirit at work among God's people: "Now the Lord is the Spirit, and where the Spirit of the Lord is, there is freedom. And all of us with unveiled faces, seeing the glory of the Lord as though reflected in a mirror, are being transformed into the same image from one degree of glory to another; for this comes from the Lord, the Spirit" (2 Cor 3:17–18).

As the Holy Spirit animates the church to share in the divine life and thus brings glory to God, the community of God's people grows. In the next chapter, the focus is on the nature and the purpose of that community: the church.

EXERCISES

1. Often discussions about the Trinity become defensive and argumentative. Interreligious dialogue can quickly digress into a debate about who is really monotheistic and who is really polytheistic. There is no question that Christian monotheism is different from Islamic or even Jewish monotheism. However, the expansion of the monotheism to include relational unity in God's oneness has the potential to create space for more fruitful dialogue on a host of different levels.

    Discuss the following questions: How could a relational understanding of the Trinity as God's "community-of-being" or God's "being-in-relation" offer a corrective to some of the interreligious debate? What possibilities do you see for using a relational understanding of the Trinity to talk about care for creation and about humanity's relation to God? What analogies can be drawn between a relational Trinity and other relational human interactions like marriage, leadership, and community living?

2. The Holy Spirit is the link between the risen Messiah Jesus and the church, the means by which the Christian community experiences the power of the resurrected one and the transformation into his likeness "from one degree of glory to another" (2 Cor 3:18). The emphasis on growth is tied to the invitation to ongoing renewal, vigilant resistance, critical thinking, gift deployment, cultural engagement,

and mutual discernment—all in the context of the collective entity called the body of the risen Lord, which lives for others.

Discuss the following questions: Even though Western personal identity is mostly located in the individual, what correctives can the NT emphasis on collective personal identity offer? What does the NT emphasis on the collective entity called the body of Christ say about salvation? About discipleship? About our life together? What insight is there in the NT writers' description of spiritual gifts? What is their purpose? How can discussions about spiritual gifts become abusive or unhelpful? What suggestions do you have for improving conversation about gifts of the Spirit and their deployment?

13

Ecclesiology

The Identity and Mission of the Gathered Messianic Community of God

WHAT DO THE NT writers say about the church? One thing is clear; they do not see the church as just another religious gathering with a newly discovered deity, worship pattern, or morality. As Kraus notes, the church began as a messianic movement within Judaism (1991:161). This chapter has five objectives: (1) to clarify Jesus's relation to the church, God's people, and the reign of God; (2) to explore the NT images that describe the church; (3) to summarize the church's vocation; (4) to discern the church's interaction with culture; and (5) to map out the practices of the church flowing from its character as a political reality.

DID JESUS START THE CHURCH?

What is the starting point of the church? Did Jesus start the church? This is a loaded question. The answer is both no and yes. God began to call a people together long ago. Already with Abraham (Gen 12:1–3) and at Israel's deliverance from Egypt (Exodus 15) God was gathering a people to participate in God's mission enterprise, the *shalom* project begun long ago of completing creation. So, no, Jesus could not have started the church, since there already was an identifiable people of God (Lohfink 1984). However, Jesus did gather and focus that people of God, enabling them to be what God had always intended them to be: "a light to the nations" (Isa 49:6). So in this sense, yes, Jesus did launch the *end-time* form of the people of God.

Jesus came preaching the kingdom of God (Mark 1:14-15). His proclamation was intended to renew God's original call upon Israel to live out its mandate as God's mission people. So, Jesus's mission was to establish the reign of God in visible form. The shape of that visible and renewed people is seen most clearly in the church, an outpost of God's inbreaking reign in these last days.

Only twice do we find Jesus talking about the church (*ekklēsia* = Greek for "gathering" or "assembly") in the Gospels, and both instances are in Matthew's narrative (Matt 16:17-19 and 18:15-20). In Matt 16:17-19, Jesus makes clear that his mission is to build the church on a rock. The rock is a powerful symbol in Judaism. It is the sacred point of contact between heaven and earth already from the time of Jacob's dream (Genesis 28). The rock is the place where God is especially present to protect, to save, and to accomplish God's creation purposes. Thus, the church is identified with the rock in that it is here that God's final invitation comes for all to find their home in God's reign, now fully disclosed in Messiah Jesus. The Christian testimony, to be precise, is that "the rock was Christ" (1 Cor 10:4; see also 1 Cor 3:11).

John Toews observes that Jesus makes two assertions about the church on the rock (1989:8-9). First, "the gates of Hades will not prevail against it" (Matt 16:18). The "gates of Hades" is a way of referring to Satan. In other words, Satan and the powers of the demonic will not be able to overcome the church built on the rock. Why? Because Jesus builds the church with the promise that the presence and power of God is mightier than the presence and power of the demonic. Second, the church is engaged in "binding and loosing." The language of "binding and loosing" is used regularly by NT writers to denote the binding of Satan and the loosing of people from demonic powers (Mark 3:27; 7:34-35; Matt 12:22-32; Luke 13:16; John 20: 21-23; Rev 20). Included in the "binding and loosing" language is the church's mandate ("keys") to engage in ethical discernment as to what is right and/or wrong, what is consistent and inconsistent with God's reign, what is necessary to restore relationships, and what will or will not promote God's mission to complete creation. Thus, the church on the rock is triumphing over the powers of Satan and is even now involved in liberating captives from the demonic powers (Rom 16:20).

In Matt 18:15-20, Jesus elaborates on the "binding and loosing" theme by showing just how the church as a community of ethical discernment goes about taking seriously its responsibility for one another. The passage outlines incremental steps for processing broken relationships and for promoting reconciliation (first, go privately to share the grievance you have with a member; if this fails, go with several other members to attempt restoration; only if this too is unsuccessful does the whole church community get involved). There is a mutuality involved in holding each one accountable for his or her words and actions in the Christian community. Contrary to popular practice, what one does really is the local church's business; and the local church's business really is the business of each one. It means confronting those whose behaviors are harmful, and implementing creative restoration programs. The church is an outpost of the kingdom, discerning and demonstrating what it means to live as God's gathered people in these last days.

And what if these efforts to promote reconciliation among church members fail? What does Jesus mean by "let such a one be to you as a Gentile and a tax collector" (Matt 18:17)? Tim Geddert offers this helpful and timely interpretation.

> When every effort fails, we finally have the right to kick them out of the church, right? No! Just the opposite. We never seek and are never given the right to dispense with a fallen member. Rather, we take one more step, the most radical step of all, in our ceaseless efforts to gain the person back again. We treat them like a "Gentile" and a "tax collector." ... It means that if all our attempts so far have failed, we try it the other way around. We no longer view the person as a brother or sister who is going astray; rather, we view the person as someone who needs to be won to the fellowship ... It was not the person's sin that caused the break with the church. It did not happen because somebody missed the target. Nor is the person on the outside because the attempted reconciliation failed. What's more, the church did not cut off the person from the community. Rather, the person removed himself or herself by not listening to the church—by withdrawing from the mutual accountability that defines us. Therefore, we now accept what the person has chosen to become: an outsider to the community. We hope that readiness to come back will be the result of their "time out." We have never given up working toward reconciliation. (2008:55-56)

NT IMAGES DESCRIBING THE CHURCH

Jesus not only renewed the people of God; he also commissioned his disciples to proclaim the gospel to all people and to build the church among all peoples of the world (Matt 28:16-20). But how did the NT writers conceptualize the church? It may be surprising to note that they provide no theological definition of the church. Instead, as we have seen elsewhere on other topics, they provide a series of diverse images that capture one aspect or another of the church, but no definitive statements. Toews has grouped into five categories the many diverse metaphors used by the NT writers to talk about the church (1989:3-26).

First, *people-of-God* images are some of the most powerful images for the church. This is one of the ways that we know that the early Christians did not think of themselves as starting something new. They were convinced that they were part of God's election of Israel as witnessed in the OT. However, they were also convinced that membership in God's people had been radically redefined by Jesus. No longer was inclusion a matter of Jewish identity (circumcision, food laws, and holy-day laws, i.e., "works of law"); now in these last days God's Spirit has been poured out on all people (Joel 2:28-29) so that Gentiles too have an opportunity to join God's elect. They are included now because this is seen as the fulfillment of the promise given to Abraham (Gen 12:1-3). A list of the people-of-God images includes references to the church as

- Israel (Matt 1:21; 2:6; 4:16, 23; Luke 2:31-32; 7:16; Rom 11:26; Eph 2:12; Heb 8:10)
- a chosen race (Luke 1:17; 77; 2:10; Acts 13:17-31; 15:14; 18:10; Rom 9:25-26; 11:1; 15:10; 1 Pet 2:4-10)
- a holy nation (John 11:50; 18:14; Acts 3:23; 7:34; Titus 2:14; Heb 10:30; 1 Pet 2:4-10)
- the twelve tribes (Matt 19:28; Jas 1:1; Rev 21:12-14)
- the patriarchs (Rom 9:5; 15:8)
- the circumcision (Eph 2:11-16; Phil 3:3)
- the seed of Abraham (Rom 4:1, 16; Gal 3:7)
- the exodus (Heb 11:22)
- the house of David (Luke 1:69)
- the flock (John 10:16; Acts 20:28-29; 1 Pet 5:2)
- the sheep (Matt 15:23; John 10:16; Heb 13:20)

Ecclesiology 315

- the followers of the Lamb who reign with him (Rev 5:6-14; 7:9-17; 17:14)
- the Holy City (Heb 13:12; Rev 21:2)
- Jerusalem (Luke 2:38; Gal 4:26; Heb 12:22; Rev 21:10)
- the temple (Mark 14:58; 15:38; 1 Cor 3:16; 2 Cor 6:16; Rev 21:22)
- the priesthood (Heb 2:17; 1 Pet 2:4-10)
- the festivals (1 Cor 5:8; Col 2:16-23; Heb 4:9).

Second, *community* images also describe the church. Often these images are read as referring to an individual Christian. However, the NT writers usually use them in the plural sense to define the corporate nature of the church. A list of the community images includes references to the church as: saints (1 Pet 1:15-16), faithful ones (Col 1:2; Rev 17:14), righteous ones (Rom 2:13; 1 Pet 3:12; 1 John 3:7), followers (Mark 1:17; 8:34; John 10:4, 27; 1 Pet 2:21; Rev 14:4), disciples (John 13:35; Eph 4:20-21), the Way (Acts 19:9, 23; 22:4; 24:14, 22), witnesses (Acts 1:8; Heb 12:1), confessors (Rom 10:9; Phil 2:11; 1 John 4:3), slaves (Rom 6:15-23; Gal 5:13), servants (1 Cor 4:1), friends (John 15:13-15), the household of God (1 Pet 4:17), children of God (Matt 5:9; Rom 8:14; Gal 3:26), brothers and sisters (Mark 3:31-35), brotherhood/sisterhood (1 Cor 6:5; 1 Pet 2:17; 5:9), the Name (Acts 5:42), and the gathering together (Matt 16:18; 18:17; 1 Cor 16:19).

Third, *cosmic* images picture the church in universal and all-encompassing terms. Here, the church is understood as more than a people and a community; the church also points to the fulfillment of God's promises. This fulfillment is so grand and complete that cosmic categories are the only ones appropriate to describe what God is doing through the church. A list of cosmic images includes references to the church as new creation (2 Cor 5:17), first fruits (Rom 11:16; 1 Cor 15:20-23; Jas 1:18; Rev 14:4), new humanity (Rom 8:23; Gal 4:5; Col 3:10), Sabbath rest (Heb 4:9-11), and light (John 12:35-36; Acts 26:18).

Fourth, *body* images for the church are uniquely Pauline. These images exploit three aspects of the human body—the body itself, parts or members that combine to form the body, and the head as command center of the body. All the body images express the dual themes of solidarity (unity) and interdependence (diversity) shared by believers in their new life together as the church. A list of body images includes references to the church as: the body of life (Col 2:11-15), the body of Christ (1 Cor 12:27), the members of Christ (1 Cor 6:15), the body and the blood (1 Cor 10:16; 11:23–26), the diversity of ministries (Rom 12:4–8; 1 Cor 12:4–30), head of the cosmic spirits (Eph 1:22–23; Col 2:8–10, 19), head of the church (Eph 4:15–16; Col 1:18), the body of this head (Eph 5:23; Col 1:24), the unity of Jews and Gentiles (Eph 3:6), the growth of the body (Eph 4:4–16; Col 2:19), and the fullness of God (Eph 4:4–6).

Fifth, there are many *independent* or freestanding images and metaphors illustrating one or more aspects of the church's identity. A list of independent images includes references to the church as: salt of the earth (Matt 5:13), a letter from Christ (2 Cor 3:2–3), fish and fish net (John 21:5–8), boat (Matt 14:33), ark (1 Pet 3:20), unleavened bread (1 Cor 5:8), branches of the vine (John 15), God's planting (1 Cor 3:6), God's building (1 Cor 3:9), building on the rock (Matt 16:18), pillar and bulwark (1 Tim 3:15), virgins (Matt 25:1), elect lady (2 John 1), bride of Christ (2 Cor 11:1; Rev 21:9), wedding feast (Matt 22:1), wearers of white robes (Rev 7:9), clothed with good works (1 Tim 2:9–10), citizens (Eph 2:19), strangers/foreigners (Heb 11:13), dispersion (Jas 1:1), ambassadors (2 Cor 5:20), poor (Matt 5:3), and hosts with guests (Rom 16:23).

So, what can be said with regard to these NT images for the church? Toews notes at least four things (1989:21–22): (1) There is a diversity of images, suggesting that no one image can be selected as the baseline for a theology of the church. (2) Even though the images differ greatly, they all speak of one reality: the church of Messiah Jesus. Every image points beyond itself to the people in whom God is working. (3) All the images have a common referent, Jesus, the Christ. Jesus is the one who gathers God's church. In Jesus, all have access to their true identity as God's children. (4) The story of Jesus defines the nature of the church. The pictures of him—priest, self-offering, shepherd, king, second Adam, perfect and true human being, servant, first fruits, witness, holy one—define and redefine the metaphors of the church. However, the church's defining center remains stamped by the crucified Lord, whose hands remain scarred (Luke 24:39) and whose garments remain stained by the blood of self-giving sacrifice (Rev 12:11; 19:13).

THE VOCATION OF THE CHURCH

Based on the multiplicity of images describing the church, what can be distilled as its fundamental character or nature? What is the church's vocation? Emerging from these metaphors five things can be said about the nature of the church. First, the church is a people called into existence by God. Instances of this call grow with intensity and precision as Israel's story unfolds (e.g., creation launch, Abraham and Sarah, Isaac and Rebekah, Jacob and Rachel, the exodus from Egypt, Moses and Miriam, David, the prophets, and now finally Jesus of Nazareth). It is God's people; it is not its own. Now in these last days, the gospel proclamation is that this people is reconstituted as an *inclusive* people (embracing all peoples and nations) and as an *exclusive* people (gathered around Jesus as *the* Lord).

Second, the church is a people among and through whom God is present in history to liberate people from evil (Jude 20–23), to engage in ethical discernment about how to live together (Matt 18:15–20; Acts 15:6–29; 1 Cor 5:12; 6:2), and to point as a sign to God's coming reign (2 Cor 5:17–21). In presenting itself to the world, the church provides an attractive alternative to enmeshment with the deceptive domination system of evil in all its manifestations. What is the domination system? According to Walter Wink, "it is characterized by unjust economic relations, oppressive political relations, biased race relations, patriarchal gender relations, hierarchical power relations, and the use of violence to maintain them all" (1998:39). The gospel proclamation rings clear, inviting all to give up the life of alienation and lies in order to become a part of what God is now doing in Jesus. The vision of John the seer captures this potential:

> And the one who was seated on the throne said, "See, I am making all things new." Also he said, "Write this, for these words are trustworthy and true." Then he said to me, "It is done! I am the Alpha and the Omega, the beginning and the end. To the thirsty I will give water as a gift from the spring of the water of life. Those who conquer will inherit these things, and I will be their God and they will be my children." (Rev 21:5–7)

Third, the church is a people in history and with a history of living and partnering with God in God's creative and transformative activity to complete creation—God's *shalom* project. The history of God's people in the Judeo-Christian tradition is one of growth and development with some steps forward and some steps backward, but the net gain remains positive. Christian history offers many shining examples of faithfulness and plenty of embarrassing stories of greed, abuse, and violence. Yet in all this mix the NT writers chart two affirmations that serve as goalposts through which successive generations of God's people move forward (1 Cor 3:10–15): (1) The outcome of God's project is *certain* because it remains subject to God, the relentless one who sticks with humanity and creation to make sure that the *shalom* project is accomplished (Eph 3:8–13). (2) The journey from now to the assured outcome is *uncertain* because it remains subject to human beings who respond unevenly to God's call to build communities of hope that challenge the domination system, and that advocate for the least, the lost, and the left out (Jas 1:27). For better or worse, the interplay between these two poles marks the history and development of God's people.

The church's vocation to carry forward the mission of God to complete creation comes with huge affirmation and huge responsibility; it is tied to real consequences. This is highlighted by Jesus in striking terms, according to the Fourth Evangelist's rendition of Jesus's postresurrection appearance.

> Jesus said to them again, "Peace be with you. As the Father has sent me, so I send you." When he had said this, he breathed on them and said to them, "Receive the Holy Spirit. If you forgive the sins of any, they are forgiven them; if you retain the sins of any, they are retained." (John 20:21–23)

While the presence and power of the Holy Spirit offer much promise to the church in its God-given mission of forgiveness and restoration, the consequences of the church's failure are also lasting and devastating. When the church withholds forgiveness, sin is allowed to continue its viral infection from generation to generation in the various networks and systems that link human beings together. The church's vocation is to partner with God in moving creation toward completion; God's *shalom* project is for all creation.

Fourth, the church is the community or body of God's risen Messiah, the Lord Jesus. The whole is subordinate to the one who is prior to and greater than the parts. As head, the Lord Jesus defines the meaning and interrelationship of the parts that now constitute the body of the risen Lord, filling out the ancient commission of Israel. It is likely that the church came to see itself in these terms, because Jesus probably saw himself in these terms.

Most likely Jesus linked the "Son of Man" expressions (Ps 8:4; Ezek 2:1–10; Dan 7:13, 27) for the first time with Isaiah's servant and prophetic texts (Isa 42:1–4; 49:1–6; 50:4–11; 52:13–53:12; 61:1–11) and found in them a multivalent, open-ended "Help Wanted" advertisement with the built-in flexibility of referring to Israel, a remnant within Israel, and a representative individual, the Messiah. For the OT prophets, as Caird notes, "the group had a collective personality which could be embodied in an individual, and the individual was bound up with the life of the group" (1994:316). Therefore, it is probable that "Jesus used the 'Son of Man' expression in a variety of ways, and may have adopted it precisely *because* of its value in conveying the multivalent ambiguity inherent in the concept of 'the one and the many.' In this case the expression would come close to Isaiah's Servant. The Son of Man is a 'job description' for the New Israel, with Jesus inviting any and all applicants to join with him in fulfilling God's full intention, first for Israel, and then for all the nations of the earth" (Caird 1994:379–80).

Thus the Son of Man terminology functions to include all those who would respond to the gospel's invitation to join Jesus in sharing with him the demands that the kingdom is making on the Israel of the new age by filling out Jesus's existence on earth in anticipation of the new Jerusalem. For at the cross and resurrection, asserts Caird, "the humanity of Jesus ceased to be individual and becomes corporate" (1994: 292). In this way, "Jesus' primary intention was not to found what we would call a Church, but to reconstitute the nation of Israel according to the promises of Daniel and the other Old Testament prophets" (Caird 1994:384).

Fifth, the church is the new creation of God in the world that simultaneously realizes *and* points to the intention with which creation was launched. It shares already in the new-creation life by its attachment to the risen Lord, but it also continues to live within the old age, giving witness to and awaiting what is yet to be when God's reign is realized "on earth as it is in heaven" (Matt 6:10). Such a two-dimensional reality explains the sometimes-precarious existence of the church in its social and political engagements in the world; they must necessarily be *indirect*. How can engagement be indirect? Paul uses the graphic image of "the dregs" (1 Cor 4:13) to illustrate evidence of the church's indirect engagement. The church is *not* like the soap that cleans a sink full of soiled dishes, but more like the orange-colored tomato ring that remains after washing a load of spaghetti-stained dishes—the dregs give evidence of grime absorption, the mark of the church. Just as the cross unmasked evil's ancient death-dealing ways (Col 2:15), evil is undone indirectly—and the resurrection confirms Jesus's way to be indeed God's way.

Thus, God makes victory over death accessible to all who are baptized into the risen Lord; they are now able for the first time to refuse to play according to the old way of death within the domination system. While the powers will not be able to hear the church's critique fully (because they are guided by self-preservation and self-interest), this does not release the church from its obligation to stand up and unmask the powers through *indirect* action (i.e., exposing, sensitizing, testifying, and creating alternative systems). Paul understands that *direct* action against evil will not work. So, in the present, he says, it is better to be wronged than to do wrong (1 Cor 6:7), and ultimately "to overcome evil with good" (Rom 12:21). Furthermore, in contemporary terms, the church's indirect engagement with evil in society will rule out legislating Christian morality, engaging in vigilantism, and promoting violence to achieve even justifiable ends.

In the meantime, the church lives empowered by Christ's Spirit to invite one and all to abandon their rebellion against God and to choose life. In addition, the Christian community shaped by the norm of Jesus fully embraces the mandate to give witness to the powers of evil, inviting the powers also to abandon their death-dealing ways. This is how God continues to reorder the ruling authorities (Rom 13:1). Thus even the Christian's responsibility for helping to defeat evil is based on the refusal to meet evil on its own terms. Why? To crush the evil adversary with violence is to be vanquished by evil, because this means accepting evil's standards as normative (Yoder 1971:63). Again, this is not a doctrine of passivity or acquiescence to unproven affirmations. No, it is to live out of the same trust in God that Jesus pioneered and perfected (Heb 12:2).

THE CHURCH'S INTERACTION WITH CULTURE

Given these characteristics of the church, how has the church positioned itself with respect to culture through the centuries? H. Richard Niebuhr (1951) elaborated essentially five ways that the church has thought of itself in relation to human cultures.

(1) The church *of* culture: Here the church is immersed in culture to such a degree that it should be indistinguishable from culture.

Ecclesiology

Churches taking this approach hold that culture and church should be virtually interchangeable. The key adjective for church in this view would be *cultural*.

(2) The church *above* culture: Here the church is above culture in that it transcends the particularities of culture. Churches following this approach claim to be unaffected by culture, going about their business in the same way regardless of location or time. The key adjective for church in this view would be *transcendent*.

(3) The church *against* culture: Here the church aims to have little, if anything, to do with culture. Churches subscribing to this view isolate themselves from culture in an effort not to be contaminated by culture, because culture is viewed as dangerous and ungodly to the core. The key adjective for the church in this view would be *separate*.

(4) The church and culture *in paradox*: Here the church lives in a paradoxical relationship to culture. The church tries to be loyal to both Christ and culture at the same time. For churches following this pattern, the working strategy is to separate personal from public ethics. Personal ethics are shaped by Christ, but by definition, public ethics are different in that they are shaped by culture. The key adjective for the church in this view would be *dual*.

(5) The church *transforming* culture: Here the church aims to overtake culture "one elected official at a time," in an effort to Christianize the culture. Churches taking this path have as their goal to infiltrate culture, to take it over, and to fix it. The key adjective for the church in this view would *reparative*.

While the five ecclesial models do help to explain the varied ways that churches have historically thought of themselves in relation to culture, and while each taps into some aspects of the church's identity and vocation, a sixth model is not mentioned by Niebuhr: namely, the church as *outpost* of God's kingdom. This sixth model attempts to capture more adequately all five characteristics of the church's identity and vocation outlined in the previous section. The key adjectives for the church in this sixth view are *missional* (identity) and *invitational* (method). Here, as George Hunsberger observes, "the church displays the first fruits of the forgiven and forgiving people of God who are brought together across the rubble of dividing walls that have crumbled under the weight of the cross. It is the harbinger of the new humanity" (1998:103).

But why the image of an outpost for the church? An outpost picks up on the character of the church as representative of God's kingdom, *not* the sum total of God's rule in the world. Instead, the church is the end-time form of the people of God gathered around Jesus—living by the Spirit, participating in God's reign, partnering in God's mission, and inviting all to recognize who they are and who they are becoming. As a sign of the coming rule of God, the church is an anticipatory representation of the "new order of creation," living now out of the resources of the end, when all things will be made new. It is both missional *and* invitational.

Thus, the church as an outpost of God's kingdom aims to be an alternative or contrast society. It invites people to recognize at last their identity as God's beloved; they are invited to renounce their death-dealing rebellion and its resultant alienation. It invites people to engage their potential as human beings, finally now made possible by Messiah Jesus; in the church, folks are invited to appropriate their calling and partner with God in completing creation through Jesus. During these last days, the church remains a sign to culture until the end. The church employs no coercion or covert tactics, no abandonment or disdain, no segregation or compartmentalization, no disinterest or disengagement. Instead, the church, *until the end* is missional, extending God's invitation to one and all—to discover authentic life within their culturally located community of Jesus. Thus, when Jesus returns, the church is ready to join him, the returning victor (1 Thess 4:17), in completing the ordering of all creation around Jesus (Eph 1:9–14; Phil 2:10–11; Col 1:15–20). And in this way, God's kingdom is established in its fullness as "the new Jerusalem, coming down out of heaven from God" (Rev 21:22—22:7).

How could such a conceptualization of the church be diagrammed? Below is a diagram that attempts to sketch the church both as *sign* to culture and as *outpost* of God's kingdom.

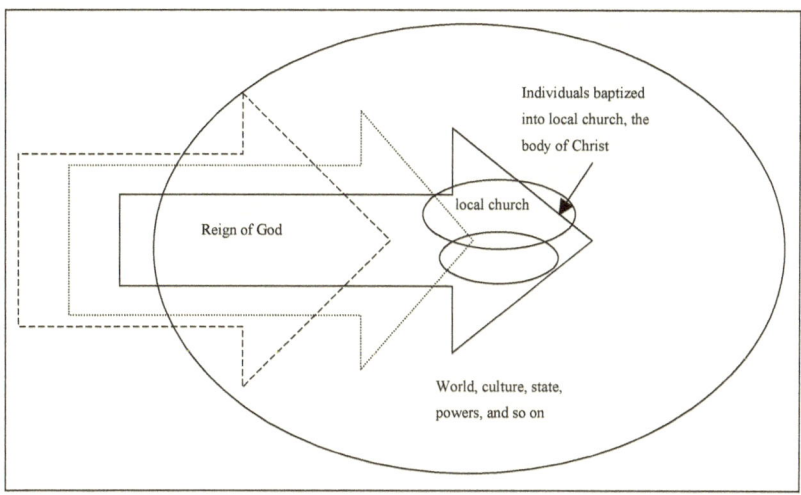

TABLE 13.1 The Church as Sign to Culture and Outpost of God's Coming Reign

As an outpost of God's kingdom, the church carries a mandate not limited to forming religious institutions that serve the larger political and social order. The NT vision of the church's mission is bigger. While God is not limited to the agency of the church, the conviction that moves the NT writers is that God has chosen the church as the primary instrument to reveal God's plan for human history (Kraus 1991:185). In Ephesians the Pauline ecclesial mission is characterized as follows:

> Although I am the very least of all the saints, this grace was given to me to bring to the Gentiles the news of the boundless riches of Christ, and to make everyone see what is the plan of the mystery hidden for ages in God who created all things; so that through the church the wisdom of God in its rich variety might now be made known to the rulers and authorities in the heavenly places. This was in accordance with the eternal purpose that he has carried out in Christ Jesus our Lord, in whom we have access to God in boldness and confidence through faith in him. (Eph 3:8–12)

Thus, the church must take seriously its role as messianic community, inviting the "powers and principalities" along with their human representatives in all sectors of society to abandon policies and practices characterized by the "domination system," and to join God's *shalom* project of completing the creation enterprise. Regardless how the church is received, the witness of the church must be faithful to the end-time shape of things, even in the present. According to Kraus, "the church's ministry is robbed of its eschatological, messianic dimensions if it neglects crucial aspects of its witness to God's universal rule and justice (Matt 6:33) and relegates that sphere to civil and political agencies" (1991:185). Given that the church is an outpost of God's kingdom, all the church's interactions have political implications.

THE CHURCH AS A POLITICAL REALITY

In popular usage the word *political* is often defined by what governments do, or what elected politicians do for their constituents, for better or worse. There is much ambivalence about "being political" in the Christian community. Some think it is absolutely necessary for Christians to be involved in all aspects of life—politics not excluded; after all, is not the church involved in political things like making decisions, assigning roles, and distributing powers? Others think that Christians should avoid political involvements; after all, is there not a separation between church and state?

John Howard Yoder (2001) argues that because the church is a body, it is necessarily political in the most basic sense of the word, and that the real question is not if but how the church is political. According to Yoder,

> The Christian community, like any community held together by commitment to important values, *is* a political reality. That is, the church has the character of a *polis* (the Greek word from which we get the adjective *political*), namely, a structured social body. It has its ways of making decisions, defining membership, and carrying out common tasks. That makes the Christian community a political reality in the simplest meaning of the term . . . The difference between church and state or between a faithful and an unfaithful church is not that one is political and the other not, but that they are political in different ways. (2001:viii, ix)

The local church's life together as an outpost of the kingdom of God includes a vocational calling not only to represent God's reign but also to function as a social organism, a *polis*, where the stuff of life—power, rank, money, conflict, memories, feelings—is negotiated from a new center stamped with the cruciform image of Jesus. Yoder (2001) lists five practices drawn from the NT writings that function as a pattern for the church's political witness before the watching world.

First, as we have already seen, the church practices "binding and loosing," involving moral discernment, naming, forgiveness, liberation, restitution, discipline, and reconciliation. The aim is always restorative, not punitive. In other words, the Christian community is equipped not with a code to protect but with a decision-making potential such that the community's action *is* God's action (Acts 15:28). Thus the inevitable conflicts that arise when people live together are negotiated within a redemptive dialogue, which is "not merely a palliative strategy for tolerable survival . . . but a mode of truth-finding and community-building" (Yoder 2001:13). Whether or not such activity is successful in the short-term, it is by such activity that the church models for the world what both are ultimately called to be and do.

Second, the church practices "breaking bread together," sharing the eucharistic meal in memory of Jesus with thanksgiving to God. Initially, this practice grew out of the community's practice of gathering to eat together for material sustenance. According to Yoder, "the meal Jesus blessed that evening and claimed as his memorial was their *ordinary* partaking together of food for the body" (2001:16). Luke notes that the first disciples' common life manifested itself in four activities: "They devoted themselves to the apostles' teaching and fellowship, to the breaking of bread and the prayers" (Acts 2:42). Whenever they gathered for the common meal (an extension of the Jewish tradition of table fellowship), they demonstrated the economic formation that characterized the new social reality that the Jesus movement represented. It spoke of hospitality, community formation, and economic solidarity, as all participants had their basic needs met—a mark of the messianic age. Again, the political and social implications are clear.

Third, the church practices "baptism and the new humanity," where baptism signals a person's introduction or initiation into the "new" people of God. The old-age barriers of rank and status are being rendered inoperative within the newly reconfigured people of God, as people are added to the body of the risen Lord. This new humanity transcends the differences in status and rank (Jew/Gentile, male/female, slave/free; Gal 3:28) that previously divided people. Baptism marks the interethnic and interclass inclusivism that signals a new phase in world history begun by Messiah Jesus. According to Yoder, "the primary characterization of that newness is that now within history there is a group of people for whom it is not exaggerating to call a 'new word' or a 'new humanity'" (2001:37).

Even though the egalitarian movement of the NT writers was betrayed for centuries within Christian history, the equality message within the practice of the early church continues to call Christian communities everywhere and at all times to give witness to the "new humanity" gathered around Jesus as it continues to take shape. This is the mission of God before the watching world.

Fourth, the church practices "the fullness of Christ." This is the Pauline language (Eph 4:11–13) to describe the new mode of group relationships in which every member of the body of Christ "has a distinctly identifiable, divinely validated, and empowered role" (Yoder 2001:47). The diversity of enablements along with the complementarity of giftings and roles give witness to a pattern of social organization profoundly different from those typically practiced both then and now, where a group's power is located in just a few individuals. The early Christian practice of power sharing and gift deployment (Rom 12:3–8; 1 Cor 12:1–30; Eph 4:1–16) was social activity not culturally available at the time and has been unevenly appreciated or continued through Christian history. The counterintuitive and countertraditional practice of early Christian community organization provides a powerful alternative to the "business-as-usual" hierarchies of domination that characterize so many social realities, including religious institutions. Sadly, however, Paul's vision has yet to be consciously and consistently lived out. Yoder offers the following analysis:

> Soon, as we have already seen, the sweeping Pauline vision was lost. Because no central authority existed in the early churches, it probably never generally won out in the first place. The notion that there are several ministries remained for a while—deacon and deaconess, lector, exorcist—but the conviction that *every* member of the body is charismatically empowered for a nameable role was soon lost. We need not ask whether the "blame" for this loss should be assigned to a resurgence of patriarchal social habits or to the assimilation of pagan notions of sacrificial cult or to certain threats of disorder which someone felt a need to ward off or to the domination of later generations by the habits of churches which had never heard or accepted the Pauline message in the first place. We often forget that what we call the New Testament canon was not that for two centuries . . . This specimen should make us aware that the New Testament contains resources for critique and renewal that have not yet been tapped. (2001:57, 59)

The fourth practice of every-member empowerment is a dimension of the gospel vision that remains on the church's agenda and, thus, the social impact of the practice before the watching world remains to be seen. For example, ecclesiastical debates over who can or cannot be "ordained" fall far short of the radical social reality envisioned by the early Jesus communities. It would be far more radical and more appropriate to reorient the notion of ministry, ordination, and mission, "so that there would be no one ungifted, no one not called, no one not empowered, and no one dominated" (Yoder 2001:60).

Fifth, the church practices "Spirit-moved deliberation" such that the will of God is discerned as consensus arises within a local Jesus community through uncoerced and open conversation (Acts 15:28). There is special concern not to overrule the unconvinced or absent voices by majority vote or parliamentary closure. Why? Because until everyone who wants to speak to an issue has spoken, the Spirit of Christ is not clearly known (1 Cor 14:26). The commitment to hear even from the "opposing side" or "dissenting voices" is connected to the insight that one's adversary is part of one's truth-finding process; in a very real way, the adversary needs to hear me, and I need to hear the adversary. Can local manifestations of the body of Christ be permitted to arrive at conclusions validated by consensus? Will this not result in chaotic diversity? In anarchy? In fragmented denominational structures? Yoder responds in two ways and offers the following assessment:

> A reasonable part of the answer is to say that such decentralization, founded in the belief that the Spirit speaks to and through everyone, will enable wholesome and realistic flexibility in adapting to local occasions and needs. The stronger, more theological, part of the answer is, however, that because Jesus Christ is always and everywhere the same, any procedure that yields sovereignty to the direction of his spirit will have ultimately to create unity. What does not create unity is centralized power tactics of the Caesars, the Inquisitors, or any other patriarchs or paternalists. A monarchical decree is quicker than careful listening, but is usually wrong. A quick majority vote may reach a decision more rapidly but without resolving the problem or convincing the overpowered minority, so that the conflict remains . . . Because God the Spirit speaks in the meeting, conversation is the setting for truth-finding. (2001:69–70)

The fifth practice of consensus-based discernment instructs local ecclesial communities on how to hold meetings and make decisions in the power of the Spirit. While different outcomes may result from such deliberation processes in one community compared with another, a discernable familial resemblance is able to span the diversity and hold them together in the unity of Christ. Jesus communities—on the local level as well as on the denominational level, in different times, cultures, and contexts—continue to find resources for living together by holding three values simultaneously: self-differentiation, connectedness, and nonjudgmentalism. A sobering yet liberating realization is that all ecclesial verdicts, whether acknowledged or not, carry the disclaimer "interim decision," as the final judgment remains in the hands of God, the ultimate arbiter.

These five apostolic practices prescribe a social process that is profoundly political and yet one that differs markedly from contemporary Western political thought. Precisely for this reason, these five ecclesial ideals offer concrete ways that the gospel of Christ lives out its testimony before the watching world, inviting it to abandon rebellion and choose a *theonomous* relationship with God. After all, according to Yoder, "the believing body of Christ is the world on the way to its renewal; the church is the part of the world that confesses the renewal to which all the world is called" (2001:78).

In the next chapter, the last one, our attention is focused on sketching out the NT vision for the goal and character of the completion of creation; this is the study of the "last things" or eschatology.

EXERCISES

1. As Western society moves to a post-Christian or post-Christendom framework, and loses shared values about God, morality, family, and so on, the church is confronted with some real challenges. There are all sorts of possible Christian responses; these could be described as isolationist, concessionist, and critical-engagement.

    Discuss how you feel about the major societal and cultural shifts happening in the Western world. Are there any losses that you mourn? If so, what are they? Are there opportunities that capture your imagination? If so, what are they? Where have you encountered isolationist or concessionist behavior? If so, what did you learn from these encounters? How does an approach of critical-engagement differ from either the isolationist or concessionist approaches? How does your host culture promote or distort the values championed by the NT witness to God's rule? In what ways could the church enhance its engagement with your host culture?

2. Select a church tradition; it could be your own or one in which you are interested. Research its founding narrative: What are its key values, beliefs, confessions, and practices? Trace the trajectory of its growth and development over the years from its birth. How has it changed? What appears to have remained constant through the changes? Can you locate the church's tradition on Niebuhr's typology of the ways that churches relate to culture? If so, where does it fit? What is the evidence for your assessment? Talk with some representatives of the church tradition and discuss your research. If you were a church consultant, what assets could you highlight and what suggestions could you make to these representatives of God's reign?

14

Eschatology

Picturing the Goal and Completion of Creation

W E HAVE LEFT ESCHATOLOGY for last. It seems appropriate to study the NT writers' vision of the "last things" and the "future hope" for creation in the last chapter of a NT theology book. This chapter has three objectives: (1) to trace the development of eschatology and the afterlife within Judaism, (2) to describe three contemporary forms of eschatology, and (3) to explore the NT images of the final judgment.

THE MEANING AND DEVELOPMENT OF ESCHATOLOGY AND THE AFTERLIFE

The word *eschatology* is a slippery term. The reason for this is that not everyone means the same thing by the term. While it is a relatively new word, first used in 1845, it has been the source of much controversy and dispute. Part of the difficulty with the word eschatology is that it has come to mean two very divergent forms of the future hope.

Initially, the nineteenth-century term *eschatology* referred to the ultimate destiny of the *individual* (death, judgment, heaven, and hell). However, the term was soon also used to cover the biblical teaching about the destiny of the *world* and the working out of God's purposes in and through God's people, the nation of Israel (e.g., dispensationalism; see below). That is, the term *eschatology* began to refer to the historical significance of Israel as a nation. The problem is that these two different forms of eschatology (individual and national) began to be mixed together in the assumption that the finality associated with death, judgment, heaven, and hell for individuals was also linked to a national eschatology and the unfolding of world affairs. In order to make this mixture work, the biblical writers' imagery picturing the Day of the Lord was increasingly read with a dangerous form of literalism, which was used to timetable the prospects of the world's nations. In this view, the world wars of the last century and the global conflicts of this century are seen as evidence in support of such a reading of biblical eschatology.

The complexity of the issue is exacerbated by the diversity of meanings attached to the last things in the Bible itself. In the OT almost the only kind of future hope we find is in *historical* terms. Almost all the books in the OT were written before some began to appreciate the *individual* dimensions of an afterlife in the intertestamental times. By the NT times, among both Jews and Christians, there is a well-established view of life beyond death. This development between the testaments means that it is not always easy to discern whether a biblical text is dealing with national or individual eschatology.

So how did the development of eschatological thinking take place within Judaism? We can say that most of the period covered by the OT shows no evidence of individual eschatology or belief in afterlife for individuals. This makes sense, given the collectivist understanding of identity among ancient peoples. For example, the death of a patriarch is described as being "gathered to his people" (Gen 25:8). When Jacob gives his final speech, he does *not* say, "I am going up to a better place in heaven." He says, "I am about to be gathered to my people. Bury me with my ancestors—in the cave in the field of Ephron ... There Abraham and his wife Sarah were buried; there Isaac and his wife Rebekah were buried; and there I buried Leah" (Gen 49:29–33). When Joseph dies, he asks that his brothers promise to bring his bones with them when they go to Canaan (Gen 50:24–26; Exod 13:19). The point is that God's blessings are experienced in the present with one's people, the clan. The emphasis is on the continuity of life in the people, not in an afterlife of an individual. God's blessings (e.g., health, wealth, family, and the like) and judgments (e.g., disasters, wars, and so forth) are all achieved in real time, in the historical life of the clan and nation.

Still, the OT does provide the grounds on which postexilic Hebrews developed an understanding of the afterlife, probably with some help from their Hellenistic neighbors. In addition to the patriarchal experience, the OT clearly testifies to God's power over the forces of death and destruction. For example, the psalmist is convinced that nothing can separate one from the presence of God, even if one is far away in a place called Sheol, the shadowy existence of death. He says, "If I make my bed in Sheol, you are there" (Ps 139:8). It was not a great leap before the promise of an everlasting life with God was interpreted by some postexilic Hebrew people in a manner that filled out the biblical texts' meaning, since God's people could never be out of God's reach. Consider these psalms: "I wait for the Lord, my soul waits, and in his word I hope; my soul waits for the Lord" (Ps 130:5) and "You do not give me up to Sheol, or let your faithful one see the Pit" (Ps 16:10).

No doubt some Jews found the Greek worldview partially helpful in their own developing view of the afterlife. The Greeks based their view of the afterlife on Plato's idea that the physical world was merely a shadow of the ideal—there was a clear division between body and soul (see Plato's Myth of the Cave). The body (*sōma*) was the earthly prison for the eternal soul (*psychē*). After a loved one's death, Greek families continued to commune with the dead person's immortal soul by eating with them and seeking their advice. While Jews did not believe that human beings were immortal souls entombed in mortal bodies, the line between Semitic and Greek views should not be drawn too starkly; recall Saul's encounter with the medium of Endor, who conjures up the soul of the dead Samuel (1 Samuel 28).

During the Second Temple period, apocalyptic Judaism (beginning in 200 BCE) transformed Judaism in some radical ways. The growing conviction was that God must intervene and bring an end to the corruption of human history and the oppression of God's people. Things are just so bad that no nation on earth can legitimately carry out God's judgments as in the days of old. If there is to be a new age, it must begin with a chosen agent who brings God's rule from the outside.

Thus, Israel's servant texts (Isa 42:1-4; 49:1-6; 50:4-11; 52:13—53:12) and Son of Man terminology were filled with great anticipation; they were interpreted to refer to a righteous Israelite remnant and especially to a messianic freedom fighter for the people of Israel (Dan 7:13). The presence of Qumran community and other apocalyptic and messianic movements around the time of Jesus of Nazareth are evidence of these ideals, although Jesus's nonviolent version of messianism was a unique framing of these traditions. Still, from these tentative beginnings a belief in an afterlife of the individual and in a general resurrection of the righteous at the end of time rapidly matured during Israel's apocalyptic period (Dan 12:2), until by the NT times all but the Sadducees accepted it (2 Macc 12:39–45).

An important observation needs to be made at this point. The growing conviction among the Israelite people of an afterlife for the individual must not be confused with the Greek idea of the immortality of the soul separate from a body. How then did the NT writers imagine their confidence of "remaining in the presence of God" beyond death? Paul is the one who articulates most clearly what must have been the common early Christian view. For them, the language of "resurrection" became associated with the afterlife, since the risen dead would need bodies in order to carry on (1 Cor 15:42–49). Unlike the Greek world, the Semitic world had no disdain for the body and did not see a soul as existing separately from a body. This explains why Paul had such trouble with the young Corinthian Christians whose inherited worldview was Greco-Roman paganism. They thought Paul was unsophisticated by talking about resurrection of the body. Paul insists (1 Cor 15:35–41), on the contrary, that it is *they* who are fools to think that souls would not have an appropriate body (Hays 1997:270).

Apparently, Paul's instructions were not well understood by his Gentile converts, who mixed Paul's gospel with popular Greek ideas of the "immortality of the soul." Paul argues vigorously (1 Cor 15:42–49) for a highly nuanced idea of a "bodily resurrection," which is not a natural or physical body (so as to exclude a walking corpse), but neither is a disembodied spirit (so as to exclude a ghost). Instead, Paul describes resurrection as a "spiritual body" in order to show the continuity (it is a body!) and discontinuity (it is spiritual!) between the natural order and the resurrected order.

Furthermore, the end is not about winged flight, where God's people escape the earth as creation burns up in massive destruction. Instead, Paul uses the image of the traditional Roman victory march where the cheering crowds run out of the city gates to join the returning, triumphant soldiers making their way back into the city under the archway and through the streets (Sanders 1991:30). The people's shouts of celebration and victory accompany the soldiers as they enter the city with plunder and captives in tow. Paul says, "Then we who are alive, who are left, will be caught up in the clouds together with them to meet the Lord in the air; and so we will be with the Lord forever" (1 Thess 4:17). Thus, the existing world gathers around the Lord Jesus, so as to bring to completion at last the creation project begun so long ago—the transformation of all things (Rom 8:18-25), as the "new Jerusalem" comes down to earth from heaven (Rev 21:2).

To picture the afterlife of the individual, the NT writers use two ways of talking about this event (Caird 1994:271-73). They describe it as: (1) entry into the final state at the time of death, so that one is "with Christ" (Phil 1:23); and (2) the "sleep of death" until all are roused at the last trumpet (Phil 3:20-21). For some Western thinkers these assertions fail what is called the "law of noncontradiction." The perceived problem is that both assertions cannot be true at the same time. However, the biblical writers were not oriented by Western logic, and these kinds of paradoxical assertions are frequent in the biblical literature, as we have seen already. This feature of Semitic style, known as *parataxis*, refers to the happy positioning of two apparently contradictory ideas side by side (Caird 1994:262).

But are these assertions—being with Christ *and* waiting for the last trumpet—really contradictory? Not necessarily, but two comments are needed here. First, the NT writers were likely speaking about the same thing, but from different perspectives. To the sleeping person, the next thing one remembers is waking. The passage of time is not experienced. This makes every death equidistant from eternity. Second, the NT writers also do not appear to anticipate that their language about the afterlife of the individual would be taken with "flat-footed literalness" (Caird 1997:248). Thus, both assertions can be held together.

Still, we need to be very clear about one thing: for most Jews, the term *resurrection* denoted a single event when the ages changed, when the old-world order came to an end, and all the righteous are raised to receive new bodies (Dan 12:2). So when the early Christians gave witness to the resurrection of Jesus, this shattered their inherited "symbolic map" of the way they had perceived the world to work. The first Christians picked up the pieces of their shattered map, so their newly reconstructed map necessarily was limited to the end-of-the-world language of the old map for that which was not yet the end of the world, but clearly stamped with the character of the end; the only tool in their toolbox capable of accounting for their experience was end-of-the-world language! As it turns out, this was this tool that proved most adequate to articulate their new concept of eschatology, one that was mediated by their religious experience of the risen Lord among them, which changed and expanded in several ways their previous understanding of the last things. For example, as we have seen already, Jesus became identified as the "first fruits" of the general resurrection that was yet to come; thus, the old age and the new age must necessarily overlap for a time (1 Cor 10:11), and the Day of the Lord must be expanded to include both the initial coming (Col 3:1) *and* the final coming or return of the Lord at the end of time (1 Cor 15:51–52).

THREE CONTEMPORARY FORMS OF ESCHATOLOGY

Unfortunately, it would be wrong to say that the stretching of the term *eschatology* has been uniformly understood. As we have seen, the term *eschatology* has been stretched from the historical concerns of the patriarchs to include individual afterlife (in the biblical narrative), and from an individual's afterlife to include the destiny of the world in relation to Israel (in contemporary Western Christian history). It would be more correct to say that the term *eschatology* has been extremely divisive in NT theology. Well-meaning Christians have generated more heat than light in their articulations of the *eschaton*. Today much of eschatological teaching is characterized by an unhelpful and even dangerous flat-footed literalness. Two very common forms are described below before a third form is considered as an alternative.

First, *consistent eschatology*: this view emerged in the nineteenth century and argued that the *parousia* expectation must have become obsolete and embarrassing for the early church, after Jesus did not return. Adherents to this view contend that when Jesus handed himself over to the authorities to be killed, it was his attempt to force God to bring the end of the old world and usher in the new. Jesus expected God to intervene. As this did not happen, Jesus died under a dark cloud of disappointment. Paul and the early Christians re-interpreted this disappointment by asserting that through a mystical union with Christ, initiation into the messianic kingdom could be actualized. Advocates of consistent eschatology point to the apparent contradictions in the speeches of Jesus. In Mark, Jesus says that the end cannot happen for a long time (Mark 13:7), *and* Jesus says that the disciples are to be ready for it at any moment (Mark 13:30–32). This, it is claimed, is not consistent—it sounds like "hurry up and wait."

Paul's instructions in 1–2 Thessalonians are also not seen as consistent in this view. Paul encourages the young church to be ready at any moment since the Day of the Lord comes "like a thief" (1 Thess 4:13—5:11). Then he tells these same Christians that the Day could not happen yet as a number of things need to transpire first (2 Thess 2:1–12). Again, this is not consistent—at least according to the "law of noncontradiction"—and can only mean, it is claimed, that Jesus and Paul were mistaken. Disillusioned, but not defeated, the early Christians tried to salvage the embarrassing situation by adding a new feature—delay— to the tradition in order to account for the nonreturn of Jesus, calling it the "delay of the *parousia*."

The problem with consistent eschatology is that it assumes that the apparent contradictions mean one exhortation was *early* (pre-Easter) and the other *late* (post-Easter), because Jesus and Paul could not have held both at the same time. Or could they have? As we have seen on several occasions, this Western assessment does not give sufficient sensitivity to *parataxis*, which was a common form of self-expression in the Semitic world. Consistent eschatology suffers from flat-footed literalness.

Second, *dispensational eschatology* also emerged in the nineteenth century, and grows out of another type of "consistent" reading of biblical literature. However, here the focus is on the literal interpretation of biblical symbols and images. Fundamental to dispensationalism is the conviction that God's plan for saving the world unfolds in historically distinguishable "dispensations" or "economies," each of which is subject to a particular revelation for that time period. There is step-by-step action as God's timetable unfolds so that the content of saving faith varies with each successive dispensation. Usually seven dispensations are identified:

(1) Innocence (before the Fall)
(2) Conscience (from the Fall to Noah)
(3) Human Government (from Noah to Abraham)
(4) Promise (from Abraham to Moses)
(5) Law (from Moses to Christ)
(6) Grace (the church age)
(7) the Kingdom (the millennium).

This sevenfold schema of world history was popularized in America by the *Scofield Reference Bible,* published first in 1909 and revised in 1917 and again in 1967.

Using a literalist-interpretation method, dispensationalism attempts to translate the symbolic language of the apocalyptic genre in Daniel and Revelation into a literal map forecasting the political outcomes still in the future. Of particular interest is Revelation 20:1–6, where the millennium is read as a literal thousand-year reign of Christ before the final judgment. Key to the scheme is distinguishing God's program for Israel from God's program for the church. Specifically, the church does not begin in the OT, but at Pentecost. Neither does the church carry forward the promises made to Israel in the OT. Instead, the church is in one dispensation, and the kingdom of God is in the following dispensation where Israel is again the central focus. During the present, church dispensation, individuals are saved by trusting in Jesus. However, in the future kingdom dispensation during the millennium, Israel accepts Jesus as its political Messiah, and the nation of Israel carries out the Messiah's political rule. In this way, the nation of Israel wages war against evil until evil is eventually defeated. However, just before the inauguration of the thousand-year reign, the church is "raptured" out of the world to escape the intense backlash of evil (tribulation) at Messiah Jesus's return with his iron rod and military might. Following evil's defeat at the Last Battle of Armageddon, the Millennium closes, ushering in the Eternal State.

The problems with dispensational eschatology are numerous.

(1) Separating the church from Israel runs counter to Paul's entire argument in Romans, not to mention Jesus's teaching in the Sermon on the Mount ("Do not think that I have come to abolish the law or the prophets; I have come not to abolish but to fulfill," Matt 5:17).

(2) Separating the church from the kingdom of God severs the continuity that Jesus announced and illegitimately brackets out the ethical implications of Jesus's preaching (e.g., the Sermon on the Mount) as not applicable to the church age.

(3) Dispensationalism suggests that Messiah Jesus comes at the *parousia* in a different way (as a sword-wielding warrior) from the Messiah that was crucified and raised (as the suffering servant). Such a revision calls into question the normative character of God's self-disclosure in Jesus of Nazareth.

Like consistent eschatology, dispensational eschatology also suffers from flat-footed literalism. Is there an alternative? Yes!

Third, in contrast to both of the above constructions, *metaphorical eschatology* argues that the NT writers were essentially consistent, although in a *paratactical* sense (Caird 1994:243–67). The NT writers believed literally that the world had had a beginning in the past and would have an end in the future (unlike their pagan neighbors, who saw time as an endlessly rotating wheel). The goal was certain even if all the parts between the beginning and end were not fully known. Furthermore, the NT writers regularly used end-of-the-world language metaphorically to refer to that which they well knew was *not* the end of the world (Caird 1997:256).

For example, Jesus himself said that the "end" of Jerusalem would happen within a generation (which happened); however, only God knows the time of the final end (Mark 13:28–37). Jesus was referring to the pending crisis within Israel. According to Caird, "Jesus believed that Israel was called by God to be the agent of [God's] purpose, and that he himself had been sent to bring about that reformation without which Israel could not fulfill its national destiny" (1994:365–66). For Israel to reject its mission could only lead to destruction. Was this the end of the world? No, the destruction of the temple (70 CE) was a sign of the end, not the end itself. Still, the warning issued by Jesus is still worth heeding, regardless of how long time would continue following the destruction of the temple. Jesus announces that the time is short, and that Israel must choose between two conceptions of its national destiny: one that is self-serving, or one that is missional. The consequences of this decision are real. Since God is constantly calling God's servant Israel to account, the end is constantly impacting upon the present. So at one level, the destruction of Jerusalem is the end; but on another level, it points to the end (Caird 1994:256). Is this inconsistent? No, it is totally consistent with the evocative language and imagery of the prophetic tradition that Jesus embodied as Israel's Messiah.

Let us examine another passage of Scripture. Paul instructs young people contemplating marriage to "remain as they are" (1 Cor 7:20, 24, 26), not because the time is short chronologically before the end, but because "the old regime is beginning to disintegrate" (Caird 1994:253), and they should expect to live under harsh pressure to give up their newly found primary allegiance to the Lord. So they are instructed not to give in to the temptation to place anything other than God's kingdom at the center of their lives: not ethnic status, not civil status, and not sexual status (Matt 6:33; Gal 3:28). Instead, they are to "remain as they are" in their newly found identity as God's beloved through Jesus Christ. Is this inconsistent? No, Paul also uses the same kind of urgency and crisis language of the prophetic tradition, not in a flat-footed, literal way, but rather to impress upon his young churches the consequential nature of joining Jesus in filling out the Israel of the new age; for to confess God's kingdom as central is to reorient all relations, making them all subject to the lordship of Jesus.

Certainly many times the NT writers do insist on the "nearness of the end" (Luke 21:5-36; Rom 13:11-14; 1 Cor 7:29-31; 15:51-52; Phil 4:5; 1 Thess 4:15-17; 2 Thess 2:1-12; Heb 10:25; Jas 5:8-9; 1 Pet 4:7; 1 John 2:18; Rev 22:20). However, these appear to be metaphorical references employed for their evocative and formational value, because whenever people do misunderstand them to be literally speaking about the end in chronological or temporal terms (say, in a few years), these people are portrayed as people in error (Luke 21:8; John 21:23; 2 Pet 3:3-10). Instead, it is the nature of the end that people do not know how long it will last. Evidently the "nearness" language of the NT writers has more to do with a relational nuance (as in, "I like it when you sit near me") than a temporal nuance (as in, "it is nearly time for dinner"). It is the relational nuance of "near" that is affirmed by the NT writers, as the end-time reality powers the ethical and behavioral norms of God's end-time people, even in the now time. Believers, therefore, are always encouraged by the NT writers to be fully engaged in their societies, actively anticipating and living out of God's rule in the present.

The key to metaphorical eschatology is the conviction that the end continues to impact the present. In this reading, the character of the end-time period continues because of God's patience, as God "desires everyone to be saved and to come to knowledge of the truth" (1 Tim 2:4), and therefore "the good news must first be proclaimed to all the nations" (Mark 13:10). In the meantime, metaphorical eschatological discourse carries forward the prophetic and apostolic tradition of calling God's people to consequential living. In other words, as a consequence of the new identity that believers share in their attachment to the risen Lord, the focus remains on formation and ethical living. The NT writers' eschatological discourse uses the evocative imagery of the end to exhort the church to ethical faithfulness; it is not to cause fear but to motivate with hope.

During the extension of the end-time period—the period from the beginning of the end (at the cross/resurrection) to the end of the end (at the close of this age)—the church lives in tension. On the one hand, it prays "thy kingdom come" (Matt 6:10; Rev 22:20), but on the other hand, it lives alert and engaged in faithful, missional, and invitational living. The church holds up the sign of the kingdom, as an outpost of what is coming. Eschatological discourse is intended to encourage faithfulness and to discourage speculative calendarization. The center point of metaphorical eschatology is the faithfulness and triumph of God in Jesus Christ. Jesus is God's Yes to all creation, and Jesus is humanity's Yes to God (2 Cor 1:20). God's work of salvation on behalf of humanity was accomplished once and for all in the representative person of Jesus: the one who finally and fully unified the human and the divine in a way that "God had intended from all eternity to be the destiny of the human race" (Caird 1994:337). In this way, metaphorical eschatology attempts to take seriously the symbolic character of the NT writers' apocalyptic language, allowing it to continue to encourage, challenge, and correct God's people today, as it did in the first century, with the hope of Christ's return at the close of this age.

THE FINAL JUDGMENT

All that remains in this chapter about "last things" is a frank and open discussion about the NT witness to the final judgment and the consequential character of human beings living in God's world with the mandate to steward (Gen 1:28; Ps 8:6-8) and complete creation with God (Eph 3:8-12). So, what are the NT images of the final judgment? The NT writers use language that has given rise to four basic interpretations of the final judgment (Kraus 1991:212-15). Each of them is but a partial picture, often raising more questions. In other words, each interpretation illuminates some aspect of the final judgment but if pushed too hard or taken exclusively proves less helpful and even distracting. Let's review each one.

First, *literal eternal punishment* (Matt 25:1-46) describes a scenario where those who die without acknowledging Jesus as God's Messiah are punished eternally in hell. The NT image behind this interpretation is Gehenna, the smoldering garbage dump outside Jerusalem (Matt 5:22;

18:9). Gehenna is understood to refer to the punishing fires of hell, and the word *eternal* is taken chronologically as "everlasting." The strength of this interpretation is that it certainly provides a vivid picture of the serious consequences of ongoing rebellion against God and continued allegiance to the death-dealing ways of sin. However, a punitive hell does not deal satisfactorily with God's goodness. If evil continues to be punished in hell, then evil still exists and will never be eradicated. Can God be happy with a scenario where most of the world burns in eternal punishment? This is not a very successful rescue plan. Furthermore, how can that which undergoes destruction never be destroyed?

Second, *annihilation of evil* (2 Pet 3:3–15) is built on the NT image of the purifying heat of the refiner's fire. This scenario imagines Jesus's return in a different fashion from the way he lived and ministered during his life. Here, instead of unmasking the powers of evil by challenging them at Golgotha as the suffering servant, Jesus returns to take direct action: he bombs the enemy to nothingness. In fact, all creation is burned up and dissolved by intense heat and fire, but the righteous ones are rescued to repopulate the new heaven and earth. The strength of this interpretation is that it also provides a powerful reminder of the fact that evil will be defeated in the end. However, in this scenario, the Creator sustains staggering losses as most of creation is destroyed. How effective is this rescue operation? According to Gen 8:21, God promises never to destroy the world again. Furthermore, this solution also gives evil the last word, since in the end God uses evil's instrument of death to wipe out creation.

Third, *conditional immortality* (Rev 21:1–8) is constructed on the NT image of the heavenly throne-room scene of ultimate judgment. This interpretation imagines a scenario where heaven is seen as the final stage in life's journey. Heaven provides the realization of the fullness of God's presence. This view takes the Semitic idea of embodiment seriously, since only those acknowledging the rule of God will have their souls embodied; only they pass the throne of judgment to eternal life. All the rest remain dead because, having removed themselves from the love of the Father, they cannot live. Without access to the Tree of Life, sinful humanity simply dies and stays dead—they perish. Hell is the self-chosen state of the nonliving, or "the second death." The strength of this interpretation is that it takes seriously the consequences of human choices. However, this scenario also has problems. Again, God's salvation plan seems impotent and ultimately limited by human beings. God seems weak and not very loving. Can you imagine a parent saying to the child, "Go ahead play in the traffic; I warned you, but if you insist, go ahead and get yourself killed"?

Fourth, *creation completion* (Col 1:9–20) is assembled on the NT image of creation's having a beginning, a middle, and eventually an end. This interpretation describes yet another scenario where Christ's victory over sin, evil, and death is for all creation. In Christ, all things are reconciled to God the Father. In the end, love does overcome evil and all is perfected. God's invitational love is indefatigable and ultimately triumphant. Paul is convinced that one day "all Israel" will be saved (Rom 11:25), meaning presumably representatives from all the nations (Gen 12:1–3). However, this scenario should not be confused with universalism, which holds that all ways, whether good or evil, eventually lead to God without any need to abandon rebellion against the Creator. Rather, the picture is one in which God never withdraws the offer of life (Luke 15).

In this scenario, unbelievers who enter death experience the shock and pain of entering a lighted room, accustomed as they are to living in darkness. Those who persist in refusing to embrace the light will only experience more pain, not less, in hell. However, God is able to outwait "even the vilest offender" (as in the old Fanny Crosby hymn, "To God be the Glory") who turns at last to abandon the ways of death, darkness, and destruction so that "at the name of Jesus every knee should bend" (Phil 2:10). The strength of this interpretation is that it tries to balance God's sovereignty with human freedom and to imagine judgment as clarification, illumination, and discernment—not as vindictive punishment.

However, this scenario also has its challenges. It requires the recalibration of the church's mission toward a more asset-based mission as opposed to a need-based mission. Questions to the world in an asset-based mission might include, e.g., what do you have to begin with? Who are you? How can we continue the transformation together? Also, the imperatives of Christian discipleship require reorientation toward a more centered-set approach, as opposed to bounded-set approach. Questions about discipleship in a centered-set approach might include, e.g., what direction are you moving? How goes the journey? How can we mutually encourage one another along the way? Still, in the end, this view of the final judgment is dependent on the rational capabilities and good judgment of human beings. How reasonable is this? What about those who appear incapable of good choices, no matter how many chances they are given?

All four of these scenarios of the final judgment are interpretations that emerge from the imagery used by the NT writers. Should they be reduced to one? Should some be ruled out? Should one be given preference? This journey through NT theology has emphasized the diversity of NT voices and images. So at one level, it is *impossible* to reconcile these four NT images of the final judgment. Any one scenario effectively eliminates the other three. However, at another level, each scenario does illuminate some aspects of the NT writers' witness to the final judgment. To eliminate any would be to claim more than we can or should, as all four derive from NT imagery. Still, there are three things that ought to be said when constructing a biblical theology of the final judgment.

First, however the concept of the final judgment is imagined, it must be shaped by the self-disclosure of God in Jesus. It is theologically inconsistent to say that God will abandon God's character of *agape* love at some point in the future. Jesus is not expected to operate differently in the end than he did during his ministry; the old-age notion of redemptive violence does not get reactivated in the end. At the same time, it is equally inconsistent to imagine that God could "wink" at evil, as if it did not matter. God's face is firmly set against evil and will not allow it to have the final word.

Second, however the final judgment is conceived, it must not let human cooperation or human freedom be trivialized, manipulated, or eliminated. Both double predestination and universalism trample on this fundamental freedom characteristic of God and the humanity created in God's image.

Third, however the final judgment is conceptualized, it must keep the church's mandate clearly focused on God's mission to invite all creation and every individual to authentic life and to unalienated relationship. The invitation is to return home, to rediscover one's true and prior identity as God's beloved. God's mission is not about providing "hellfire insurance," but about the tremendous opportunities to experience authentic living from now on. The gospel invitation is to come along now and begin to experience authentic living; it will only get more difficult to come along if one persists in rebellion. There is much to miss, even now, by insisting on choosing the consequences of hell: alienation from God.

See C. S. Lewis's insightful and provocative argument for heaven and hell in *The Great Divorce*.

No better image can close the discussion of the last things and the future hope than the one painted by John the seer. It is a glorious picture emphasizing the unmediated presence of God with God's people, the drawing up of the human into the divine, the coming down of God to dwell fully with humanity, the completion of the creation project begun so long ago, the multinational character of God's *shalom* project, the celebration of human ingenuity, the open access to further creation projects, and the absence of evil.

> I saw no temple in the city, for its temple is the Lord God the Almighty and the Lamb. And the city has no need of sun or moon to shine on it, for the glory of God is its light, and its lamp is the Lamb. The nations will walk by its light, and the kings of the earth will bring their glory into it. Its gates will never be shut by day—and there will be no night there. People will bring into it the glory and the honor of the nations. But nothing unclean will enter it, nor anyone who practices abomination or falsehood, but only those who are written in the Lamb's book of life. (Rev 21:22–27)

EXERCISES

1. The development of the afterlife tradition in Judaism predisposes one to anticipate growth in the human understanding of the divine. This is a given, since growth is built into creation by God's design and its completion is yet to be realized. However, such an admission does not necessarily mean that all theological developments are equally helpful or worthy of endorsement.

   One religious ideal that has crept into some forms of Christianity is the Greco-Roman notion of the immortality of the soul. It comes up in many popular Christian expressions such as when parents at the birth of a child are acknowledged as "welcoming baby Jordan into their family." Such a statement could be construed to mean that baby Jordan existed as an immortal soul in heaven prior to birth, waiting for the appropriate body and family to be born into. This theological development, unlike the afterlife development, does not have a link to Judaism. Why? Because it trivializes the body and undermines the creative work that parents do making a baby "out of nothing." In the

Judeo-Christian tradition both the body and creation are affirmed as a testimony to God's own creative power. Jordan did not exist before conception, and Jordan's body, soul, and spirit are bound together in a complete whole.

Another popular expression of the immortality of the soul occurs at the other end of the life cycle: at funerals. Consider the excerpt below from Richard Hays's commentary on 1 Corinthians 15 (1997:279). What thoughts go through your mind as you read this story? How could you design a funeral service that takes seriously both the Christian confession of the resurrection of the body at the end of time and the reality of death's grip during these last days of the old age?

> In a culture that evades telling the truth about death, the teaching of the resurrection comes as a blast of fresh air. If asked, "What do we hope for after death?" many devout Christians would answer with sentimental notions of their souls going to heaven and smiling back down on the earth. Such ideas have virtually no basis in the Bible, and those who exercise the teaching office in the church should seek to impress upon their congregations that the predominant future hope of the New Testament writers is precisely the same as the hope presented here in 1 Corinthians 15: resurrection of the body at the time of Christ's *parousia* and final judgment.
>
> I have never forgotten a conversation I had with a young woman in my church years ago. I will call her "Stephanie." Her eighteen-year-old sister (whom I will call "Lisa") had been killed in a car accident. All the members of her family were saying things like "Lisa is so much happier now in heaven; she was always such an unhappy child here" or "God must have wanted her to be with him" or "I just know that Lisa is watching us now and telling us not to be sad." Stephanie was infuriated by such sweet, pious talk, for it seemed to deny both the reality of Lisa's death and its tragedy. Yet Stephanie felt guilty, because as a Christian she thought she ought to believe the pious things her family was saying. Thus, it came as a liberating word to her to learn that Paul speaks of death as a destructive "enemy" that will be conquered only at the end of this age. First Corinthians 15 enabled her to acknowledge soberly that Lisa was now really dead and buried in the ground, while at the same time realizing that she could hope to hold Lisa in her arms again, in the resurrection. Obviously, such matters must be handled with the greatest pastoral sensitivity, but we need to find ways to communicate these matters more clearly in

the church. The resurrection of the dead is, after all, the classical teaching of the New Testament and the Christian tradition; we might find that such teaching would go a long way to promote healthier attitudes towards death and life in our congregations.

TABLE 14.1 A Reflection on the Resurrection of the Dead Occasioned by Lisa's Funeral

2. Some debate the relation between the church and Israel. The debate manifests itself in the ways that some Christians think about foreign policy and other theological topics. For example, how Christians think of creation, God's mission, Jesus's life and ministry, the church's witness, what it means to be human, and the world's future—all of these huge topics are included in the way Christians think about the church's relation to Israel.

Essentially, all Christians embrace one of three views on the relation of the church to Israel. See diagrams below. Each of these views raises specific questions regarding God's purpose for creation. Consider each model with the analysis and pertinent questions. Compare and contrast the three models. How do they differ? Which do you find most compelling, and why? What areas of further exploration are raised for you?

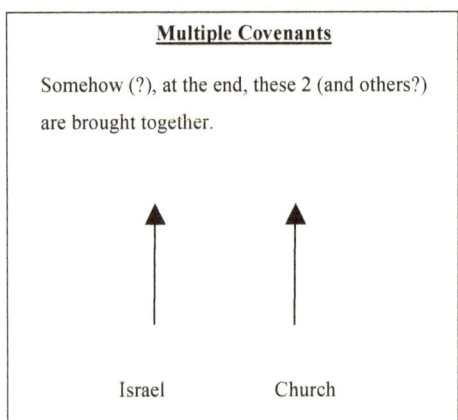

Typically associated with dispensationalism and two- (or multiple-)covenant theology, although differently. The state of Israel carries on without challenge from Christianity. In dispensationalism, God requires a strong, militant Israel to destroy evil and usher in the rule of Jesus at the end of time. Thus the church cheers (supports) Israel's militant foreign policy, since it will benefit in the future from Israel's military might in the final battle of Armageddon. There is no mission to Israel in dispensationalism, since Israel cannot be asked to follow the way of Jesus before it has killed off evil. No mission to Israel in two-covenant theology either, since God has covenants with all religious traditions, and no one needs to convert to a particular one.

<u>Questions:</u>

How does the dispensational church reconcile its approval of military soloutions with its confession that Jesus demonstrates God's preferred way of being? What is the role and significance of Jesus for these Christians? How does the multiple-covenant church reconcile its lack of mission with Jesus's testimony to Jesus's own challenge to the religious establishment's crooked behavior and beliefs? What is the character of Jesus's mission for these Christians?

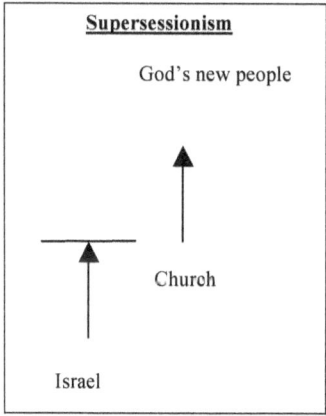

Supersessionism (church *supersedes* Israel) is also associated with displacement theology (church *displaces* Israel as God's people). In both of these views, the promises to Israel in the OT are transferred to the church. God no longer requires Israel, since it has already played its role of providing the context for Jesus to be born and raised. Israel's rejection of Jesus signals the next stage in the development of God's people. The NT characterizes God's new covenant people such that there is sharp division between OT and NT, with the NT superseding the OT. Mission to Jews continues, as they must now abandon Israel and become Christians to be saved.

<u>Questions:</u>

How does the church reconcile this view with its confession that God is faithful and does not abandon God's people? How is Jesus's life and ministry understood by these Christians?

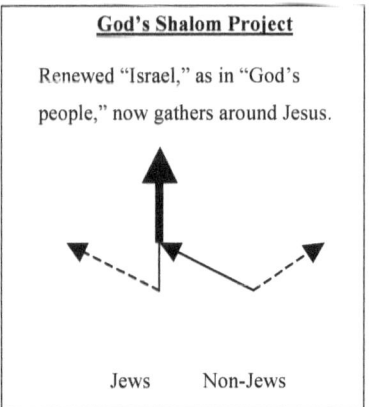

God's people have been under construction from the beginning of tim. This is God's Shalom Project. Israel is not abandoned or superseded by the church. Renewed Israel (thickest arrow) is gathered in Jesus to be both the "saved" and "saving" nation as intended by God from the beginning (Gen 12:1–3). The secular state of Israel is not automatically included, just as no nation (or individual, for that matter) is automatically included in God's people. Mission to Jews and non-Jews continues, as all are invited to give up their rebellion against God and recognize the *potential* that characterizes all people, as all are stamped with God's image.

Questions:

How does the church, as representative of God's end-time people, resist the seductive allure of old-age solutions (redemptive violence, ethnocentrism, etc.), when these still appear to work very well in these last days of the old age? How is Jesus's witness to God's preferred way of living practically embraced by these Christians?

TABLE 14.2 Three Views on the Church's Relation to Israel

3. The NT writers' apparent confidence in God's ultimate victory and their conviction that the future hope can inform the present strikes some people as embarrassingly naive or as hopelessly delusional. They ask: how rational is it to love your enemy? Can evil really be overcome with good? Is Jesus's return to finish the creation enterprise plausible? Come on, really! The NT writers' eschatological exhortations invite readers to a conversion of the imagination—to see the present situation with resources funded by the future. At one level, the utilitarian question of effectiveness does not apply. Why? Because Christians

do not live this way *in order* to get anything, but because this is how God's end-time people behave. Of course, at another level, a pragmatic prudence is reasonable in order to live at peace with others as much as possible (Rom 12:18; Heb 12:14). Nevertheless, regardless of the immediate effects, the conviction of God's ultimate victory and the public righting of wrong fortifies the believing community in the meantime, even when evil appears still to have the upper hand.

Discuss the following questions: Do you find the NT writers' end-time (eschatological) language embarrassingly naive or hopelessly delusional? If so, why might this be? What suggestions do you have for understanding the NT writers' apocalyptic language without descending into date-setting, doomsday fanaticism or into nationalistic, military triumphalism or into disengaged, irrelevant pietism?

Epilogue

NT THEOLOGY OUGHT TO be both descriptive and constructive—this is the argument that has occupied us in *New Testament Theology: Extending the Table*. I have argued that NT theology is *descriptive* in that it deals with the accounts that the NT writers narrate of their experience with Yahweh, the God of Israel, in the light of Easter. It is *constructive* in that it joins the diverse testimonies of the NT writers into a textured and thick space within which contemporary followers of Jesus continue to be shaped by the ancient yet living Spirit of God.

The NT theology that I have set out in the preceding chapters has the ambitious goal of adopting a method that is historical, thematic, and theological in orientation. It explores the conversation taking place "around the table," where the writers of the NT share their guiding vision of God's saving work among them and their passion for the Christian church engaged in God's mission. As is to be expected, differing perspectives are developed at the NT conference table. On most any topic, a spectrum of convictions emerges. Instead of finding this to be disturbing, the compilers of the NT canon held together the differing perspectives without reduction, forming a creative tension that is deep and rich. It is precisely within this interpretive space that ongoing community reflection, discernment, and praxis can take place.

Listening in on the table conversation, we have heard the NT writers' conviction that the launch of God's creation project is full of potential, but certainly not yet complete. God's purpose from the start, rather, is to grow a partner people that works with God to bring about the realization of the creative potential of the universe—and to carry it farther and further! This is God's project—continually creative, profoundly relational, and lovingly mutual.

The NT testimony is that Jesus is part of a long line of Israel's prophets, calling Israel back to God's foundational creation project of bringing wholeness and hope to all the nations—thus calling Israel to be both the gathered and the gathering people of God. However, there is more. Jesus is unique; as God's chosen one, he makes possible for the first time creation's liberation from the death-dealing grip of sin's reign, and the realization of God's purpose for creation. In this way, Jesus unleashes and embodies the end-time prototype of the new-creation humanity, the humanity that will carry forward the creation project to its goal. God keeps promises. In Jesus, humanity finally "gets" God's righteousness and preferred way of undoing evil.

God's purposes, according to the NT writers, cannot fail. In Jesus, human beings are finally empowered to be who they were created to be, even though their complete redemption is still not yet realized. By the Spirit of the risen Lord, the church—representative of God's end-time people—gives witness to all creation by speaking truth to power wherever it is located, by resisting the empire's dehumanizing and destructive ways in all its manifestations, by challenging the ethnocentrism of culture, by confronting the oppression of religiosity, by exposing the ineffective trust the state has in redemptive violence, and by inviting all to abandon rebellion against God's creation purpose, in order to find their true identity as God's beloved by joining God's renewed Israel. In the end, the NT confession is that God is patient and will be sure to make it possible for all to choose life, even though the possibility of remaining aligned to death, dysfunction, and decay continues to be real, since God is one, and God is fair.

And so, the table conversation continues. Refusing to set out new tables or get rid of a few (the temptation has always been to say *more* or *less* than the biblical witness), my project has been to find ways to *extend* the NT witness in ways appropriate for today. While this might be understood as traditional (taking seriously the biblical text), I believe it is also quite progressive (taking seriously the context within which the biblical witness lives). This is the constructive dimension of biblical theology—building within the canonical resonance space an understanding of a host of contemporary topics that speak today in a compelling and invitational way. Through much thoughtful and lively deliberation over the centuries, the NT writings continue to be sorted and organized by faith communities around the world under topical headings like Christology, anthropology, ecclesiology, eschatology, and so on. In this way, the impulse to theological discernment that brought the NT writings together in the first place, continues to nurture and fund communities of Jesus for a life of faithful witness to God's inbreaking rule. Thus, NT theology plays the role of "extending the table," giving contemporary faith communities a way of connecting with God's people from the dawn of time to the end of time.

Bibliography

Aland, Kurt, editor. 2006. *Synopsis of the Four Gospels: Greek-English Edition*. 12th ed. Peabody, MA: Hendrickson.
Alexander, Loveday C. A. 1993. "Chronology of Paul." In *Dictionary of Paul and His Letters*, edited by Gerald F. Hawthorne et al., 115–23. Downers Grove, IL: InterVarsity.
Attridge, Harold W. 1989. *The Epistle to the Hebrews: A Commentary on the Epistle to the Hebrews*. Hermeneia. Philadelphia: Fortress.
Banks, Robert. 1994. *Paul's Idea of Community: The Early House Churches in their Cultural Setting*. Peabody, MA: Hendrickson.
Bartholemew, Craig. 2005. "Biblical Theology." In *Dictionary for Theological Interpretation of the Bible*, edited by Kevin J. Vanhoozer et al., 84–90. Grand Rapids: Baker.
Baur, Ferdinand C. 1875. *Paul: The Apostle of Jesus Christ; His Life and Work, His Epistles and His Doctrine: A Contribution to the Critical History of Primitive Christianity*. 2 vols. Translated by A. Menzies. London: Williams & Norgate.
———. 1973. *Vorlesungen über neutestamentliche Theologie*. Darmstadt: Wissenschaftliche Buchgesellschaft. 1st ed 1863.
Beker, J. Christiaan. 1980. *Paul the Apostle: The Triumph of God in Life and Thought*. Philadelphia: Fortress.
Beasley-Murray, George R. 1993. "Baptism." In *Dictionary of Paul and His Letters*, edited by Gerald F. Hawthorne et al., 60–66. Downers Grove, IL: InterVarsity.
Bornkamm, Günther. 1963. "The Stilling of the Storm in Matthew." In *Tradition and Interpretation in Matthew*. Edited by G. Bornkamm et al., 52–57. Philadelphia: Westminster. 1st German edition 1948.
Brown, Raymond E. 1979. *The Community of the Beloved Disciple*. New York: Paulist.
Bultmann, Rudolf. 1953. "New Testament and Mythology." In *Kerygma and Myth*, edited by Hans-Werner Bartsch, 1–44. London: SPCK.
———. 1951. *Theology of the New Testament*, vol. 1. Translated by Kendrick Grobel. New York: Scribner.
———. 1955. *Theology of the New Testament*, vol. 2. Translated by Kendrick Grobel. New York: Scribner.
Caird, George B. 1959. "The Exegetical Method of the Epistle to the Hebrews." *Canadian Journal of Theology* 5:44–51.
———. 1995. *New Testament Theology*. Completed by Lincoln D. Hurst. Oxford: Clarendon.
———. 1997. *Language and Imagery of the Bible*. Grand Rapids: Eerdmans. Originally published, 1980.

Childs, Brevard S. 1970. *Biblical Theology in Crisis*. Philadelphia: Westminster.
———. 1985. *The New Testament as Canon: An Introduction*. Philadelphia: Fortress.
———. 2008. *The Church's Guide for Reading Paul: The Canonical Shaping of the Pauline Corpus*. Grand Rapids: Eerdmans.
Conzelmann, Hans. 1982. *The Theology of St. Luke*. Translated by Geoffrey Buswell. Philadelphia: Fortress. 1st German edition, 1954.
Crossan, John Dominic, and Jonathan L. Reed. 2001. *Excavating Jesus: Beneath the Stones, Behind the Texts*. San Francisco: HarperSanFrancisco.
Cullmann, Oscar. 1967. *Salvation in History*. Translation drafted by Sidney G. Sowers and completed by the editorial team at SCM Press. London: SCM.
Dunn, James D. G. 1990. *Unity and Diversity in the New Testament: An Inquiry into the Character of Earliest Christianity*. 2nd ed. London: SCM.
Ehrman, Bart D. 2004. *The New Testament and Other Early Christian Writings: A Reader*. 2nd ed. New York: Oxford University Press.
———. 2008. *The New Testament: A Historical Introduction to the Early Christian Writings*. 4th ed. New York: Oxford University Press.
Ewert, David. 2000. *How to Understand the Bible*. Scottdale, PA: Herald.
Fee, Gordon D., and Douglas Stuart. 2003. *How to Read the Bible for all Its Worth*. 3rd ed. Grand Rapids: Zondervan.
Ferguson, Everett. 2003. *Backgrounds of Early Christianity*. 3rd ed. Grand Rapids: Eerdmans.
Finger, Thomas N. 1989. *Christian Theology: An Eschatological Approach*, vol. 2. Scottdale, PA: Herald.
Fuller, Reginald H. 1989. "New Testament Theology." In *The New Testament and Its Modern Interpreters*, edited by Eldon J. Epp and George W. MacRae, 565–84. The Bible and Its Modern Interpreters 3. Philadelphia: Fortress.
Gamble, Harry. 1995. *Books and Readers in the Early Church: A History of Early Christian Texts*. New Haven: Yale University Press.
Geddert, Timothy J. 2000. "Working Together for Good (Romans 8:28)." *Mennonite Brethren Herald* 39/13:4–5.
———. 2001. *Mark*. Believers Church Bible Commentary Scottdale, PA: Herald.
———. 2008. *All Right Now: Finding Consensus on Ethical Questions*. Scottdale, PA: Herald.
Gilbert, Pierre. 2001. "Human Free Will and Divine Determinism: Pharaoh, a Case Study." *Direction* 30:76–87.
Girard, René. 2001. *I See Satan Fall Like Lightning*. Translated by James G. Williams. Maryknoll, NY: Orbis.
González, Justo L. 1990. *Mañana: Christian Theology from a Hispanic Perspective*. Nashville: Abingdon.
Green, Joel B., and Mark D. Baker. 2000. *Recovering the Scandal of the Cross: Atonement in New Testament & Contemporary Contexts*. Downers Grove, IL: InterVarsity.
Gundry-Volf, Judith M. 1993. "Expiation, Propitiation, Mercy Seat." In *Dictionary of Paul and His Letters*, edited by Gerald F. Hawthorne et al., 279–84. Downers Grove, IL: InterVarsity.
Guthrie, Donald. 2001. *New Testament Theology*. Downers Grove, IL: InterVarsity.
Hasel, Gerhard F. 1978. *New Testament Theology: Basic Issues in the Current Debate*. Grand Rapids: Eerdmans.
Hays, Richard B. 1997. *First Corinthians*. Interpretation. Louisville: Westmindster John Knox.

Hiebert, Paul. 2000. "Spiritual Warfare and Worldviews." *Direction* 29:214-24.
Hunsberger, George R. 1998. "Missional Vocation: Called and Sent to Represent the Reign of God." In *Missional Church: A Vision for the Sending Church in North America*, edited by Darrel L. Guder, 77-109. Grand Rapids: Eerdmans.
Hurst, Lincoln Douglas. 1990. *The Epistle to the Hebrews: Its Background of Thought*. Society for New Testament Studies Monograph Series 65. Cambridge: Cambridge University Press.
Hurtado, Larry W. 1998. *One God, One Lord: Early Christian Devotion and Ancient Jewish Monotheism*. 2nd ed. Edinburgh: T. & T. Clark.
Isaak, Jon M. 1995. "Hearing God's Word in the Silence: A Canonical Approach to 1 Corinthians 14:34-35." *Direction* 24:55-64.
———. 2002. *Situating the Letter to the Hebrews in Early Christian History*. Studies in the Bible and Early Christian History 53. Lewiston, NY: Mellen.
———. 2003. "The Christian Community and Political Responsibility: Romans 13:1-7." *Direction* 32:32-46.
———. 2004. "Baptism among the Early Christians." *Direction* 33:3-20.
Jeremias, Joachim. 1958. *Jesus' Promise to the Nations: The Franz Delitzsch Lectures for 1953*. Studies in Biblical Theology 24. London: SCM.
Johnson, Luke Timothy. 1998. *The Religious Experience in Earliest Christianity: A Missing Dimension in New Testament Studies*. Minneapolis: Fortress.
———. 1999. *The Writings of the New Testament: An Interpretation*. Rev. ed. with the assistance of Todd C. Penner. Minneapolis: Fortress.
———. 2003. *The Creed: What Christians Believe and Why it Matters*. New York: Doubleday.
Käsemann, Ernst. 1964. "The Problem of the Historical Jesus." In *Essays on New Testament Themes*, 15-47. Studies in Biblical Theology 41. London: SCM. 1st German edition, 1954.
———. 1969. "The 'Righteousness of God' in Paul." In *New Testament Questions for Today*, 168-82. Philadelphia: Fortress. 1st German edition, 1961.
Kelber, Werner H. 1997. *The Oral and the Written Gospel: The Hermeneutics of Speaking and Writing in the Synoptic Tradition, Mark, Paul, and Q*. Voices in Performance and Text. Bloomington: Indiana University Press.
Kingsbury, Jack Dean. 1983. *The Christology of Mark's Gospel*. Philadelphia: Fortress.
Kraus, C. Norman. 1991. *God our Savior: Theology in a Christological Mode*. Scottdale, PA: Herald.
Kuhn, Thomas S. 1970. *The Structure of Scientific Revolutions*. 2nd ed. Chicago: University of Chicago Press.
Kümmel, Werner Georg. 1975. *Introduction to the New Testament*. Translated by Howard Clark Kee. Rev. ed. Nashville: Abingdon.
———. 1973. *The Theology of the New Testament according to Its Major Witnesses*. Translated by John E. Steely. Nashville: Abingdon.
Ladd, George E. 1993. *A Theology of the New Testament*. Rev. ed. Edited by Donald A. Hagner. Grand Rapids: Eerdmans.
Lampe, Peter. 2003. *From Paul to Valentinus: Christians at Rome in the First Two Centuries*. Translated by Michael Steinhauser. Edited by Marhsall D. Johnson. Minneapolis: Fortress.
Lewis, C. S. 2001. *The Great Divorce: A Dream*. San Francisco: HarperSanFrancisco. Original publication, 1946.

Lohfink, Gerhard. 1984. *Jesus and Community: The Social Dimension of Christian Faith*. Translated by John P. Galvin. Philadelphia: Fortress.

Luther, Martin. 1960. "Prefaces to the New Testament." In *Luther's Works*. Vol. 35, *Word and Sacrament 1*, edited by Helmut T. Lehmann and E. Theodore Bachmann, 357-411. Translated by C. M. Jacobs. Luther's Works. Philadelphia: Muhlenberg. 1st German edition 1522.

———. 1961. "Two Kinds of Righteousness." In *Martin Luther: Selections from his Writings*, edited with an introduction by John Dillenberger, 86-96. Anchor Books. New York: Doubleday. 1st German edition, 1519.

Mack, Burton L., and Vernon K. Robbins. 1989. *Patterns of Persuasion in the Gospels*. Foundations & Facets. Literary Facets. Sonoma, CA: Polebridge. Reprinted, Eugene, OR: Wipf & Stock, 2008.

Magarshack, David, translator. 1982. *The Brothers Karamazov*, by Fyodor Dostoyevsky. Penguin Classics. London: Penguin. 1st Russian edition, 1880.

Malina, Bruce J. 2001. *The New Testament World: Insights from Cultural Anthropology*. 3rd ed. Louisville: Westminster John Knox.

Marshall, I. Howard. 2004. *New Testament Theology: Many Witnesses, One Gospel*. Downers Grove, IL: InterVarsity.

Martens, Elmer A. 1975. "Realizing the Vision: Through Biblical Theology." In *The Seminary Story: Twenty Years of Education in Ministry (1955-1975)*, edited by A. J. Klassen, 35-40. Fresno, CA: Mennonite Brethren Biblical Seminary.

———. 1998. *God's Design: A Focus on Old Testament Theology*. 3rd ed. North Richland Hills, TX: Bibal.

———. 2005. "A Personal Tour." *Christian Leader* 68/9:13-15.

Martin, Ralph P. 1981. *Reconciliation: A Study of Paul's Theology*. New Foundations Theological Library. Atlanta: John Knox.

Martyn, J. Louis. 1979. *History & Theology in the Fourth Gospel*. 2nd ed. Nashville: Abingdon.

Matera, Frank J. 2007. *New Testament Theology: Exploring Diversity and Unity*. Louisville: Westminster John Knox.

Mead, James K. 2007. *Biblical Theology: Issues, Methods, and Themes*. Louisville: Westminster John Knox.

Meeks, Wayne A. 1983. *The First Urban Christians: The Social World of the Apostle Paul*. New Haven: Yale University Press.

Metzger, Bruce M., and Bart D. Ehrman. 2005. *The Text of the New Testament: Its Transmission, Corruption, and Restoration*. 4th ed. New York: Oxford University Press.

Morgan, Robert C., editor and translator. 1973. *The Nature of New Testament Theology: The Contribution of William Wrede and Adolf Schlatter*. Studies in Biblical Theology, 2nd ser., 25. London: SCM.

———. 1992. "Theology (NT)." In *The Anchor Bible Dictionary*, edited by David Noel Freedman, 6:473-83. 6 vols. New York: Doubleday.

Neufeld, Thomas R. Yoder. 2007. *Recovering Jesus: The Witness of the New Testament*. Grand Rapids: Brazos.

Niebuhr, H. Richard. 1951. *Christ and Culture*. New York: Harper.

Nouwen, Henri. 1994. *The Return of the Prodigal Son: A Story of Homecoming*. New York: Doubleday.

Olson, Dennis T. 2006. "Biblical Theology." In *The New Interpreter's Dictionary of the Bible*, edited by Katherine Doob Sakenfeld, 1:461-65. 5 vols. Nashville: Abingdon.

Ott, Bernhard. 2004. *God's Shalom Project.* Translated by Timothy J. Geddert. Intercourse, PA: Good Books.
Penner, Todd, and Caroline Vander Stichele, editors. 2005. *Moving Beyond New Testament Theology? Essays in Conversation with Heikki Räisänen.* Publications of the Finnish Exegetical Society 88. Göttingen: Vandenhoeck & Ruprecht.
Rad, Gerhard von. 1962. *Old Testament Theology,* vol. 1: *The Theology of Israel's Historical Traditions.* Translated by D. M. G. Stalker. New York: Harper & Row.
———. 1965. *Old Testament Theology,* vol. 2: *The Theology of Israel's Prophetic Traditions.* Translated by D. M. G. Stalker. New York: Harper & Row.
Richardson, Alan. 1958. *An Introduction to the Theology of the New Testament.* London: SCM.
Sanders, E. P. 1977. *Paul and Palestinian Judaism: A Comparison of Patterns of Religion.* Philadelphia: Fortress.
———. 1991. *Paul.* Past Masters Series. Oxford: Oxford University Press.
———. 1993. *The Historical Figure of Jesus.* London: Penguin.
Sanders, E. P., and Margaret Davies. 1989. *Studying the Synoptic Gospels.* London: SCM.
Sandmel, Samuel. 1974. *A Jewish Understanding of the New Testament.* Augmented ed. New York: Ktav.
Sandys-Wunsch, John, and Laurence Eldredge. 1980. "J. P. Gabler and the Distinction between Biblical and Dogmatic Theology: Translation, Commentary, and Discussion of His Originality." *Scottish Journal of Theology* 33:133–58.
Schlatter, Adolf. 1973. "The Theology of the New Testament and Dogmatics." In *The Nature of New Testament Theology: The Contribution of William Wrede and Adolf Schlatter,* edited by Robert C. Morgan, 117–66. Studies in Biblical Theology 2/25. London: SCM. 1st German edition, 1909.
Schmithals, Walter. 1997. *The Theology of the First Christians.* Translated by O. C. Dean Jr. Louisville: Westminster John Knox.
Schreiner, Thomas R. 2008. *New Testament Theology: Magnifying God in Christ.* Grand Rapids: Baker Aacademic.
Schüssler Fiorenza, Elisabeth. 1989. "Revelation." In *The New Testament and Its Modern Interpreters,* edited by Eldon J. Epp and George W. MacRae, 407–27. The Bible and Its Modern Interpreters. Philadelphia: Fortress.
Spener, Philip J. 1964. *Pia Desideria.* Translated, edited, with an introduction by Theodore G. Tappert. Seminar Editions. Philadelphia: Fortress. 1st German edition, 1675.
Stegemann, Ekkehard W., and Wolfgang Stegemann. 1999. *The Jesus Movement: A Social History of Its First Century.* Translated by O. C. Dean Jr. Minneapolis: Fortress.
Stendahl, Krister. 1962. "Biblical Theology, Contemporary." In *The Interpreter's Dictionary of the Bible,* edited by George A. Buttrick et al., 1:418–32. 4 vols. Nashville: Abingdon.
———. 1976. "The Apostle Paul and the Introspective Conscience of the West." In *Paul among Jews and Gentiles, and Other Essays,* 78–96. Philadelphia: Fortress.
Strecker, Georg. 2000. *Theology of the New Testament.* Completed by Friedrich Wilhelm Horn. Translated by M. Eugene Boring. Louisville: Westminster John Knox.
Sundberg, Albert C. 1973. "Canon Muratori: A Fourth-Century List." *Harvard Theological Review* 66:1–41.
Thielman, Frank. 2005. *Theology of the New Testament: A Canonical and Synthetic Approach.* Grand Rapids: Zondervan.
Throckmorton, Burton H., editor. 1992. *Gospel Parallels: A Comparison of the Synoptic Gospels.* 5th ed. Nashville: Nelson.

Toews, John E. 1989. "The Nature of the Church." *Direction* 18:3–26.

———. 2004. *Romans.* Believers Church Bible Commentary. Scottdale, PA: Herald.

Vanhoozer, Kevin. 2005. "Systematic Theology." In *Dictionary for Theological Interpretation of the Bible,* edited by Kevin Vanhoozer et al., 773–79. London: SCM.

Vanhoye, Albert. 1963. *La Structure Littéraire de l'Epître Hébreux.* Studia neotestamentica. Studia, 1. Paris: Desclée de Brouwer.

Via, Dan O. 2002. *What Is New Testament Theology?* Guides to Biblical Scholarship. New Testament Series. Minneapolis: Fortress.

Wink, Walter. 1998. *The Powers that Be: Theology for a New Millennium.* New York: Doubleday.

Wisse, Frederik. 1972. "The Epistle of Jude in the History of Heresiology." In *Essays on the Nag Hammadi Texts in Honour of Alexander Böhlig,* edited by M. Krause, 133–43. Nag Hammadi Studies 3. Leiden: Brill.

———. 1978. "Gnosticism and Early Monasticism in Egypt." In *Gnosis: Festschrift für Hans Jonas,* edited by Barbara Aland, 431–40. Göttingen: Vandenhoeck & Ruprecht.

———. 1986. "The Use of Early Christian Literature as Evidence for Inner Diversity and Conflict." In *Nag Hammadi, Gnosticism & Early Christianity,* edited by Charles W. Hedrick and Robert Hodgson Jr., 177–90. Peabody, MA: Hendrickson.

Wrede, William. 1906. *Das literariche Rätsel des Hebräerbriefes.* Forschungen zur Religion und Literatur des Alten und Neuen Testaments 8. Göttingen: Vandenhoeck & Ruprecht.

———. 1907. *Paul.* Translated by Edward Lummis. London: Philip Greene.

———. 1971. *The Messianic Secret.* Translated by J. C. C. Greig. Library of Theological Translations. Cambridge: James Clarke. 1st German edition, 1901.

———. 1973. "The Task and Methods of New Testament Theology." In *The Nature of New Testament Theology: The Contribution of William Wrede and Adolf Schlatter,* edited and translated by Robert C. Morgan, 68–116. Studies in Biblical Theology 2/25. London: SCM. 1st German edition, 1897.

Wright, N. T. 1992. *The New Testament and the People of God.* Christian Origins and the Question of God 1. Minneapolis: Fortress.

———. 1999. "The Future of Jesus." In *The Meaning of Jesus: Two Visions,* by Marcus J. Borg and N. T. Wright, 197–204. San Francisco: HarperSanFrancisco.

———. 1996. *Jesus and the Victory of God.* Christian Origins and the Question of God 2. Minneapolis: Fortress.

———. 2003. *The Resurrection of the Son of God.* Christian Origins and the Question of God 3. Minneapolis: Fortress.

Yoder, John Howard. 1971. "Peace without Eschatology?" In *The Original Revolution: Essays on Christian Pacifism,* 52–84. Christian Peace Shelf Series 3. Scottdale, PA: Herald.

———. 2001. *Body Politics: Five Practices of the Christian Community before the Watching World.* Scottdale, PA: Herald.

Index of Authors

Aland, Kurt, 104, 236, 237, 355
Alexander, Loveday C. A., 59, 355
Attridge, Harold W., 194, 355
Augustine, 121, 205, 242

Baker, Mark D., 94, 245, 249, 283, 291, 356
Banks, Robert, 67, 355
Bartholemew, Craig, 230, 355
Baur, Ferdinand C., 11, 12, 70, 71, 355
Beasley-Murray, George, 79, 355
Beatty, A. Chester, 13
Beker, J. Christian, 73, 355
Bodmer, Martin, 13
Bornkamm, Günther, 122, 355
Brown, Raymond E., 149, 165-67, 355
Bultmann, Rudolf, 4, 12, 15, 25-31, 36, 73, 116, 117, 122, 131, 160, 161, 355

Caird, G. B., xi, xviii, 19, 20, 30, 36, 42, 46, 92, 114, 117, 118, 120, 125, 128, 129, 133, 134, 162-64, 172, 176, 181, 195, 213, 224-26, 239, 240, 244, 253, 272, 277, 281, 283, 292, 295, 319, 334, 338, 340, 355
Childs, Brevard S., 4, 65, 67, 68, 167, 192, 356
Christmann, Wolfgang J., 1
Clement of Alexandria, 146, 148, 151, 156, 167, 171, 190, 212
Conzelmann, Hans, 132, 133, 135, 356
Crossan, John Dominic, 13, 356
Cullmann, Oscar, 14, 356

Davies, Margaret, 106-8, 110, 111, 359
Diest, Henricus A., 1
Dostoyevsky, Fyodor, 53, 358
Dunn, James D. G., 15, 356

Ehrman, Bart D., 52, 61, 64, 67, 141, 160, 185, 216, 220, 221, 232, 235, 237, 356
Eldredge, Laurence, 3, 359
Eusebius, 111, 121, 147, 148, 151, 190, 193, 205, 212, 222
Ewert, David, xvi, 281, 356

Fee, Gordon D., 109, 356
Ferguson, Everett, 13, 356
Finger, Thomas N., 292, 294, 356
Fuller, Reginald H., 21, 356

Gabler, Johann P., 2, 11, 14, 359
Gamble, Harry, 58, 66, 68, 187, 204, 356
Geddert, Timothy J., xvi, xix, 113, 120, 121, 259, 270, 278, 305, 307, 313, 356, 359
Gilbert, Pierre, 278, 356
Girard, René, 93, 120, 182, 198, 214, 356
González, Justo L., 304, 356
Green, Joel B., 94, 245, 249, 283, 291, 356
Gundry-Volf, Judith M., 99, 356
Guthrie, Donald, 10, 356

Hasel, Gerhard F., 1, 356

Hays, Richard B., 91, 333, 345, 356
Hiebert, Paul, 209, 211, 275, 357
Hunsberger, George R., 321, 357
Hurst, Lincoln Douglas, xviii, 194, 355, 357
Hurtado, Larry W., 274, 305, 357

Irenaeus, 72, 110, 121, 146, 148, 167, 171, 190, 205, 212, 254
Isaak, Jon M., 78, 149, 195, 268, 357

Jackson, Shirley, 297
Jeremias, Joachim, 49, 125, 357
John of Damascus, 47
Johnson, Luke Timothy, xvii, xviii, 30, 31, 35–38, 40, 41, 52, 63, 67, 108–10, 112, 118, 121, 125, 126, 148–50, 153, 157, 165, 166, 168, 172, 173, 175, 177, 189, 191, 197, 202, 203, 208, 209, 213, 218, 219, 273, 289, 305, 307, 308, 357
Josephus, 32, 143, 221
Justin Martyr, 111

Käsemann, Ernst, 97, 131, 132, 357
Kelber, Werner H., 113, 122, 357
Kingsbury, Jack Dean, 115, 357
Klassen, A. J., xv, 358
Kraus, C. Norman, xvii, xviii, 278, 279, 285, 296, 303, 304, 311, 323, 324, 340, 357
Kuhn, Thomas S., 71, 357
Kümmel, Werner Georg, 14, 59, 63, 64, 66, 146–48, 151, 160, 161, 167, 170, 171, 177, 190, 192, 205, 216, 357

Ladd, George Eldon, 14, 73, 357
Lampe, Peter, 13, 357
Lewis, C. S., 88, 280, 344, 357
Lohfink, Gerhard, 311, 358
Luther, Martin, 69, 70, 98, 148, 169, 170, 200–204, 358

Mack, Burton L., 156, 358
Malina, Bruce J., 32, 79, 358

Marshall, I. Howard, 14, 358
Martens, Elmer A., xv, xvi, 100, 102, 358
Martin, Ralph P., 73, 358
Martyn, J. Louis, 149, 358
Matera, Frank J., 14, 358
Mead, James K., 4, 358
Meeks, Wayne A., 32, 358
Metzger, Bruce M., 232, 235, 237, 358
Milton, John, 277
Morgan, Robert, 22, 358–60

Neufeld, Thomas R. Yoder, 253, 358
Niebuhr, H. Richard, 320, 321, 329, 358
Nouwen, Henri, 279, 358

Olson, Dennis T., 4, 22, 358
Origen, 190, 212
Ott, Bernhard, 21, 359

Papias, 111, 113, 121, 146, 148, 167, 171, 220, 221
Penner, Todd, 4, 357
Pliny, 33, 221

Rad, Gerhard von, 4, 359
Reed, Jonathan L., 13, 356
Richardson, Alan, 310, 359
Robbins, Vernon K., 156, 358
Rowling, J. K., 250
Rylands, John, 13

Sanders, E. P., 59, 66, 70, 73, 77, 96, 106–11, 145, 203, 333, 359
Sandmel, Samuel, 195, 359
Sandys-Wunsch, John, 3, 359
Schlatter, Adolf, 14, 24, 25, 28, 359
Schmithals, Walter, 12, 359
Schreiner, Thomas R., 10, 359
Schüssler Fiorenza, Elisabeth, 183, 359
Spener, Philip J., 2, 359
Stegemann, Ekkehard W., 13, 359
Stegemann, Wolfgang, 13, 359
Stendahl, Krister, 22, 69, 359
Strecker, Georg, 12, 359
Stuart, Douglas, 109, 356

Suetonius, 33, 140, 221
Sundberg, Albert C., 190, 359

Tacitus, 33, 221
Thielman, Frank, 14, 359
Throckmorton, Burton H., 104, 141, 359
Toews, J. B., xv
Toews, John E., xv, xvi, xvii, xix, 16, 44, 81, 97, 312, 314, 316, 360

Vander Stichele, Caroline, 4, 359
Vanhoozer, Kevin J., 230, 355, 360

Vanhoye, Albert, viii, 196, 360
Via, Dan O., 4, 22, 360

Wink, Walter, 41, 209, 211, 212, 317, 360
Wisse, Frederik, 68, 72, 110, 151, 160, 166, 191, 204, 217, 218, 360
Wrede, William, 11, 24, 25, 28, 71, 113–15, 122, 160, 194, 360
Wright, N. T., 15, 90, 134, 360

Yoder, John Howard, 184, 296, 320, 324–28, 360

Index of Scriptural Passages and Other Ancient Writings

OLD TESTAMENT

Genesis

1–3	299
1:1—2:3	209
1–2	276
1:1–2	296
1:1	272, 289
1:2	242, 252, 301
1:27	288
1:28	340
2:17	296
3	289
3:1–24	209
3:1–19	296
6:5–6	289
8:21	341
11:1–9	136
12–50	272
12:1–4	276
12:1–3	81, 139, 242, 252, 281, 311, 314, 342, 348
12:3	126, 148
17:24	204
25:8	331
28	312
28:12	209
31:19–35	273, 305
35:2–4	273, 305
45:7–8	102
49:29–33	331
50:20	211, 281
50:24–26	331

Exodus

1:15–22	143
3–15	272
3:14	272
9:12	211, 278
9:34	211, 278
12:46	155
13:19	331
15	311
15:3	271, 283
19–40	272
20:1–7	273, 305
20:7	272
32:12	279

Leviticus

1–7	272

Deuteronomy

6:1–9	81
21:22–23	77, 273
21:23	37
29:28	279
32:8–9	273, 275, 305
32:35	279

Joshua

5:13–15	41, 209

Judges

6:34	301

Index of Scriptural Passages and Other Ancient Writings

1 Samuel

2:1–10	137
8–12	272
8:1–22	278
12:14–15	278
28	332

2 Samuel

7:11–16	37
7:16	278
14:17	296

1 Kings

3:9	296
22:19	41, 209

2 Kings

21:1–16	81
22:13	279

Job

27:3	301

Psalms

8	49, 195, 276, 287
8:4	117, 318
8:5–6	275
8:6–8	340
16:10	332
23:1	271
27:1	101
27:26	101
29:11	101
45:4–5	37
75:7	271
89:26	271
95	49, 195
95:3	271
109	101
110	38, 196, 276, 287
110:1	38, 49, 57, 94, 273
118:22	39, 49, 57, 273
130:5	332
131:2	271
137:4	39
139:8	332

Isaiah

2:2–4	125
6:9–10	124, 130, 281
7:14	124, 144
9:1–2	124
11:1	124
24–27	170
40	274, 305
42	49, 252
42:1–4	124, 319, 332
45:1–8	81
45:22–23	94
46:9–11	51
49	49, 252
49:1–6	319, 332
49:5–6	125
49:6	48, 124, 126, 282, 290, 312
50:4–11	319, 332
51:9–11	289
52	49, 252
52:13—53:12	81, 319, 332
53	49, 138, 252
53:4–5	49, 57
53:4	124
53:5	39
55:8–9	130, 279
59:1	225
60:1–6	144
61	49, 252
61:1–11	319
61:1	301
62:11	124

Jeremiah

3	279
3:8–14	280
16:19	271
18:1–3	124
31	196
31:15	124, 144
32:4–5	81

Ezekiel

2:1–10	318
37:3–6	276
38–39	170

Index of Scriptural Passages and Other Ancient Writings

Daniel

1:1–2	102
7–12	170
7:13–14	82
7:13	49, 117, 119, 252, 318, 332
7:14	172
7:27	318
12:1–12	63
12:2	37, 333, 334

Hosea

2:19	280
11:1	124, 144

Joel

2	170
2:13	102
2:28–29	314
2:28	273

Micah

4:1–2	43
5:2	124

Habakkuk

1:5–11	81

Zechariah

8:23	125
9–14	170
9:9	39, 49, 57, 124, 273
11:12–13	124
14:8–9	125

APOCRYPHAL / DEUTEROCANONICAL WRITINGS

2 Maccabees

12:39–45	333

NEW TESTAMENT

Matthew

1:1—4:16	123
1:1–17	126
1:18	242, 252
1:21	126, 314
1:22–23	242, 252
1:23	122, 124
2:1–12	108
2:1	143
2:6	124, 314
2:13–23	108
2:15	124
2:18	124
2:19	143
2:23	124, 143
4:1–11	108
4:15–16	124
4:16	314
4:17—16:20	123
4:17	123
4:23	314
5–7	123
5:3	316
5:9	315
5:10	246
5:13	316
5:17	337
5:20	138
5:22	340
5:34–73	206
6:10	47, 319, 340
6:12	289
6:13	233
6:33	268, 324, 339
7:7–8	205
8:17	124
8:23–27	122
9:1–8	108
9:6	116
9:27–31	125
10	123
10:34–36	277
10:34	89

Index of Scriptural Passages and Other Ancient Writings 367

12:18–21	124	26:30—27:54	154
12:22–32	312	27:9–10	124
12:22	125	27:35	233
13:13	130, 281	28:16–20	314
13:14–15	124	28:16	141
13:28	295	28:18–20	126
13:44	108	28:20	122, 242, 252
13:45–46	108		
13:47–50	108	**Mark**	
14:33	114, 316	1:1—8:26	118
15:21–28	125	1:12	108
15:23	314	1:14–15	312
16:17–19	312	1:15	119, 246
16:18	126, 312, 315, 316	1:17	315
16:21—28:20	123	1:34	114
16:21	123	2:1–12	108
17:21	233	2:10	116, 118, 219
18	123	2:12	308
18:11	233	3:12	114
18:15–20	312, 313, 317	3:27	312
18:17	126, 313, 315	3:31–35	243, 284, 315
18:23–25	108	4:11	246
19:28	314	4:12	130, 281
20:25–28	132	4:30–32	119
20:29–34	125	4:35—5:43	120
21:1	107	4:41	118
21:5	124	5:43	114
21:14	125	6:45–52	120
21:33–46	126	6:50	273
21:41	127	6:52	114, 120
21:42–45	127	7:16	233
21:43	127	7:34–35	312
22:1–14	126	7:36	114
22:1	316	8:1–21	120
22:7–14	128	8:18	120
22:7	128	8:27—16:8	118
22:39	205	8:27–33	118
22:44	38	8:30	114
23:9	285	8:31	119
23:14	233	8:34	119, 120, 315
23:37–39	106	8:38	116, 118, 158, 284
24–25	123	9:9	114
24:33	206	9:31	119
25:1–46	340	9:44	233
25:1–12	108	9:46	233
25:1	316	10:13–27	246
26:21–25	105	10:17	246

Mark (continued)

10:29–30	285
10:33	119
10:39	119
10:42–45	132
10:44	119
10:45	121, 138, 198, 245
11:1–9	120
11:15–19	48, 259
11:23–24	205
11:25	284
11:26	233
12:10–12	127
12:31	205
12:36	38
13	123, 134, 226
13:1–36	48
13:3–37	63
13:4	58
13:7	335
13:8	293
13:10	339
13:26–27	119
13:26	118
13:28–37	338
13:30–37	293
13:30–32	336
13:32–36	227
13:32	284
14:12–25	153, 154
14:18–21	105
14:22–25	120
14:22–24	155
14:26—15:39	154
14:36	284
14:53–65	154
14:58	48, 291, 315
15:13–14	86
15:28	233
15:34	37, 46, 120
15:38	315
16:7	141
16:8	32, 113
16:9–20	233, 234, 235

Luke

1:1—9:51	136
1:1–4	135
1:1	135, 140
1:5–80	108
1:17	314
1:28	233
1:35	137, 242, 252
1:46–55	137
1:52–53	137
1:69	314
1:77	314
2:1–52	108
2:4	143
2:10	314
2:25	139
2:31–32	314
2:38	315
2:39	143
3:22	137
3:38	136
4:1–13	108
4:1	137
4:16–30	139
5:17–26	108
5:24	116
6:20	137
6:24	138, 206
9:51—24:53	136
9:55–56	233
10:18	277
10:21	137
10:27	205
10:29–37	108
11:4	289
12:51–53	277
13:16	312
13:33	140
13:34–35	106
14:21–23	128
15	279, 342
15:11–32	108
15:13	138
15:30	138
16:19–31	108
17:36	233
18:1–8	108
19:8	138
19:19	245

Index of Scriptural Passages and Other Ancient Writings 369

19:28	107	3:13	158
19:38	107	3:14	163
20:17–19	127	3:16–17	256, 282
20:42	38	3:16	161, 246
21:5–36	339	3:31–36	158
21:8	339	3:31	160
21:28	227, 245	3:34	159
21:38	157	4:1–42	152
22:19–20	135	4:21–23	162
22:19	138	4:25	162
22:21–23	105	4:46–54	155, 157
22:25–27	132	5:1	152
22:29–30	139	5:2–9	157
22:37	138, 139	5:3–4	233
22:39—23:49	154	5:19–20	163
24:13	141	6	151
24:18	141	6:1–15	157
24:26–27	139, 245	6:4	152
24:27	31	6:16–21	157
24:33	141	6:33	158
24:39	29, 94, 316	6:38	158
24:44–45	50, 239	6:41	158
24:44	31	6:42	158
24:45	31	6:50	158
24:47	141, 246	6:51	158
24:49	141	6:58	158
24:52	141	6:68	276
24:53	157	7–8	291
		7	151
John		7:10	152
1:1–18	157, 243, 257	7:28	158
1:1–10	256	7:38	306
1:1–5	282	7:53—8:11	157, 233, 234, 235
1:1	240, 252	8	151
1:5	157	8:14	158
1:12	157, 164	8:28	163
1:14	161	8:36	227
1:18	158, 162	8:42	158
1:19—12:50	157	9:1–41	157
1:29	153, 155	9:22	151, 153
1:33	163	10:4	315
2:1–11	152, 155, 157	10:10	276
2:13–22	152, 259	10:16	314
2:13	152	10:17	91
2:17–22	153	10:18	163
3:1–21	152	10:27	315
3:11–15	163	10:36	159

John (continued)		20:31	120
11:1–57	152, 157	21	167
11:42	159	21:1–25	157, 158
11:50	314	21:5–8	316
11:51	246	21:23	339
12:12	152		
12:16	153	Acts	
12:32	158, 163, 164, 239	1:1—12:25	136
12:33	31	1:1	135, 140
12:35–36	315	1:4	141
13:1—20:31	157	1:8	137, 141, 306, 315
13–17	151, 166	1:15–26	139
13:1—17:26	158	2:1–11	139
13:1–38	152	2:4–11	136
13:1–11	153	2:4	137
13:3	158, 159	2:11	46
13:35	315	2:14–39	46
14:6–7	160	2:16–17	306
14:6	257	2:22	46
14:18–26	306	2:23–24	47
14:25	153	2:34	38
14:30–31	245	2:42–47	138
14:30	163	2:42	325
15	316	3:12–26	46
15:13–15	315	3:23	314
16:13–15	50	3:24	48
16:13	306	4:8	137
16:33	227	4:12	245, 257
17	244	4:13	207
17:3	159, 246	4:32–35	138
17:5	163, 164	5:3	138
17:15	161	5:42	315
18:1—20:31	158	6:3	270
18:14	314	6:5	137
18:28	154	7:34	314
18:37	162	8:14–25	141
19:14–18	153	8:32–33	138
19:14	154	8:37	233
19:30	154, 162	8:38	79
19:31–33	154	9:1–2	37
19:32–33	155	9:17	137
20:9	153	9:18	39
20:20	161	9:23–31	59
20:21–23	306, 318	10:34–43	46
20:21	159	10:38	49
20:22	306	10:40–42	50
20:30–31	157	10:44–48	136, 306

Index of Scriptural Passages and Other Ancient Writings

10:44	137	24:14	315
10:47	139	24:22	315
11:22	141	25:9–12	60
11:27–30	59	25:11	59
12:25	141	26:18	246
13:1—28:31	136	26:2–23	46
13:5	141	26:18	315
13:13	141	26:23	48
13:14	141	28:17–28	139
13:17–31	314	28:17	141
13:26–41	46	28:20	141
13:43	51	28:29	233
14:1	141	28:30–31	136
14:15–17	256	28:30	66
15	19, 20, 59		
15:1–29	59	**Romans**	
15:6–29	59, 139, 270, 317	1:1–6	74
15:14	314	1:1	76
15:19–21	140	1:5	44, 77, 81
15:28–29	59	1:16–17	76
15:28	137, 325, 327	1:16	44, 74, 125, 245
15:29	140	1:17	97, 246
15:34	233	1:18–32	92
16:4	141	1:18–31	282
16:11–15	285	1:18	86
17	32	1:19–21	256
17:1	141	1:20	225
17:10	141	1:21	308
17:14–27	256	2:1	225
17:16–34	46	2:6	203
18:4	141	2:9–10	125
18:10	314	2:13	315
18:11	59	2:14–16	256
18:12	59	2:16	76
18:19	141	3:9–20	209, 278
18:22	59	3:9	225, 230, 289, 295
18:32	33	3:19	288
19:9	315	3:21–26	74, 85, 99, 202, 243, 245, 282
19:23	315	3:21	50, 97
20:28–29	314	3:22	97, 202
20:28	135, 138	3:23	225, 289
20:31	64	3:24–26	77, 86
21:17–26	59, 60	3:24	245
22:1–21	46	3:25	245
22:4	315	3:29–31	275
24:2–21	46	3:30	76
24:6–8	233		

Romans (continued)

4:1	314	8:14	315
4:3–5	203	8:15–16	306
4:10–12	204	8:15	246, 284
4:16	314	8:17	63
4:24–25	77	8:18–25	84, 246, 334
4:25	84	8:21	95, 246
5	240, 290, 300	8:22–25	288
5:1	202	8:22	209
5:5	306	8:23	246, 306, 315
5:8	246	8:24	226
5:9	86	8:29	94
5:11	246	8:31–39	84
5:12–21	74, 78, 87, 243, 256, 277, 282	8:35–39	92
		8:38	92, 230
5:12	242, 288	9–11	131, 140, 243, 280
5:14	82	9:5	314
5:16	87	9:11	246
5:18–21	92, 202, 211	9:25–33	207
5:18	256	9:25–26	314
5:21	83	10:4	44, 48, 77, 86, 202, 291, 297
6:1–14	88	10:9	315
6:1–12	83, 210	10:10	226
6:3–4	78	10:14–17	78
6:3	246	11:1	314
6:4	94, 275	11:16	315
6:7–10	92	11:25–36	278
6:10	93	11:25–26	275
6:12	84, 275, 294	11:25	342
6:13	89	11:26	44, 314
6:15–23	315	11:28	246
6:22	227, 245, 246	12:1–2	79
6:23	276	12:3–8	326
7:7–12	202	12:4–8	316
7:7–11	44	12:9–21	58, 283
7:4–6	92	12:17–19	101, 279
7:24	225	12:18	349
7:25	226	12:19	283
8	70, 244	12:21	320
8:1–27	90	13:1–7	89, 268
8:1–11	79	13:1	268, 320
8:1	246	13:3	140
8:3	306	13:11–14	339
8:4	250	13:11	74, 227
8:9–11	306	14	66
8:9	302, 306	14:17	246
8:13	89	15:8	314

Index of Scriptural Passages and Other Ancient Writings

15:10	314	6:3	94, 209, 211, 275
15:16	76	6:5	315
15:19	76	6:7	320
15:28	60, 66	6:9–11	306
15:31	59	6:11	302
16:1–16	66, 285	6:15	316
16:1–2	60	6:17–19	78
16:20	84, 94, 211, 227, 275, 287, 312	7	90, 226
		7:8	66
16:22	62	7:10	58
16:23	316	7:20	134, 338
16:24	233	7:24	134, 338
16:25	74, 76	7:25–35	63
		7:26–31	293
1 Corinthians		7:26	134, 338
1:1	62	7:29–31	85, 339
1:9	85, 86	7:29	134
1:17–18	83	7:31	83
1:18	77, 227	7:36	294
1:22	77	8:4–7	295
1:23–25	80	8:6–7	66
1:23	37	8:6	244, 274, 275
1:26–31	32	9:1	80
1:30	246	9:5	190
2:2	77	9:12	76
2:6–16	306	10:4	312
2:6–8	83, 92	10:11	74, 83, 273, 294, 335
2:6	277, 283	10:16	316
2:7–8	47	10:19–22	275
2:8–9	80	10:19–20	295
2:8	42, 83, 92, 250, 275, 276	10:23–33	140
3:6	316	11:2–16	66
3:9	316	11:11	285, 294
3:10–15	xiii, 263, 318	11:23–26	316
3:11	312	11:23	58
3:13	201, 275	12–14	306
3:16–17	48	12:1–30	326
3:16	315	12:3	306, 307
4:1	315	12:4–30	316
4:9	210	12:4–6	302
4:13	319	12:7	307, 308
5	66	12:8–10	308
5:1–13	140	12:11	308
5:8	315, 316	12:13	79
5:12	317	12:14	308
6:2–3	84, 276	12:18–21	308
6:2	317	12:18	308

1 Corinthians (continued)

12:21	308
12:24–25	308
12:26	308
12:27	308, 316
12:28	308
13:10	308
14:12	307
14:26–40	66
14:26–28	308
14:26	307, 327
14:29	307
14:33–36	66
14:34–35	285
14:35	267
15	93, 300, 345
15:1–8	41
15:3–11	77
15:3–4	57, 92, 276, 282
15:3	246
15:4	46
15:5–9	95
15:8	80
15:15	95
15:19	95
15:20–28	84
15:20–26	44
15:20–23	315
15:20	90, 94
15:23–28	83
15:23	74, 90
15:24–26	74
15:25	94, 227
15:26	92
15:35–41	333
15:38	29
15:42–49	333
15:44–46	95
15:44	29
15:45–49	211
15:45	83, 282, 290, 301, 306
15:47	83
15:50–57	245
15:50	29, 94, 246
15:51–52	335, 339
15:53	84
15:55–57	226
15:54–57	84
15:56	138, 190, 295
15:57	74
16:1–4	44
16:19	315

2 Corinthians

1:1	62
1:20	85, 86, 340
1:22	90, 306
2:12	76
2:14	74
3:2–3	316
3:6	306
3:17–18	309
3:17	246
3:18	246, 289, 301, 309
4:3	76
4:4	83
4:6	91, 240, 244, 256, 274, 305
5	300
5:10	74
5:14–21	245
5:16–21	88, 211
5:16	40, 83, 84
5:17–21	317
5:17	46, 74, 83, 89, 92, 246, 315
5:18–21	243
5:18–19	246
5:18	46
5:19	92
5:20	316
5:21	242
6:16	315
7:1	227
8–9	44
9:13	76
10:14	76
11:1	316
11:7	76
11:14	295

Galatians

1:1	62
1:4	80, 83, 84

1:11–12	80	1:9–14	322
1:12	60, 74	1:10	65
1:15–20	44	1:14	227, 306
1:15	57	1:22—23	316
1:16	34, 57, 77	2:4–7	246
1:18—2:1	59	2:10	246
1:18	59	2:11–16	314
2	19, 20	2:12–21	74
2:1	59	2:12	314
2:6	140	2:14	74
2:8	207	2:19–22	48
2:9–10	59	2:19	316
2:10	44, 140	2:20	65, 291
2:11–14	140	3:5–6	81
2:15–21	245	3:6	65, 316
2:16–17	77	3:8–13	318
2:16	100, 202	3:8–12	323, 340
2:19–20	81	3:9	210
2:20	100	3:10	92, 230
3:5	306	3:12	100
3:6–8	97	4:1–16	326
3:7	314	4:4–16	316
3:19	41, 209, 295	4:4–6	302, 316
3:22	100	4:7	308
3:26	315	4:11–13	326
3:27	246, 282	4:15–16	316
3:28	32, 285, 294, 325, 339	4:20–21	315
4:1–7	245, 257	4:30	227
4:3	83	5:21—6:9	64
4:4	240	5:23	316
4:5	246, 315	5:26	227
4:6	284, 306	5:30	233
4:9	83	5:32	65
4:26	315	6:10–17	295
5:1	227, 306	6:12	74, 92, 227
5:6	203		
5:13–14	306	**Philippians**	
5:13	315	1:1	62
5:22–26	306	1:20	227
5:22	307	1:23	334
6:11	62	1:27	76
6:14	83	1:28	74
6:15	246	2:5–11	243, 277
		2:6–11	94, 245
Ephesians		2:10–11	322
1:1	64, 65	2:10	342
1:5	246	2:11	74, 315

Philippians (continued)

2:12	227
3:3	314
3:6	37
3:9	100
3:10–11	74
3:20–21	334
3:20	227
4:5	74, 339

Colossians

1:1	62
1:2	315
1:9–20	342
1:13	74
1:14	246
1:15–20	74, 322
1:15–19	243
1:15–16	294
1:15	40, 90, 282, 290, 297
1:16	92, 94
1:18	64, 316
1:24	316
1:27	65
2:2	60
2:7	65
2:8–10	316
2:8	64, 83
2:9	240
2:11–15	315
2:11	246, 306
2:15	41, 74, 77, 80, 83, 92, 93, 138, 198, 211, 227, 230, 243, 245, 276, 284, 320
2:16–23	315
2:19	316
2:20–23	64
2:20	83
3:1	63, 335
3:3	79
3:6	279
3:10	240, 315
3:18—4:1	64

1 Thessalonians

1:1	62
1:4	246
1:5	76
1:8	77
1:9–10	77
1:9	76, 77
2:2	76
2:8	76
2:9	76
2:19	83
3:2	76, 237
3:13	83
4:13—5:11	133, 336
4:13–18	63, 83
4:15–17	339
4:17	322, 334
5	90
5:2–11	84
5:5	74
5:9	74
5:10	246

2 Thessalonians

1:1	62
1:8	76
2:1–12	63, 133, 336, 339
2:14	76
3:6–13	133

1 Timothy

1:11	76
2:1–3	101
2:4	339
2:9–10	316
2:11–12	285
2:11	66
2:15	66
3:1–13	66
3:15	316
4:3	66
5:14	66
5:17–22	66
6:11–19	74
6:12	246

2 Timothy

1:8–10	74
1:8	66
1:13–14	67

Index of Scriptural Passages and Other Ancient Writings 377

2:8	76	6:20	197, 198
2:11–13	279	7:1–28	194, 198
3:1–8	74	7:11–28	243
3:16	246	7:22	197
		7:26	198
Titus		8:1—9:28	196
1:1–3	74	8:1–7	211
2:14	314	8:1	198
		8:2	197
Philemon		8:6	198, 291
1	62	8:10	314
		8:13	196, 198
Hebrews		9:5	245
		9:11—10:18	194
1:1–4	256	9:11–28	199
1:1–3	243	9:11–14	245
1:1–2	255	9:11	91, 198
1:1	195	9:12	227
1:2	197	9:14	233, 302
1:5—2:18	196	9:15	198, 245
1:6	197	9:22	198
1:13	38, 227	9:23–28	211, 245
2:4	306	9:24	91
2:5–18	195, 287	9:27–28	199, 276
2:10	197	10:1–25	245
2:11	197	10:1–18	291
2:17	198, 315	10:11 14	199
3:1—4:16	196	10:12–14	91
3:1—4:14	196	10:13	227
3:1–6	194	10:14	199
3:1	197, 198	10:18	246
3:3	197	10:19–25	199
3:6	239	10:19	199
3:14	200	10:21	198
4:9–11	315	10:23	239
4:9	315	10:25	339
4:14—5:14	194, 198	10:30	314
4:14	198	10:35–36	200
4:15	242, 252	11:1—12:29	196
5:1—7:28	196	11:1—12:2	256
5:5	198	11:1–40	194, 199, 200
5:7–9	211	11:1	200
5:8–10	241, 253	11:9	199
5:8–9	199	11:10	200
5:9	197, 242, 252	11:12	199
5:10	198	11:13	49, 200, 316
6:1	199	11:17	199
6:4	239		

Hebrews (continued)

11:22	314
12:1-2	199, 200, 285
12:1	21, 210, 267, 315
12:2	197, 241, 253, 294, 320
12:11	246
12:14	245, 349
12:22	315
12:24	198
13:12	315
13:20	197, 314
13:22-25	194
13:22	193
13:23	193, 195

James

1:1	204, 314, 316
1:5-6	205
1:17	207
1:18	315
1:19-20	205
1:22	203
1:27	203, 206, 318
2:1-7	206
2:8-13	206
2:8	205
2:14-17	206
2:17	203
2:21-23	203
3:5-12	206
3:5-6	205
3:13	205
3:18	101, 246
4:1-2	207
4:4	207, 225
4:6-10	207
4:7-8	205
4:8	227
4:11-12	206
4:13-17	207
5:8-9	339
5:9	206
5:12	206
5:13-16	206

1 Peter

1:1	207
1:2	245
1:11	213
1:15-16	315
1:18-19	288
1:18	227
1:19	213
1:20	246
1:22—2:3	213
2:4-10	207, 314, 315
2:9	210
2:10	207
2:11—3:17	213
2:11-12	214
2:11	212
2:12	308
2:13	208
2:16	227, 246
2:17	208, 315
2:20	213
2:21	210, 211, 212, 213, 315
2:24	210
3:12	315
3:16	215
3:18-22	211, 212
3:18	213, 243
3:20	316
3:21-22	210
3:22	227
4:1	213
4:7	339
4:12-19	214
4:12-17	315
4:14-15	213
4:14	233
4:17	315
5:2	314
5:5-9	207
5:8-9	227
5:9	215, 315
5:10	210, 215
5:12	208
5:13	208

2 Peter

1:1	215
1:5	215
1:10	246

Index of Scriptural Passages and Other Ancient Writings 379

1:16	218	5:11–13	165
1:20–21	216	5:13	246
2:1–22	215	5:19	165
2:1	218		
2:7	218	**2 John**	
2:12–22	217	1	316
2:18	217	7	168
3:2	216	10	168
3:3–15	341		
3:3–10	339	**3 John**	
3:14–17	188	9	167
3:15–16	55, 69, 216	11	168
3:15	110, 188	12	167
3:16	218		

Jude

1	215
3	215
4–16	215
11	217
16	217
20–23	317
20	215
21	246

1 John

1:2	165
1:5	165
1:6	165
1:7–10	227
1:8–10	169
1:10	165
2:2	245
2:4	165
2:8–10	165
2:15	165
2:18	339
3:1	165
3:7	315
3:9	165
3:11	169
3:14–15	165
3:16–18	169
3:16	246
3:19	165
3:24	306
4:1–6	306
4:1	168
4:3	165, 315
4:6	165
4:7	246
4:10	245
4:12	246
4:13	306
5:3–5	227
5:3	246
5:7–8	232, 234, 235

Revelation

1:1	170
1:5	179
1:13	172
1:19	176
2–3	174, 176
2:1—3:22	187
3:21	227
4–22	174, 176
4:2	176
4:4	177
4:8	171, 176
4:11	171, 176
5:1–7	179
5:5	176
5:6–14	245, 315
5:6–9	173
5:7	180
5:9–10	181
5:9	176, 180, 181
5:10	176
5:12	180

Revelation (continued)	
6:1—8:1	176
6	181
6:1-8	173
6:10-11	184
6:16 17	283
7:1-17	176
7:4	177
7:9-17	315
7:9	180, 316
7:14	180, 184, 227
7:17	180
8:1	176
8:2—11:19	176
10:1—11:14	176
11:15	176
12:1	177
12:7-12	172, 245
12:9	182
12:10-12	245
12:10-11	180, 227
12:11	172, 181, 184, 316
12:20	246
13	182
13:11-18	184
14:1-5	177
14:1	180
14:4	180, 315
14:14	172
15:1—16:21	176
15:5	176
16:1	176
17:14	227, 315
19:6	173
19:7	180
19:8	227
19:9	180
19:11-21	245
19:13	172, 181, 184, 316
19:19	227
19:20-21	184
20	312
20:1-6	177, 179, 337
20:2	182
20:7	182
20:11-15	279
20:11-14	245
20:12	181
20:14-15	184, 227, 297
20:14	183
20:15	181, 182
21	300
21:1-8	341
21:1	175
21:2	315, 334
21:5-7	317
21:5	240
21:6-7	184
21:8	183
21:9	172, 180, 182, 316
21:10	182, 183, 315
21:12-14	177, 314
21:22—22:7	276, 322
21:22-27	180, 344
21:22-26	183
21:22	48, 291, 315
21:27	180, 181, 182, 225
22:1-5	180
22:2-5	183
22:2	177
22:6	209
22:20	179, 339, 340

EARLY CHRISTIAN WRITINGS

Augustine

Against Julian

5.54	242

Harmony of the Evangelists

1.2.4	121

On Marriage and Concupiscence

2.29.51	242

Eusebius

Ecclesiastical History

3.24.7-13	151
3.25	190
3.39.3	148
3.39.15	111
3.39.16	121

6.14.7 151
6.25.3 190

Irenaeus
Against Heresies
3.1.1 121
3.11.7 111

John of Damascus
De fide orthodoxa
2.29 47

Justin Martyr
Apology
1.19.7 111
Dialogue with Trypho
106.3 111

JEWISH AND ROMAN HISTORICAL WRITINGS

Josephus
Antiquities
18.3.3 33
20.9.1 33

Pliny
Letters
10.96 33

Suetonius
Claudius
5.25.4 33
Nero
16 140

Tacitus
Annals
15.44.2–8 33

www.ingramcontent.com/pod-product-compliance
Lightning Source LLC
Chambersburg PA
CBHW022226010526
44113CB00033B/513